Lecture Notes in Computer Science   1477

Edited by G. Goos, J. Hartmanis and J. van Leeuwen

T0223206

Springer

Berlin
Heidelberg
New York
Barcelona
Budapest
Hong Kong
London
Milan
Paris
Singapore
Tokyo

Kurt Rothermel   Fritz Hohl   (Eds.)

Mobile Agents

Second International Workshop, MA'98
Stuttgart, Germany, September 9-11, 1998
Proceedings

 Springer

Series Editors

Gerhard Goos, Karlsruhe University, Germany
Juris Hartmanis, Cornell University, NY, USA
Jan van Leeuwen, Utrecht University, The Netherlands

Volume Editors

Kurt Rothermel
Fritz Hohl
Institut für Parallele und Verteilte Höchstleistungsrechner (IPVR)
Breitwiesenstr. 20/22, D-70565 Stuttgart, Germany
E-mail: {Kurt.Rothermel,Fritz.Hohl}@informatik.uni-stuttgart.de

Cataloging-in-Publication data applied for

Die Deutsche Bibliothek - CIP-Einheitsaufnahme

Mobile agents : second international workshop ; proceedings / MA
'98, Stuttgart, Germany, September 9 - 11, 1998. Kurt Rothermel ;
Fritz Hohl (ed.). - Berlin ; Heidelberg ; New York ; Barcelona ;
Budapest ; Hong Kong ; London ; Milan ; Paris ; Singapore ; Tokyo :
Springer, 1998
  (Lecture notes in computer science ; Vol. 1477)
  ISBN 3-540-64959-X

CR Subject Classification (1991): C.2, D.2, D.1.3, D.4.2-6, I.2.11

ISSN 0302-9743
ISBN 3-540-64959-X Springer-Verlag Berlin Heidelberg New York

© Springer-Verlag Berlin Heidelberg 1998
Printed in Germany

Typesetting: Camera-ready by author
SPIN 10638724   06/3142 – 5 4 3 2 1 0   Printed on acid-free paper

Preface

The concept of mobile agents has attracted tremendous attention in the last few years. It offers unique opportunities for structuring and implementing distributed systems, and a wide range of applications has been identified for mobile agent technology, including electronic commerce, telecommunication services, network management, and collaborative work.

This book constitutes the formal proceedings of the 2nd International Workshop on Mobile Agents, held in Stuttgart (Germany), September 9-11, 1998. The goal of this workshop was to provide a forum for the presentation and discussion of the latest research work in the field of mobile software agents. This workshop — following the successful MA'97 held in Berlin — was supported by Gesellschaft für Informatik (GI), IEEE ComSoc, Informationstechnische Gesellschaft (ITG), and International Federation for Information Processing (IFIP).

The call for papers for MA'98 attracted 45 submissions from 12 countries. Each submission was reviewed by three members of the program committee, and finally 21 papers were accepted for the workshop. There were 7 paper sessions complemented by 3 invited keynotes: "Present and future trends of mobile agent technology" by Danny Lange (General Magic, USA), "Mobile agent applicability" by Dag Johansen (University of Tromso, Norway), and "Wide-area languages" by Luca Cardelli (Microsoft Research, UK).

Looking at the contributions to MA'98 one can recognize a strong emphasis on applications for mobile agent technology: one keynote speach and two paper sessions were exclusively dedicated to applications. Other topics covered by the workshop included

* agent migration
* communication concepts and protocols
* transactional agents and fault-tolerance
* tracking and termination mechanisms
* security issues
* agent languages, systems, and standards (OMG MASIF)

Many people have contributed to make this workshop a success. We would like to thank the program committee members for their timely and in-depth reviews, which contributed greatly to constituting a very solid workshop program. Our thanks also go to Michael Matthiesen for his involvement in organizing this event. We express our special thanks to Stephanie Klöpf and the members of the Distributed Systems Research Group for their great help in making all kinds of arrangements for this workshop.

September 1998   Kurt Rothermel, Fritz Hohl

Organizations

Organized by:

University of Stuttgart

Supported by:

Gesellschaft für Informatik (GI)
IEEE ComSoc
Informationstechnische Gesellschaft (ITG)
International Federation for Information Processing (IFIP)

Committees

Chair

Kurt Rothermel   U. Stuttgart, Germany

Program Committee

Michel Banatre	IRISA, France
Paolo Ciancarini,	U. Bologna, Italy
Oswald Drobnik	U. Frankfurt, Germany
Dag Johansen	U. Tromso, Norway
Günter Karjoth	IBM, Switzerland
Johannes Klein	Tandem Computers, USA
David Kotz	Dartmouth College, USA
Rivka Ladin	Tandem Computers, Israel
Winfried Lamersdorf	U. Hamburg, Germany
Danny Lange	General Magic, USA
Thomas Magedanz	TU Berlin, Germany
Keith Marzullo	U. California at San Diego, USA
Friedemann Mattern	TU Darmstadt, Germany
Manuel Mendes	Pont. U. Catolica, Brasil
Kinji Mori	Tokyo Institute of Technology, Japan
V. K. Murthy	U. Ballarat, Australia
Radu Popescu-Zeletin	GMD, Germany
Guy Pujolle	U. Versailles, France
Kurt Rothermel	U. Stuttgart, Germany
Fred B. Schneider	Cornell University, USA
Otto Spaniol	RWTH Aachen, Germany
Ralf Steinmetz	U. Darmstadt, Germany
Vipin Swarup	MITRE, USA
Christian Tschudin	ICSI, USA
Hugo Velthuijsen	PTT Telecom, Netherlands
Wolfgang Zimmer	GMD, Germany

Organization Committee

Fritz Hohl	U. Stuttgart, Germany
Michael Matthiesen	U. Stuttgart, Germany

Table of Contents

Mobile Agent Systems

Security

Invited Talk

Communication

Applications II

Present and Future Trends of Mobile Agent Technology

Danny B. Lange

General Magic, Inc.

Sunnyvale, California, U.S.A

danny@acm.org, http://www.acm.org/~danny

Abstract

Mobile agents are an emerging technology that makes it very much easier to design, implement, and maintain distributed systems. We have found that mobile agents reduce the network traffic, provide an effective means of overcoming network latency, and perhaps most importantly, through their ability to operate asynchronously and autonomously of the process that created them, help you to construct more robust and fault-tolerant systems.

What is the current state of commercialization of mobile agent technology? Where is research heading in this field? How will standardization efforts impact the future of this technology? Those are just a few questions I will cover in my talk. I will in particular cover the impact of Java and report on current efforts to create a standard Java Agent API. I will also cover some of the deficiencies in present approaches to agent mobility and throw light on recent attempts to overcome these problems.

About the Speaker

Danny B. Lange is director of Agent Technology at General Magic, Inc. located in Sunnyvale, California. Prior to joining General Magic, he was a visiting scientist at IBM Tokyo Research Laboratory, where he invented the Java Aglet and was the chief architect of IBM's Aglets Software Development Kit. Danny received an MS and PhD in computer science from the Technical University of Denmark.

References

1. Lange, D.B. and Oshima, M.: Programming and Deploying Java™ Mobile Agents with Aglets™, ISBN 0-201-32582-9, Addison-Wesley, 1998.
2. Aridor, Y. and Lange, D.B.: Agent Design Patterns: Elements of Agent Application Design, In Proceedings of the Second International Conference on Autonomous Agents (Agents '98), ACM Press, 1998, pp. 108-115.
3. The Object Management Group: The Mobile Agent System Interoperability Facility, OMG TC Document orbos/97-10-05, The Object Management Group, Framingham, MA., 1997.

The Shadow Approach: An Orphan Detection Protocol for Mobile Agents

Joachim Baumann, Kurt Rothermel

IPVR (Institute for Parallel and Distributed High-Performance Systems)
Breitwiesenstraße 20-22
D-70565 Stuttgart
EMail:Joachim.Baumann@informatik.uni-stuttgart.de

Abstract. Orphan detection in distributed systems is a well researched field for which many solutions exist. These solutions exploit well defined parent-child relationships given in distributed systems. But they are not applicable in mobile agent systems, since no similar natural relationship between agents exist. Thus new protocols have to be developed. In this paper one such protocol for controlling mobile mobile agents and for orphan detection is presented.

The 'shadow' approach presented in this paper uses the idea of a placeholder (shadow) which is assigned by the agent system to each new agent. This defines an artificial relationship between agents and shadow. The shadow records the location of all dependent agents. Removing the root shadow implies that all dependent agents are declared orphan and eventually be terminated. We introduce agent proxies that create a path from shadow to every agent. In an extension of the basic protocol we additionally allow the shadow to be mobile.

The shadow approach can be used for termination of groups of agents even if the exact location of each single agent is not known.

1 Introduction

A mobile agent is regarded as a piece of software roaming the network on behalf of a user, e.g. searching for information in different databases, buying a flight ticket and renting a car, or trying to find the cheapest flower shop. Mobile agents seem to be the solution to many of the problems in the area of distributed systems. But while the idea of mobile agents is quite appealing, and while many researchers are working in this area, some very important problems have not been solved. Most of the research concentrates on providing the basic system support for migration, communication, the security of the platform underlying the agent system and for the asynchronous operation of agents. Some solutions for these problems already exist and have been implemented in different agent systems (e.g. [12], [4], [8], [14], [7], [6]). But until now no protocols exist for orphan detection in mobile agent systems.

Orphan detection in an agent system is very important both from the user's and from the system side, because a running agent uses resources which are valuable to both user and system. The user has to pay for resources (at least in principle), and the system has only a limited amount of them. So if the user does not need the results of a distributed computation in progress anymore, he wants to be able to terminate the computation to minimize the resulting cost. With an orphan detection mechanism the user simply declares the agents to be terminated as orphans. Orphan detection guarantees that the now useless agents can be determined by the system and ended, thus freeing the resources they have bound. In this paper we will present a new protocol, the shadow protocol, that allows both control of mobile agents and orphan detection. The paper is organized as follows: Sect. 2 presents our agent model. In Sect. 3 the shadow protocol is presented with different extensions and optimizations. Sect. 4 presents related work, and in Sect. 5 the conclusion and outlook is given.

2 The Agent Model

In this section we will give you a short overview of our agent model, that has been described in more detail in [12], [1] and [4]. Our model of an agent-based system - as many other models - is mainly based on the concepts of agents and places. Places provide the environment for safely executing local as well as vis-

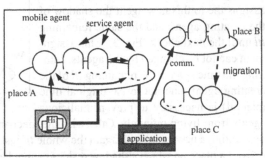

Fig. 1. The Agent Model

iting agents. An agent system consists of a number of (abstract) places, being the home of various services. Agents are active entities, which may move from place to place to meet other agents and access the places' services. Each agent is identified by a globally unique agent identifier. An agent's identifier is generated by the system at agent creation time. The creating place can be derived from this name. It is independent of the agent's current place, i.e. it does not change when the agent moves to a new place. In other words, the applied identifier scheme provides location transparency. A place is entirely located on a single node of the underlying network, but multiple places may be situated on a given node. For example, a node may provide a number of places, each one assigned to a certain agent community, allowing access to a certain set of services or implementing a certain prizing policy. Places are divided into two types, depending on the connectivity of the underlying system. If a system is connected to the network all the time (barring network failures and system crashes), a place on this system is called *connected*. If a system is only part-time connected to the network, e.g. a user's PDA (Personal Digital Assistant), the place is called *associated*.

3 The Shadow Protocol

In this section we discuss the basic Shadow Protocol with its agent proxies, the extension that allows the shadows to be mobile, and discuss possible optimizations.

3.1 The Idea

In the shadow concept each application creates one or more shadows, a data structure on a connected place. The place where the shadow is created does not necessarily have to run on the same host on which the creating application runs. Each agent created by

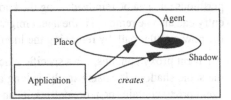

Fig. 2. The Creation of a Shadow

the application depends on such a shadow (Fig. 2). The agent is dependent of the shadow instead of the application. As long as the shadow exists in the system, no contact of agents to the application itself or to the computer system on which the application runs is necessary. In regular intervals (called *time to live* or *ttl*) the system checks for each agent if the associated shadow still exists. If the shadow does no longer exist, the agent is declared to be an orphan and is removed.

If an agent creates a new agent, the system assigns the to this new agent the shadow of the creating agent, and the same remaining *ttl* until the next check (Fig. 3). This assignment cannot be changed by the agents. Limiting the time span to the remaining *ttl* of the creating agent (and not to the original time interval) is necessary to prevent malicious

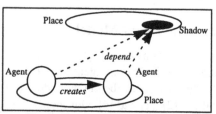

Fig. 3. Creating a New Agent

agents from living infinitely. Otherwise the mechanism could be circumvented simply by creating a new agent with again the whole *ttl* just before the life span of the old agent ends. If a place on which a shadow resides cannot be reached, the system tries to contact the place several times. If still the place cannot be reached, the shadow is presumed no longer existent and its associated agents are killed. The disadvantage of this approach is that regardless of what an agent does, it has to connect to its shadow's place in regular intervals. The advantage on the other hand is that we have a worst-case time bound for the termination of agents through removing the shadows. This upper bound is exactly the sum of *ttl* of the agents and the timeout for contacting.

Until now the protocol only allows passive termination. By removing a shadow all dependent agents are declared orphans, and after the *ttl* it is guaranteed that all agents have been removed by the orphan detection. By adding the *path* concept to this protocol, we also allow active termination, i.e. termination of an agent while its *ttl* is greater 0. Agent proxies are structures at each place that keep track of the movement of all agents dependent of a specific shadow, thus creating a path leading to the agent. By storing the place at which the agent got checked the last time we can find the beginning of a path for every agent. Even if the path gets lost, the agent will contact the shadow after the *ttl*.

If an agent arrives at a place where not yet an agent proxy for this shadow exists, one is created (Fig. 4). As soon as the agent migrates to another place, the destination (being part of the path leading to the agent) is stored in the proxy together with the *ttl*.

When the end of the *ttl* is reached, the agent's shadow gets a request for extending the agent's life, and thus the new place of the agent is made known to the shadow (Fig. 5). The path entries stored in the different agent proxies along the agent's way is now superfluous and can be removed using the knowledge about the *ttl* stored in the proxy. An entry can also be removed if the agent migrates back to this place (this simply optimizes the now circular path by removing the loop).

An agent proxy contains, for a specific place, all path segments of agents belonging to the same shadow. It exists exactly as long as there is a path entry in it. As soon as the agent proxy contains no more entries, it can be removed as well. This is especially helpful if the agents are actively terminated, i.e. the system actively sends messages to terminate the agents as fast as possible. In that case, all entries are removed from the agent proxy, allowing the system to delete the proxy as well.

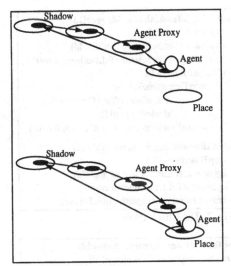

Fig. 4. Proxie Paths

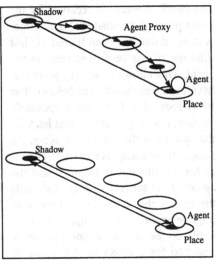

Fig. 5. Regular Update of Proxies

3.2 The Protocol

We will discuss the different parts of the protocol separately. The protocol is presented in an object-oriented pseudo-code notation.

The place on which the agent resides, decrements in regular intervals the *ttl* of the agent. As soon as the *ttl* of the agent is 0, a message is sent back to the home place of the shadow, containing the id of agent and shadow. At the same time a timer is started with a timeout, and the agent enters the *check phase* (Fig. 6). To allow greater flexibility each shadow (and thus the group of associated agents) can have a timeout of its own. This allows for a loophole by setting a very long timeout. But this can be corrected by introducing a per-place timeout. The timeout finally chosen is the minimum of agent timeout and place timeout.

```
Regular Intervals:
   for each agent
      agent.timeToLive - -;
      if (agent.timeToLive == 0)
         sendCheck(agent.shadowHome, currentPlace,
                  agent.shadowId, agent.id);
         startTimer(min(place.TimeOut,agent.timeOut),
                  agent.proxy, agent);

onArrival(agent)
   agentproxy = proxyList.find(agent.shadowId);
   if(agentproxy == null)
      agentproxy = new Proxy(agent.id, agent.timeToLive,
                  agent.shadowHome, currentPlace);
      proxyList.add(agentproxy);
   else
      agentproxy.add(agent.agentId, agent.timeToLive);
   agent.proxy = agentproxy;
   agentList.add(agent);
   agent.start();

onLeaving(agent, target)
   if (agent.timeToLive > 0)
      agentList.remove(agent);
      agent.proxy.setTarget(agent.id, target));
      startTimer(  agent.timeToLive + agent.timeOut,
                  agent.proxy, agent.id);
      SendAgent(target, agent);
   else
      SendException (agent);
```

Fig. 6. System Methods

The check message is received by the home place of the shadow. First a timer is stopped that has been started the last time the *ttl* has been sent back to the agent. This allows to detect agents that have been terminated (see below). The *ttl* is requested from the responsible shadow, and if greater 0 is sent back by the system to the requesting agent. As soon as the message is received, the timer for the timeout is stopped, and the agent's *ttl* is set (see Fig. 7). This ends the agent's check phase and allows it to migrate again. When an agent arrives at a place, the list of agent proxies is searched for a proxy of that agent. If none exists, a new one is created, and the agent gets a reference on it. As soon as an agent wants to leave, its *ttl* is checked. This is done to prevent an agent who is in the check phase to migrate. If it is not in the check phase, the information in the agent proxy is updated to point to the target place. At the same time a timer is started that removes the path after the sum of remaining *ttl* and timeout (see Fig. 6). The shadow can decide on a case-by-case basis if an agent's life time is to be extended, and by which interval.

In Fig. 8 we present an example policy, that for all of the agents returns the same *ttl*. This method checks first if an agent entry already exists for this agent (in case a newly created agent contacts the shadow), updates the information about the location of the agent, and returns the *ttl*. The shadow is also called if the system has detected (via the timeout), that an agent has been terminated. The simplest policy is to remove the related entry from the list. We now discuss the reaction to the different timeouts (see Fig. 9). One possible reaction to the timeout of the check message has been sketched out above. Here we present a

```
receiveCheck(from, shadowId, agentId)
    stopTimer(agentId);
    shadow = shadowList.find(shadowId);
    timeToLive = shadow.timeToLive(from, agentId);
    if (timeToLive > 0)
        startTimer(timeToLive
                   + shadow.getTimeOut(agentId),
                   shadow, agentId);
        sendAllowance(from, agentId, timeToLive);
receiveAllowance(agentId, timeToLive)
    stopTimer(agentId);
    agent = agentList.findAgent(agentId);
    agent.timeToLive = timeToLive;
    proxyList.setTime(agentId, timeToLive);
```

Fig. 7. The Check Phase

```
timeToLive(from, agentId, shadowId)
[here an example policy is presented]
    shadowproxy = listOfProxies.find(shadowId);
    agententry = shadowproxy.get(agentId)
    if( agententry != null)
        agententry.target = from;
    else
        agententry = new AgentEntry(from, agentId,
                                    timeToLive);
        shadowproxy.add (agententry);
    return agententry.timeToLive;

remove(agentId)
[implement policy]
    agentproxy = listOfProxies.find(agentId);
    agentproxy.remove(agentId);
```

Fig. 8. Methods in the Shadow Object

```
onTimer(proxy, agent)              // check timeout
[here an example policy is presented]
    agentList.remove(agent);
    agentproxy.remove(agentId);
    if(agentproxy.entries() == 0)
        proxyList.remove(agentproxy);

onTimer(agentproxy, agentId)      // path redundant
[implement policy]
    agentproxy.remove(agentId);
    if(agentproxy.entries() == 0)
        proxyList.remove(agentproxy);

onTimer(shadow, agentId)          // ag. terminated
    shadow.remove(agentId);
```

Fig. 9. System: Reaction to Timeouts

simple alternative; the agent is removed at once. The next timeout affects the paths. As soon as an agent migrates, the path segment pointing to its new location is created, and a timer started. As soon as this timer ends, we know that the path information in the shadow itself has been updated, and this part of the path can safely be removed. The last method is called if an agent has not tried to contact the shadow for the sum of *ttl* and timeout. In this case the agent has terminated. The shadow method (see Fig. 9) is called to react to it.

Finding Agents. If we want to actively terminate a specific agent, we have to find it first. This can be done with the help of the information stored in the agent proxies. If the agent is in the local list of active agents, it is already found. If not, the related agent proxy is searched. If it is not found, an error is returned. If it is discovered, a *find request* is sent to the target found in the proxy. At the target place the list of active agents is again examined. If the agent is found, a success message is sent back. If not, the related agent proxy is searched again. If no proxy exists, an error is sent back. Otherwise, the message is sent on. This

```
find(agentId)
    if (agentList.find(agentId) != null)
        return(this);
    agentproxy = shadowList.find(agentId);
    if(agentproxy != null)
        sendFind(agentproxy.target(agentId), this, agentId);
    else
        return(notFoundError);

receiveFind(searcher, agentId)
    if (agentList.find(agentId) != null)
        sendFound(searcher, this, agentId);
    if((agtproxy = proxyList.find(agentId)) != null)
        sendFind(agtproxy.target(agentId), searcher, agentId);
    else
        sendError(searcher, notFoundError, agentId);

receiveFound(from, agentId)
    return(from);

receiveError(error, agentId)
    if (error == notFoundError)
        return(error);
```

Fig. 10. Finding Agents

is repeated until the agent is found or the path ends (see Fig. 10).

3.3 Mobile Shadows

In cases where many of the agents depending on a shadow move somewhere far away (i.e. communication costs are high), every one of the agents has to contact the shadow independently, resulting in unnecessarily high communication costs. If the migration behaviour is known in advance, the shadow can be placed in a way that reduces the communication cost. But in many cases the behaviour is not known in advance, or the group moves as a whole from area to area (e.g. from one organization to another). In these cases it would be much better if the shadow moved with the agents. Possible policies where to place the shadow could be:

• at a place where the communication cost to all dependent agents would be lowest.

• where one agent important for the computation is situated. If the place becomes unavailable (e.g. crashes), both shadow and agent would not be reachable, and the other dependent agents would be terminated.

While in the first case the shadow would have to be persistent, in the second case it would have to be transient to implement the policy.

To move a shadow two problems have to be dealt with. The first is that the agents depending on the shadow have somehow to be notified about the new location of the shadow. The second is that the application still has to be able to reach the shadow, e.g. in case it wants to terminate the agents. Both problems can be solved similar to the approach used with the agent proxies. When a shadow moves, a shadow proxy stays behind. Thus over time a shadow path is built. By contacting the copy at the home place in regular intervals this path can be cut short. As alternative to intervals at which to cut the path short, a maximum path length would be suitable. But using a maximum path length adds communication along the path, because as soon as the maximum path length has been reached the shadow proxies along the path have to be notified that they are no longer needed. A combination of these policies seems the most flexible.

Now, when an agent requests a new *ttl*, the shadow might already have moved somewhere else. In this case, the request is sent to the new place of the shadow. If the shadow already has moved again, the request is forwarded along the path of shadow proxies until the shadow itself is reached. The shadow sends a new grant back to the agent together with its new place. The next time the agent sends its request directly to the new place.

The shadow proxies can be removed as soon as the path is no longer needed and no agent still has the reference to a shadow proxy. Thus the maximum of agent and shadow *ttl* is the maximum time the proxy has to be hold. One exception has to be made though. The first proxy, that stays at home, cannot be removed as long as the shadow is elsewhere.

The Protocol. We first examine the shadow part of the protocol. Moving the shadow to another place creates a path to the target and starts a timer. After the timeout of this timer the path has to be deleted. The path is created by leaving a shadow proxy behind. Removing the shadow is done by sending a message along the path (see Fig. 11). Each shadow gets a *ttl*, after which it must contact its home place. This time is not necessarily the same as for the agents.

```
move(target)
    if (timeToLive != 0)
        sendShadow(target, this);
        if(currentPlace != null)        // part of path
            pathTimeOut = timeToLive + timeOut;
            startTimer(pathTimeOut, shadow);
        currentPlace = target;

terminateShadow()
    if (currentPlace != null)        // shadow moved
        sendTerminate(currentPlace, id);
    delete(this);
```

Fig. 11. Additional Shadow Methods

In regular intervals this *ttl* is decremented. As soon as the shadow's *ttl* is 0, the shadow enters the check phase. A message containing the shadow id and its current place is sent to the home place and a timer is started (see Fig. 12). The check message for the shadow contains the new place of the shadow. If the shadow proxy at home still exists, it is updated and the *ttl* is sent back. If the answer

```
Regular Intervals:
[agent related part stays the same]
    for each shadow
        if (shadow.homePlace != place.name())
            shadow.timeToLive--;
        if (shadow.timeToLive == 0)
            sendCheck(shadow.homePlace,
                      shadow.id);
            startTimer(shadow.timeOut,
                       shadow);
```

Fig. 12. Extended System Methods:
Regular Intervals

is not received until the timeout, the shadow is removed (more complex reactions with retries can be chosen instead).

As soon as it is received, the timer is stopped and the *ttl* is set (see Fig. 13). The shadow proxies creating the path between home place and shadow get a similar timeout after the sum of *ttl* of the shadow, of the agent (see below) and the communication timeout. At that point the path is redundant and can be removed (see below). This way the path created by the shadow is cut short in regular intervals. If the shadow comes back to its home place, the shadow proxy is replaced by the original.

```
onTimer(shadow)        // this path seg. is redundant
    shadowList.remove(shadow);
receiveAllowance(shadowId, timeToLive)
    shadow = shadowList.find(shadowId);
    stopTimer(shadow);
    shadow.timeToLive = timeToLive;
receiveCheck(from, shadowId)
    shadow = shadowList.find(shadowId);
    if(shadow != null)
        shadow.currentPlace = place;
        sendAllowance(from, shadowId,
                          shadow.timeToLive);
```

Fig. 13. Additional System Methods: Checking the Shadow

In the basic protocol the agent check message is sent to the shadow's home place. Now it is sent to the place from which the last *ttl* message has been received. This is done by storing it in an additional attribute. If the shadow moves between two such messages, the check message is sent to a shadow proxy (somewhere on the path) instead of the original. The shadow proxy now forwards this agent check message along the path. The original, upon receiving the message, sends back the *ttl* and its own place. The path is superfluous as soon as the shadow's place is known at the home place **and** no agent still references a part of it (see Fig. 14).

```
receiveCheck(from, shadowId, agentId)
    stopTimer(agentId);
    if(currentPlace != place.name())
        sendCheck(currentPlace, from,
                        shadowId, agentId);
    else
        shadow = shadowList.find(shadowId);
        timeToLive =
                    shadow.timeToLive(from, agentId);
        if (timeToLive > 0)
            startTimer(timeToLive
                       + shadow.getTimeOut(agentId),
                     shadow, agentId);
        sendAllowance(from, place.name(),
                        agentId, timeToLive);
receiveAllowance(shadowPlace, agentId, timeToLive)
    stopTimer(agentId);
    agent = agentList.findAgent(agentId);
    agent.timeToLive = timeToLive;
    agent.shadowHome = shadowPlace;
    proxyList.setTime(agentId, timeToLive);
```

Fig. 14. Changed System Methods: Extending the Agent's Life

Together with sending back the *ttl* to the agent the shadow starts a timer. If after this timeout the agent did not send a check message, the shadow knows that the agent has terminated. But since the timeout is detected at a place and not inside the shadow, the information might only reach a proxy and not the shadow itself. In this case the shadow has to be informed. Thus a message is sent along the path containing the information that the agent has terminated. Every proxy sends the information onward until it reaches the shadow. Now the agent entry is removed (see Fig. 15).

```
onTimer(shadow, agentId)          // agent terminated
    shadow.remove(agentId);
    if (shadow.currentPlace != place.name() )
        sendRemoved(   currentPlace, shadowId,
                                 agentId);
receiveRemoved(shadowId, agentId)
    shadow = shadowList.find(shadowId);
    if(shadow != null)
        if(shadow.currentPlace != place.name())
            sendRemoved(   currentPlace, shadowId,
                                 agentId);
        else
            shadow = shadowList.find(shadowId);
            shadow.remove(agentId);
```

Fig. 15. Changed System Methods: Detecting Terminated Agents

3.4   Optimizing the Communication

As soon as more than one agent belongs to a shadow, optimizations of the communication are possible. Three optimizations exist:

- If two agents belonging to the same shadow come to the same place, the *ttl* of the one with the lower remaining time interval is set to the *ttl* of the other one. This works with an arbitrarily large number of agents on a place and happens conveniently at the arrival of a new agent.

- If an agent's shadow has been checked, then this information also gets transferred to all other agents belonging to the same shadow on the same place as the agent.

- The combination of shadow and agent proxies creates a spanning tree that follows the agents' movements with the shadow as the root. The tree can be optimized by simply using common paths for the parts of the paths that are the same for different agents. This effectively reduces the number of messages that flow without changing the functionality. Furthermore, the agents on nodes along the tree can be updated simultaneously.

The proxies allow to find an agent, e.g. to terminate it actively. But with all of the mentioned optimizations the path to a specific agent can be lost. This can happen if an agent gets additional *ttl* from another agent, and the path assuming the original *ttl* is removed. The optimizations make it impossible to terminate a specific agent.

The interesting point though is that this doesn't matter for the termination of the whole group of agents. If the termination message is sent to all known proxies, then these proxies forward the termination message along all of the paths they are part of. Ultimately this termination message reaches all of the agents, even those no longer directly known to the shadow. The path segment for an agent exists exactly for the current *ttl* of the agent. So if it got additional time, then at that place the agent proxy holds the path from that place for that remaining time. Every time an agent gets additional time from another agent, there exists a valid path to that other agent. So, by first following the path to the other agent, and then the still valid path to our agent, every agent gets the termination message. This way, all of the mentioned optimizations can be used without compromising functionality for the group as a whole.

3.5 Fault Tolerance

Our fault model contains two types of failures, node failures (fail-stop) and network partitions. It is important to note that from the viewpoint of a node these failures are not distinguishable. By introducing a path of proxies the fault sensitivity of the protocol is increased. If only one of the nodes containing a proxy is not reachable, either through node failure or network partitioning, the path is broken. Different mechanisms have to be used for the two different kinds of paths. While in the case of a broken agent proxy path only one agent is no longer reachable until its *ttl* is 0, in the case of a broken shadow proxy path the agents trying to extend their life are threatened. The mechanism employed for the agent proxy paths has already been presented in Sect. 3, and is only discussed briefly. The mechanism used for shadow proxy paths has not yet been discussed in the protocol section and is examined in the following in detail.

Agent Proxy Path. By introducing the *ttl*, after which the agent has to contact the shadow's place, it is guaranteed that even if the path is broken, the new location of the agent can be identified after the *ttl* (as a worst-case bound), as long as either the network partition is short-term, or agent place and shadow place are in the same partition. If after the *ttl* (plus the timeout) the agent has not contacted the shadow, the shadow knows that the agent does not exist any longer (either because it has terminated or has been declared orphan and removed by the system).

Shadow Proxy Path. Two strategies are possible for dealing with a broken shadow proxy path. The first strategy does not change the characteristics of the protocol, but manages only short-term failures. It lets the last shadow proxy of the still-existing path try to contact the next shadow proxy again. The problem though is that the new *ttl* has to be sent to the agent before the system decides to terminate it.

The second strategy allows for longer failures but changes the worst-case bound for passive termination of the agents (the worst-case bound is 2*ttl* in this variant). If the last shadow proxy detects the break, it sends a new *ttl* back to the agent, but with the *home* place of the shadow as the new location. The new *ttl* is the minimum of the remaining shadow *ttl* and the agent *ttl*. If the shadow would have been removed, then the shadow proxy would know about it (and would have been removed as well). Thus the shadow still exists and it is correct to send the allowance. The home place of the shadow is sent instead of the location of the next shadow proxy in the path, to guarantee that the agent has a valid place to send the request for the next *ttl*. If the *ttl* of the agent is shorter than the remaining time of the shadow proxy path, then the next request will be sent along the same path (that hopefully is connected again). If the *ttl* of the path is shorter, then the agent will contact the home place of the shadow when the shadow itself has requested a new *ttl*. This means that the home place holds the new location of the shadow and forwards the request correctly.

4 Related Work

In the area of mobile agent systems the current research concentrates on the basic system support. But now that many different agent systems existing support the functionality needed to realize applications, mechanisms providing the functionality presented in this paper are essential. Thus the problem areas of orphan detection and termination of agents are beginning to evoke the interest of the research community. But apart from the mechanisms developed at the University of Stuttgart (see [5] describing a group concept or [2] discussing an energy concept and a path concept) no publications present similar functionality for mobile agent systems. However, in the area of distributed systems many algorithms exist that solve similar problems. The area of distributed algorithms, and especially distributed termination detection (in [9] and in [13] a discussion of many algorithms can be found) and distributed garbage collection (one example is the work on Stub Scion Pair Chains [11]), has to be seen as related work.

But two differences prevent the use of these algorithms for mobile agent systems. First of all, the fault model is different. The possibility of network partitions or node crashes does not exist in the fault model used for most distributed algorithms. Mobile agent systems explicitly include these faults in their fault model. Furthermore, the fault model supports the asynchrony of agents. The second difference is the autonomy of the "objects" in question that very much influences the processing model. A process (or object) in the distributed system area is not normally seen as autonomous. Here a process is seen as a cooperating part of a larger application. For a mobile agent the autonomy is one of the important prerequisites. This autonomy leads to the problem that a malicious agent might try to remove itself from the control by the system. These differences make it impossible to use the existing distributed algorithms in the area of mobile agent systems. It might be possible to use one such algorithm as the basis for a new design tailored to the needs of mobile agent systems. But the changes in the fault model and in the processing model effect so many changes in the algorithm itself that a *correct* transformation would be problematic at best. Nevertheless we believe that in principle it is possible to transform these algorithms correctly into algorithms that take the peculiarities of mobile agent systems into account. The key to this is an automatic transformation that, used on e.g. an algorithm for distributed garbage collection, turns it into a orphan detection and / or termination algorithm for mobile agent systems. An analogon to such an algorithm exists for the automatic transformation of termination detection algorithms into distributed garbage collection algorithms [10].

5 Conclusion and Future Work

In this paper we presented the shadow protocol. The shadow protocol has still some disadvantages: it introduces additional communication into the system and resources (memory) are bound to store the different path information. But the advantages outweigh the disadvantages by far: the mechanism is robust against malicious or faulty agents, the path information is updated without additional communication costs (no outdated path information exists), and the time until all agents are terminated in the worst case can be determined exactly. The presented protocol has been implemented in our agent system Mole (for a description of Mole see [12], [1], and [4]).

We will examine the area of fault tolerance in detail. The presented mechanism is robust against short time network partitioning and system faults, but does not cope well with lasting faults. We will investigate in which way the shadow concept can be made fault resilient by replication of the control structures.

Comment: This paper does not contain the full protocol as an appendix due to space restrictions. For the complete description please refer to [3].

Acknowledgements: Parts of the protocol have been implemented by M. Zepf. The comments of F. Hohl, M. Schwehm and M. Straßer improved the quality of the paper.

A References

1. J. Baumann, F. Hohl, N. Radouniklis, K. Rothermel, M. Straßer. "Communication Concepts for Mobile Agent Systems", in Mobile Agents '97, LNCS 1219, Springer-Verlag, pp. 123 - 135, 1997.
2. J. Baumann. „A Protocol for Orphan Detection and Termination in Mobile Agent Systems", Tech. Report 1997/09, Fac. of Computer Science, U. of Stuttgart, 1997.
3. J. Baumann, K. Rothermel. "The Shadow Approach: An Orphan Detection Protocol for Mobile Agents", Tech. Report 1998/08, Fac. of Computer Science, U. of Stuttgart, 1998.
4. J. Baumann, F. Hohl, K. Rothermel, M. Straßer. „Mole - Concepts of a Mobile Agent System", in WWW Journal, Special Issue on Software Agents, to appear.
5. J. Baumann, N. Radouniklis. „Agent Groups for Mobile Agent Systems", in Distributed Applications and Interoperable Systems, H. König et al., Eds., Chapman & Hall, pp. 74 - 85, 1997.
6. J. Baumann, C. Tschudin, J. Vitek. "Mobile Object Systems: Workshop Summary", Workshop Proceedings for the 2nd Workshop on Mobile Object Systems, in Workshop Reader ECOOP '96, d-punkt.verlag, pp. 301 - 308, 1996.
7. General Magic, "Odyssey Web Site". URL: http://www.genmagic.com/agents/
8. IBM. "The Aglets Workbench". URL: http://www.trl.ibm.co.jp/aglets/
9. F. Mattern. "Verteilte Algorithmen", Springer-Verlag, 1989.
10. G. Tel, F. Mattern. "The Derivation of Distributed Termination Detection Algorithms from Garbage Collection Schemes.", ACM TOPLAS 15:1, pp. 1-35, 1993.
11. M. Shapiro, P. Dickman, D. Plainfossé. "SSP Chains: Robust, Distributed References supporting acyclic Garbage Collection", Tech. Report No. 1799, INRIA, Rocquencourt, Frankreich, 1992.
12. M. Straßer, J. Baumann, F. Hohl. "Mole - A Java Based Mobile Agent System", in Workshop Reader ECOOP '96, d-punkt, pp. 327 - 334, 1996.
13. G. Tel. „Distributed Algorithms", Cambridge University Press, 1994.
14. J. E. White. "Telescript Technology: The Foundation of the Electronic Marketplace", General Magic, 1994.

An Approach for Providing
Mobile Agent Fault Tolerance

Flávio M. Assis Silva[1], Radu Popescu-Zeletin

Technical University Berlin/GMD FOKUS
Kaiserin-Augusta Allee 31, 10589 Berlin, Germany
{flavio, zeletin}@fokus.gmd.de

Abstract. This paper presents a fault-tolerance protocol for mobile agent executions that tolerates long-term failures of agencies. If the agency where an agent execution is being performed fails for a long-time, the execution can be recovered and continue at another agency. This is not only important for avoiding a mobile agent execution to become blocked, but it also contributes for enforcing the autonomy of organizations in an open environment emitting mobile agents to execute applications that cross the boundary of autonomous organizations. The protocol presented in this paper is based on mobile agent replication and is a variation of the protocol described in [6]. Our protocol differs from the work in [6] mainly in the sense that an agent can execute more than a single atomic transaction at an agency; it integrates distributed storage of recovery information; and it supports partial recovery of the activity carried out at an agency. The motivation of this work is on building a support for the execution of open nested transactions with a set of mobile agents.

1 Introduction

Supporting *reliable* mobile agents executions is an important functionality to be present at a mobile agent execution infrastructure. Once issued by its user, a mobile agent (or simply *agent*) should be able to execute its activity and *eventually* provide the results of its execution, independently of failures. In particular, a mobile agent execution should be resilient to long lasting failures of *agencies* (the logical "place" where mobile agents execute), in order to avoid that the execution becomes blocked [1][5][6]. If the agency where an agent is executing fails for a long time, a new copy of the agent should be activated in another agency to recover and continue the activity of the failed agent. Providing such an agent fault tolerance allows an agent-based execution to explore alternatives and to achieve its end as fast as possible. Furthermore, in this way the executions of mobile agents in an environment of autonomous systems become more independent of particular policies applied at the agencies where mobile agents execute, thereby contributing to enforce the autonomy of organizations emitting

---

[1] The work of this author is partially supported by CNPq (Conselho Nacional de Desenvolvimento Científico e Tecnológico), Brazil.

mobile agents. Both are important requirements for mobile agent-based applications in open environments.

The description of protocols for agent fault tolerance that tolerate long-term failures of agencies has not been much considered in the literature. The most closely related work is [5], [6] and [7]. In [5] so-called *rear guards* are used to provide agent fault tolerance. No protocols, however, are described. In [7], the author concentrates on the problem of protecting agents against being subverted by malicious hosts. We do not consider this problem in this paper. In [6], a specific algorithm was described for mobile agent fault tolerance, but which is coupled with the execution of a single atomic transaction by an agent at an agency. If a new agent is activated to perform recovery of a failed agent, the state of the execution backtracks to the point before the beginning of the execution at the agency. We present here a variation of this protocol which supports that agents can execute other types of activities than only a single atomic transaction (for example, two independent atomic transactions, in parallel, on autonomous service providers); incorporates distributed storage of recovery information and partial recovery of the activities executed at an agency. The motivation of this work is on building a support for the execution of an open nested transaction model [9] with a *set* of mobile agents. In such applications it is necessary that *child* agents are created and controlled reliably. This paper is part of ongoing work in this direction.

This paper is structured as follows. Section 2 presents a description of the environment where mobile agents execute and the failure model considered. Section 3 describes in general terms our approach for providing mobile agents fault tolerance. Section 4 describes details of the approach introduced in section 3. Section 5 provides concluding remarks.

2 System Model and Failure Semantics

The whole environment where agents execute is called the Distributed Agent Environment (DAE). In the DAE an agent executes its task by moving from an *agency* to another. Each agency is associated with a set of *application services*. Application services represent application-related services, which agents can access to achieve their application goals, like, for example, bank services, flight-ticket reservation services, etc. An agent goes to the agency where an application service is to access it *locally*.

Each agency has a local *stable storage*, i.e., a storage which survives failures. Agents execute in volatile memory. We consider *fail-stop* semantics for each executing component, i.e., each executing component fails by stopping, without performing incorrect actions.

Fail-stop semantics for an agency means that when an agency fails, all the agents that were running at that agency in the moment of the failure fail as well. We consider that agents are correctly programmed and are able to handle exceptions without crashing. A mobile agent, therefore, only fails if the agency where it is running fails.

In an environment of autonomous systems it cannot be expected in general that failed systems recover from failures in a short period of time. We consider, however, that agencies *eventually* recover from failures. When an agency recovers from a failure, it performs its recovery procedures using information stored locally. In particular, it creates a new copy of each agent that was running at the agency when the failure occurred. Each new created agent performs its own recovery. The specific recovery actions performed by an agent are not part of the protocol presented in this paper. They are, however, coordinated by this protocol.

The communication channels are assumed to be reliable, i.e., with no damaged, duplicated or out-of-sequence messages and a message will eventually reach the destination (if the sender and the receiver do not fail and they can communicate). There is no bound, however, on communication delays. The network may become partitioned, but we consider that the network *eventually* recovers from failures as well.

Each agency has an *input queue*. An agent sent to an agency is put its input queue. Operations on these queues are considered to be subject to transactional semantics, i.e., a set of queue operations can be performed inside a transaction. The effects of the operations are only visible if the transaction commits. If the transaction aborts, the effects of the operations are cancelled on the queue (the state of the message queue will be the same as before starting the transaction).

3   Making Agents Fault-Tolerant

As in [6] and [7], a mobile agent executes in a sequence of *stages*. The first stage begins when the mobile agent is launched for execution. A new stage then begins (and the previous terminates) when the mobile agent moves to a new agency. To provide agent fault-tolerance, copies of the agent are additionally sent to a non-empty *set of other agencies*.

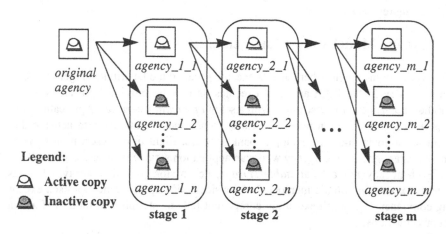

Fig. 1. The general agent execution model

Figure 1 represents the movement of a mobile agent executing a certain task. The agent intends to perform actions at agencies *agency_1_1*, *agency_2_1*, ..., *agency_m_1*, i.e., at the uppermost agencies in Figure 1. As it can be seen, at each stage copies of the agent are sent to the desired agency and to a set of *n-1* other agencies. For example, in *stage 1*, copies of the agent were sent to agencies *agency_1_1*, *agency_1_2, ..., agency_1_n*. The *n-1* additional agencies are used primarily for performing exception handling. When the execution terminates at a stage, copies of the agent are sent to the agencies at the next stage and the copies at the current stage are destroyed.

At each stage, one copy of the agent starts executing the activity. If this copy fails, some other copy recovers and resumes the execution of the failed agent. The fault tolerance mechanism can be seen as composed of three subproblems: managing the activation of a new copy of the agent when the currently active agent fails; providing mechanisms for supporting consistent recovery of the state of the activity; and managing the initiation and termination of stages.

The first subproblem is solved with an *election protocol* (for example, [3][8]). In general terms, the protocol is applied in the following way. Each agency participating in a stage is assigned a priority. At each agency *agency_i* there is a *Monitoring Component* (MC). The agency with the highest priority is the agency to where the agent intends to go to execute there. At the beginning of a stage, the agent at the agency with the highest priority begins to execute. This agent is denominated the *leader*. The MCs at the other agencies monitor the current leader. If an MC (or MCs) detects that the leader failed, an election protocol involving the MCs of all running agencies of the stage is carried out. This protocol is used to vote another agency where the copy of the agent will be activated to resume the execution of the failed agent. In other words, the protocol will *elect a new leader*. The MCs at the other agencies begin to monitor the new leader. If the new leader is later considered failed by an MC, the election process is repeated.

The second subproblem is addressed by replicating recovery information. While an agent is executing its activity, recovery information is primarily stored at the agency where the agent is running. Part of the recovery information is, however, also stored at the repositories of the other agencies taking part in the stage. It is convenient to describe the local repository of an agency as being composed of two parts: the LCD (Local Context Database) and the LDCD (Local component of the Distributed Context Database). The LCD is used to store recovery information locally. The set of LDCDs of the agencies taking part in a stage is called the DCD (Distributed Context Database) for that stage (see Figure 2). The DCD represents the distributed repository of recovery information.

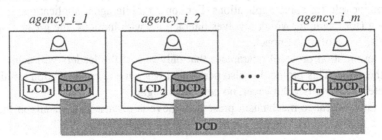

Fig. 2. Local and distributed repositories

The exact pieces of information that are stored locally, i.e., the ones necessary for local recovery, or distributed, i.e., the ones necessary for recovering the activity from long-term failures, are defined by the application. The agent fault-tolerance protocol will automatically recover agents and will provide them with relevant events to coordinate the recovery process. For example, an event indicating if a *short-term failure* (i.e., a failure that persisted (probably) for a short time period) or a *long-term failure* (i.e., a failure that persisted (probably) for a long time period) occurred. By handling these events, the application can implement a specific recovery logic.

A failure is considered short-term if the failed agent continues to be considered the leader by the MC at the agency. If the agent is not considered the leader any longer, it receives an indication of a long-term failure.

When a new leader resumes the execution of the activity, it uses the recovery information at the DCD to perform recovery. The recovery mechanism described in this paper guarantees that a new elected leader always reads from the DCD the description of the state of the execution to which the last leader will eventually backtrack. In this way, the failed agent eventually cancels its effects (if there is any) after the state stored at the DCD and the new agent continues from that point on. The recovery activities of the leaders are said to be *synchronized*.

The third subproblem, i.e., management (initiation and termination) of stages, is performed by a *stage termination protocol*. This protocol is carried out when a leader achieves the end of the execution at a stage and wants to move to another agency in order to continue executing its activity. A transaction is firstly executed which mainly: puts the information about the agent (its id, code and current state) and additional control information at the input queue of each agency of the next stage; and stores a *termination flag* at the DCD. If this transaction commits, the next stage can begin and the actions to terminate the current stage will start (i.e., the copies of the agent and all recovery information at the current stage will be deleted from the agencies that took part in it). This transaction can abort for some reasons detailed later. If it aborts because some of the new set of agencies are not available, a new set of agencies may be chosen.

The transaction is committed using a *three-phase commitment protocol* (3PC) [2]. The use of this protocol alleviates the possibility of blocking due to failure of a *single* node present in the protocol described in [6][1], but at the cost of less efficiency. For mobile agent executions in an open environment, however, reliability seems to us to play a major role for some applications. For some mobile agent applications intrinsically long (for example, which involves interactions with humans) the greater latency seems also to be of little impact.

The termination protocol guarantees that only one of the leaders will achieve the end of the stage. This protocol is also performed when the agent execution terminates (completely). Obviously, however, no new stage begins.

The fault tolerance mechanism presented above is discussed in details in the following.

---

[1] A blocking situation occurs, for example, if the so-called orchestrator with the highest priority enters the ready state and the agency where it is fails (see [6] for details).

4 Detailed Description of the Fault Tolerance Protocol

4.1 The Stage State Table (SST)

Each agency maintains a local table, called *stage state table* (SST). The SST is used to keep information in stable storage about the execution of the stages at the agency. When an agency restarts execution after a failure, it uses the information at the SST to perform its recovery.

Each entry in the SST has fields for storing the *stage id*, the list of addresses of the agencies taking part in a stage, the priorities of the agencies, the current stage state and a set of *terminating agencies* (this set will be used during the termination protocol (see section 4.4)). The SST has an entry for each stage in which it takes part.

The group of agents used for achieving fault tolerance is globally uniquely identified by a *group id*. This id does not change while the execution moves from one stage to another. The stage id is a concatenation of the group id and a stage index. The index begins with 1 (first stage) and is incremented sequentially when a new stage starts.

A stage can be in one of the following states:

- ACTIVE: the copy of the agent at the agency is a leader and is executing its normal activity (not processing a long-term failure). Each agent knows if it is running at the highest priority agency or not;
- MONITORING: the local copy of the agent is idle and the MC at the agency is currently performing monitoring of a leader at another agency;
- PROCESSING_LONG_FAILURE: the stage enters this state at an agency if it was in the ACTIVE state and the monitoring process detects that a new leader was elected (long-term failure). During this state the local agent copy performs a backtrack to the last state stored by it at the DCD. After performing the recovery, the stage enters the MONITORING state;
- TERMINATING: the agent at the agency was a leader (ACTIVE state), it achieved the end of the execution of the stage and the transaction that initiates the next stage already committed. The termination protocol was started and is being controlled from this agency (see section 4.4);
- ABORTING: the end of the stage was achieved by a leader at another agency. During this state the stage is being terminated locally. If there were a leader active at the agency, during this stage it will perform a backtrack to the last state stored by it at the DCD.

At the agency with the highest priority the stage begins in the ACTIVE state. At the other agencies it begins in the MONITORING state. The description of the states above indicates the stage state changes that may occur.

4.2 Receiving an Agent at an Agency

When an agent is transmitted to another agency (put in its input queue), the following information is sent: the copy of the agent (its id, code and current state), the *stage id* and the list of the addresses of the agencies taking part in the stage with their respective priorities.

Consider firstly that when an agent arrives at an agency there is no stage being processed at that agency with the same group id. We will consider the case when there is such a stage later in section 4.6.

After the agent is received at the queue, an ACID transaction will eventually be run locally that: gets the arrived information from the input queue; creates an entry in the SST for the stage; stores the agent's code and state at the local repository (LCD) at the agency; registers the stage id and the list of agencies addresses and priorities at the SST; and if the agency has the highest priority, sets the stage state field to *ACTIVE*. Otherwise, the stage state field is set to *MONITORING*.

If this transaction commits, the agent becomes locally recoverable at the agency. If the transaction aborts, the information returns to the input queue. If this transaction commits and the agency has the highest priority, the agent will be put to run. Otherwise, monitoring of the leader (agent at the agency with the highest priority) begins.

4.3   Handling Long-term Failures

Managing the Recovery Information at the DCD. The algorithm used for managing the replicated data in the DCD must provide *one-copy serializability* [2] (the correctness criterion used for replicated data) *while being fault-tolerant*. With one-copy serializability, the replicated repository (the DCD) behaves as if each object has only one copy, as far as the user can tell.

Furthermore, an access to the DCD should be able to be integrated with other operations inside a transaction. This is necessary for the termination protocol (see section 4.4) and for supporting the creation of child agents. An access to the DCD should be able to be performed inside the same transaction that creates the child agent's first stage. Since in our concept we use 3PC for committing transactions that initiate stages, an access to the DCD should be able to be performed inside a transaction being committed with 3PC.

The *quorum voting* replication strategies [2] preserve availability and consistency in environments with the failure semantics considered in this paper. A quorum voting algorithm works in such a way that a read or write operation at the replicated data only succeeds if the operation succeeds, respectively, in a *read* or *write quorum*. The definition of the quorums is done in such a way that each write quorum of a replicated datum has at least one copy in common with every read quorum and every write quorum of the datum. *Majority* is a special case of quorum, where all processes have equal weight.

An approach that fulfils the above requirements is, therefore, a combination of a quorum voting replication strategy with 3PC[1]. We are considering firstly the use of a combination of a majority voting strategy with a 3PC protocol. An approach integrating group communication is being investigated.

Election Protocol and Synchronization of Leaders. In the presence of communication failures, the election protocol may result in the election of more than one leader. We need a protocol to synchronize (coordinate) the actions of the leaders, so that we

---

[1]   The 3PC does not eliminate blocking, but causes blocking less frequently than 2PC.

have the effects of *exactly one* of the agents.

A simple form of achieving synchronization of the leaders in this way is by using the DCD. Consider that each time an agent is elected the leader, the leader is indicated by a *leader id* that differentiates this election from previous elections. Each time a leader is elected, its first action is to access the DCD to set the value of a variable *current_leader* to its leader id. If the variable is not in the DCD, it is created. Any time a leader accesses the DCD (read or write some recovery information), the access is only performed if it continues to be the current leader, i.e., if the value of *current_leader* is equal to its leader id. If it is not, that means that a new leader was elected and the access is rejected. The agent will then cancel the effects of its actions backward until the last state stored by it at the DCD (if there is something to be cancelled). In order for the agent to access the DCD again, it must be elected again. If it is elected, it will obtain a new leader id.

Observe that, since the accesses to the DCD are serialized, each leader will only be able to access the DCD while the value of *current_leader* remains equal to its leader id. Therefore, no access of a leader can be performed between two accesses of some other leader. If a leader detects that another leader changed the value of *current_leader*, it will cancel the effects it caused after the last state stored by it at the DCD. The leader that changed the *current_leader* variable started exactly from this state. The leaders are, therefore, synchronized.

Considering that the DCD works with a majority voting strategy, the election algorithm could be made to elect a leader only if the agent has the votes from the majority of the agencies. Otherwise the leader might not be able to start executing, since there might be no quorum for accessing the DCD (reading the recovery information in the DCD and modifying the value of *current_leader*). This modification, however, is not strictly necessary for the approach to work.

4.4 Termination Protocol

Each agency has a *termination controller* (TC) which controls the execution of the termination protocol at the agency. Consider that in stage i the end of the execution (request to move) was achieved by the leader executing at agency *agency_i_j*. The termination protocol then begins. Let TC_j represent the TC component at *agency_i_j*.

Firstly the TC_j starts an ACID transaction that carries out the following steps:

a) increments the index of the stage id;
b) sets the state of this stage in the SST to *TERMINATING*; and
c) stores in the DCD a flag indicating that the stage is finished (*termination flag*);
d) puts in the input queue of each agency of the next stage the following information: the agent (its id, code and current state), the next stage id and the list of addresses of the agencies involved in the next stage with their respective priorities.

If the id of the leader terminating the stage is different from the value of *current_leader* at the DCD, the transaction aborts and the agent starts processing a long-term failure (the stage enters the PROCESSING_LONG_FAILURE state). If the copies of the agent cannot be transmitted to the agencies of the next stage, the transaction is aborted and a new set of agencies can be chosen. Observe that if the transaction fails, the termination protocol is cancelled completely and it might be started by another leader at another agency. Since this transaction is committed with 3PC, failures of this agency does not block the termination protocol.

If this transaction commits, the TC_j sends a TERM_STAGE(*agency_i_j*, stage_id) message to the TCs at each other agency of the terminating stage and waits for a TERM_ACK (*agency_i_k*, *stage_id*) message from each of them. The TC_j sends the TERM_STAGE messages periodically until a TERM_ACK message is received from each agency. When a TERM_ACK message arrives, the TC_j inserts the sending agency id (*agency_i_k*) in a set of terminating agencies and confirms with a FORGET(stage_id) message. The set of terminating agencies is a field of the stage's SST entry.

Consider that the other agencies of the stage are in the MONITORING state (i.e., monitoring the leader at *agency_i_j*). When a TERM_STAGE message arrives at such an agency, say *agency_i_l*, the stage enters the ABORTING state, the TC_l stores an indication that it received the TERM_STAGE message, and it sends a TERM_ACK to the TC_j, i.e., the TC of the agency received as parameter of the TERM_STAGE message. TC_l then waits for a FORGET message. When this message arrives, an atomic transaction is executed that deletes the information about the stage at this agency (the agent copy, the recovery information at the LCD_j, the entry at the SST and the indication that a TERM_STAGE message arrived). The stage then terminates at that agency. After having received a TERM_STAGE message an agency periodically sends the TERM_ACK message until it receives a FORGET message.

When the TC_j receives an ACK message from all agencies in the stage, it considers the stage terminated and executes a new atomic transaction to delete the resting information about that stage, i.e., the agent copy, the local entry about the stage in the SST, the recovery information at the LCD_j (local LCD) and the recovery information at the DCD.

Let us now consider other possible situations. Whenever a leader tries to access the DCD and it finds the stage termination flag, the stage state is set to ABORTING and the leader performs the backtrack to the last state stored by it at the DCD. When it terminates, the stage at that agency must also terminate. The agency then simply waits for the TERM_STAGE message and behaves as described above.

If the TERM_STAGE message arrives at an agency and the stage state is either ACTIVE or PROCESSING_LONG_FAILURE, the stage turns into the ABORTING state. In both cases the local TC responds with a TERM_ACK message and behaves as described above. The local recovery information is only deleted when the FORGET message arrives *and* the local recovery actions are done. If the stage is unknown at the agency when a TERM_STAGE message arrives, the message is ignored.

A TERM_ACK message may arrive at an agency that coordinated a termination protocol after the information about the stage was deleted. In this case, the message is simply replied with a FORGET message.

4.5   Recovery and Indication of Failures

When an agency recovers from a failure, each entry of the SST is processed. The executed recovery actions are the following, depending on the stage state:

a) ACTIVE: a new copy of the agent is created, the agent is notified a short-term fail-ure[1] and the monitoring process is activated. After performing the recovery from the short-term failure, the agent continues executing as a leader. The leader id continues the same as before the failure;

b) MONITORING: it simply activates the monitoring process;[2]

c) PROCESSING_LONG_FAILURE: a new copy of the agent is created, monitor-ing is activated, and the agent is notified a *processing_long_failure* signal. With this signal the agent continues its interrupted recovery actions. When the agent indicates that it terminated processing the long-term failure, the stage enters the MONITORING state and the copy of the agent remains idle;

d) TERMINATING: TERM_STAGE messages are sent to agencies to which no such message was sent yet (if there is any). The local TC then behaves as indicated in section 4.4;

e) ABORTING: if the recovery actions are not complete yet, a new copy of the agent is created and the agent is notified a *processing_long_failure* signal. If the recep-tion of a TERM_STAGE is registered but no FORGET was received yet, send a TERM_ACK message. If no TERM_STAGE was received, the local TC waits for it. The behaviour is then as described in section 4.4.

If the monitoring component at an agency recognizes a leader at another agency while the stage at the agency is at the ACTIVE state, the local copy of the agent receives a long-term failure signal and the stage enters the PROCESSING_LONG_FAILURE state. The same actions as in item (c) above then happens. A stage enters the ABORT-ING state when a TERM_STAGE message arrives or a *termination flag* is found in the DCD.

4.6 Handling Stages with the Same group id at the Same Agency

In the previous sections we did not consider the possibility that a stage should be ini-tialized at an agency which already has some other stage or stages with the same group id (as part of its stage id). This situation may happen because a stage may begin before the previous stages completely terminated. A stage can only be initialized at an agency if all other stages with the same group id are either in the TERMINATING state or in the ABORTING state. In the latter case, all local recovery actions must have already been performed, i.e., the local TC is just waiting for a TERM_STAGE or FORGET message.

To achieve that, when the information about a new stage is read from the input queue, it is checked if there is some previous stage at the agency with the same group id which is not either in the TERMINATING state or in the ABORTING state. If there is,

---

[1] Observe that the failure could have been a long-term failure. A short-term failure is, however, indicated optimistically. If the failure was indeed a long-term failure, the monitoring process will eventually reveal it or the agent will realize when it accesses the DCD.

[2] The monitoring process detects the leader to monitor automatically.

it is forced to enter the ABORTING state (observe that in this way there can be at most one such stage). Only when the condition of the previous paragraph holds can the new stage start. Furthermore, the information from the input queue is processed in such a way that each stage with the same group id is processed in FIFO order. I.e., it may happen that a transaction that sends an agent to an agency commits before a transaction that sends an agent to the same agency with the same group id, but with a smaller stage index. The former stage must be processed *after* the second. The latter, however, for sure arrived at the agency firstly.[1]

4.7   A Brief Informal Discussion of the Protocol

In section 4.3, it was informally shown that the leaders are synchronized and so the execution can go forward with each leader continuing the execution from the point where the last stopped. Since an agent knows if it is running at the highest priority agency or not, it can act appropriately on the last state read, i.e., execute the activity forward or perform recovery.

Only one leader will achieve the TERMINATING state, i.e., will start the next stage. This is true, due to the serializability of the accesses to the DCD and the use of the *termination flag*. If a leader stores the *terminating flag* at the DCD, that means that the next stage will eventually begin (the transaction initiating the stage committed) and no other leader will be able to commit another terminating stage transaction.

The concept is built on a set of protocols that are based on majority: the 3PC, the majority voting and the election protocol. If a majority of the agencies of a stage are connected (can communicate with each other) for a sufficient long time, a leader can be elected. Each participant of an access to the DCD or of a transaction that terminates a stage will be able to complete the transaction if it is connected with the majority of the components involved in the transaction (in the former case a majority of the agencies of the stage, and in the latter case the agencies of the next stage and the agencies of the current stage involved in the storage of the *termination flag*). In particular, accesses to the DCD and the transaction that terminates a stage will not be blocked if only the agency that initiated the transaction fails.

In [6] the transport of the copies of the agent to the next stage might block if a single node fails, as explained in section 3. Using 3PC is more expensive, since it implies a higher latency to the terminating protocol. The 3PC protocol, however, is less subject to blocking.

5   Concluding Remarks

We consider that the additional resiliency of 3PC might be important in supporting mobile agent-based applications in an open environment, since, in such an environment, the notion about the availability level of each system is imprecise. Furthermore, some types of applications of mobile agents will be intrinsically long-lasting. For example, applications which involve interactions with humans. For such applications the greater latency of the agent transport may not have great impact.

---

[1]   This type of checking must be extended to support hierarchies of agents (child agents).

Our main motivation on this work is to build a support for executing open nested transactions with multiple mobile agents, what creates the need for handling the creation and control of child agents reliably. In this case it seems that the frequency of use of the DCD might be a function of the number of child agents and some of the costs are paid together. For example, registering the creation of a child agent at the DCD can be performed in the same transaction that initiates the first stage of the child agent. This cost, however, must be paid anyway when a child is created.

Observe that the concept presented in this paper represents a functionality upon which a layer implementing a recovery logic for the applications should be built. We are considering the construction of this layer for an open nested transaction model being executed by multiple agents.

The approach presented in the paper represents a form of *primary-backup* replication strategy. The implementation of such strategies are commonly based on group communication [4]. We are considering firstly a mechanism for managing the replicated data at the DCD based on a quorum voting and 3PC. That is a form of performing a registration at the DCD and the actions that start/terminate a stage together within the same transaction. More investigation, however, is being done to analyse the integration of group communication in the concept.

The presented work is part of a still ongoing work on building a support for the execution of open nested transactions with multiple agents. A prototypical implementation is being developed at the Technical University Berlin and at GMD FOKUS.

References

1. Assis Silva, F.M., Krause, S. A Distributed Transaction Model based on Mobile Agents. Proceedings of MA'97. Lecture Notes in Computer Science 1219. K.Rothermel, R.Popescu-Zeletin (Eds.). Springer-Verlag. 1997
2. Bernstein, P., Hadzilacos, V., Goodman, N. Concurrency Control and Recovery in Database Systems. Addison-Wesley Publishing Company. 1987
3. Garcia-Molina, H. Elections in a Distributed Computing System. IEEE Transactions on Computers. C-31(1):47-59. January, 1982
4. Guerraoui, R., Schiper, A. Fault-Tolerance by Replication in Distributed Systems. Proc. of Reliable Software Technologies. Lecture Notes in Computer Science 1088. 1996
5. Johansen, D., van Renesse, R., Schneider, F.B. Operating system support for mobile agents. Proceedings of the 5th IEEE Workshop on Hot Topics in Operating Systems. Orcas Island, Wa, USA. May, 1995
6. Rothermel, K., Straßer, M. A Protocol for Preserving the Exactly-Once Property of Mobile Agents. Technical Report 1997/18. University of Stuttgart, Department of Informatics. October, 1997
7. Schneider, F.B. Towards Fault-tolerant and Secure Agentry. Proceedings of the 11th International Workshop on Distributed Algorithms. Saarbrücken, Germany. September, 1997
8. Stoller, S.D. Leader Election in Distributed Systems with Crash Failures. Technical Report 481. Indian University, Dept. of Computer Science. May 1997, Revised July 1997
9. Weikum, G., Schek, H.-J. Concepts and Applications of Multilevel Transactions and Open Nested Transactions. In Database Transaction Models for Advanced Applications. A.K.Elmagarmid (ed.). Morgan Kaufmann Publishers. USA. 1992

Transparent Migration
of Java-Based Mobile Agents
Capturing and Reestablishing the State of Java Programs

Stefan Fünfrocken

Department of Computer Science, Darmstadt University of Technology,
Alexanderstr. 6, D 64283 Darmstadt, Germany
Email: fuenf@informatik.tu-darmstadt.de

Abstract. In this paper we describe a way to save and restore the state of a running Java program. We achieve this on the language level, without modifying the Java virtual machine, by instrumenting the programmer's original code with a preprocessor. The automatically inserted code saves the runtime information when the program requests state saving and reestablishes the program's runtime state on restart. The current preprocessor prototype is used in a mobile agent scenario to offer transparent agent migration for Java based mobile agents, but could generally be used to save and reestablish the execution state of any Java program.

1 Introduction

Mobile agents are programs that can move from one host to another. These programs can initiate their own transfer by executing a special instruction in their code. To migrate an agent, some state information of the agent program has to be saved and shipped to the new destination. At the target destination the agent program is restarted. Ideally, the moved agent (or program) can be restarted in exactly the same state and at the same code position as it was before migration. If migration exhibits this property, it is called *transparent* or characterized as *strong migration* [1]. If the program has to prepare its migration by explicitly storing its state in some variables and is started again at the new location, and if the programmer has to provide explicit code to read and reestablish the stored state, migration is called *non-transparent* or characterized as *weak migration*. Both mechanisms require the capturing of state information and the reestablishment of the saved state during restart.

Capturing and reestablishing the state of a running program is a well-known issue in different areas of computer science [9]. For example, it is used in distributed operating systems to provide load balancing functionality. In such a scenario, the state of a program in execution (i.e., the process state) is captured and sent to some other host with low load. The receiving host creates a local process that has exactly the same state as the process whose state was captured. State capturing can also be used to provide fault tolerance or persistence [6] in a distributed system. The state of programs or processes is captured at regular intervals and is written to stable secondary storage. When the system restarts after a crash or regular system shutdown, the saved information is used to reestablish the processes and continue operation.

Our application scenario is the migration of mobile agents from one host to another. This differs from process migration for 'traditional' purposes (e.g., load balancing) in the sense that migration is initiated by the program itself and not by an external control instance. Although the developed mechanism is designed for the mobile agent scenario, it can be used by every Java program to save and load the runtime state.

To capture the state of a program one has to know what exactly comprises that state. The state can be divided into the following different parts: the code of the program, the data of the program (located in its variables), and the runtime information (consisting of the program counter, the call stack, and a few more items). One problem in capturing the state of a program is that the required information is located in different places: the program variables are accessible from within the program itself (i.e., on the language level), but in contrast to this, all the runtime information is located in lower hierarchy levels (e.g., the program counter, which is located in the process executing the program). The state capturing mechanism has to collect all that information, and consequently there has to be a way to extract the information from the system.

2 Capturing and Reestablishing State in Java

Java is an object oriented programming language. Thus the state of each Java program comprises the state of all the objects that exist at the time the capturing takes place, the method call stack resulting from the method invocations during the program execution, and the program counter. Since Java is an interpreted language that requires an interpreter (the Java Virtual Machine, or VM for short) to execute Java programs, the method call stack and program counter information is located in the interpreter and not in the process executing the interpreter. It would be sufficient to have access to the information inside the VM to capture the state of a Java program.

Currently the Java VM only supports the capturing of all object states, known as serialization [10], but it does *not* support the capturing of the method call stack which includes all local variable values of methods or the capturing of the program counter. Because of this, transparent migration of processes or mobile agents is not possible in Java so far.

There are systems [7, 8, 4] that provide the required state capturing of Java programs. However, they modified the Java VM. In contrast to this, we aim at a solution that does not require the modification of the VM or any underlying component. We found that it is indeed possible to capture the state of a Java program at the language level.

Our mobile agent scenario requires that the state capturing process is initiated by the program itself at the language level and not at some lower hierarchy level (i.e., from outside the program). To capture the state of a Java program, we developed a preprocessor that instruments the user's Java code by adding code that does the actual state capturing, and reestablishes the state on restart at the target machine. We do this instrumentation by parsing the original program code using a Java based parser generated with the JavaCC-tool [5] from a Java 1.1 grammar. Our preprocessor uses and modifies the parse tree from which the new code is generated.

Since additional code introduces time and space penalties (see section 3.3), we only instrument the code where it is necessary and make sure that the additional code is executed only when necessary (i.e., when state capturing occurs).

2.1 Capturing the State

Java object serialization offers an easy, although rather inefficiently implemented way to dump the state of all Java objects that exist in the program. This state consists of the values of all variables (i.e., class and instance variables) of each object, which represent each object's internal state, and the information about the type of each object. By using object serialization, a large part of the information (all language level information) required to reestablish the program's state can be captured. What is missing, however, is information located in the virtual machine: the method call stack with the values of each method's local variables, and the current value of the program counter.

To capture the missing state information of the program, the preprocessor inserts code that saves the values of all local variables of methods and program counter related information. Consider the program in Figure 1 which defines local variables for the method mymethod of class Myprogram and uses state saving to save the value of new variables.

```
class Myprogram {                                    ...
    // definition of variables                           saveState();
    ...                                                  ...
    public void mymethod(int i, real j, MyObject m){     }
        int k;                                           ...
        Hashtable h;                                     int v = 10;
        ...                                              ...
        saveState();                                     saveState();
        ...                                              ...
        if ( k == 5 ) {                                  }
            Vector x = new Vector();               }
```

Fig. 1. Program using state saving

There are two things to keep in mind: First, local variables may be defined anywhere in a method's code. When defined in a block, the variable is visible in that block only (e.g., Vector x in the example). When the program requests state saving, only those variables can be saved that are visible at the current program position (only those variables are on the stack). Second, the inserted code that saves the values of the local variables should be executed only in the case when the program initiates the state capturing process, which is done by calling a special method (saveState[1] in the example) a programmer can use. Our system provides this special method as an extension to the Java language.

Because of efficiency reasons we instrument only those methods that might initiate the state capturing process when called. Since this can happen at the end of a method call chain, we have to detect which methods initiate the state capturing process indirectly by calling other methods that initiate that process. We do this by fixed-point-iteration starting with the method that initiates state capturing.

Since the current state is located in the method call stack of the VM, we have to be able to traverse that stack and execute the state saving code our preprocessor inserted in each method that possibly might be on the stack during state saving. In addition, no further code of the program must be executed after the state saving process is initiated. To conform to both requirements, we use the Java error mechanism. Similar to Java exceptions, errors can be thrown and successively caught. When thrown, the normal flow of execution stops immediately. An error can be caught by a catch clause of a try statement. If not caught, the error is propagated up the method call stack. This is automatically done by the exception/error handling mechanism of the Java VM. We make use of this behavior to traverse the method call stack and save all local variables of each of the methods currently on the stack: The method that initiates the state saving process throws an error. Our preprocessor inserts an encapsulating try-catch statement for each method that might initiate the state saving. The code that saves the local variables of such a method is located in the catch clause of the inserted try-catch statement. After executing this code, the error is re-thrown thus propagating it up the stack to the calling method, which in turn catches the error leading to the execution of the variable saving code in this method. This is done until the stack is completely deconstructed. In this way, the state saving code is only executed when state saving is requested. Thus the code of class Myprogram shown above is transformed to the code depicted in Figure 2.

Using an error instead of an exception to realize state saving has the advantage that errors don't have to be declared in the method's signature.

To save all local variable values we use a special save object which is inserted by our preprocessor in the top level class of the Java program. In addition to that, all methods that might be part of the state saving process are passed the reference to this special object. Because of this, all relevant method signatures have to be instrumented. Furthermore, we provide the class with the code for the special method that initiates the state saving process. By this way, the method can be called as a local method. Unfortunately, this leads to problems in the inheritance tree when such methods are part of an interface which the class has to implement. So far, our solution to this problem is to generate a new interface incorporating the instrumented method signatures. We are currently

---

[1] In our mobile agent scenario this method is called go. For presentation of the general case we will use the more generic name saveState in this paper.

```
class Myprogram {                                  catch ( Migration mig} {
// variables are saved by normal serialization         save(x);
...                                                     save(h); save(k);
public void mymethod(int i, real j, MyObject m){        save(m); save(j); save(i);
    int k;                                              throw mig;
    Hashtable h;                                    }
    ...                                              ...
    try{                                         }
        saveState();                             ...
    }                                            int v = 10;
    catch ( Migration mig} {                     ...
        save(h); save(k);                        try{
        save(m); save(j); save(i);                   saveState();
        throw mig;                               }
    }                                            catch ( Migration mig} {
                                                     save(v);
    ...                                              save(h); save(k);
    if ( k == 5 ) {                                  save(m); save(j); save(i);
        Vector x = new Vector();                     throw mig;
        ...                                      }
        try{                                     ...
            saveState();                      }
    }
```

Fig. 2. Transformed code of class Myprogram

investigating a solution that does not need to instrument the method signature in order to avoid this overhead.

After saving and deconstructing the stack, all state information is held in the special save object. Since this object is part of the top-level program class, its value can be saved by the normal object serialization mechanism. The final step in the state saving procedure is to initiate the serialization of the program's current object graph. This is done in the catch clause of the top-level object, inserted by the preprocessor, which also carries the save object.

Depending on the purpose of the state saving mechanism, the captured state (i.e., the serialization information) can be written to a file – in the case of check-pointing – or to a network socket – in the case of state transfer, as in mobile agents applications.

2.2 Reestablishing the State

Capturing the state of a running Java program is only half the way: it must also be possible to construct a process and program state from the saved state information that is equivalent to the state of the process and program from which the state was saved.

From the program's point of view the flow of control should be continued directly after the statement that initiated the state saving process. Since the Java VM provides no means to load a saved state, we have to do the re-establishment on our own. This task requires rebuilding the program's object graph and its objects states, rebuilding the method call stack, and reestablishing the values of the local variables of each method on the rebuilt method stack.

Rebuilding the object graph and the object states. Most of the program's state can be automatically reconstructed from the serialization information provided by the normal deserialization process Java offers. This process results in an object graph which exhibits the same connectivity and object state properties as the object graph that represented the program at serialization time. What is missing is the method call stack which is not automatically rebuild.

Rebuilding the method call stack. Since our save object (which keeps the relevant information) is part of the program's object graph, we can make use of that information to fill all the local method variables with the correct values once we recreated the method call stack. To do so, we just call again all relevant methods in the order they have been on the stack when the state capturing took place. To prevent re-execution of already executed method code, we have to skip all the code parts of each method which have been executed before the state capturing took place. But we do have to call the method that was next on the call stack during state saving.

To ensure this, we introduce code regions and an artificial program counter. The artificial program counter indicates for each modified method which code statements were already executed and therefore have to be skipped when the method call stack is rebuilt. It is not necessary to modify the artificial program counter after every instruction: successive statements that do not initiate state saving can be treated as a compound region and therefore the artificial program counter is updated only before and after such a compound region.

Region boundaries are introduced by the methods that may lead to state saving. Each such method forms a region by itself, which also encapsulates the state saving code. To skip the already executed code regions, each region is guarded by an if-statement that checks whether the artificial program counter indicates that the specific region has to be entered or skipped. Since the methods that might initiate a state saving process may be located in control flow statements that may possibly be nested, we have to introduce code regions for each control flow statement. The code regions of nested control flow statements are formed by applying the code region modifications of the outer statements before the inner statements.

Code regions for control flow statements introduce the problem that the control flow decision (which was already decided before state saving by evaluating the condition of the statement) cannot simply be decided again on restart by just re-executing the whole statement or re-evaluating the condition. Consider for example the while loop of Figure 3, where a method checkresource is called and might initiate state saving for the purpose of checkpointing.

Assume that checkresource has initiated state saving for i = 3. On restart, this loop should continue – after returning from checkresource – with statement5 and i=3. This means to skip the initialization part, the evaluation of the condition, the first two iterations and to skip i++; statement2 and statement3 of the third iteration. Now assume that the state saving will be initiated in the last iteration (i.e., i=4 in the condition). After evaluating the condition to true, the

```
// init i somewhere to 0
while (i<5) {
    i++;
    statement2;
    statement3;

    //method might initiate state saving
    checkresource(res[i]);

    statement5;
    statement6;
}
```

Fig. 3. Transforming loops

loop body is executed and i is set to 5 immediately. Because of this, it is not possible to restore the value of i immediately before the while loop to the value saved in the captured state (which yields 5). This would result in skipping the pending execution of **statement5** and **statement6** on restart. Because of this, the loop condition has to be saved in a generated variable which is restored on restart for re-evaluation. This modification applies also to do-while, and **for** loops accordingly. For loops are transformed into **while** loops before the actual modification takes place.

Setting the values of local variables. When the program initiates state saving, all local variables of each method on the method call stack are saved in our save object. On restart, the method stack is rebuilt as described above. Now we have to set all local method variables to the correct values (i.e., the values that we saved in the save object). To achieve this we insert declaration code for each variable that sets the correct value. For a variable there are two possibilities to get its value: the original initial value as provided by the programmer in the case of a normal program start, and the value stored in the save object in the case of program restart. Since the actual value assignment is done in an **if** statement, all variables are initialized to an irrelevant default value, to satisfy the Java compiler. Since variable declarations are possible anywhere in the Java code, extra code is inserted at the position of each variable declaration, which also leads to correct variable visibility. Figure 4 code shows the transformation.

2.3 Threads

In Java it is not possible to transfer the state of running threads by the means of object serialization. Since every Java program is executed as a thread by the Java VM, our converter is able to save the state of a single thread. To save the state of all program threads, we simply use a new save object for each thread, that stores the method stack information of the associated thread. On restart, all threads that existed at the time of state saving are newly created and read their runtime information from their save object. Saving the runtime information of each thread is simple, but there are other problems that require attention: since

```
real i;                              // init j
int j = 7;                           int j = 0;
Integer x = new Integer(5);          if ( restart ) j = so.restore(j);
                                     else j = 7;

Is transformed into:                 // init x
                                     Integer x = null;
    // init i                        if ( restart ) x = (Integer) so.restore(x);
    real i = 0.0;                    else x = new Integer(5);
    if ( restart ) i = so.restore(i);
```

Fig. 4. Transformation for local variables.

threads run concurrently, one cannot predict at what time a thread that requests state saving will initiate state saving and in which state all other threads will be at this moment. From the point of view of all other threads, state saving could occur at every instruction. Because of this, we would have to be prepared to save the thread state after each instruction. That, however, would lead to the insertion of state saving code after each instruction which clearly is rather inefficient.

State saving occurs rarely, and usually only after certain amount of work has been done by the program. Because of this, we need the help of the programmer: he or she has the knowledge which program statements should be executed prior to state saving. We provide the programmer with a new method called `allowGo()`, that when called, indicates that the calling thread is ready to save its state. By this way, state saving occurs only if all running threads have called this new method or initiated state saving. This can be seen as barrier synchronization of all running threads. The new method checks if another thread requested state saving. If not, it returns immediately, otherwise it blocks the current thread until all running threads called the synchronization method. Accordingly, the method that requests state saving blocks the calling thread until all running threads allow state saving by a call to the new method.

3   Discussion

We provide a mechanism by which it is possible to collect and reestablish the state of a running program. In the application area of mobile agents this allows strong migration. We do this by a mechanical transformation of code written for transparent migration into code written for non-transparent migration. By this way we allow a programmer to program code that assumes transparent migration for a system that only provides non-transparent migration.

Of course, transparent migration is not a necessity: it is always possible to provide the same program functionality by explicitly coding a program specific migration mechanism on top of a non-transparent system. However, it is more convenient to use an automatic (i.e., transparent) mechanism. The question then is the cost (in terms of run time penalties and additional code) of this mechanism.

It is up to the programmer to decide, whether he or she is willing to pay the cost of our mechanism in order not to have to design and code the restart of the program explicitly. In our opinion our preprocessor offers the comfort of writing code for transparent migration at a reasonable cost.

3.1 Limitations of Full Transparency

Since the use of our converter is targeted towards the mobile agent scenario, some more general aspects concerning full transparency have to be considered: when moving a running program to another environment, this environment will usually differ from the former one. In contrast to scenarios where the saved program is restarted at the same machine (e.g., checkpointing), moving the saved state to a different machine before restarting it is inherent in the mobile agent scenario. However, changing the environment between saving and restarting introduces additional difficulties when providing fully transparent migration.

One aspect is the problem of references into the local environment such as file handles. In general, hiding the differences of environments from the program is difficult and hard (if ever) to achieve, and this is why transparent migration is often considered expensive [1]. For files this would require a distributed system layer that allows to open a file, disconnect temporarily from the file, and reconnect to the open file some time later from some other place. This might be possible for appropriate filesystems (cf. NFS, CORBA), but basically the same has to be done for all local system resources. This clearly is beyond the scope of our prototype system. Because of that, we offer - at a reasonable cost - 'almost' transparent migration: the flow of control starts right behind the statement that initiated migration, and the state of the migrated program is the same as the old program, except for the references into the environment. This means that we require the programmer to be aware of these 'environment problems'. Furthermore, we require that he or she tags variables that carry local references as 'transient', and that code for local resource accesses can react to errors that result from 'old' resource handles or from new handles that from the program's point of view represent a resource in an unexpected state.

3.2 Limitations of Language Level Instrumentation

Our preprocessor instruments code and our mechanism requires that all methods that might initiate state saving are instrumented. This causes a problem when using program libraries. Normally, libraries come without source code. Because of that, we cannot instrument the library code. In most cases this is not a problem, since these calls do not initiate state saving by themselves. But if the library call results in a callback to a program's method that can initiate state saving, the uninstrumented library code will prevent the correct state saving and restoring. Because of this, we require that callback methods do not initiate state saving directly or indirectly by a method call. This is not a real limitation because the callback method could raise a flag that indicates to initiate state saving to another method. This of course requires a second thread of execution.

The same problem arises when using dynamic loading of code during runtime (e.g., Class.forName). Since it is not possible to know at convert-time which code is loaded at runtime, the current prototype cannot handle this case.

3.3 Overhead

Instrumenting and inserting code introduces time and space overheads. Since we add code to the program, there is always a file size space penalty: the code is blown up. At run time there is also a memory space penalty: we have to store all local variables of methods. But at the same time, the method stack is deconstructed, so that the maximum required memory size does not grow.

The time penalty at compile time consist of the runtime of the preprocessor that has to instrument the original code and the time the compiler needs to compile the additional code. The time penalty at runtime can be divided into the additional runtime during normal program execution, the time that is needed to collect the program state after the state saving process is initiated, and the time that is needed to reestablish the program state before normal program execution continues.

The additional code that is always executed at runtime consists mainly of the code parts that *organize* the re-establishment of the control flow (in contrast to the code that actually *does* the re-establishment). For each variable initialization an if-statement has to be evaluated that checks whether the program is running after a restart or migration, or whether it is the first program start. Each code region is guarded by an if-statement that checks whether the guarded code segment has to be skipped while reestablishing the program state. In addition, the artificial program counter has to be modified at the end of each code region. The code that is responsible for saving the program state is not executed when the program runs in normal mode.

All overheads depend on how often in the code the state saving method is called, how many other methods call a method that initiates state saving, and how many local variables have to be saved. Since we instrument only those methods that could be on the stack while saving the state, the instrumentation overhead is as small as possible. Preliminary measurements for the overhead of the instrumentation during normal program execution shows the following results:

No	Tested code	Orig	Instr	Overhead
1	100 loops: saveState + Factorial	260ms	300ms	15%
2	100 loops: saveState + Factorial + IO	2553ms	2653ms	4%
3	100 loops: encapsulated saveState + Factorial	262ms	311ms	19%
4	100 loops: encapsulated saveState + Factorial + IO	2520ms	2695ms	7%

No program did initiate state saving, to avoid measuring the overhead resulting from actually saving the program state. As the tests show, the overhead resulting

from a saveState call is approximately 5 to 20 percent. We also measured the
Bytecode blow up factor of the instrumentation:

No	Original	Instrumented	Blow-up factor
1	1047 Byte	4916 Byte	4.7
2	1333 Byte	4866 Byte	3.65
3	1175 Byte	5058 Byte	4.3
4	1322 Byte	5198 Byte	3.93

Note that in our preliminary tests almost all instructions of the original code
have been instrumented, this is not the case in 'normal' agent code. Because of
this we expect the blow up factor of realistic agent code to be smaller. Also, one
should compare the instrumented code with code written for non-transparent
migration providing the same functionality.

3.4   Related Work

To our knowledge, providing transparent migration or save and restart possibility
for Java is done in a few other projects only [4, 7, 8], and providing it on the
language level (i.e., without modifying the Java VM), is done in our project
only.

Concerning transparent agent migration, one should mention Telescript [11],
an interpreted, object oriented programming language that was designed for
mobile agents by General Magic. Because the design of Telescript was tailored
especially for mobile agents, the language had a lot of agent specific features
(e.g., object ownership, read only object references) including transparent migration of agents. Transparent migration was implemented inside the Telescript
interpreter (called engine), which did all the state saving, and did not provide
migration of multiple (agent) threads (called processes). Unfortunately, General
Magic stopped the development of Telescript.

Concerning state saving of programs or processes in general, there are a
several systems [2, 6] that use state saving mechanisms to provide for example
transparent process migration or persistence. Since these systems are especially
designed for this task, the state saving mechanisms are coded into the operating
system, interpreter, or runtime system itself in order to provide fast and efficient
access to the state information of every process.

All approaches differ from our approach by the fact that they have full control
over the implementation of the underlying system (i.e., the language interpreter
or operating system). In contrast to this we aim at not modifying the Java
interpreter at all.

3.5   Future Work

Currently the preprocessor has some limitations which we will eliminate in the
near future. An interesting extension would be the possibility to transform the

byte code of a program or using the reflection classes Java offers to do some parts of the transformation at runtime. We plan to study the feasibility of both ideas.

4 Summary

We presented a way to allow Java programs to save their state in such a way that the program can be restarted with exactly the same state and at exactly the same code position. This is achieved by using code instrumentation and Java's object serialization mechanism. The code instrumentation of Java programs is done by a preprocessor that analyzes the original program and adds code that saves the current runtime state and makes it possible to reestablish that state on restart.

The instrumentation also supports state saving in the presence of multiple program threads, but in this case the cooperation of the programmer is required by using a special method to indicate that a thread is ready to save its state.

The current preprocessor prototype is used in the WASP project [3] to allow transparent migration for mobile agents written in Java.

References

1. Baumann J., Hohl F., Rothermel K., Straßer M., *Mole - Concepts of a Mobile Agent System*, to appear in: WWW Journal, Special issue on Applications and Techniques of Web Agents, 1998
2. Douglis F., Ousterhout J., *Transparent Process Migration: Design Alternatives and the Sprite Implementation*, Software - Practice and Experience (SPE), Volume 21, Number 8, August 1991, pp 757-785
3. Fünfrocken S., *How to Integrate Mobile Agents into Web Servers*, Proceedings of the WETICE'97 Workshop on Collaborative Agents in Distributed Web Applications, Boston, MA, June 18-20, 1997, pp 94-99
4. Gray R., *AgentTcl: A Transportable Agent System.*, Proc. CIKM'95 Workshop of Intelligent Information Agents, 1995
5. Java Compiler Compiler, http://www.suntest.com/JavaCC/
6. Mira da Silva M., *Mobility and Persistence*, Chapter in Mobile Object Systems. LNCS 1222, Springer-Verlag, 1997, pp 157-175
7. Peine H., Stolpmann T., *The Architecture of the Ara Platform for Mobile Agents*, In: Rothermel K., Popescu-Zeletin R. (Eds.), *Mobile Agents*, Proc. of MA'97, Springer Verlag, Berlin, April 7-8, LNCS 1219, pp 50-61
8. Ranganathan M., Acharya A., Sharma S., Saltz J., *Network-aware Mobile Programs*, Proceedings of Usenix'97, Anaheim, CA, 1997
9. Smith J.M., *A Survey of Process Migration Mechanisms*, Operating System Review, Volume 22, Number 3, July 1988, pp 28-40
10. Sun Microsystems, *Object Serialization Specification*, JDK Online Documentation 'docs/guide/serialization/spec', 1996, 1997
11. White J.E., *Telescript Technology: The Foundation for the Electronic Marketplace*, Whitepaper by General Magic, Inc, Sunnyvale, CA, USA

Infrastructure for Mobile Agents: Requirements and Design

Yariv Aridor and Mitsuru Oshima

IBM Research, Tokyo Research Laboratory
Yamato-shi, Kanagawa-ken, JAPAN
E-mail: tayariv|moshima@trl.ibm.co.jp

Abstract. Mobile agent technology makes it possible to reduce network traffic, overcome network latencies and enhance robustness and fault-tolerant capabilities of distributed applications. However, it is sometimes difficult or even impossible to take full advantage of these technical benefits because of the lack of an appropriate infrastructure for overcoming problems related to connectivity (e.g. access through firewalls), security, location transparency, and use of proprietary tools. This paper discusses these problems and introduces the requirements for various infrastructure components and their implementation with the aim of enhancing the practicality and accelerating the deployment of mobile agents.

1 Introduction

The ability of mobile agents to travel autonomously from one host in a network to another and to use distributed resources locally, makes it possible, among other things, to overcome network latencies, reduce network loads and even enhance the robustness and fault-tolerant capabilities of distributed applications. The ubiquity of the Internet along with the resolution of heterogeneity problems by Java [5] and script languages [3], facilitates the use of mobile agents in distributed systems.

However, it is sometimes difficult and even impossible to take full advantage of mobile agents due to lack of appropriate infrastructure which enables to overcome problems related to connectivity (e.g., access through firewalls), security, location transparency and usage of propriety tools. These problems are discussed ahead in this paper.

During their work on the deployment of Aglets [4], a Java-based mobile agent system developed in IBM Japan, the authors identified several required components of a comprehensive infrastructure to enhance the practicality and accelerate the deployment of Aglets and more generally, to make mobile agents a pervasive technology. For example, it should be possible to pull agents into hosts that are not directly reachable by agents (e.g., hosts behind firewalls), to locate agents transparently and to control agents from different types of client environments (e.g., hand-held devices, browsers and desktops). These infrastructure components are the subject of this paper.

In this paper, the term "infrastructure" refers to network components (e.g. servers) as well as the services and components used by the run-time layer of a mobile agent system (e.g., the implementation of its basic functionality). Thus, agent servers, naming services, and even security services are considered parts of the infrastructure of mobile agent systems. To the best of our knowledge, the infrastructure components discussed in this paper received so far very little, if any, attention in the literature.

The rest of the paper is organized as follows: section 2 identifies the requirements for infrastructure components which are described in the following sections 3-6. These also discuss related works. The last section concludes the paper.

2 Requirements for Infrastructure for Mobile Agents

A basic infrastructure of mobile agent systems is composed of stand-alone "agent servers" and "agent clients". The former are hosts with fixed network connections, which run special engines and daemons to create, run, and launch agents onto the network or to receive agents from the network and allow them to resume their execution. An agent engine uses a language interpreter and an agent system. The latter is composed of a security manager, shared resources (e.g., whiteboards) and run-time services for agents (e.g., dispatch and communication).

The "agent clients" are software environments that allow clients to create and control agents locally (in which case they run agent engines) or directly at remote hosts. The following describes some limitations of this infrastructure with respect to the practicality and widespread deployment of mobile agents, identifying motivation for new infrastructure components.

Communication. For inter-agent communication, agents should be located by means of various schemes. For example, the most convenient way for multiple agents, working in parallel on a specific task at different hosts, to locate and communicate with each other would be to use a shared naming server. Otherwise, communication with agents originated at a specific host can be most efficiently established from that particular host, by using local logging information which indicates their location.

Thus, mobile agent applications should benefit from naming services that (1) provide location transparency for agents and (2) use multiple locating schemes, subject to performance and security requirements. Such naming services are described in section 4.

Mobility. Mobility is limited if destination hosts are temporarily unavailable (e.g., shutdown), have dynamically assigned network addresses (e.g., when dialup network connections are used) which cannot be resolved or are protected by firewalls. For example, a search agent cannot return to its origin to report results if that origin is a mobile computer connected to the network only for short durations of time. An infrastructure component, providing a general and asynchronous way to pull agents, is introduced in section 3.

Management and Control. It should be possible to control agents from thin-client environments (e.g., hand-held devices) or web browsers (i.e., HTML-based interface) as well as to integrate support for mobile agents in familiar user interfaces. Thus, clients will not be restricted to use proprietary software or to become familiar with new user interfaces in order to take advantage of mobile agents, thus allowing mobile agent technology to become more ubiquitous. A desktop-like tool for agent management and an HTML-based user interface for mobile agents are described in sections 5 and 6, respectively.

3 Agent Box

While traveling, mobile agents may have problems in reaching their destination hosts. For example, these hosts may be temporarily disconnected from the network, be located inside firewalls, or have unknown addresses (e.g. if dialup network connections are used). In some cases, simple solutions in the form of polling (e.g., repeatedly trying to dispatch the agents) work although they consume a lot of network resources. In other cases, such as when a host is located behind a firewall, such solutions never succeed.

Another solution is to pull agents; that is to say, a host initiates a request to receive an agent from a remote host. This can be done by means of the retract operation, which is unique to Aglets [1]. However, (1) this operation can only pull a single known agent at a time, and (2) in practice, it would be necessary to write extra code allowing the target agent to suspend retract operations until it has completed its current task (including the release of local resources) and is ready to be pulled.

A general and asynchronous mechanism for overcoming problems of connectivity in distributed systems is queuing (e.g. e-mail and message-oriented middleware) [9]. In the context of mobile agents, hosts that may not be reachable by agents can use private queues (termed "agent boxes"), located at remote sites, where incoming agents can be queued and later be pulled by these hosts when they become available or reconnected to the network. In addition, hosts behind firewalls can use private queues outside their firewalls from which they can pull agents and host them. Agents inside agent boxes can be saved as streams of code and data and protected against unauthorized clients.

An agent box has also other benefits:

- It facilitates sharing of agents. In clusters of machines, agents can be pulled from a shared queue and run them simultaneously, for example, to improve load balancing.
- It provides a secured solution for accepting agents inside firewalls or security domains. Internal hosts will pull agents from agent boxes located outside these domains or firewalls. The agents themselves will be authenticated by the corresponding agent box server just before they are queued. The main advantage over other solutions like external dedicated aglet server is that with an agent box server aglets are not active and so malicious aglets cannot harm the server. A similar idea was recently introduced in [2].

Figure 1 shows a usage model of agent boxes that incorporates some of the aforementioned benefits. Consider, for example, a company that provides mobile

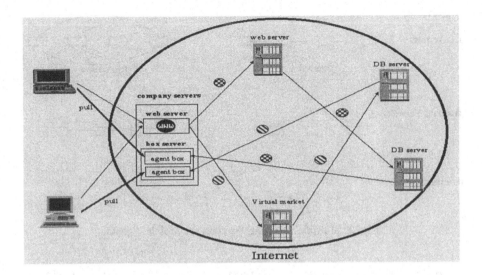

Fig. 1. A Usage Model for Mobile Agents Using Agent Boxes.

agent-based services (e.g., e-commerce agents and remote monitoring agents) via home pages (see section 6). Once a client downloads these pages and instantiates mobile agents (denoted by the circles), an agent box is created (with an expiry date) at the company's servers and the agents are initiated with the address of the box. The client is notified of its box's address via HTML pages created dynamically when its agents are created. The agents will provide the services, after which they will be queued in the client's box. [1]

The client, running an "agent client" configured to utilize its box, will pull the agents from the box after being reconnected to the Internet and becoming ready to host them. The key features of this model are that it (1) overcomes the problems of connectivity with clients' machines (2) keeps private the network addresses of clients' machines (which might be preferable for some clients).

As part of Aglets, we implemented a prototype of an aglet box server. The following design decisions were taken:

- Aglets are queued in agent boxes via the **dispatch** operation for transfer to remote hosts. [2]
- A **dispatch** operation to an aglet box returns successfully, immediately after the agent is queued.
- A proprietary message (i.e. not an aglet operation) is used to transfer aglets from the boxes to their final destination. At the destination, the aglets are instantiated as if they were all received directly from the network.

---

[1] While a mail box could be considered as an alternative to an agent box, in practice, clients might not want to expose their e-mail addresses or may not use e-mail readers capable of receiving and instantiating mobile agents.

[2] In this case, the **dispatch** operation uses the address of a specific aglet box, instead of an aglet server.

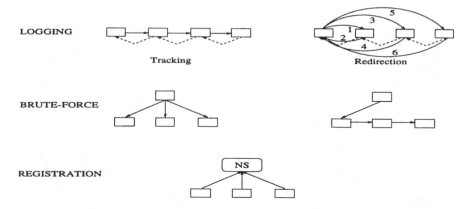

Fig. 2. Multiple Locating Schemes for Mobile Agents

– Sending messages to aglets queued in boxes causes an exception which indicates that these messages cannot be handled as messages which are sent to aglets which have been serialized and saved on disks at some hosts.

We believe that the above integration of agent boxes in Aglets is also applicable in the context of other mobile agent systems, with minor modifications. The idea of an agent box is similar to that of a docking system used by Agent TCL [3]. The latter is a server, paired with a laptop, in which agents, originally sent to the laptop, can be queued while the laptop is disconnected. From the available documentation, we realized that a docking system is a system-level mechanism which is used to overcome connectivity problems only while laptops are disconnected, whereas an agent box is a more explicit mechanism which can be used at the application-level, to support all the other aforementioned benefits.

4 Naming Services

Locating agents in the network enables remote inter-agent communication and remote agent management. For example, the owner of a remote agent wants to send it a control message (e.g., dispose) or customize its behavior. Another example is a case of multiple agents dispatched to different hosts in order to perform tasks in parallel which later need to communicate in order to exchange temporary results or to synchronize. This section discusses several schemes for locating mobile agents and for the delivery of messages between them and presents their application in the context of Aglets.

4.1 Schemes for Locating Agents

Figure 2 shows three basic schemes for locating agents. Rectangles denote hosts while arrows denote massaging for locating agents. These schemes are:

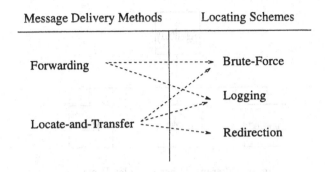

Fig. 3. Methods for Message Delivery Between Mobile Agents

Logging. An agent is located by following trail information, indicating its next destination, left in every agent server it already visited. Trail information for disposed agents can be garbage-collected according to, for example, the expired time or explicit notification by agents.

Agents can be located by trail information via two approaches, as shown in Figure 2. While redirection involves more communication than tracking, it is a simpler approach; intermediate hosts don't have to dedicate resources to initiate requests and wait for their results. In both cases, one possible enhancement is, after an agent has been located, to update its current location in previously visited hosts (see dashed lines in figure 2) so that next time, it can be directly located from any of these hosts.

Brute Force. An agent is located by searching for it in multiple destinations. Searching can be done in parallel or in sequence.

Registration. An agent updates its location in a predefined directory server that allows agents to be registered, unregistered or located. Other agents use the directory to locate the agent.

In practice, communicating agents need to agree in advance upon a naming server. Such agreement can be simplified by adopting an architecture in which every agent server is associated with one available naming server. Then, if aglets share the same origin or arrive at the same host (see the aforementioned cases at the beginning of this section), they can simply share the default naming server associated with their origin instead of locating and exchanging explicit addresses of naming servers, in advance.

The selection of a specific location scheme is subject to security and performance requirements. The following are some examples:

– The Logging scheme needs to know the origin of the target agent or any other host it has previously visited. Otherwise, the Registration or the Brute-Force schemes might be preferable to searching for trail information itself. A typical case in which Registration is used is that of multiple agents, working in parallel on a specific task at different hosts, which try to locate and establish communication with each other. In this case, the trail information necessary

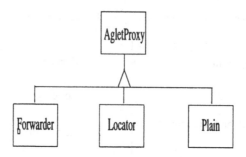

Fig. 4. Different Types of Aglet Proxies

to them for locating each other is not available.
- The Brute-Force scheme is simple to implement within an application; agents can be used to locate other agents. In addition, it is independent of external mechanisms like trail information or external naming servers. Thus, if agent hosts contacted for tail information or naming servers are overloaded or temporarily unavailable, it it still possible to locate agents by the Brute-Force scheme.

4.2 Methods for Delivery of Messages between Aglets

There are two basic methods for delivery of messages, as indicated by figure 3:

Locate-and-Transfer. An agent is located after which the message is transferred directly to it; in this case, two separate phases are used.
Forwarding. Locating a receiver aglet and the delivery of a message to it are both done in a single phase (e.g. the message may be redirected by using trail information).

There are two main differences between these methods of message delivery:

- Locate-and-Transfer may not always give the locations of agents accurately, since they may be dispatched during the second phase of message transfer. With Forwarding, such cases can be eliminated, since agents are located "on-the-fly" during the delivery of messages to them[3].
- Forwarding may be more efficient than Locate-and-Transfer in the presence of small messages. Otherwise, it might be more efficient to locate an agent and then transfer a large message directly to it.

Each of the above methods can use multiple locating schemes, as shown by figure 3. For example, Forwarding can be done by redirection of messages (the Logging scheme) or by broadcasting messages to multiple hosts where agents may be located (the Brute-Force scheme).

---

[3] During forwarding, messages are temporarily queued while the receiver aglets are being transferred [11].

4.3 Naming Services for Aglets

As part of the Aglets, we prototyped naming services to provide aglets with location transparency and message delivery. These services have the following key features:

- Applications can benefit from multiple methods for message delivery based on multiple locating schemes.
- While a scheme for delivery of messages to an aglet is defined at the application level, the aglet system handles all the low-level details for communicating with that aglet even after it has been dispatched to other hosts.

Aglets communicate by message-passing; a sender aglet sends a message to a proxy object representing the receiver aglet, after which the proxy forwards the message to its aglet. The integration of naming services in aglets is done by implicit use of different types of proxies, all of which are instances of subclasses of an `AgletProxy` base class, as shown in figure 4. Using these three types of proxies, messages can be delivered in any of the ways indicated by the arrows in figure 3. The specific type of proxy objects to be used is determined as follows:

- Forwarding based on the logging scheme (via tracking) is naturally the default method of message delivery, since it does not require any application specific information such as a specific naming server. The following is a segment of code for sending a message to a remote aglet:

```
AgletProxy  p= <create an aglet>;   // Forwarder proxy is created
...
if (p!=null) {
    p.dispatch(<destination>);
}
...
p.sendMessage(msg); // a message is forwarded.
```

Once an aglet is created, it has a **Forwarder** proxy. Before being dispatched to a new destination, the aglet creates trail information at the current host, specifying its next location. The **Forwarder** proxy uses the trail information to later forward messages to this aglet.
- Registered aglets can be located by a **Locator** proxy. The following is a segment of code for sending a message to an aglet that is registered at the naming server associated with the current aglet server.

```
AgletFinder finder = <an object which encapsulates access
                      to a naming server>;
AgletProxy p = finder.lookupAglet("Aglet A");
if (p!=null) {
    p.sendMessage(msg);  // a message is transferred
}
...
p.sendMessage(anotherMsg); // another message is transferred
```

The **lookupAglet()** returns a `Locator` proxy for aglet A, that maintains the address of the naming server. Then, whenever it is used to send a message to aglet A, it will find its current location via that naming server (assuming that aglet A updates its location at that naming server every time it is dispatched to a new destination) and transfer the message.

- If the location of remote aglets is known (e.g., if location information was previously made known to other aglets), then the `Plain` proxy is used to simply transfer messages to these aglets, as shown by the following code segment:

```
AgletProxy  p = this.getAgletContext().getProxy(url,id);
if (p!=null) {
    p.sendMessage(msg);  // a message msg is transferred
}
```

The location of the receiver aglet and its identifier are represented by the **url** and **id** objects. The **getProxy()** returns a `Plain` proxy object, which sends the message to that aglet.

Few other mobile agent systems support naming services for location transparency of agents based on limited schemes: Voyager [7] supports only forwarding of messages (based on the Logging scheme) while Odyssey [6] supports Registration via an interface to a naming server, which is configured with an agent system. In contrast, MOA [10] supports multiple schemes. In comparison with Aglets, MOA uses special location objects to encapsulate the current location of an agent, as well as the specific locating scheme to locate it. Before an agent is located, its location object needs to be located in naming servers. Finally, as mentioned earlier, MASIF standardizes the locating of agents via Registration for heterogenous type of agents [8].

5 Agent Viewers

Clients may want to use interactive tools to manage (e.g., to create, dispatch and dispose agents) local agents in their "agent clients". Figure 5 shows an innovative desktop aglet viewer in which aglets and locations are represented as icons. Operations such as **dispatch** and **dispose** are performed by dragging and dropping icons of aglets (e.g. the bee icon at the top-left corner) onto icons of locations (e.g., icons with title prefixes of "atp") or the Trash icon (bottom-right corner), respectively. Future versions will have icons of itinerary objects (i.e., objects encapsulating multiple locations and a scheme for routing between them) in order to be able to save hot "itineraries" (e.g., lists of database servers in which to repeatedly search for or monitor information) or even pop-up windows to allow remote communication with aglets. Although we do not expect all clients to use this tool as it is, it presents some initial ideas for embedding support for mobile agents in current desktop user interfaces.

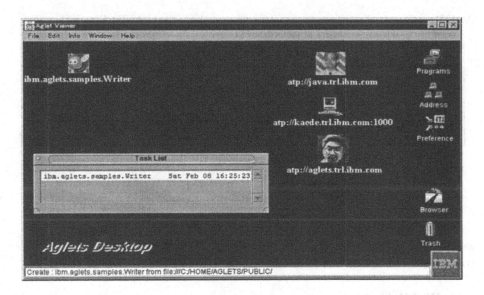

Fig. 5. A Desktop Aglet Viewer

6 Integration with the Web

The World Wide Web is a de facto ubiquitous infrastructure. Thus, new software technologies for operations such as audio/video streaming or pushing information are being integrated with the Web (e.g., using the HTTP protocol to deliver messages) to allow widespread deployment. The same motivation holds for mobile agents. For example, the ubiquity of Web browsers makes them perfect client tools for creating and communicating with remote agents. Clients are not required to install any proprietary software or familiarize themselves with new user interfaces. This section describes the advantages of the integration between mobile agents and the Web, in the context of Aglets.

6.1 Aglets inside Applets

Aglets, which are written in pure Java, can be created and launched by applets. These applets are downloaded with an aglet library to support manipulation of aglets. [4] Since an applet can establish communication only with its original host, aglets launched by it are transparently transferred to a special router server running at the original host, after which they are dispatched by that router to their destination hosts.

Compared with stand-alone "aglet clients", clients do not have to install any kind of software (not even Java) in order to run aglets inside applets. In addition, aglets that are downloaded together with their applets and run inside the browsers can be authenticated as part of the applet authentication and

---

[4] Alternatively, the aglet library can be installed as a plug-in, to improve performance.

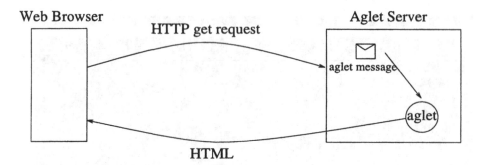

Fig. 6. Message-flow in HTTP Messaging

controlled by the applet security manager. They are likely to be more readily accepted by clients, at least in the near future, than stand-alone "aglet clients" with proprietary security mechanisms.

6.2 HTTP Messaging

The idea behind HTTP messaging is the usage of HTML as a user interface for remote agents. In Aglets, this is done via HTTP messaging: HTTP requests are used for the delivery of messages *directly* to remote aglets. These HTTP requests use a URL of the form:

`http://mall.server:port/aglets/YourShopingAglet/report?type=brief`

The path and arguments parts of the URL include the identity of a receiver aglet (e.g., YourShopingAglet), the message type (e.g., report) and parameters (e.g., type), respectively. The location of an aglet is specified by the host part of the URL.

As shown by figure 6, upon receiving such an HTTP request, an aglet server locates the receiver aglet and delivers the message directly to it. The aglet handles the message and sends a reply which is carried back by the corresponding HTTP response. The reply can be an HTML page created dynamically. Clients can create remote aglets by sending messages to known stationary aglets to create them. Moreover, by using naming services, the server can locate and forward messages to aglets that have already dispatched themselves to other hosts.

In practice, web sites and kiosks offering aglet-based services allow clients to control aglets within HTML pages; clients only need to click on HTML links that are actually HTTP messages to aglets in order to create remote aglets or send messages to remote aglets. In addition, (1) aglets can return HTML pages that are created dynamically to present actual results or to initiate communication with their users and (2) links that are HTTP messages to aglets can be saved as bookmarks so that clients can easily reconnect to their aglets whenever they want. No additional information needs to be saved.

HTTP messaging is a very lightweight mechanism. As such, it is applicable to a broad range of clients devices.

7 Conclusion

We have presented some requirements and designs of several infrastructure components in order to enhance the practicality of mobile agents and to accelerate their deployment on the Internet. Deployment is not considered simply in terms of how well mobile agents are integrated with the existing infrastructure (e.g. the Web), but also in terms of usage models (e.g. agent boxes) that are likely to be adopted by, for example, the Internet community.

Another aspect of deployment to be considered is the compatibility between software models of mobile agents and other models. For example, how compatible are the models of Java-based mobile agents with a component model like Java Beans. This issue influences the necessity for programmers to learn propriety models and the adequacy of available development environments (e.g., Beans editors) for development of mobile agent applications, thus indirectly influencing the deployment of mobile agents.

8 Acknowledgments

We would like to thank Danny B. Lange, the inventor of aglets, for pointing out the significance of the subject and for fruitful discussions. We are also grateful to Mike McDonald of IBM Japan for checking the wording of this paper.

References

1. Lange B. D. and Oshima M. *programming and deploying Java mobile agents with Aglets*. Forthcoming book, Addison-Wesley, 1998.
2. Ad Astra Eng. Jumping Beans. http://www.JumpingBeans.com.
3. Kotz D. et al. Mobile agents for mobile Internet computing. *IEEE Internet Computing*, 1(4):58–67, 1997.
4. IBM. Aglets Workbench. http://www.trl.ibm.co.jp/aglets.
5. Arnold K. and Gosling J. *The Java Programming Language*. Addison-Wesley, 1996.
6. General Magic. Odyssey. http://www.genmagic.com/agents/odyssay.
7. ObjectSpace. Voyager. http://www.objectspace.com/voyager.
8. OMG. Mobile Agent System Interoperability Facility (MASIF). OMG TC Document ORBOS/07-10-05, 1997.
9. Orfali R., Harkey D., and Edwards J. *The Essential Client/Server Survival Guide*. Wiley Computer Publishing, 1996.
10. Milojicic D. S., LaForge W., and Chauhan D. Mobile objects and agents (MOA). In *Processing of the USENIX Conference on Object-Oriented Technologies and Systems (COOTS)*, April 1998.
11. Kim W. and Agha G. Efficient support for location transparency in concurrent object-oriented programming languages. In *Proceeding of Supercomputing*, 1995.

MASIF
The OMG Mobile Agent System Interoperability Facility

Dejan Milojicic[5], Markus Breugst[3], Ingo Busse[3], John Campbell[5†],
Stefan Covaci[3], Barry Friedman[2‡], Kazuya Kosaka[4], Danny Lange[2††],
Kouichi Ono[4], Mitsuru Oshima[4], Cynthia Tham[2‡‡],
Sankar Virdhagriswaran[1] and Jim White[2]

[1]Crystaliz, [2]General Magic, Inc., [3]GMD Fokus, [4]IBM, [5]Open Group
† John Campbell is currently with the Sun Microsystems, East
‡ Barry Friedman is currently with Cisco
†† Danny Lange was with IBM during the initial part of MASIF
‡‡ Cynthia Tham is currently with Freegate

Abstract. MASIF is a standard for mobile agent systems which has been adopted as an OMG technology. It is an early attempt to standardize an area of industry that, even though popular in the recent past, still has not caught on. In its short history MASIF has raised interest in industry and academia. There are already a number of projects pursuing MASIF reference implementation. MASIF addresses the interfaces between agent systems, not between agent applications and the agent system. Even though the former seem to be more relevant for application developers, it is the latter that impact interoperability between different agent systems. This paper describes two sets of interfaces that constitute MASIF: MAFAgentSystem and MAFFinder (the acronym MAF is used for historical reasons). MASIF extensively addresses security. The paper provides a brief description of MASIF and its interfaces, data types and data structures.

1. Introduction

Mobile agents are a relatively new technology, but there are already a number of implementations, such as AgentTcl [6], Aglets [4], MOA [8], Grasshopper [12], and Odyssey [7]. These systems differ widely in architecture and implementation, thereby impeding interoperability, rapid proliferation of agent technology, and growth of the industry. To promote interoperability and system diversity, some aspects of mobile agent technology must be standardized. MASIF [1] is a collection of definitions and interfaces that provides an interoperable interface for mobile agent systems. It is as simple and generic as possible to allow for future advances in mobile agent systems. MASIF specifies two interfaces: *MAFAgentSystem* (for agent transfer and management) and *MAFFinder* (for naming and locating).

The original intent for MASIF was to keep it simple for the first phase and only deal with the minimal features needed for interoperability. For example, MASIF defines parameters in the agent profile to specify the requirements the agent has on the receiving agent system. This allows an agent system to support as many agent profiles as its implementation allows. Language interoperability is just one of the parameters in the agent profile. This is not a big limitation because Java is becoming the de facto standard. Therefore, interoperability in this document is not about language interoperability. MASIF is about interoperability between agent systems written in the same language expected to go through revisions. Language interoperability for active objects that carry "continuations" around is difficult, and it is not addressed by MASIF. Furthermore, MASIF does not standardize local agent operations such as agent interpretation, serialization/deserialization, and execution. In order to address interoperability concerns, the interfaces have been defined at the agent system rather than at the agent level. MASIF standardizes:

- *Agent Management.* One can envision a system administrator managing agent systems of different types via standard operations in a standard way: create an agent, suspend it, resume, and terminate.

- *Agent Transfer.* It is desirable that agent applications can freely move among agent systems of different types, resulting in a common infrastructure, and a larger base of available system agents can visit.

- *Agent and Agent System Names.* Standardized syntax and semantics of agent and agent system names allow agent systems and agents to identify each other, as well as clients to identify agents and agent systems.

- *Agent System Type and Location Syntax.* The agent transfer cannot happen unless the agent system type can support the agent. The location syntax is standardized so that the agent systems can locate each other.

The MASIF, in its current form, provides the features required for the first level of interoperability which is the transport of agent information where the information format is standardized. Once the information is transferred from one agent system to another, how the agent system deals with the parameters internally is an implementation matter and not addressed by the MASIF standard. Such information includes agent profile which describes the language, serialization, and other requirements the agent has on the current agent system. MASIF makes it possible for an agent system to understand the requirements the agent has on its system because we believe that it is the first step in end to end interoperability.

Function	Addressed by MASIF	Complexity
agent management	yes	straightforward
agent tracking	yes	straightforward
agent communication	no	n/a
agent transport	yes	complex

Table 1. Interoperability addressed by MASIF and implementation complexity.

Table 1 describes the types of interoperability MASIF addresses, and estimates the complexity of agent systems required to support it. *Agent management* allows agent systems to control agents of another agent system. Management is addressed by interfaces for suspending, resuming, and terminating agents. This is straightforward to implement. *Agent tracking* supports locating agents registered with MAFFinders (naming service) of different agent systems. This is also straightforward to implement. *Agent communication* is outside the scope of MASIF, and it is extensively addressed by CORBA [2]. *Agent transport* defines methods for receiving agents and fetching their classes. This requires cooperation between different agent systems, and it is complex to achieve.

There are other aspects that should be standardized when the industry is more mature. The security issues become complex when an agent makes a multi-hop between security domains. Most security systems today deal only with single-hop transfer. Standardizing multi-hop security should be delayed until security systems can handle the problem. Today's mobile agent systems use different languages (e.g. Tcl and Java). The effort to convert between encodings is too complex. When the code and serialization formats are similar, it should be possible to build standard bridges between different agent system types.

2. Basic Concepts

An *agent* is a computer program that acts autonomously on behalf of a person or organization. Most agents are programmed in an interpreted language for portability. Each agent has its own thread of execution, so tasks can be performed on its own initiative. A *mobile agent* is not bound to the system where it begins execution. It has ability to transport itself from one system in a network to another. *Agent state* (execution state and the attributes) and code are transported while an agent travels. An *agent's authority* identifies the person or organization for whom the agent acts. *Agent names* are required for identification, management operations, and locating. Agents are named by their authority, identity, and agent system type, whose combination has a unique value. An agent's identity is a unique value within the scope of the authority that identifies a particular agent instance.

An *agent system* is a platform that can create, interpret, execute, transfer and terminate agents. Like an agent, an agent system is associated with an authority that identifies the person or organization for whom the agent system acts. An agent system is uniquely identified by its name and address. A host can contain one or more agent systems. An *agent system type* describes the profile of an agent. For example, if the agent system type is Aglet, the agent system is implemented by IBM, supports Java as the Agent Language, uses Itinerary for travel, and uses Java Object Serialization. MASIF recognizes agent system types which support multiple languages and serialization methods. A client requesting an agent system function must specify the agent profile (agent system type, language, and serialization method) to uniquely identify the requested functionality.

An agent transfers itself between *places*. A place is a context in which an agent executes. It is associated with a location, which consists of the place name and the address of the agent system where the place resides. An agent system can contain one or more places and a place can host one or more agents. If an agent system does not support places, then it acts as a default place. When a client requests the location of an agent, it receives the address of the place where the agent is executing.

A *region* is a set of agent systems of the same authority, but not necessarily of the same agent system type. Regions allow more than one agent system to represent the same person or organization. A region may grant a richer set of privileges to one agent than to another agent with a different authority, e.g. an agent with the same authority as the region may be granted administrative privileges. A region can be the same as an identity domain of CORBA security if its authority equals domain's identity. Region can be regarded as a security domain.

Serialization is the process of storing an agent in a serialized form, sufficient to reconstruct the agent. Deserialization is the inverted process. The serialized form must be able to identify and verify the classes from which the fields were saved. *Codebase* specifies the location of the classes used by an agent. It can be an agent system or non-CORBA object such as Web servers. In *remote agent creation*, a client program interacts with the destination agent system to request that an agent of a particular class be created. A client can be an agent or another program. The client authenticates itself to the destination agent system, thereby establishing the authority and credentials that the new agent will possess. Then it supplies initialization arguments and, if necessary, the class needed to instantiate the agent.

During *agent transfer,* the destination place and the quality of communication service are identified. The latter is not specified by MASIF, it is left open to agent system implementors. When the destination agent system agrees to the transfer, the source agent's state, authority, security credentials, and (if necessary) its code are transferred to the destination. The destination agent system reinstantiates the agent, and resumes its execution. *Remote method invocation* on another agent or object needs to be authorized and requires a reference to the object and specification of required level of quality of service (not covered by MASIF). When an agent invokes a method, the security information supplied to the communications infrastructure executing the method invocation is the agent's authority. Most distributed object systems support remote method invocation.

3. Functions of an Agent System

a) Initiating agent transfer (sender side).
1. Suspend the agent (halt the agent's thread).
2. Identify transferable agent's state.
3. Serialize the Agent class and state.
4. Encode it for the chosen transport protocol.
5. Provide authentication info. to the server.
6. Transfer the agent.

b) Receiving an agent (receiver side).
1. Authenticate client.
2. Decode the agent.
3. Deserialize the Agent class and state.
4. Instantiate the agent.
5. Restore the agent state.
6. Resume agent execution.

Fig. 1. Algorithms for agent transfer.

Transferring an Agent. The mobile agent requests the source agent system for a transfer to the destination agent system, as a part of an internal API. When the destination agent system receives the transfer request, it executes the algorithm described in Figure 1a. Before an agent is received into a destination agent system, the destination agent system must determine whether it can support the agent profile. If it does, it accepts the agent, and executes the algorithm presented in Figure 1b. There are three cases when class transfer is necessary:

1.*Agent instantiation (remote agent creation).* When an agent is created remotely, the Agent class is needed to instantiate the agent. If the class does not exist there, then it must be transferred from the source agent system.

2. *Agent instantiation (agent transfer).* After an agent travels to another agent system, the Agent class is needed to instantiate the agent. If it does not exist there, then it is transferred from the source.

3. *Agent execution after instantiation.* After an agent is instantiated due to 1) or 2), the agent often creates other objects. If these objects' classes are not available at the destination, then they are transferred from the source or from a server.

Class Transfer. The common conceptual model is flexible enough to support variations of class transfer so that implementors have more than one method available. Specifically, the model supports:

1. *Automatic transfer of classes.* The source agent system (the class provider or the agent sender) sends all classes needed to execute the agent with each remote agent creation or transfer request. This transfer eliminates the need for the destination agent system to request classes. However, it consumes unnecessary bandwidth if the classes are already cached at the destination.

2. *Automatic transfer of the Agent class, transfer on demand of other classes.* The source agent system sends the class needed to instantiate the agent with each remote agent creation or transfer request. If more classes are needed after instantiation the agent, the destination makes requests to the class provider. If the class provider is not accessible from the destination, the destination agent system issues the request to the sender agent system by calling *fetch_class* method with the codebase as parameter. The sender locates the requested classes either by using the codebase information, or by sending a further request to another agent system associated with the codebase. The sender may have cached the classes. This approach does not require the source to determine all possible classes necessary before creating or transferring an agent, and it is more efficient as more classes are cached at the destination. However, the agent creation or transfer request fails if the destination agent system cannot access the source agent system to transfer the necessary classes, e.g. if the source agent system is a portable computer that disconnected since the agent creation or transfer.

3. *Variations of the previous two: a)* Case 2) when transferring an agent and case 1) when creating an agent remotely. When a remote agent creation is launched by a client that is not always connected, all classes are automatically transferred for remote agent creation operations. *b)* The source sends a list of class names that includes all the classes necessary to perform the specific agent operation. The destination requests only the classes that have not been cached. This approach is efficient, but it still requires the source agent system to know which classes the agent needs before making the agent creation or transfer request.

Creating an Agent. To create an agent, an agent system creates an instance of the Agent class within a default place or a place the client specifies. The Agent class specifies the interface and the implementation of the agent. It executes on its own thread. An agent system must generate a unique name for itself, and the agents and places it creates. When an agent wants to communicate with another agent, it must be able to find the destination agent system to establish communication. The ability to locate a particular mobile agent is also important for agent management.

4. Security

It is imperative for agent systems to identify and screen incoming agents. An agent system must protect resources including its operating system, file system, disks, CPU, memory, other agents, and local programs. To ensure the safety of system resources, an agent system must identify and verify the authority that sent the agent. The agent system must have the access rights of the authority. The ability to identify the agent authority enables access control and agent authentication. Also, an agent might want to keep its activities confidential, however, the MASIF expects the communication infrastructure to honor confidentiality.

Threats and Attacks. Agent systems may be vulnerable to security threats due to weaknesses in the communications infrastructure and programming languages. MASIF is mainly concerned with communications security threats, such as: denial of service, unauthorized access through agent or agent system; unauthorized modification or corruption of data, spamming, spoofing or masquerade, trojan horse, replay, and eavesdropping.

Countering Threats and Attacks. To ensure that agents act responsibly, sets of rules are defined as security policies that govern agent activities. The security and safety services that the underlying communications infrastructure and the programming language provide enforce the rules. Both agents and agent systems can have multiple security policies. The authority that the agent or agent system represents sets the policies. The particular policy is determined based on the authenticity of the communicating parties credentials, agent class, agent authority, and/or other factors. Security policies contain rules for restricting or granting agent capabilities, setting agent resource consumption limits, and restricting or granting access.

Agent System Authentication. Authentication services normally available in secure communications infrastructures include support for agent system authentication. Agent systems use communication transport calls (e.g. RPC) to transfer agents between systems. Agent systems are typically co-located with the information that their authority uses to authenticate itself. To satisfy the destination agent system's security policies, mutual authentication of agent systems may be required. Agent systems operate without human supervision (e.g. without entering a password).

Agent authentication and delegation. Agents cannot carry their encryption key with them when they travel. Instead, agent authentication uses authenticators. An authenticator is an algorithm that determines an agent's authenticity. An authenticator uses information such as the authenticity of the source agent system or launching client, the authorities of the agent and agent system involved, and possibly information about trusted authorities that can authenticate an agent. If an agent is migrating to destination agent system, the agent credentials are transferred as well. The credentials may be weakened depending on the authentication. If the client (or the server on its behalf) invokes a remote method, the client agent credentials are passed for charging or auditing.

Authenticators are divided into one-hop and multi-hop. It is currently possible to specify the behavior of and requirements for a one-hop authenticator. A one-hop authenticator can authenticate an agent traveling one hop from its source agent system. For example, an agent of authority A is executing on a source agent system of Authority A, then migrates to a destination agent system of authority B. If authenticator can successfully authenticate the source, the agent retains its authenticity on destination. If authenticator cannot authenticate the source, the agent is not defined as authenticated. MASIF currently does not address multi-hop authentication.

Authentication of clients for remote agent creation. Security services must support the authentication of non-agent system client applications. This might be done using passwords or smart cards. Authenticating a client establishes the credentials of agents.

Agent and agent system security policies. The agent and its agent system must set and enforce the access controls. If the access controls are self-defined and self-enforced, the source agent's credentials must be available to the destination system.

Level of Network Communications Security. For any communication, the requestor must be able to specify its integrity, confidentiality, replay detection, and authentication requirements. The communications infrastructure must honor these requirements, or return a failure indication to the requestor.

5. CORBA Services

This chapter contains brief descriptions of the CORBA services related to mobile agent technology (see Figure 2): naming service, life cycle service, externalization service and security service.

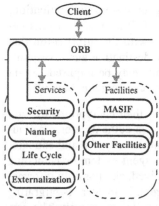

Fig. 2. CORBA Services.

5.1 Naming Service

The CORBA Naming Service binds names to CORBA objects. The resulting name-to-object association is called a *name binding*, which is related to a *naming context*. A naming context is an object containing a set of name bindings in which each name is unique. Naming contexts can be combined into a *naming graph*. A specific object can be addressed by a sequence of names that builds a path in the naming graph. Applications use the Naming Service to publish named objects, or to find an object given the name. An application typically bootstraps a reference to a naming context using the ORB::resolve_initial_references operation.

MASIF describes two CORBA object interfaces: MAFAgentSystem and MAFFinder. These objects may be published in the Naming Service. Agents acting as CORBA objects may publish themselves, and thereby allow applications to dynamically obtain object references to remote agents and interact with them using CORBA RPC. Since a CORBA object reference (IOR) comprises, among others, the name of the host on which an object resides and the corresponding port number, a mobile agent gets a new IOR after each migration, and the IOR kept by the accessing application becomes invalid. This can be solved in different ways:

ORB itself is responsible for keeping the IOR of moving objects constant. The mapping of the original IOR to the actual IOR of the migrated agent is managed by a corresponding proxy object maintained by the ORB. This is not a mandatory feature in CORBA, and MASIF does not rely on this feature.

Update the name binding after each migration, i.e. supply the Naming Service with the new IOR, is achieved either by the agent systems involved in the migration or by the migrating agent.The Naming Service maintains the actual IOR during an agent lifetime. If an application tries to access the agent after it migrated, it receives an exception and, as a result, must contact the Naming Service to obtain the new agent IOR.

The original instance (proxy) remains at home and forwards subsequent access. A disadvantage of this solution is that the proxy must be contacted by the agent after each migration in order to provide the new IOR and that the home system must be accessible at any time. If the home system is terminated, the agent cannot be accessed.

In the context of the CORBA Naming Service, each of the components is represented by one CosName.Name object. The MAFFinder object is independent of specific authorities. The identification of such an object is managed by means of a single CosName.Name object corresponding to the CORBA Naming Service.

5.2 Life Cycle Service

The CORBA Life Cycle Service defines services and conventions for managing CORBA objects. The CORBA objects can be created, deleted, copied and moved using the Life Cycle Service. Since it is necessary to transfer the agent state, the Life Cycle Service must be combined with the Externalization Service. The Life Cycle Service can only be used for CORBA objects. MASIF does not require agents to be CORBA objects. In order to provide a uniform interface for both CORBA and non-CORBA agents, new operations have been introduced. The *create_agent* and *terminate_agent* operations of the MAFAgentSystem interface (See Appendix A) can use the Life Cycle Service internally for CORBA agents.

5.3 Externalization Service

The CORBA Externalization Service provides a standardized mechanism for recording an object's state onto (and for restoring it from) a data stream. However, the implementor is free to choose other methods, e.g. Java Object Serialization. By using the Externalization Service to serialize an agent, the agent's state must be represented by a CORBA object that implements the Streamable interface. The agent system should also implement a MemoryStream object that has two purposes:

1) output an in-memory octet sequence when externalizing the agent and 2) read from an in-memory octet sequence when internalizing an agent.

```
#include <CosExternalization.idl>
typedef sequence<octet> OctetString;
// MemoryStream externalizes objects to in-memory octet.
// sequence. After calling externalize() and flush(), the octet
// representation may be accessed by calling get_octets().
interface MemoryStream : CosExternalization::Stream{
        OctetString get_octets();};
// Use MemoryStreamFactory to create a MemoryStream object.
// Call create() to make empty MemoryStream for externalization.
// Call create_from_octets() to make a MemoryStream that can
// internalize the objects from the supplied octet sequence.
interface MemoryStreamFactory {
    MemoryStream create();
    MemoryStream create_from_octets(OctetString octets);};
```

Fig. 3. Externalization and Internalizations Interfaces.

A MemoryStreamFactory interface allows for the creation of MemoryStream objects. A suggested set of interface definitions is presented in Figure 3. Once an agent is externalized, the octet sequence is passed to the remote agent system's *receive_agent()* operation to transmit the agent's state. The receiving agent system constructs a MemoryStream from the received octet sequence using the *create_from_octets()* operation. The receiving agent system then calls the MemoryStream's *internalize()* operation to reconstruct the agent's state.

5.4 Security Service

This section describes how CORBA implementations fulfill the agent security requirements discussed in Section 4. The security capabilities of current CORBA implementations can be categorized as follows:

- *No security services.* The implementation includes neither proprietary nor standardized security interfaces. This type of implementation is limited to secure environments (physically or firewall protected), or to applications that contain no data or services worth protecting. Intranet applications are a typical example.

- *Proprietary security services.* The implementation includes vendor-defined security capabilities such as authentication and access control. These services may be transparent to the application, or may be accessed via vendor-defined interfaces.They do not involve the ORB, and do not provide an acceptable level of safety.

- *Conforming to CORBA security services* (see [9] for more information about CORBA-defined security services). The implementation includes security services that conform to CSI level 0, 1 or 2 as defined in [10], and interfaces defined in [9]. The rest of the paper is related to this type of security service.

Agent Naming. The destination agent system must identify the principal on whose behalf an agent is acting. This is true even when that principal is not authenticated, because certain applications may find it acceptable to use application-defined heuristics to evaluate authenticity. An agent system provides the following information to an authorized user about an agent it is hosting (CORBA security uses the term principal instead of authority):

- The agent's name (principal and identity)

- Whether or not the principal has been authenticated (authenticity)

- The authenticator (algorithm) used to evaluate the agent's authenticity

Secure ORBs exchange security information about principals when remote operations are invoked. This information is available as a Credential object. If an ORB does not support security services, or a principal is not authenticated, the principal identity information is not available. An agent system exchanges principal information when agents are transferred. If available, the information in the Credential may be used to evaluate the authenticity of the exchanged information.

Client Authentication for Remote Agent Creation. CORBA security services offer client authentication services via the PrincipalAuthenticator object. The client invokes the authenticate operation to establish its credentials. When the client makes a request to create an agent, it makes the credentials (obtained via PrincipalAuthenticator object) available to the destination agent system. The principal for the new agent is then obtained via these credentials. The agent system uses this information to find and apply the appropriate security policies. A non-secure ORB does not provide client authentication. If a client creates an agent in a non-secure environment, the client may supply a name for the agent, but the agent will be marked as "not authenticated".

Mutual Authentication of Agent Systems. CORBA security services allow administrators to require the mutual authentication of agent systems by setting the association options for agent systems. Specifically, both the EstablishTrustInClient and EstablishTrustInTarget association options are required. Both the source and destination agent systems transfer credentials before an agent transfer occurs, making it possible to apply security policy before transferring the agent and protecting agents from illegitimate agent systems and agent systems from illegitimate agents. A non-secure ORB does not provide mutual authentication of agent systems. An agent initially marked as authenticated is marked as "not authenticated" if it visits a non-authenticated agent system.

Access to Authentication Results and Credentials. At the destination of an agent transfer, CORBA security services provide access to the credentials of the source via the SecureCurrent interface. The get_credentials operation may be used to obtain a reference to a Credentials object. The Credentials object includes the sender's principal if the sender was authenticated. The receiver of an agent transfer request may evaluate the sender's credentials to determine the identity and authenticity of the sender. If an agent invokes operations on CORBA objects, the agent needs to have the credentials for its principal for secure invocations, even if the agent is defined as non-CORBA object. In this case, the credentials object of the agent should be available at the destination. Therefore, the credentials of both the agent systems and the agents must be available at the destination.

If a secure ORB supports CSI level 2 with composite delegation, credentials of both the agent's principal and the sender agent system's principal can be made available at the receiver side. These credentials are obtained using the SecurityLevel2:Current interface (only possible if composite delegation is supported). The sender agent system can set and use the agent system's credentials for the agent transfer using SecurityLevel2:Current interface or may use the override_default_credentials on the reference of the target agent system. If the agent system's credentials are used for the agent transfer, the destination agent system can evaluate the sender agent system's principal to determine the identity and authenticity of the sender. However, the invocation credentials for the agent may become those of the agent system that is hosting the agent. This makes object invocations by any agent appear to have the authority of the agent system's principal.

Agent systems without the CSI level 2, may choose to use the agent's credentials for the agent transfer. The receiver agent system can then use these credentials for the agent's secure invocations. In this case, the sender's credentials are not available and the receiver cannot evaluate the sender agent system's principal. Note that the secure agent system can be built on top of CSI level 0 or 1 if an agent does not invoke operations on CORBA objects. In a non-secure ORB, all agent transfers and agent operation invocations are anonymous. The only identifying information available is the unauthenticated principal value that an agent system may include during an agent transfer. The ORB does not transfer or support access to credentials.

Agent Authentication and Delegation. When possible, it is desirable that secure ORB implementations propagate the agent's credentials along with the agent as it moves between agent systems. This may only be possible using composite delegation, which involves both parties in the transfer request, and propagates the credentials of the agent and the sending agent system. Upon receiving an agent's credentials, the receiving agent system should establish the agent's credentials as the invocation credentials of the agent. By doing so, operations invoked by the agent are subject to the policies associated with the agent's principal. This approach ensures the propagation of the agent's credentials during subsequent transfers. If an agent system receives an agent from an untrusted agent system, the agent system may choose to weaken the agent's credentials.

The propagation of both agent's credentials and agent system's credentials is only possible with composite delegation, which is only available with ORB implementations that conform to CSI level 2. It is not known whether ORB implementations will support delegation of credentials to application-created threads of execution. Delegation of credentials is needed to identify an agent's principals when an agent invokes a method on CORBA objects. In CSI level 0 and 1 implementations, only one of the credentials of the agent or the agent systems can be transmitted. If mutual authentication between agent systems is not required (e.g. in a trusted environment), the agent's credentials may be propagated to the destination agent system in lieu of the agent system's credentials. In non-secure ORB implementations, an agent's credentials are not propagated between agent systems.

Agent and Agent System Defined Security Policies. A CORBA object implementation may refuse to service a request. Secure ORB implementations (CSI levels 0,1, or 2) can provide the object with the credentials of the requestor, allowing objects to make their own access decisions. Typically, when a CORBA object throws exception CORBA::NO_PERMISSION of a type that indicates that a security viola-

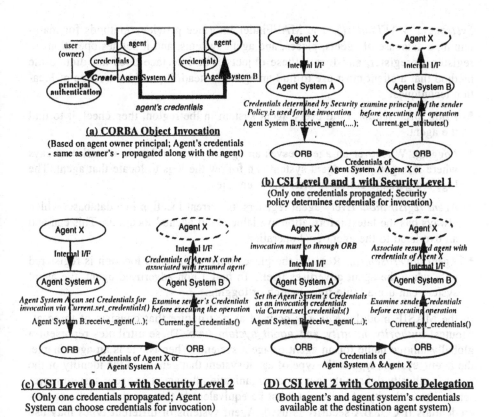

Fig. 4. Delegation of credentials in case of remote method invocation (a) and migration (b, c, d)

tion was attempted and refused. Object implementations based on non-secure ORBs do not have the requestor's credentials available. They may refuse a request based on other criteria (e.g. values of the parameters).

Security Features. Secure ORB implementations allow applications to specify the quality of security service when they invoke operations. To specify the security level, set the security features of the invoker's credentials, or set the quality of protection in an object reference. Security features set via the invoker's credentials include: integrity, confidentiality, replay detection, misordering detection, and target authentication (establish trust). Security features set via the quality of protection in an object reference include: integrity and confidentiality.

6. MASIF Naming and Locating

The CORBA services are designed for static objects, CORBA naming services applied to mobile agents may not handle all cases well. Therefore, MASIF defines a MAFFinder interface as a naming service. A client can obtain the object reference to the MAFFinder using either the CORBA Naming Service or the method *Agent-*

System.get_MAFFinder(). The MAFFinder interface provides methods for maintaining a database of agents, places, and agent systems, and it defines operations to register, unregister, and locate these objects. The interface does not dictate the method that a client must use to find an agent. Instead, it provides a range of location techniques:

- *Brute force search.* Find every agent system in the region, then check it to find the agent.

- *Logging.* Whenever an agent leaves an agent system, it leaves a mark that says where it is going. An agent system can follow the logs to locate that agent. The logs are garbage-collected after the agent dies.

- *Agent registration.* Every agent registers its current location in a database, which always has the latest information available about agents' locations. This can add an overhead to the agent *go()* operation.

- *Agent advertisement.* Register the places only. An agent's location is registered only when the agent advertises itself. To find a non-advertised agent, the agent system can use a brute force search or logging.

In the MASIF module, *Name* is defined as a structure that consists of three attributes: *authority, identity,* and *agent_system_type*. These attributes represent a globally-unique name for an agent or agent system. When Name is an agent name, the agent_system_type is the type of agent system that generated the identity of the agent. Authority defines the person or organization the agent or agent system represents. The authority of the agent must be equivalent to the principal of the agent's credentials if CORBA security is used. Agent systems of different types may use different mechanisms to generate identities. Therefore, it is possible that two agent systems of different types might generate the same authority and identifier. The responsibility for naming an agent may also differ for each agent system type. The client may be responsible for naming in some agent system, while the agent system generates a name for the agent in others.

The *ClassName* structure defines the syntax for a class name. A class name has a human-readable name and an octet string that ensures uniqueness within the scope. MASIF does not specify mechanisms to make class names globally unique. MASIF implementors are responsible for ensuring that class names are unique within the scope of the source agent system.

Figure 5 illustrates the minimum requirement for class name uniqueness, (uniqueness within an agent system). When Agent System C requests ClassOne from Agent System A, it should be unique within the scope of A. Similarly, when C requests ClassOne from B, it should be unique within the scope of B. C must distinguish between the two versions. This is necessary, for example, if D needs ClassOne to create an instance of an A type of agent. Suppose C wants to create an agent on D. If a ClassOne is involved in this creation, C uses the class_names parameter in Create_Agent to specify which ClassOne is necessary. Once D receives the class, it can rename it.

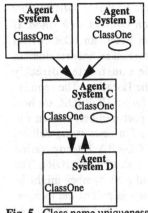

Fig. 5. Class name uniqueness.

The difference between names for the same version on the two systems can cause an unnecessary class transfer. For example, if Agent System D later attempts to transfer an agent that uses the A version of ClassOne to C, C might not recognize that the ClassOne specified in the class list for the call is the same as the class A:ClassOne that it already has. If the region administrators of the communicating agent systems agree on a globally-unique class naming scheme, the problem of duplicate names for the same class can be avoided. For example, if class names were globally unique in Figure 5, Agent System C would not encounter two classes with the same name.

In the MAFFinder interface, *Location* specifies the path to an agent system based on the name of the system, agent, or place. For example, when *MAFFinder.lookup_agent()* is called using an agent name, a Location specifying the agent system that contains the agent is returned. Once the client gets the Location (a String) of an agent system, it must convert it to the object reference of the agent system to invoke the operations offered. The Location is in one of two forms: a) a URI containing a CORBA name; b) a URL containing an Internet address. The advantage of using the CORBA Naming Service is that it is protocol independent. The advantage of using an internet address is that it is better suited to mobile agents and the Internet. To determine the format of the Location, the client parses the string up to the first colon (:). If the characters preceding the colon are "CosNaming", the string is a CORBA name; if they are "mafiiop", the string is an Internet address.

```
mafuri      :=scheme":"location
scheme      :="CosNaming"
location    :=components | "/"location
components:=component | component"/"components
component:=id"!"kind
id          :=xpalphas
kind        :=xpalphas
```

Fig. 6. Syntax of COSNaming Format.

COSNaming Location String Format. When the Location is in a CORBA name format, the client must convert the URI to the syntax of a CosNaming.Name (see RFC 1630 for URI). Once the Location is converted to a CosNaming.Name, the client uses it as the key for a search that returns the object reference. The format of a CosNaming.Name is an ordered sequence of components, consisting of two attributes: the identifier and the kind (both are strings). The location for an agent system or a place can be written in URI form using the syntax presented in Figure 6 (see RFC 1630 for a definition of xpalphas). Conversion of a CosNaming URI to a CosNaming.Name is a straightforward mapping from one to the other. In a CosNaming URI, the components are separated with slashes (/), and the identifier and kind attributes of each component are separated with an exclamation mark (!). For example, the Location containing *URI: CosNaming:/user!domain/user_name!u3* can be converted to the following CosNaming.Name: *{{"user", "domain"}, {"u3", "user_name"}}.*

mafurl	:= scheme ":" location
scheme	:= "mafiiop"
location	:= "//" [hostport "/"] agentsystem ["/" place]*
hostport	:= host ":" port
host	:= hostname I hostnumber
port	:= digit+
agentsystem	:= uchar+
place	:= uchar+
components	:= component ["&" components]
component	:= tagname "=" tagvalue
tagname	:= "TAG_ORB_TYPE" I
	"TAG_CODE_SETS" I
	"TAG_SEC_NAME" I
	"TAG_ASSOCIATION_OPTIONS"I
	"TAG_GENERIC_SEC_MECH"
tagvalue	:= uchar+

Fig. 7. Syntax of Internet-Specific naming format.

Internet-Specific (MAFIIOP) Location Conversion Method. If IIOP is used, an IOR for an agent system in another domain may be constructed directly from the Location. The requirements for an IIOP IOR are host name, port number, and an object key (an octet string defined in the CORBA Interoperation description of IIOP IOR). The host and port number might be expressed as part of the location information, and the object key for the agent system can be a string value (e.g. "AgentSystem1"). Such references may not be actual object references, since CORBA objects may migrate and thus change their IOR. The IIOP redirection capability is used to map a received reference to an actual reference. The client's ORB caches the correct version. The requesting client object is oblivious to redirection. This works for obtaining a reference to any CORBA object, and is not MASIF specific. However, CORBA does not mandate redirection. Therefore, clients also have to obtain actual IORs, e.g. by contacting a Naming Service supplied with the actual IORs of mobile objects. The location of an agent system or a place can be expressed in URL form (see Figure 7, RFC1738 describes component definitions). URLs of this type can define locations accessible via IP-based networks such as the Internet.

Even though a place is addressable via this scheme, MASIF does not mandate places as first class CORBA objects. To get a reference to an agent system, a client creates an IOR using the host, port, and agent system components of URL. If there is a place component (a path separated by one or more slashes), it is passed as an argument to operations. If there are components (equations separated by "&"), then it denotes tagged components included in IIOP 1.1 IOR. Because locations can be strings, no special data type is required for them.

Additional Location Conversion Method. For non-IP networks that do not use the CORBA Naming Service, other URIs (see RFC1630) could be developed. Those URIs are distinguished from the URL defined above by choosing different scheme tags. The location specification and mapping to an IOR will be defined.

OMG has agreed to become the naming authority for MASIF. Having a naming authority benefits the interoperability between different MASIF applications. The identifiers assigned to parameters such as agent system type and authenticator should be unique across MASIF implementations.

Agents and agent systems provide application specific properties. A client may specify the properties in order to restrict the scope of a search operation while looking for a specific agent or agent system using the corresponding lookup method of the MAFFinder interface. In order to specify a property, a client must support the application specific format of the value component of the property. The semantics and syntax of the value are identified by the name component of the property.

7. Conclusions and Future Work

The MASIF goals are to accelerate the industry and promote a higher level of interoperability between different agent systems. It is a result of the significant effort of a team comprised of experienced agent developers. Experience accumulated in developing Telescript [15], Odyssey [7], Aglets [4], Mubot [5], Grasshopper [12]and MOA [8] was incorporated into MASIF. A number of presentations given at five OMG meetings (Cape Cod, Tampa, Montreal, Ireland and East Brunswick) in front of different audiences, such as working groups (ORBOS and Common Facilities), Security SIG, Architecture Board, Technical Committee, as well as many individual OMG members who have contributed to improving the technical contents and presentation of the specification.

According to the OMG rules, after each technology submission is made, a reference implementation, in a form of a product, should follow within a year of submission acceptance. This applies only to official submitters (IBM and GMD) and not to supporters (General Magic, Crystaliz and Open Group). This is the only difference between these two different levels of participation. The latter can, and are encouraged to, pursue reference implementation as well.

The immediate feedback on MASIF is encouraging. A number of European projects are interested in adopting MASIF, for example MARINE at Italtel, MIAMI at GMD Fokus, MONTAGE at INTRACOM, Greece, MARINER at Teltec Ireland [11]. FIPA [13] has tentative plans to adopt OMG technology to avoid duplication of standardizations and repeating efforts. We believe that after the reference implementations are introduced that MASIF will increase its relevance. The developers hope that MASIF will achieve a higher level of interoperability than is the case with ORBs, i.e. that the reference implementations by different developers will interoperate. This is the ultimate goal of MASIF.

Acknowledgment

The MASIF proposal (originally MAF) is a result of a collaborative work of many contributors. It started more than three years ago as OMG issued a Request for Proposals [3] on the Mobile Agents Facility. Sankar Virdhagriswaran from Crystaliz was instrumental in creating and maintaining the CFP. The original submissions were made by Crystaliz and IBM [14]. After the first presentations, a joint proposal was made. At that time, The Open Group, GMD Berlin and General Magic joined the team. The joint proposal was soon replaced with a new one, which was eventually presented at OMG and (many times) voted upon. The co-authors of this paper contributed through various phases of project. Dan Chang and Danny Lange of IBM and Sankar Virdhagriswaran wrote the original proposals. Dan Chang was instrumental in the first joint proposal. The second joint proposal was a true joint effort, and it was led by Cynthia Tham. The major contributors were Barry Friedman and Jim White of GMI, Danny Lange of IBM, Stefan Covaci and Ingo Busse of GMD, Sankar Virdhagriswaran of Crystaliz and Dejan Milojicic and John Campbell of The Open Group. Larry Smith of IBM was driving the last phases of the project. He successfully took us through the "politicking" waters of OMG. Dejan Milojicic, Mitsuru Oshima and Markus Breugst of GMD Fokus technically led the last phases of submission. According to an approximate estimate, the invested effort in MASIF by co-submitter companies is 7.5 engineer years. We are indebted to various reviewers of MASIF and of this paper who are too numerous to be mentioned here.

References

[1] OMG MASIF, OMG TC Document ORBOS/97-10-05, also available from http://www.opengroup.org/~dejan/maf/draft10.

[2] OMG, The Common Object Request Broker: Architecture and Specification, Revision 2.0, July 1995.

[3] OMG, Common Facilities RFP 3, OMG TC Document 95-11-3, November 3, 1995.

[4] Aglets Workbench (http://www.trl.ibm.co.jp/aglets).

[5] Mubot: (http://www.crystaliz.com).

[6] Agent-Tcl, http://www.cs.dartmouth.edu/~agent/.

[7] Odyssey: (http://www.genmagic.com/agents/).

[8] Mobile Objects and Agents, Proc. of the COOTS'98 (http://www.opengroup.org/RI/java/moa/).

[9] CORBA Security Services Specification.

[10] Common Secure Interoperability Specification (CSI).

[11] ACTS Domain 5, Agent Cluster Baseline Document, editor T. Magedanz, January 1998.

[12] Grasshopper, http://www.ikv.de/products/grasshopper.html.

[13] FIPA http://drogo.cselt.it/fipa/.

[14] Chang, D., Covaci, S., "The OMG Mobile Agent Facility: A Submission", Proc. of MA'97, April 1997, pp 98-110.

[15] White, J., "Telescript Technology: Mobile Agents", General Magic White Paper.

Appendix. Interfaces, Data Structures, and Data Types

```
interface MAFFinder {
    void register_agent (in Name agent_name,  in Location agent_location,  in AgentProfile
    agent_profile,);
    void register_agent_system (in Name agent_system_name, in Location
    agent_system_location,
        in AgentSystemInfo agent_system_info);
    void register_place (in string place_name, in Location place_location);
    Locations lookup_agent (in Name agent_name, in AgentProfile agent_profile);
    Locations lookup_agent_system (in Name agent_system_name, in AgentSystemInfo
    agent_system_info);
    Location lookup_place (in string place_name);
    void unregister_agent (in Name agent_name);
    void unregister_agent_system (in Name agent_system_name);
```

```
        void unregister_place (in string place_name);};
interface MAFAgentSystem {
        Name create_agent (in Name agent_name, in AgentProfile agent_profile, in OctetString
        agent, in string place_name,
                in Arguments arguments, in ClassNameList class_names, in string code_base, in
        MAFAgentSystem class_provider);
        OctetStrings fetch_class(in ClassNameList class_name_list, in string code_base, in
        AgentProfile agent_profile);
        Location find_nearby_agent_system_of_profile (in AgentProfile profile);
        AgentStatus get_agent_status(in Name agent_name);
        AgentSystemInfo get_agent_system_info();
        AuthInfo get_authinfo(in Name agent_name);
        MAFFinder get_MAFFinder();
        NameList list_all_agents();
        NameList list_all_agents_of_authority(in Authority authority);
        Locations list_all_places();
        void receive_agent(in Name agent_name, in AgentProfile agent_profile, in OctetString
        agent, in string place_name,
                in ClassNameList class_names, in string code_base, in MAFAgentSystem
        agent_sender);
        void resume_agent(in Name agent_name);
        void suspend_agent(in Name agent_name);
        void terminate_agent(in Name agent_name);};
```

typedef short	**AgentSystemType**;	typedef sequence<LanguageMap>	
typedef sequence<octet> **OctetString**;		**LanguageMapList**;	
struct **ClassName**{		struct **AgentSystemInfo** {	
string	name;	Name	system_name;
OctetString	discriminator;};	AgentSystemType	system_type;
typedef sequence<ClassName> **ClassNameList**;		LanguageMapList	language_maps;
typedef OctetString	**Authority**;	string	system_description;
typedef OctetString	**Identity**;	short	major_version;
struct **Name**{		short	minor_version;
Authority	authority;	PropertyList	properties;};
Identity	identity;	struct **AuthInfo** {	
AgentSystemType	agent_system_type;};	boolean	is_auth;
typedef string	**Location**;	Authenticator	authenticator;};
typedef short	**LanguageID**;	struct **AgentProfile** {	
typedef short	**AgentSystemType**;	LanguageID	language_id;
typedef short	**Authenticator**;	AgentSystemType	agent_system_type;
typedef short	**SerializationID**;	string	
typedef sequence<SerializationID> **SerializationIDList**;		agent_system_description;	
typedef any	**Property**;	short	major_version;
typedef sequence<Property>**PropertyList**;		short	minor_version;
struct **LanguageMap** {		SerializationID	serialization;
LanguageID	language_id;	PropertyList	properties;};
SerializationIDList	serializations;};		

MASIF does not dictate agent system types, languages, serialization mechanisms, and authentication methods must be used to accommodate new systems. The OMG naming authority should begin with these initial values:

Language: NotSpecified (0), Java (1), Tcl (2), Scheme (3), Perl (4)
Agent system types: NonAgentSystem (0), Aglets (1), MOA (2), AgentTcl (3)
Authenticator types: none (1), one-hop (2)
Encoding mechanisms: SerializationNotSpecified (0), Java Object Serialization (1)

Automatic State Capture of Self-Migrating Computations in MESSENGERS

Christian Wicke[1,2], Lubomir F. Bic[1], Michael B. Dillencourt[1], and Munehiro Fukuda[3]

[1] Information and Computer Science, University of California, Irvine, CA 92697, USA
[2] Institut für Rechnerentwurf und Fehlertoleranz, Universität Karlsruhe, 76128 Karlsruhe, Germany
[3] Institute of Information Sciences and Electronics, University of Tsukuba, Tsukuba, Ibaraki 305, Japan

Abstract. With self-migrating computations, the main challenge is the extraction and subsequent restoration of the computation's state during migration. This is very difficult when the navigational statement may be placed anywhere in the code and hence many systems place the burden of state capture on the application programmer. We describe an intermediate approach, where the use of navigational statements is restricted to the top level of the self-migrating computation. This permits an efficient implementation of a fully transparent state capture and restoration. We demonstrate that this approach is applicable not only to interpreted mobile code but also to compiled self-migrating computations executing entirely in native mode.

1 Introduction

Self-migrating computations, commonly also referred to as mobile agents, are self-contained entities that can navigate autonomously through a network and perform various tasks in the nodes they visit. The underlying computational model is essentially a multi-threaded environment, augmented by navigational capabilities. Individual agents consist of a program and a state and are able to communicate with one another via shared or distributed memory mechanisms. Navigational capabilities permit individual computations (i.e., agents) either to move themselves or to send copies of themselves to other nodes in the network so that execution continues in the new environment.

To achieve these navigational capabilities, it is not sufficient to simply spawn a copy of the current computation, since this would cause the spawned copy to start executing from the beginning. Instead, there must be a mechanism for extracting the state of the computation at the source node, restoring it at the destination node, and causing the new or moved instance of the computation to start execution immediately following the computational statement that invoked the navigational capability. Note that this is much more difficult than a context switch. The latter also requires state capture and restoration, however, the state is only that of the processor. In particular, when the mobile agent is compiled and executing in native mode, the state that needs to be saved and restored at context switch is the contents of the hardware registers and flags of the CPU. When the agent is interpreted, its entire context switching state is maintained by the interpreter in memory and thus does not even have to be saved.

For the purposes of migration between different machines the complete state of the computation (not just the processor) must be considered. This includes, in addition to the processor registers and flags, the complete activation stack, any dynamically allocated heap memory, and all file and communication descriptors. Generating the code to automatically extract all of the above information at arbitrary points during the execution and in a manner transparent to the user is extremely difficult, requiring a major extension to the compiler or the interpreter, depending on the agents' mode of execution. Consequently, mechanisms for achieving this have been implemented in only a few systems, such as Telescript [Tel96, Whi94], Agent Tcl [Gra96], and Ara [Pei97, PS97]. Other systems provide a much lower level of support. For example, Java-to-go [LM96] requires the programmer to explicitly save and restore the state during a migration operation. Aglets [LO96] preserve the heap during migration but require that the stack and the program counter be explicitly saved by the programmer.

An intermediate approach to state capture is to restrict the points in the execution at which this can occur. This approach has been used successfully by the MESSENGERS system [BFD96], where the use of any navigational statements is restricted to only the top level of execution, i.e., the equivalent of the main program. It also prohibits the use of pointers at this level. This eliminates the need to extract/restore the activation stack as well as any data on the heap storage and hence only the computation's local variables and its program counter need to be sent along with the code during migration. This not only greatly simplifies the state capture problem but also makes its implementation very efficient.

While earlier versions of the MESSENGERS system were interpreted at the top level, thus making state capture under the above restrictions very simple to implement, we have recently developed a fully-compiled version of MESSENGERS. In this paper, we show that the strategy of limiting the possible locations at which state extraction/restoration can occur leads to a very simple implementation even when the agents are compiled and execute in native mode. The restriction is a very natural one that furthers one of the design goals of MESSENGERS, namely the clean separation of computation from coordination.

After presenting a brief overview of MESSENGERS (Section 2), we describe our approach to state capture in compiled MESSENGERS code in Section 3. In Section 4, we present performance results showing that MESSENGERS is competitive in performance with message-passing approaches to distributed computing.

2 Overview of MESSENGERS

MESSENGERS [BFD96, FBDM98] is a system that supports the development and use of distributed applications structured as collections of autonomous objects, called Messengers[1]. The MESSENGERS system involves three levels of networks. The lowest level is the *physical network* (a LAN or WAN), which constitutes the underlying computational nodes. To allow Messengers to navigate autonomously through the network and carry out their tasks, the MESSENGERS system is implemented as a collection of daemons instantiated on all physical nodes participating in the distributed computation. A daemon's task is to continuously receive Messengers arriving from other daemons, interpret their behaviors, described as programs carried as part of each Messenger, and send them on to their next destinations as dictated by their behaviors. These daemons constitute the middle layer. The *logical network* is an application-specific computation network created on top of the daemon network. At system startup, a single logical node, named *init*, is created on every daemon node. Any Messenger may be injected (from the shell or by another Messenger) into any of the *init* nodes and from these it may start creating new logical nodes and links on the current or any other daemon.

Messenger programs, referred to as *Messenger scripts*, are sequences of statements of the following types:

- *Computational statements* enable the Messenger to perform general computations. They include all standard C assignment and control statements, involving arbitrary variables and constants except pointers.
- *Navigational statements* endow the Messenger with mobility, permitting it to manipulate and move within the logical network. The *hop* statement allows a Messenger to move around the network. Its syntax is as follows:[2]

  $hop(ln = n; ll = l; ldir = d)$

  where *ln* stands for "logical node", *ll* stands for "logical link", and *ldir* stands for the link's direction. Other commands allow a Messenger to create and delete nodes and links in the logical network.
- *Function invocation statements* provide an interface to the system's environment. They permit the dynamic loading and invocation of arbitrary precompiled functions written in unrestricted C and executed in native mode.
- *Synchronization statements* allow Messengers to wait for certain conditions to occur and to signal the occurrence of conditions.

Given the MESSENGERS system's orientation toward general-purpose high-performance computing, the following design choices have been made in the compiled version:

1. An executing Messenger can only be preempted when it performs a navigational statement, a (blocking) synchronization statement, or voluntarily

---

[1] The individual autonomous objects are denoted by mixed case (Messengers), while the system as a whole is denoted by small capitals (MESSENGERS).

[2] The syntax shown here is somewhat simplified. In its full generality, a single *hop* statement supports multiple hop specifications and an elaborate set of options as specified by the navigational calculus described in [FBDM98].

gives up the processor. Hence each sequence of instructions between any such statements is automatically an uninterruptible critical section.

2. There are two types of variables: node variables, which are stationary in every logical node, and messenger variables, which are carried by a Messenger. This clearly separates a node state from a messenger state.

3. The distinction between the code at the script level of every Messenger and the C functions it invokes, provides for a clear separation between the coordination and the computation layers of an application.

These have important implication for the problem of state capture, as described below.

3 State Capture with Compiled Messengers

As described in Section 2, the current version of MESSENGERS uses a combination of interpreted code at the top (script) level while all invoked functions execute in native mode. The interpretation overhead is significant and hence a fully compiled version is currently being developed. This means that each Messenger program is compiled entirely into native code. The main difficulty is the implementation of the statements that may cause a context switch. As mentioned above, this includes (1) navigational statements, (2) blocking synchronization statements, and (3) statement that voluntarily give up the processor (including the termination of a Messenger). For each of these cases, the state of the computation must be captured and saved automatically and transparently in a data structure. In the case of a navigational statement, this data structure is sent to another node where the Messenger is recreated and continues executing. In the other two cases, the Messenger's execution is interrupted and continues on the same logical node at a later time.

As already explained in Section 1, restricting the placement of all context-switching statements to the top level of the Messenger script guarantees that the state of the computation consists of only the local variables and the program counter. This information is kept in a data structure, called the *Messenger control block*, which is maintained for each Messenger at its current logical node. To perform a navigational statement, the local variables can easily be extracted and packed into a message for transport. The main difficulty is the program counter, which cannot be carried in the form of a memory address between machines.

Our solution, which handles all context-switching statement in a uniform way, is to restructure the Messenger script into a collection of *script-level functions* as follows:

1. All statements of the original script become part of one of the new functions; that is, the original script consists of only function calls.

2. All functions are numbered and each knows (at compile time) its possible successors, i.e., the numbers of the functions to execute next. Note that, due to conditional and loop control statements, a function may have more than one possible successor, which is selected at runtime.

```
S1;                    f1(mcb) {           f2(mcb) {
SC;                      S1;                 S2;
S2;                      mcb->next_func=2;   mcb->next_func=...;
...                      //code for SC//;  }
                       }

(a)                                        (b)
```

Fig. 1. Transformation of straight-line code

3. Any statement that may cause a context switch may execute only as the *last* statement of a function. This guarantees that we only need to capture the state *between* functions. Hence instead of the actual program counter, the state can simply record the number of the next function to be executed. This is a machine-independent integer, called *next_func*, and is maintained in each Messenger control block.

Figure 1 illustrates the above transformations for straight-line code. Part (a) of this figure shows a fragment of MESSENGERS code containing a context-switching statement SC, such as a *hop*, preceded by a sequence ($S1$) of other statements and followed by another sequence of statements ($S2$).

Part (b) shows the pseudo code for the two functions into which this script is transformed. Both functions are passed a pointer, *mcb*, to the Messenger control block as a parameter. Function $f1$ starts with the sequence of statements $S1$. It then assigns 2 as the number of the function to be executed next. (This is used as an index and identifies the function $f2$.) Finally, it executes the code generated by the compiler for the statement SC. In the case of a navigational statement (e.g., *hop*), this code would extract the state of the Messenger from its control block and send a copy to all destinations as specified by the *hop* parameters.

As a result of this send, the function $f2$ is started on all nodes receiving the state. This executes the statements $S2$ and, prior to exiting, sets the value of the *next_func* variable.

If SC is not a navigational statement but a (local) synchronization statement, the code generated for this statement would dequeue the Messenger control block from the ready list and enqueued it at the appropriate waiting list. When it is later returned to the ready list, it continues with $f2$ as the next function.

The above transformations may be applied when the context-switching statements are at the top level of the script, that is, outside of any conditional and loop constructs. To satisfy the requirement that any context switching statement may execute only as the last statement of any function (condition 3 above), additional transformations must be applied, which split conditional and loop constructs into multiple functions along any embedded context-switching statements.

Figure 2 illustrates the transformation of a conditional (if-then-else) statement, where both branches contain a SC statement. To show how the conditional is integrated with its enclosing statements, the conditional shown in part (a) is preceded by a sequence of statements $S1$ and succeeded by a sequence S6.

```
        S1;                  f1(mcb) {               f2(mcb) {
        if (...) {               S1;                     S3;
            S2;                  if (...) {               S6;
            SC;                      S2;              }
            S3;                      mcb->next_func=2;
        } else {                 //code for SC//;
            S4;                      return;
            SC;                  } else {               f3(mcb) {
            S5;                      S4;                     S5;
        }                           mcb->next_func=2;       S6;
        S6;                         //code for SC//;    }
                                    return;
                                 }
                             }

            (a)                           (b)
```

Fig. 2. Transformation of conditional code

```
while (...) {              f1(mcb) {                f2(mcb) {
    S1;                       while (...) {             S3;
    if (...) {                    S1;                   S5;
        S2;                       if (...) {            while (...) {
        SC;                           S2;                   S1;
        S3;                           mcb->next_func=2;     if (...) {
    } else S4;                        //code for SC//;          S2;
    S5;                               return;                   mcb->next_func=2;
}                                 } else S4;                    //code for SC//;
                                  S5;                           return;
                              }                             } else S4;
                          }                                 S5;
                                                        }
                                                    }

            (a)                           (b)
```

Fig. 3. Transformation of a while loop

Part (b) shows the three functions resulting from this script. Each is again passed the pointer to the Messenger control block, *mcb*, as a parameter. Function $f1$ starts with the statements $S1$ and then includes the code of both branches that precede the SC statements. The then-branch sets *next_func* to 2, followed by the code generated for the SC statement. Similarly, the else-branch sets *next_func* to 3, followed by analogous code for SC. Consequently, when the Messenger resumes its execution after the SC statement, one of the functions $f2$ or $f3$ is invoked as the successor, depending on the current *next_func* value. This completes the corresponding branch and continues with the sequence $S6$.

Figure 3 illustrates the transformation of a while-loop containing a SC statement. This statement is embedded inside a conditional statement (part (a)). Part

(b) shows the two resulting functions. Function $f1$ contains the entire while-loop except for the code following the SC statement (i.e., the sequence $S3$). Instead, this branch ends with setting *next_func* to 2, followed by the code for SC. The successor function, $f2$, then contains the remainder of the path, $S3$, which is executed when the Messenger resumes execution after the SC. The sequence following $S3$ is $S5$, which ends the original while-loop. The while-loop is then replicated to continue the next iteration. Note that, instead of replicating the while-loop, function $f2$ could simply return $f1$ as its successor and terminate. The replication guarantees that no unwanted context switch will occur in the middle of the while loop. It also gives the compiler a larger window of code for better optimization. We expect this to outweigh the cost of replication, since the Messenger script level is the "coordination" level of the computation, where deep nesting of loops or conditionals is not likely to occur.

The above compilation approach guarantees that every Messenger program is a simple *linear sequence of function invocations, without any conditionals, iterative statement, or other control statements.* This permits us to replaces the current interpreter daemon in each physical node by a new daemon, which maintains the ready lists of all Messengers and repeatedly performs the following tasks:

- For all Messengers currently on the ready list, invoke the function identified by its *next_func* value; before it terminates, this function automatically updates the *next_func* value with the number of its successor function, as described above. Note that state capture as well as any movement of Messengers between the ready queue and other queues is not performed by the daemon but by the code generated by the compiler for the corresponding context-switching statement.

- After a complete pass through the ready list, receive any messages (each containing a Messenger control block) arriving from other nodes and enqueue these at the ready list.

The above discussion ignores the issue of I/O connections. Since MESSEN-GERS can run on any network, maintaining the status of file connections may not be meaningful if a Messenger hops between physical nodes that do not share a common file system. However, in the special case where a hop is between two physical nodes that access a common file, it is useful to preserve a file connection across navigational statements. This can be achieved by providing special MESSENGERS functions to open and close files instead of the standard C library functions. This permits the MESSENGERS system to keep track of all files opened by each Messenger. All the information needed to restore the file status (filename, position pointer, access permission) may be added to the messenger state. After moving to a new physical node, the files can then be reopened transparently in the same state as before the navigational statement.

4 Matrix Multiplication

In this section we contrast a distributed application using compiled MESSEN-GERS with an implementation of the same application using a message-passing approach. The application we have chosen is matrix multiplication. We selected this applications for two main reasons. First, matrix multiplication is an essential component of a very large class of numerical computations and hence is an important problem in its own right. Second, MESSENGERS is intended for general-purpose computing. Many scientific problems either use matrix multiplication directly or must solve similar numeric problems that, like matrix multiplication, are highly regular in their structure and require significant movement of data between computations. Hence matrix multiply represents a good test case for studying MESSENGERS' capabilities in this arena. This includes both its ability to describe the problem intuitively in a distributed manner and the resulting performance. We compare the MESSENGERS implementation with am implementation using PVM [GBD+94]. PVM was chosen because it is a widely available, commonly used system that supports the message-passing approach to distributed computing. We compare performance of the original interpreted MESSENGERS, th new compiled MESSENGERS, PVM, and sequential implementations.

The simplest possible implementation of matrix multiplication on a single processor is a triply nested loop, where the outer and middle loops iterate over the rows and columns of the two matrices and the inner-most loop (k) computes the inner product of a row and a column as follows: $C[i, j] = C[i, j] + A[i, k] * B[k, j]$. This naive implementation of matrix multiplication is adequate when the matrices are small. Considerable effort has gone into developing sequential algorithms that are faster for large matrices but more complex to program; see for example [Pan84, CW90]. Much of the emphasis in this research has been improving the asymptotic performance beyond the $\Theta(n^3)$ running time of the naive algorithm for $n \times n$ matrices. Even modifications that do not improve the asymptotic performance beyond $\Theta(n^3)$ can provide some useful speedup. For example, partitioning a matrix into smaller blocks and then decomposing the multiplication into a series of additions and multiplications of these blocks can result in some speedup, because multiplying the smaller sub-matrices obtained by partitioning increases cache utilization and reduces paging overhead. The precise amount of speedup depends on the specific machine architecture. Our experiments indicate that on a 110 MHz SPARCstation 5 with 32MB of memory, partitioning a 1500×1500 matrix into 9 blocks of size 500×500 results in a speedup of roughly 13%.

The main point is that the sequential algorithm can be improved by carefully orchestrating data accesses to the matrices. In general, more speedup requires more careful orchestration, which significantly increases the complexity of implementing the algorithm. When compared with parallel matrix multiplication algorithms, we observe that these are no more difficult to write than those optimized for a single processor, yet we gain the additional benefit of speedup by utilizing multiple processors. In the remainder of this section we consider a well-known algorithm for parallel matrix multiplication [GBD+94], which we implement using two very different approaches to parallel program construction—one using message-passing and the other using MESSENGERS.

The algorithm is block-oriented. The two $m \times m$ input matrices A and B, and the resulting matrix C are all partitioned into rectangular blocks of size $s \times s$. We will use $A[i,j]$ to denote the corresponding $s \times s$ block of matrix A, i.e., all elements of A with indices ranging from $(i * s)$ to $(i * s + s - 1)$ and $(j * s)$ to $(j * s + s - 1)$. Similarly, $B[i,j]$ and $C[i,j]$ denote the corresponding $(s \times s)$ blocks of B and C. Each block $A[i,j]$, $B[i,j]$, and $C[i,j]$ is assigned to a different processor, addressed using the same coordinates $[i,j]$. The blocks of C remain stationary, that is $C[i,j]$ always resides on processor $[i,j]$, while the blocks of A and B are moved between the processors according to the following three distinct phases:

1. *Distribution of A*: During each iteration, k, all blocks $A[i,j]$ whose indices satisfy the condition $j = (i + k)$ mod s are multi-cast to all processors in the same row. During iteration 0 all elements on the diagonal $A[0,0]$, $A[1,1]$, $\ldots$, $A[m-1, m-1]$ are distributed to each row. The diagonal to be distributed is then shifted one to the right. That is, during iteration 1 the elements $A[0,1]$, $A[1,2]$, $\ldots$, $A[m-1,0]$ are distributed, etc.

2. *Block multiplication*: The block of A received during the previous step is multiplied with the block B currently residing in the processor and is added to the block of C assigned to the processor.

2. *Rotation of B*: Each block of B is moved to the neighboring processor in the same column using a circular shift. That is, blocks of B residing on processors $[i,j]$ are shifted to processors $[(i - 1)$ mod $s, j]$.

After repeating the above three phases m times, the (distributed) matrix C contains the result of the complete multiplication of the matrices A and B.

4.1 Performance

We have conducted the performance comparison between interpreted MESSENGERS, compiled MESSENGERS, PVM, and sequential C implementations on a 2×2 and a 3×3 grid of processors, both using an Ethernet-based LAN of SPARCstations 5. All experiments were run on 170 MHz SPARCstations. The results are shown in Figure 4(a) and (b), The experiments on the 2×2 grid were run for matrices of size 20×20, 40×40, 60×60, 100×100, 200×200, 400×400, and 1000×1000. Thus the block sizes were, respectively, 10×10, 20×20, 30×30, 50×50, 100×100, 200×200, and 500×500.

The experiments on the 3×3 grid were run with the same set of block sizes, so the matrices were of size 30×30, 60×60, 90×90, 150×150, 300×300, 600×600, and 1500×1500. The various programs benchmarked are as follows:

- *Single Program:* A straightforward sequential matrix multiplication, with no partitioning of the matrix.
- *CM:* Compiled Messenger, as discussed in this paper.
- *IM:* The earlier (interpreted) version of Messenger.

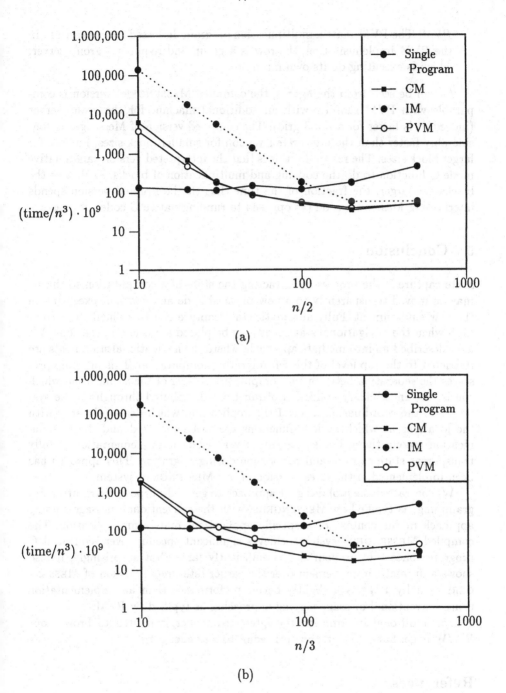

Fig. 4. Matrix Multiplication results. (a) On 4 processors arranged as a 2×2 grid. (b) On 9 processors arranged as a 3×3 grid.

– *PVM:* The PVM matrix multiplication program discussed in this section. In the PVM implementation, the row is a group and requires a group server, which is executing on its own machine.

As can be seen from the figures, the compiled MESSENGERS version is comparable with PVM running with an additional machine for the group server (indeed, it is faster for a 3 × 3 grid). The compiled version of Messenger is considerably faster than the interpreted version for smaller block sizes, but not for larger block sizes. The reason for this is that the interpreted version calls a native mode C function to do the copying and multiplication of blocks, so that as the blocks get larger, the fraction of the time that the interpreted version spends interpreting Messenger code (as opposed to running native C code) decreases.

5 Conclusion

State capture is the process of extracting the state of a computation so that it may be moved transparently to a new physical node and continue executing in the new environment. Fully automatic state capture can be difficult to accomplish when the navigational statement may be placed anywhere in the code. We have described an intermediate approach, where the navigational statements are restricted to the top level of the self-migrating computation. This not only preserves the separation between the computational layer of the application, which consists of an arbitrary collection of functions distributed throughout the system, and the coordination layer of the application, which deals primarily with the locations at which various functions are to be executed and the communication among them; it also permits a very efficient implementation of fully transparent state capture and restoration during migration. This approach has been implemented in the latest version of our MESSENGERS system.

We contrasted the mobile agent approach to general-purpose distributed programming, as typified by MESSENGERS, with the conventional message-passing approach in the context of a specific application, matrix multiplication. The compiled MESSENGERS system achieves significant speedup over sequential C programs once the problem size is sufficiently large. Not surprisingly, it also shows a dramatic improvement over the earlier interpreted version of MESSENGERS. Finally, it gives a slightly better performance than an implementation using conventional message-passing approaches as typified by PVM.

For additional information the interested reader is invited to browse our WWW page: `http://www.ics.uci.edu/~bic/messengers`.

References

[BFD96] L.F. Bic, M. Fukuda, and M. Dillencourt. Distributed computing using autonomous objects. *IEEE Computer*, 29(8), Aug. 1996.

[CW90] D. Coppersmith and S. Winograd. Matrix multiplication via arithmetic progressions. *Journal of Symbolic Computation*, 9(3):251–280, March 1990.

[FBDM98] M. Fukuda, L.F. Bic, M. Dillencourt, and F. Merchant. Distributed coordination with messengers. *Science of Computer Programming*, 31(2), 1998. Special Issue on Coordination Models, Languages, Applications.

[GBD+94] A. Geist, A. Beguelin, J. Dongarra, W. Jieng, R. Manchek, and V. Sunderam. *PVM: Parallel Virtual Machine. A User's Guide and Tutorial for Networked Parallel Computing.* MIT Press, Cambridge, MA, 1994.

[Gra96] R. S. Gray. Agent Tcl: A flexible and secure mobile-agent system. In *Proceedings of the Fourth Annual Tcl/Tk Workshop (TCL 96)*, Monterey, California, July 1996.
http://www.cs.dartmouth.edu/~agent/papers/index.html.

[LM96] W. Li and D.G. Messerschmitt. Java-to-go. Technical report, Dept. of EECS, University of California, Berkeley, 1996.
http://ptolemy.eecs.berkeley.edu/dgm/javatools/java-to-go/.

[LO96] D. B. Lange and M. Oshima. Programming mobile agents in Java with the Java Aglet API, 1996. http://www.trl.ibm.co.jp/aglets/.

[Pan84] V. Pan. *How to multiply matrices faster.* Lecture Notes in Computer Science 179. Springer-Verlag, Berlin, 1984.

[Pei97] H. Peine. An introduction to mobile agent programming and the Ara system. ZRI Technical Report 1/97, Dept. of Computer Science, University of Kaiserslautern, January 1997.
http://www.uni-kl.de/AG-Nehmer/Ara/ara.html.

[PS97] H. Peine and T. Stolpmann. The architecture of the ara platform for mobile agents. In K. Rothermel and R. Popescu-Zeletin, editors, *Proc. of the First International Workshop on Mobile Agents (MA'97)*, Berlin, Germany, April 1997. Springer Verlag, Lecture Notes in Computer Science No. 1219.
http://www.uni-kl.de/AG-Nehmer/Ara/Doc/architecture.ps.gz.

[Tel96] The Telescript reference manual. Technical report, General Magic, Inc., Mountain View, CA 94040, June 1996. http://www.genmagic.com.

[Whi94] J.E. White. Telescript technology. Technical report, General Magic, Inc., Mountain View, CA 94040, 1994.

Mobile Agent Applicability

Dag Johansen

Department of Computer Science, University of Tromsø, NORWAY **

Abstract. In this paper, we present experiences from building several mobile agent based distributed applications using the agent system TACOMA. Our hope is to demonstrate mobile agent applicability potential through some real and concrete examples. We conclude that mobile agents, even if they simplify remote installation of software, basically complement other structuring techniques in distributed applications.

1 Introduction

We have now been through a period of 4-5 years of intense focus on the mobile agent, or just agent for short, paradigm. This has resulted in infrastructures [17, 9, 12, 5, 13] which enable agents to move autonomously about in the Internet taking advantage of resources on the individual hosts. We now understand some of the technical challenges involved with, for instance, how to move an agent efficiently about or how to secure the hosts from agents.

We also have an emerging understanding of the potential in this technology, and various arguments are augmented in favour of its use. This includes arguments about utilizing the network in a much more cost-effective way [9], to arguments that agents can be used to construct new classes of applications [17]. However, despite its claimed potential, we still need some less speculative arguments.

Perhaps it is time then to sit back and reflect more about what we can use this technology for. This is what we focus on in this paper. We will attempt to avoid hypothetical scenarios for agent technologies, but restrict the validation to some real application prototypes we already have built. Neither will we discuss problems related to agent and host integrity.

In the next section, we will briefly describe the TACOMA agent system. Then, the rest of the paper is structured around three broad claims informally selected from the agent community. For each claim, we start by stating the engineering problem related to it. Then, we present applications we have built to solve this particular problem. We intend to shed light on *how* agents can be applied to solve the specific engineering problem. For each claim, we also discuss *if* agents are fundamental in this process.

** This work was supported by NSF (Norway) grant No. 112578/431 (DITS-program).

2 TACOMA - Mobile Code Infrastructure

We use the TACOMA[1] system as platform for our agent prototypes. In the next subsections, we will structure the presentation of TACOMA by showing how applications fundamentally influenced the initial design of it.

2.1 User Diversity

The first version of TACOMA was built in 1993 based on experience from the StormCast project [7]. StormCast is a project where we develope a series of large-scale distributed application prototypes in the environmental and weather monitoring domain. StormCast applications are monitoring, collecting, storing, and processing large amounts of weather data of different types. This includes raw sensor data, satellite images, and video images.

StormCast servers are typically clustered around a local area network in a single administrative domain. The APIs of these servers have been derived through an initial software analysis with a limited set of potential users. As soon as we made StormCast available on the Internet, we experienced that the APIs we supported did not meet all potential demands. At the same time, we could not reimplement the servers just to accomodate individual needs. A mechanism like remote evaluations [14], where we could install a piece of code at a remote server could possibly solve this problem. In contrast to remote evaluations, however, we needed a more asynchronous scheme where some customized client code could be permanently installed at the server for periodic execution.

This was the first design requirement for TACOMA, the need for a simple abstraction for encapsulation of code to be installed remotely, as well as its accompanying data. This is how the *folder* abstraction came into existence. A folder is basically a container for agents, data, or meta-data. This way, we can stick source code (or binaries) into a folder. A client program can now capture application level state in specific folders grouped in a uniquely named *briefcase*. Next, it can ship this briefcase over the network to another TACOMA agent using the *meet* operation. The syntax of a *meet* operation is:

meet *ag@h bc* [sync|async]

Execution causes *target agent ag* at host *h* to be executed using briefcase *bc* as argument. If an agent is to be sent through the network, *bc* will contain source code (or binaries) for it. The target agent will then extract this code from the *CODE* folder. Next, it will interpret, or compile and run this code.

2.2 Interaction Diversity

A second lesson from StormCast is the need for different interaction schemes. In a typical application, we model module interactions using RPC [1], streams, and

---

[1] Tromsø And COrnell Moving Agents. URL: http://www.cs.uit.no/DOS/Tacoma/

shared memory techniques. This need for interaction diversity is why *meet* has *sync/async* as options. When *async* is specified, the initiating agent continues executing in parallel with execution of *ag*; otherwise the initiating agent blocks.

Another motivation for the *async* option is to support the more itinerant style of agent computing. An agent can now be launched from a host without leaving any dependencies left, and it can roam from host to host.

When we measured the end-to-end latency of a *meet* [8], we noticed that the compilation of an agent at the destination host accounts for about 99% of the overall time. This motivated us to add caching to TACOMA, so that we do not need to transfer code or compile it next time an agent visits a host previously visited. The *meet* abstraction can now be used to program in, for instance, RPC style (agent code is cached at the destination), remote evaluation style (briefcase contains code), or to move one or a set of agents itinerantly about in the Internet.

2.3 Language Diversity

A third lesson from StormCast is the need for language diversity. We never build any StormCast application using *a* single programming language; a typical StormCast application is a mixture of C, C++, Java, Perl, and Tcl. As a result, TACOMA supports agents written in C, C++, ML, Perl, Python, Scheme, Tcl/Tk, and Visual Basic.

2.4 Platform Diversity

A fourth lesson from StormCast, is the need for platform diversity. StormCast applications are always running in a very heterogeneous environment. Part of StormCast is typically running on top of UNIX workstations clustered around a 10 Mbit/s Ethernet. Client PCs or workstations are connected to the application through modems. Logging devices with proprietary operating systems are connected through satellite, packet radio, or modem communications.

This experience influenced the decision to make TACOMA easily portable across multiple platforms; not providing automatic state-capturing is one consequence of this. TACOMA is now running on top of most flavours of UNIX (from Linux to HP-UX 11.0), Windows 95, Windows NT, and some Personal Digital Assistant (PDA) systems (Windows CE and PalmPilot). TCP/IP is the common glue between TACOMA systems.

3 Claim: "Agents Support Extensibility"

An initial motivation for TACOMA was the need for *extensible servers*. Extensibility implies that client code can be installed over the network local to server computers, much the way remote shell facilities or remote evaluations work. This is also one of the frequent claims about agents, and we will present our experience with TACOMA agents in this context.

3.1 The Motivating Problem

In a distributed application based on client/server structuring techniques, clients depend on the static API provided by the server. If this API is inadequate, a client might need to send a sequence of requests to the remote server. One problem with this is the amount of messages needed to carry out the desired functionality. Another problem is the dependency on a stable and connected network while these operations take place.

A rich API, where the server provides much more functionality, can avoid these two problems. First, the client will only need to send a single request to the server. Second, the network connection is only needed for the single request and the single reply.

However, a rich API is not without problems. First, the server API can be too rich and complex for the application programmer. Then, user requirements might vary over time, which require servers to be updated.

3.2 The TACOMA Application Approach

Agent technology can potentially be used to solve these API problems. The idea is to use servers with APIs that hardly, if ever change. Simultaneously, the servers can receive, install, and execute client specific code (agents). Ideally, the network is only used when the agent is moved and when the potential result propagates to its recipient.

We have built several extensible servers based on TACOMA, and we will detail a StormCast service based on this extensibility idea.

The Specific Problem - StormCast. The Internet based StormCast application serves users in the order of thousands each day throughout the year[2]. This is a diverse user group, and even the same weather alarm might trigger different responses. For instance, when a low pressure area suddenly is pushing through, a fisherman might delay the planned fishing trip and take a day off. A windsurfer, on the other hand, might also take a day off, but to hit the beaches and the rough sea.

The specific problem we approached was to build an extensible StormCast server that accepts user specified alarms as agents. These are installed and run periodically by the servers, and the remote user is notified if certain alarm threshold values, or combinations of several values, are exceeded.

The Design and Implementation - StormCast. We have built an agent based alarm service for StormCast. The architecture of this alarm service is illustrated in Figure 1. First, the user can compose a weather alarm in a WWW browser form. Through CGI scripts written in Python, the alarm is installed at the remote server(s). A copy of the source code and meta data is also stored in a

---

[2] URL:http://www.cs.uit.no/DOS/StormCast

database at the server for error recovery purposes. Next, the alarm is executed periodically using data received from remote sensors in StormCast. The user can be totally disconnected from StormCast while the agent acts autonomously on his behalf. He can now receive specialized alarm messages or periodic updates through a cellular phone, email or web browser (selective push implemented in DHTML).

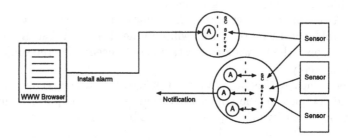

Fig. 1. Extensible StormCast Alarm Servers.

Experiments - StormCast. The StormCast Alarm Servers are running on PPro 200MHz computers equipped with 128 Mbytes RAM. They are running FreeBSD 2.2 and TACOMA v.1.2 and are clustered on the same 10 Mbit/s Ethernet.

We were insterested in an estimate of the cost of installing a single weather agent, and the cost of running several weather agents simultaneously. First, we measured the time it takes to install an agent at the remote server. Using *gettimeofday()*, we measured the time from the user did a submit in his browser, until an install acknowledgement was received. An average of 10 tests gave us an installation time of 1.5 seconds.

We also measured the time it takes to execute 1.000 alarms already installed. The alarm simply checks the current temperature, and notifies a user if an alarm value is exceeded. The average time of 10 test runs was 8.23 seconds, which means that a single agent execution accounts for 8.23 milliseconds. This excludes the time it takes to notify the user.

3.3 Discussion

The architecture presented in Figure 1 has shown to be very convenient in Storm-Cast. Through TACOMA, personalized weather agents can be dynamically installed and executed at remote servers. Installation through CGI scripts accounts for a few seconds at most, which is acceptable. The run-time environment also handles load well.

We have structured other distributed applications using the same architecture, and we have identified three general patterns in how to use such extensible servers:

- (1). *Server patching*; the agent is installed to provide a new server API. The agent is installed as an extension to the server, and clients can access this remote agent through, for instance, TCP/IP in a regular client/server interaction.
- (2). *Client agent*; the agent executes like a remote evaluation. The agent is basically shipped to the server for execution on behalf of the client. A potential result can be propagated back to the client, or the agent can move along to another host. Generally, no extra server API is provided for remote access.
- (3). *Periodic agent*; the agent is more permanently installed on the server and is executed periodically. This agent normally acts autonomously on behalf of the remote client. Only upon certain events, will it initiate a dialogue with a remote client.

A fundamental question is if agents are vital in solving this type of engineering problems. At the conceptual level, the answer is no. Agents basically supplement other structuring techniques like, for instance, remote shell facilities, remote evaluations and various process migration techniques [16, 3]. Currently, we also see other areas where this fundamental structuring mechanism is applied. Extensible kernels like, for instance, the Exokernel [11] uses the same concept at the operating system kernel layer. Another example is active networks [15], where, for instance, user specific routing mechanisms (agents) can be injected in the network. Similar ideas are also emerging in database systems, where SQL based databases can install some client Java code (agent) and allow it to run close to the database server(s).

The best argument for agents in this context, is its *ease of use*; agent technology provides a very simple way of installing and relocating code in a distributed application.

Ease of use is also related to *how to compose agents*. We consider this problem to be vital in an applicability context. A programming expert can write agents easily in any of the languages supported by TACOMA, but this scheme is too complex for a less experienced user. Our approach has been to introduce high-level agent specification languages and by using visual programming techniques. For instance, we have made a high-level boolean based specification language for users of the StormCast Alarm Service. This WHALE (WeatHer Alarm Language Environment) language consists of a set of boolean expressions which can be used like this[3]:

(temperature > 10.0 and humidity < 50.0) or (windspeed >10)

Additionally, the user can specify how to be contacted when the alarm is triggered. The WHALE run-time system on the TACOMA server, evaluates these expressions (agents) and notifies the user if *TRUE*.

To support users with little, if any, programming language experience, we have also built a visual programming environment for the TACOMA NT. The

---

[3] This service can be accessed at URL:http://www.cs.uit.no/DOS/StormCast

programmer can compose agents out of existing software components. A component or complete agent is represented by icons on the screen or in the NT Explorer hierarchy. Next, an icon can be dragged and dropped over the network icon or a specific host icon. This results in an installation and execution of the agent.

4 Claim: "Agents Improve Performance"

Agents are often claimed to potentially improve performance; either can bandwidth be saved or the number of messages between a client and a server can be reduced. Our research approach has been to build the same set of realistic distributed applications using two different paradigms. We used the commonly known client/server design pattern, and we used an agent-based design pattern.

4.1 The Motivating Problem

In a distributed environment, it is common that data is gathered and stored at centrally located servers. Client computers can subsequently pull data from these servers over the network for local processing.

A general problem with this scheme is that the amount of data to be transferred can require far too much bandwidth or number of messages on the wire. Maybe there are concrete applications that would benefit if the client computation was moved to the remote server(s), only returning the result of the computation. A proof of concept would be an application where the agent version out-performed the client/server version.

4.2 The TACOMA Application Approach

We have been searching for potential candidates for agent computing in the domain that motivated the initial TACOMA; multi-media Internet StormCast applications. The TACOMA Image Server and the TACOMA Video Server are probably the most promising and realistic applications we built in this context.

The Specific Problem - Images. The motivation for the TACOMA Image Server was problems identified in the application domain of Tromsø Satellite Station (TSS). TSS reads down and process data from polar orbiting satellites (ERS-1, ERS-2, JERS-1, RADARSAT, NOAA), and have a data archive in the order of Terabytes. TSS distributes satellite images to customers world-wide using the Internet, and this is not without practical problems.

First, we can not assume that remote clients can access an on-line Terabyte database by shifting through images. Enough bandwidth is one problem, ensuring the property rights of the satellite images another. Meta-data is used today as an approach, but this is not optimal since very much information can have been lost in the annotation process.

Another problem, which is of a general nature for images, is that the human perception is in the loop. Details can be overlooked by the human, or the data set can contain interesting information not visualized properly. We see automation of this task as something lending itself to agent technology, where agents can parse through the raw data used to produce an image.

The Design and Implementation - Images. We built the TACOMA Image Server to solve these problems. This is an extensible image server where remote users can install and run personalized agents. An agent can, for instance, parse through all new data sets from a specific geographical area.

The TACOMA Image Server uses a PostgreSQL database on a set of HP 720 workstations running HP-UX 9.05 and TACOMA v.1.2. We receive and store a daily feed of satellite data from TSS. To be able to compare an agent approach with a client/server approach, we used this server in two fundamentally different ways.

First, we built an agent that could be shipped from the client and installed at the TACOMA Image Server. All data processing can then be done at the server. This agent implemented in C has a size of 2.9 Kbytes. Input to the agent is an AVHRR (Advanced Very High Resolution Radiometer) data set. This data set typically contains 5 layers of 2000*2000 pixel images. Each pixel is represented by a 12 bit grey color value aligned on 16 bit boundary. The output from the agent sent back to the client is the total amount of pixels within certain gray-levels. In the StormCast context, this can be used to determine, for instance, amount of snow cover in the mountains[4].

Next, we built a client/server version providing exactly the same functionality for the end user. However, the client now pulls over the necessary data from the TACOMA Image Server and process it locally.

Experiments - Images. We conducted experiments and compared the agent and the client/server implementations. The platform used was two HP 720 work-stations (64 Mbytes RAM) running HP-UX 9.05 and TACOMA v.1.2. The work-stations were connected on the same segment of a 10 Mbit/s Ethernet under normal load.

We instrumented the software with *gettimeofday()* calls to measure end-to-end latencies. The sequence we measured was the time of (a) shipping the agent over the network, (b) installing and running it, (c) returning the result back to the client machine, and (d) printing of the result. To compare, we measured the client/server implementation from (a) the client started downloading a remote AVHRR data set, (b) processing of the data set, and (c) printing of the result.

Figure 2 is a plot of average response time for varying data sizes. We report data from 10 samples, with relative standard deviation between 1 - 7 %. Since

---

[4] Another TACOMA agent is in daily use at URL: http://dslab0.cs.uit.no:8080/sat/. This TACOMA agent and a neural network is used in StormCast 5.0 to determine weather conditions at, for instance, North Cape.

TCP/IP is used, we varied the TCP buffer size as shown in the plot to determine how much this influenced the client/server performance.

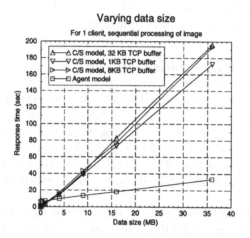

Fig. 2. TACOMA Image Server, response time versus data size.

It can be argued now that the agent approach has room for performance improvement. For instance, the client sending the agent remotely for processing, might also provide cycles to the processing. The idea is to combine the client/server model with the agent model by carefully sharing the load between the TACOMA Image Server and the client host.

We experimented with this combination using two HP C-160 workstations running HP-UX 10.20 and TACOMA v.1.2. on a dedicated 10 Mbit/s Ethernet segment. We report data from 100 samples, with relative standard deviation between 1-8% for all.

Figure 3 is a plot of average response time of the different approaches. The two extremes are the pure client/server and agent approaches. The hybrid model varies with respect to how much data is processed by an agent at the server (20%, 40%, 60%, 80%).

Since this type of processing is relatively little CPU-intensive, we also added some extra (but artificial) computation to the application. Figure 4 is a plot of the same experiment, but this time the computation also computes the square root of each individual pixel value. This extra computation implies that the hybrid model now outperforms the pure agent model.

The Specific Problem - Video. In StormCast, we have been capturing and storing video images and video sequences the last 5 years. The amount of this data is in the order of 6 Gigabytes, and more is added every day. We have been interested in supporting customized searches on raw video data in a video archive, but where dependency on annotation information is avoided.

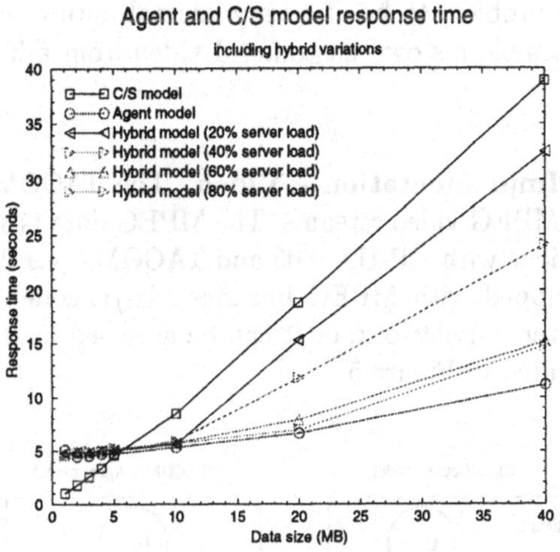

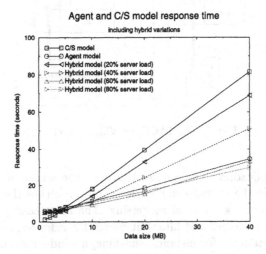

Fig. 3. Combining the agent and client/server models.

Fig. 4. Impact of adding processing to the computation.

We consider this problem to be of a very general nature. For instance, this way a client can assemble his own customized video from a huge on-line video store.

The Design and Implementation - Video. The TACOMA Video Server stores and retrieves MPEG video streams. The MPEG data is stored in flat files on HP 720 workstations with HP-UX 9.05 and TACOMA v.1.2. The TACOMA Video Server is equipped with MPEG libraries (de-/encode). The server can either be accessed over the network, or it can be accessed by a local TACOMA agent. This is illustrated in Figure 5.

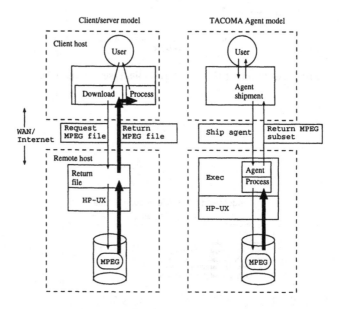

Fig. 5. The TACOMA Video Server.

The agent application ships an agent over to the server for processing of MPEG data, while the client/server implementation fetches the entire MPEG stream over the network for local processing. The functionality of both is to parse MPEG video streams and filter out particular video sequences. This can be a sequence containing, for instance, sunshine, a wind-surfer, or a boat. The application parses every frame and matches with parameters given by the user; this includes color values and coverage percentage. The output of the processing is a subset of MPEG video that matches the parameters.

Experiments - Video. We ran similar experiments with the TACOMA Video Server as we did with the TACOMA Image Server, but got no surprising results. Depending on how much sequences found in an MPEG stream, we experienced cross points where the agent approach outperformed the client/server approach. The important point was not whether this happened at 0.5 Mbytes in one particular case, or at 3 Mbytes in another. The importance is that we experienced all these cross points.

We then replaced the 10 Mbit/s Ethernet connection with a 14.400 baud modem connection and experimented with it. Figure 6 is a plot of average response time for varying data size from one of the experiments. The time measured for the client/server approach includes (a) receiving of the entire MPEG stream, (b) processing of the stream, and (c) displaying any found sequences. The time measured for the agent approach includes (a) shipping of the agent, (b) installing and running it, (c) returning of the result, and displaying of the found sequences. The size of this agent implemented in C is 13.4 Kbytes. We report data from 10 samples, and relative standard deviation for this particular experiment is between 5-9%. In this particular case, no sequences were found.

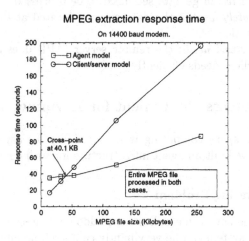

Fig. 6. MPEG filtering application.

4.3 Discussion

Experience from two TACOMA servers indicates that there are application domains where the agent paradigm outperforms the client/server paradigm. This is not surprising, taken all the qualified claims about this issue. For instance, we showed that the agent version of the TACOMA Image Server application clearly outperformed the client/server version when realistic image sizes were used. For a 36 Mbytes image, the agent approach runs more than 5 times faster. This was on a 10 Mbit/s local area network, and a wide-area network setting with less capacity would make this difference even larger. Also, the dependency on the TCP buffer size was almost negligible in this context.

We also showed that hybrid design models can be used. The TACOMA Image Server is an example where part of the computation can be done by an agent at the server, while the rest can be computed at the client. In the particular experiments with data-intensive applications, we noticed that the pure agent model still performed best. However, the hybrid model can be an alternative if the type of processing is more CPU-intensive.

A fundamental question is if agent technology is needed for this type of engineering problems. The answer is no again, assuming the server already provides a rich API or other techniques can be used to install code at the server. Yet, we advocate agents for this type of problem, but use the same arguments as for extensible servers. We have just shown that an extensible server also can gain performance wins.

The type of agent applications we have found promising in a performance context can be characterized by being:

- (1). *Data-intensive*; large data sets need to be processed.
- and (2). *Remotely located*; the data sets are located at the other end of a network connection.
- and (3). *Specialized needs*; the remote server (API) does not support very personalized client needs efficiently.

5 Claim: "Agents Convenient for Asymmetric Systems"

One argument for agent computing is its suitability for asymmetric environments [10]. We have built an agent infrastructure for such environments.

5.1 The Motivating Problem

In a real distributed environment, hosts are seldomly homogeneous. Some of the client hosts in the system can be very lightly equipped, making it impossible to run some computations locally. Such computations can benefit from running at a highly dedicated remote host exhibiting better or more specialized resources.

5.2 The TACOMA Application Approach

In TACOMA, we have added support for asymmetric environments. There are two different approaches to this based on whether the client is running TACOMA or not.

Thin Clients running TACOMA. We have built TACOMA Lite, a TACOMA system running on the PalmPilot and on Windows CE devices [6]. This PDA environment is characterized by low connectivity, little main memory and little, if any, secondary memory, low capacity processors, and weak power supplies. To accomodate the differences between the PDAs and the well-equipped, tightly connected TACOMA clusters, we added a *hostel* gateway in between. We use the hostel to, for instance, permanently store data associated with the PDA (in *file cabinet* folders), and as a proxy to mask disconnections.

We have built several agent applications running on TACOMA Lite. The overall design of these applications is similar. First, it consists of a client part composing and shipping one or several agents off into the network. Second, there is the agents executing remotely. As a rule, these agents operate asynchronously from the client. Third, we have an agent returning to the PDA with a result. We have implemented a generic GUI agent for this user interaction; one functionality is that new agents can be launched again based on the user response.

The TACOMA Stock Ticker application is one example resembling this architecture. The remote part of the application is a set of agents fetching on-line stock information. Periodically, they perform personalized queries on a set of public web pages. This information can be combined with other sources of on-line information obtained by other TACOMA agents. If relevant information is found, the user is contacted. This can be done by a result agent sent to the hostel for forwarding to the PDA, as a short text mail to the user's cellular phone, or as an email.

Another PDA agent example is the TACOMA Mobile Diary. The application is used to maintain calendar information for the individual users. This data is replicated at the PDA and in file cabinets at the hostel. Extra functionality provided by the agent launched from the PDA, is to visit a number of hostels containing calendar information. This itinerant agent can be used to, for instance, schedule a meeting involving a group of people.

One general problem with the PDA environment is partitioned networks. The PDA is by default disconnected, and this can result in inconsistency problems. This can be resolved by the user if he always synchronizes any local calendar updates with the remote hostel. This pessimistic concurrency control approach is not always practical or possible. A more optimistic approach is to relax the requirement that users always should synchronize with the hostel, and rather resolve any conflict if inconsistency problems arise. One approach is simply to launch a new itinerant scheduling agent which terminates the old meeting and schedules a new.

A third PDA agent example is the StormCast weather alarm applications. Weather agents can also be launched from a PDA, much the same way as described for the browser approach. The PDA combined with a cellular phone is a powerful combination when users are mobile and disconnected. The user is notified through the highly available cellular phone whenever a remote StormCast alarm is triggered. The cellular phone is basically an interrupt mechanism, and the user acts as an interrupt handler. The user can now decide to, for instance, synchronize his PDA with the hostel to receive a result agent with much more information about the alarm.

Thin Clients not running TACOMA. We have relaxed the requirement that a distributed system should comprise a collection of peers [10]. We have suggested an architecture well suited for hosts with limited capabilities; an architecture with thin clients, well-equipped servers, and gateway functions between them. The net effect is that TACOMA only needs to run on the server side of the connection, while the clients must be able to launch an agent and to receive the result. The idea is to use and adapt to ubiquitous Internet facilities.

Any client device supporting a web browser can now act as launching pad for a TACOMA agent. The agent is represented as data in an HTML form and is sent to the gateway over an HTTP connection. The gateway converts this data into a TACOMA agent and does a regular *meet* with the TACOMA destination server.

Similarly, we can launch a TACOMA agent as an email. A filter at the destination TACOMA server parses any incoming email and forwards any email marked as being a TACOMA agent to the TACOMA firewall.

We have built several applications using this infrastructure. The weather information retriever is one example, where we have had a StormCast weather service based on this concept operational for almost 3 years[5].

The TACOMA Web CV application is another example. This application is a specialized web crawler where itinerant agents can move among a set of TACOMA NT servers. These servers support searches in free text documents, documents which can be retrieved from a distributed data repository.

The functionality of this application is to match employers with potential employees. Individual users can store personal meta-data in a database on one of the TACOMA servers. This meta-data also contains a URL to more information stored local to the user. This can be a more complete CV or other documents that agents can pull over to the server and parse. Employers can now launch different types of search agents running until a match is found.

Agents can also roam among a set of servers matching people into work groups based on individual skills. Additionally, employers can use the application to post job openings.

5.3 Experiments

An infrastructure where agents are off-loaded to remote servers is based on the assumption that the servers scale. We have been interested in investigating how well a TACOMA server scale, and we experimented with the TACOMA Image Server.

The experiements were done on the same 10 Mbit/s local area network configuration as previously described with two HP 720 workstations. We kept the data fixed to 36 Mbytes, an amount typical for a normal satellite image. Then, we varied the number of clients using the TACOMA Image Server two different ways. The client/server implementation sends n simultaneous requests to the server. All the server does is to push the requested data over to the clients for processing. The agent approach transfers n agents from n client hosts to the server for processing. Only the result is sent back to the clients.

---

[5] A TACOMA agent can be shipped to the Arctic fetching latest weather conditions at URL: http://www.cs.uit.no/DOS/Tacoma/Webdemo.html

The clients are all started (almost) simultaneously by a script running on an additional host. We measured the time a single client experienced from being started by the script, to the result was displayed.

What we learned from this experiment, was that the agent solution scaled very well initially. For instance, a client hardly noticed the difference if 2 or 4 other clients had shipped agents to the same server for execution. At the same time, we experienced that the client/server approach scaled relatively bad. Adding a new client implied that the server had to push additional 36 Mbytes to the client, a time consuming operation.

However, adding the 7th agent to the load brought down the entire TACOMA server. We reproduced this crash at the same scaling point, and we traced it to happen when *gcc* started to compile the agent. Adding the 7th concurrent compilation was too much in this case.

To solve this particular scaling problem, we increased the number of servers and added an intermediate broker (global scheduler) to the loop. The agents were now sent to the broker, who dispatched them round-robin among the existing servers. Figure 7 is a plot showing how this impacts the scale beyond the critical point. We report data from 10 samples, and relative standard deviation for this particular experiment is between 1-7%. With the broker, we can still just start ($i*6$) agent compilations simultaneously, $i = number\ of\ servers$.

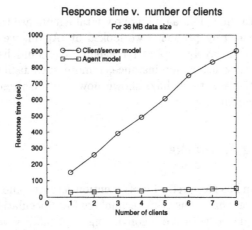

Fig. 7. Comparing the agent and client/server implementations.

5.4 Discussion

We have presented a very heterogeneous platform for distributed computing where agents are applied. Thin clients or common WWW facilities can be used to launch agents for execution at well-equipped TACOMA servers. This scheme assumes that servers can handle extra load, which we do not consider a main technical or conceptual problem; a service provider experiencing extra use of his service is likely to add extra resources due to income motives.

We showed a design scheme where a third-party, a broker (scheduler), was added to the loop. The agent is sent to this intermediate broker, and the client does not need to know exactly where the agent is forwarded and run. We find this extra mediator layer [18] very useful in an asymmetric agent environment. A user of thin clients often does not have time or resources to program an agent. A scheme where he can compose one or a set of agents and hand them off to this mediator structure is a more likely model for novice users.

The concept of deploying autonomous alarms and filters out in the network acting on behalf of the (mobile and disconnected) user, is a concept where we find agent technology appealing. When this is combined with cellular telephony as a highly connected interrupt channel, we can program very powerful, personalized, autonomous agents and deploy them out in the network. Our examples also show that a closely related claim, that *agents support mobile computing*, is valid.

This programming model can also be used to *increase the level of fault-tolerance* of a distributed application otherwise implemented as a client/server computation. The asynchronous computing model supported in TACOMA enables co-location of tightly coupled (normally distributed) modules. This makes them less dependent on lengthy network sessions; all that is needed is an available network when the agent is launched and sent to the server, and when the result is sent back.

The fundamental question, again, is how vital agents are to be able to solve the particular engineering problems we looked at. Again, we do not find any strong arguments that solely applies for agents. We could have implemented the same functionality using, for instance, remote shell facilities and manual operations. With the agents we have shown how to utilize remote resources in an *easy* and *transparent* manner.

6 Concluding Remarks

The agent paradigm has garnered a lot of attention recently, and we see an emerging understanding of what to use this technology for. Speculative arguments are gradually being replaced with more convincing applicability validations [12, 4]. We have also implemented a series of agent prototypes to better understand agent applicability aspects, and we can draw some conclusions.

First, agents are a convenient way to install client software at remote hosts. This push model complements the more pull oriented style of computing as illustrated by, for instance, Java applets. Other techniques can be used to install software remotely, but this is easy and transparent when agents are used. Also, agents are convenient when data is brought along with the agent.

Second, the way we have used an agent system like TACOMA most successfully, is to build extensible servers. An extensible server can receive, install and execute client specific software and potentially reduce the use of the network. An extensible server is also useful in a management context, since the server API can be dynamically extended through agents.

Third, the asynchronous nature of agents is important. Agents can now be off-loaded from mobile devices in a controlled manner and executed on other hosts while the mobile device is disconnected. The task delegated to the agent can be to watch for occurence of specific events, to search for personalized information, or to orchestrate a sequence of events.

Fourth, we are somewhat surprised that we could not find more convincing itinerant style computations. We have implemented agent applications for 5 years now, and the itinerant agent style seems to be more the exception rather than the rule. This can change, if new classes of applications are emerging. Electronic commerce is one such example, where personalized tasks can be delegated to shopping agents moving about in the Internet interacting with on-line services. However, we can not draw too many conclusions about agents and electronic commerce until a widely deployed system is in active use.

Finally, agents have shown to be a very convenient structuring technique for the distributed applications we have built. 5 years ago, we needed a better mechanism for dispatching of software to remote hosts. Now, we have built the same applications again with TACOMA. The parts of the applications that are mobile, have now been implemented fairly easily by using this agent system. However, until more convincing agent applications exist, our conclusion about agent applicability resembles a previous conclusion [2]; agents are basically com-plementary to other structuring techniques and it is the aggregate advantage of agents that make them attractive.

Acknowledgements

I would like to thank Robbert van Renesse and Fred B. Schneider for many discussions on agents and TACOMA the last 5 years. I also gratefully acknowl-edge the contributions of Kjetil Jacobsen, Kåre J. Lauvset, Nils P. Sudmann and Michael Susæg.

References

1. A. D. Birrell and B. J. Nelson. Implementing Remote Procedure Calls. *ACM Transactions on Computer Systems*, 2:39–59, February 1984.
2. David Chess, Colin Harrison, and Aaron Kershenbaum. Mobile Agents: Are They a Good Idea? Technical report, IBM Research Division, T.J. Watson Research Center, March 1995.
3. D. L. Eager. The Limited Performance Benefits of Migrating Active Processes for Load Sharing. *ACM Performance evaluation review*, 16(1):63–72, 1988.
4. A. Fugetta and G. Vigna. Understanding Code Mobility. *IEEE Transactions on Software Engineering*, 24(5):342–361, 1998.
5. Robert Gray, David Kotz, Saurab Nog, Daniela Rus, and George Cybenko. Mobile agents: The next generation in distributed computing. In *Proceedings of the Sec-ond Aizu International Symposium on Parallel Algorithms/Architectures Synthesis*

(pAs '97), pages 8–24, Fukushima, Japan, March 1997. IEEE Computer Society Press.

6. K. Jacobsen and D. Johansen. Mobile Software on Mobile Hardware – Experiences with TACOMA on PDAs. Technical report, Department of Computer Science/University of Tromsø, December 1997.

7. D. Johansen and G. Hartvigsen. Architectural Issues in the Stormcast System. *Springer-Verlag, Lecture Notes in Computer Science, Dagstuhl Seminar*, pages 1–16, 1995.

8. D. Johansen, N. P. Sudmann, and R. van Renesse. Performance Issues in TACOMA. In *11th Europeean Conference on Object-Oriented Programming*, 3rd. Workshop on Mobile Object Systems, June 1997.

9. D. Johansen, R. van Renesse, and F. B. Schneider. Operating System Support for Mobile Agents. In *Proceedings of the 5th Workshop on Hot Topics in Operating Systems (HOTOS-V)*, pages 42–45. IEEE Press, May 1995.

10. D. Johansen, R. van Renesse, and F. B. Schneider. Supporting Broad Internet Access to TACOMA. In *Seventh ACM SIGOPS European Workshop*, pages 42–45, June 1996.

11. M. Frans Kaashoek, D. Engler, G. Ganger, H. Briceno, R. Hunt, D. Mazières, T. Pickney, R. Grimm, J. Jannotti, and K. Mackenzie. Application Performance and Flexibility on Exokernel Systems. In *Proceedings 16th ACM Symposium on Operating System Principles*, pages 52–66, October 1997.

12. M. B. Dillencourt L. F. Bic, M. Fukuda. Distributed Computing using Autonomous Objects. *IEEE Computer*, 29(8), August 1996.

13. H. Peine and T. Stolpmann. The Architecture of the Ara Platform for Mobile Agents. In *Proceedings of the First International Workshop on Mobile Agents*, April 1997.

14. J.W. Stamos and D.K. Gifford. Remote Evaluation. *ACM TOPLAS*, 12(4), October 1990.

15. D. L. Tennenhouse and D. J. Wetherall. Towards an Active Network Architecture. *Computer Communication Review*, 26(2), April 1996.

16. M. M. Theimer, K. A. Lantz, and D. A. Cheriton. Preemptable Remote Execution Facilities in the V System. In *Proceedings of the 10th Symposium on Operating System Principles*, pages 2–12, 1985.

17. J. E. White. Telescript technology: The foundation for the electronic marketplace. General Magic white paper, General Magic Inc., 1994.

18. G. Wiederhold. Mediators in the architecture of future information systems. *IEEE Computer*, 25(3):38–49, April 1992.

An Agent Based Application for Personalized Vehicular Traffic Management

Alexander Schill[1], Albert Held[2], Wito Böhmak[3], Thomas Springer[1], and Thomas Ziegert[1]

[1] Dresden University of Technology, Department of Computer Science, Institute for Operating Systems, Databases, and Computer Networks, Mommsenstr.13, D-01062 Dresden, Germany {schill,springet,ziegert}@ibdr.inf.tu-dresden.de
[2] Daimler-Benz AG, Research and Technology 3, Wilhelm-Runge-Str. 11, D-89081 Ulm, Germany held@dbag.ulm.DaimlerBenz.COM
[3] Work was done while Wito was research assistant at the Institute for Operating Systems, Databases, and Computer Networks of Dresden University of Technology. witob@parallax.co.uk

Abstract. Traffic telematics applications, like road traffic management, operate in an extremely dynamic mobile computing environment. The Mobile Agent paradigm here becomes a promising alternative to the conventional client/server approach. In this article we evaluate the application of Mobile Agent Technology in the area of vehicular traffic management and introduce a general application partitioning model which facilitates the combination of asynchronous and autonomous operation, data filtering and scheduling in a user specific manner. A sample application and performance results are presented.

1 Introduction

Recently research on Mobile Agents and *Mobile Agent Systems (MAS)* has attracted much interest. Mobile Agents facilitate the support of heterogeneous distributed systems, the reduction of network traffic and a smaller overall delay by encapsulating protocol steps into an agent, send it over the wire and let it return when results are available. When mobile computers are part of a distributed system, the Mobile Agent paradigm becomes a promising alternative to the conventional *client/server* approach. In this article we focus on a partitioning technique for mobile computing applications in the domain of traffic telematics based on the mobile agent paradigm.

The article is organized as follows: in Sect. 2 we take a closer look at the three domains we want to integrate, namely: mobile computing, mobile agents and traffic telematics. Section 3 gives an overview of our application partitioning model. A sample application is presented in Sect. 4 and Sect. 5 contains some concluding remarks.

2 Foundations

2.1 Mobile Computing

Mobile computing environments add a notable amount of complexity to all common problems of distributed systems and cause a couple of new ones such as location management, frequent disconnections, resource scarcity on the mobile hosts side, etc. A great deal of research effort was undertaken trying to solve these problems in general (see [9, 14, 27] for system infrastructures) and separately (see [3] for priority based filtering of data, [4] for security issues, [6] for location management, and [15] for disconnected operation). Recently several research projects in the area of mobile computing have been applying agent technology to enable distributed applications in environments with mobile hosts (see [8, 12]). In the scope of this paper we concentrate on the issues of communication (in connected, weakly connected and disconnected mode) and application partitioning. Here we see the following problems:

- determination of appropriate actions as a result of events and associated information (*QoS* of varying communication media, cost, resource availability) caused by frequent system reconfigurations resulting from the movement of mobile hosts, users and applications or parts of the latter,
- the reduction of the amount of data directed to a mobile host, based on its age and priority,
- and the optimal placement and efficient transfer of application components to reduce expensive interactions over the wireless link and to enable autonomous processing in the wired part of the network during disconnections.

2.2 Mobile Agents

Mobile agents can be seen as another tribe growing from the *client/server* programming paradigm. In some cases they provide a better support for heterogeneous infrastructures. Participating nodes have to supply the interpreter (or *virtual machine (VM)*) for the underlying programming language and some infrastructure (places, services,...). Mobile agents or agent systems are mostly based on an interpreted language like *Java* [11] or *TCL* [24]. Some examples for agent systems can be found in [16, 21, 7, 2]. However, applications for mobile agents are still evolving. Today applications exist in the fields of information retrieval [18], management of large heterogeneous networks [5] and the support of intermittent connected network devices [8, 12] namely mobile computing. The most promising feature of mobile agents which makes them attractive for the use in systems with mobile computers is their ability to migrate freely between so called *places*[1]. It enables disconnected operation not only on the client side of a mobile connection. The mobile host can leave a proxy agent in the wired network in preparation of a prolonged phase of disconnection which will handle

---

[1] The term is borrowed from [29]. Places offer services for visiting mobile agents within the networked environment.

communication attempts directed to itself or gather information needed when the mobile computer is re-connected to the network. With mobile agent technology nothing more than an agent execution environment is necessary to install proxies for mobile hosts.

2.3 Traffic Telematics

Traffic telematics[2] is a generic term for products and services that give us more comfort in everyday vehicular traffic. Traffic telematics applications manage a continuous road traffic flow, provide value added services to passengers and drivers (adaptive guidance, information and entertainment) and result in an increased safety on our roads. They operate in an extremely dynamic environment of mobile computing. The high velocity of the mobile subscribers/machines and a fast changing environment require a maximum level of flexibility and adaptability. In this context agent technology seems a very promising alternative compared to the conventional 2 or 3-tier client/server approach. In this article we focus on a partitioning technique for mobile computing applications in the domain of traffic telematics based on the mobile agent paradigm.

3 An Application Partitioning Model

In terms of the client/server paradigm, application partitioning may be described as slicing the client into pieces/components. In mobile computing environments especially the introduction of an intermediate application component, which remains in the wired part of the network, becomes extremely useful. The intermediate agent handles interactions for the client and sends only important data over the error prone, low bandwidth and cost intensive wireless link. Application partitioning improves the adaptability of applications in environments with changing communication characteristics.

We introduce a hierarchical application partitioning technique. Figure 1 illustrates our application model. We distinguish 3 different additional entities.

The *Proxy Agent (PA)* either migrates in the wired part of the network following the path of the mobile node or will be issued when needed. It holds a certain level of knowledge about the usual user behavior (mobility and communication patterns, their most common applications, their preferences) and the system's state (available services, quality of network links and communication resources of the mobile host, etc.). A PA could be restricted to a single application, but there are some issues which do not permit this option. The PA remains in the wired part of the network during intermittent or disconnected phases. It consists of two functional parts (see Fig. 1). The first one is the same for all PAs within the system (a PA belongs to a host or user) and includes generic algorithms for filtering and scheduling of prioritized data. Scheduling of data delivery to the mobile host can be based on urgency, age and the amount of data. This is a

---

[2] Telematics combines telecommunications and informatics.

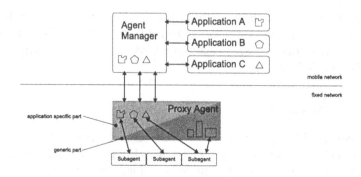

Fig. 1. The communication and placement of the models entities.

rather common issue in mobile computing and therefore all applications should share this functionality.

The following application specific issues exist: (a.) the way of filtering information (rules), (b.) the way of determining information sources within the network, and (c.) the parameterizations of the placement of additional filtering agents (where and how many in parallel). Therefore the second part of the Proxy includes context specific (semantic) information and routines. Summarizing the tasks of the PA we derive the following set of functions: *retrieving, filtering, queuing* and *scheduling* of data, according to the quality of the network link and application and user specific constraints (see the detailed view of the proxy in Fig. 2). The Proxy itself is able to send *Subagents (SA)* throughout the system. The SAs represent application tasks which may be performed simultaneously such as collecting and filtering of relevant information from various information sources. Subagents can be taken from a pool of containers with generic, customizable functionality, or must be provided by the application developer. The functionality of SAs is limited to a specific task and they need not be manageable in the same way as the proxy. The proxy issues SAs in an asynchronous manner. If a SA delivers no results the PA informs the application or creates a new one directed to an alternative location according to application specific rules. The third building block of our model is the *Agent Manager (AM)*. It represents the user interface of the proxy agent and provides generic and application specific status information. It allows the user to interact with the PA. In case of uncertainty in the decision process (where to place additional SAs, whether to deliver a large amount of urgent data or not) the AM enables the Proxy Agent to ask the user for help.

We believe that priority and content based filtering of application data (which has to be transferred over the network) facilitates the development of applications for the traffic telematics domain. Agent technology takes away the need to install proxies at all possible locations of a mobile host. Our model introduces a kind of application level routing. The information about the spatial and temporal importance of specific application data can only be found at this level.

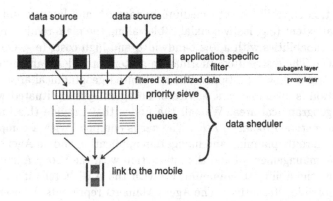

Fig. 2. The Proxy Agent in detail.

[30] proposes stationary proxies situated in the wired network. These proxies filter and delay lower priority data. This approach relies on fixed hosts that act as filter proxies as well as on *foreign agents*. Filtering takes place on the network level (specific, pre-installed filters are applied to incoming and outgoing data streams, e.g. TCP-streams). They also mention the possibility to have an agent-like proxy with the ability to move like the mobile host. Unfortunately this idea does not fit well in their approach of combining the *foreign agent* of *mobileIP* [25] with the proxy functionality. [19] proposes the so called *Mobile Floating Agent* concept, where agents manage resources for the mobile host within the wired network. These agents fulfill generic, but not application specific resource allocation and data caching on behalf of the user.

4   A Sample Application

This section describes a sample application of hierarchical application partitioning based on mobile agent technology. The scenario was taken from the domain of *Intelligent Transportation Systems (ITS)* (see [28]). We consider a *Proactive Route Planning System*. It is intended to support a trouble-free journey by car from location A to location B. The use of agent technology permits the mobile user to stay in touch with the latest information about changes in traffic conditions (congestion, incidents, road barriers) and let him react in time (e.g. select possible alternative routes) in case of changing traffic situations.

4.1   Preliminaries

We assume the existence of distributed agent and information systems. The systems nodes are dispersed over a comparatively large geographical area (e.g. Europe) and interconnected via a high bandwidth, low latency and low cost wired network (see Fig. 3). Additionally we assume the existence of wireless communication capabilities with medium bandwidth and latency and a limited geographical extent (e.g. leaky coaxial cable[3] along the main roads) and of communication capabilities with a low bandwidth and high costs (e.g. *GSM* [22] or *Mobitex* [26]). The distributed information system provides traffic information; this means traffic flow conditions within a limited geographical area. The traffic information is available as a service of an agent system situated within the respective geographical area. We call the nodes that provide this information *Traffic Information Provider (TIP)*. The car is equipped with a computing device running a route planning and navigation application and an Agent Manager enabling the management of and the interaction with the Proxy Agent. The application has the ability to communicate with the AM. It tells it the intended route and possible alternatives. The Agent Manager represents the user interface of our Proxy Agent and visualizes the application tasks passed to it. The Proxy Agent, like every mobile agent, has the ability to migrate between the locations of the distributed agent system and grants our user access to the distributed traffic information system. A PA acts on behalf of the user. Additionally, we use in this example *Traffic Information Agents (TIA)*, which act as subagents of the Proxy Agent. A TIA gathers topical information about the traffic conditions along the intended route of our sample user.

In the remainder of this section we explain the functionality of the different components and describe the interactions between them.

Route planning and navigation application The route planning and navigation application leads the driver by acoustic and optical instructions to the desired destination. This functionality is equivalent to conventional in-car navigation systems. The new dimension is an implementation according to our model (see Sect. 3). The application therefore has the ability to interact with our Agent Manager, which represents the mobile side of our Application.

Proxy Agent The PA represents the application component, which is delegated to the wired part of the network. In case of specific events it delivers results back to the application. It procures information or monitors information sources and delivers extracted and filtered information to the user. Generally speaking the PA is responsible for a dynamically adapting reliable data transfer over the last (usually wireless) link to the mobile host. Obviously it should follow the mobile host for performance and reliability reasons. The PA as an application component situated within the wired part of the network enables the timely information delivery to the user in case of traffic disturbances.

Agent Manager The AM remains on the mobile host serving as interface between the PA and the user. It presents results returned from the PA and facilitates the interaction with the user during decision processes (i. e. when congestion exceeds the given limit in time or length, the user will be asked whether the alternative route should be taken or not).

---

[3] A leaky coaxial cable could be installed along the road and provides communication media with data transmission rates of 64 or 512 kbps (see [23]).

Traffic Information Provider Local radio stations usually deliver only insufficient information about the current traffic conditions. We therefore introduce local Traffic Information Providers. TIPs constantly monitor the regional traffic conditions and are able to provide timely information about them. The information is accessible as a service provided by locations within the agent system. The migration to one of these nodes enables mobile agents to access this data source and to collect all relevant information. Specific information within the continuous flow (road from A to B is congested) triggers events within the agent's control flow which in turn results in a notification of the agent's creator (PA).

A global and "smart" traffic information system could deliver the same functionality. We register and ask for information about our intended route, or ask for a notification, when problems on our route occur. This solution obviously bears an enormous management expenditure on the part of the information system. It has to serve thousands of requests and has to send multiple messages over the network (depending on the possible degree of query parameterization, when a precise description of the requested information is possible, only the management expenditure remains).

Our approach reduces the number of messages (interactions) on the part of the network and management expenditure on the part of the information system. It facilitates the decentralization of information sources and attempts to minimize the effort on the part of the information provider. The time from the design to the provision of special services is reduced. Within this consideration, we neglect the load on the local processors, running the agent's code.

Traffic Information Agents The PA has the ability to create mobile subagents. In our example scenario we call these agents: Traffic Information Agents. These agents fulfill application tasks of modest complexity. TIAs move to the next TIP along the intended route and notify the PA, if problems occur. If not, they vanish after a given time-out interval or by an explicit termination message from the PA. TIAs enable the simultaneous procurement of information from various traffic information sources. Therefore alternative routes can be monitored in advance. TIAs subscribe to the service offered by a local TIP.

4.2 The Scenario

Assume a user wants to travel from Prague to Budapest. Therefore he assigns his Route Planning System within his car or office to find the optimal route (Prague - Jihlava - Bratislava - Budapest, see Fig. 3). No further action on the part of the user is needed and he is able to start his journey immediately.

The AM gets the information about the intended route and possible alternatives. It creates a Proxy Agent an leaves it in the wired network. The PA knows about the intended route and about the alternatives. It holds the IDs of the user and the application (to be able to contact the application in case of problems on the current route) and its own and the user's location.

The knowledge base of the proxy includes additional filter conditions (it must know which length of tailback triggers the delivery of a notification to the

Fig. 3. The sample scenario.

application) and some rules describing when to notify the application (QoS and cost criteria, in our example costs and latency are not considered, in case of problems the agent always notifies the application). The application notifies the PA about the begin and the end of the journey and whenever it reaches a new *cell* of the local wireless system. The PA itself now creates some TIAs to monitor main traffic junctions on the intended route and possible alternatives. It sends a maximum number of TIAs in advance according to the rules supplied by its creator. In our example the PA sends one agent to Prague and one to Jihlava in order to monitor the local traffic information. The PA advises the TIAs which information should be filtered and when they should notify the PA. Each TIA must notify the PA only when disturbances along the monitored route occur. The PA uses formalized knowledge from its knowledge base to deduce the necessary filter information. It determines the successor of the planned migration target place for the current route. A TIA sent to Prague, for example has to monitor the road to Jihlava. In this case the TIA must notify the PA if disturbances on the road to Jihlava occur.

The traffic information systems periodically broadcast messages about changes in traffic conditions. Therefore TIAs receive a lot of redundant messages over time (a message about a congestion of 3 km length between Jihlava and Bratislava is sent periodically until the congestion dissolves). TIAs do not terminate after the delivery of a notification about an incident. They remain alive until their lifetime expires or an explicit request for termination is received from the PA. When a TIA has sent its first message, it will not send any further messages until the congestion exceeds the next threshold (in our example this will be two times the old length). If the congestion dissolves, a mandatory message is sent by the TIA.

Let our TIA which is located in Jilhava, now send a message about a congestion of 3 km in the direction to Bratislava to the PA. The PA deduces a correction of the route and the alternative route (see Fig. 3) via Vienna. If the TIA located in Znojmo has not sent a notification about traffic disturbances yet, the PA assumes the correctness of the alternative route. Then it tries to send a message to the last known address of the application[4] (local wireless connection). If this fails it establishes a GSM-connection. The application notifies the driver of the problems on the road to Bratislava and suggests a redirection to Vienna (it presents also additional parameters of the new path: duration, etc.). Let us assume, that our user accepts the suggestion and so the application informs the PA about this decision. Then the PA terminates the TIA at the location Brno. Our driver reaches his destination without any further disturbances. After arrival in Budapest, the application sends a termination command to the PA. The PA has already terminated all TIAs because it has periodically received the current location of the application/user.

4.3 Implementation Details

The implementation of our agent system is based on the ObjectSpace Voyager core technology API [2]. It supports most of the services necessary in an agent environment and is implemented in 100% Java. This was one of the reasons to use Java as the implementation language. Furthermore, we select it because of features like object orientation, platform independence, multithreading capability and the remote method invocation mechanism (RMI) integrated in the JDK since version 1.1 [20]. Our agent system consists of agent nodes based on Voyager programs and two basic classes for agents (LocalAgent, MobileAgent) derived from the agent class of the Voyager core package. We have also implemented a basic (central) naming service using the Voyager directory class. An agent system node is represented by the class `AgentService`. It starts a Voyager program on the given port, creates a local directory service and registers the node at the global naming service. It also has RMI interfaces for querying and managing the load of the node and for the initialization of new agents, e.g. obtaining a reference to the global naming service.

The basic class for agents is the class `LocalAgent`. It contains a simple knowledge base and objects for the communication via KQML[5] messages and for the analysis of KIF[6] expressions. Local agents only register at the local directory service. Although they inherit the `moveTo()` methods from the Voyager agent

---

[4] The application updates the PA whenever it reaches a new local region.

[5] KQML (see [17]) is a language and a protocol for supporting the exchange of knowledge among agents. Each message in KQML is a part of a dialogue between sender and receiver and can contain several KIF statements.

[6] KIF [10] is a formal language for the representation and exchange of knowledge among programs.

they are not able to migrate, because there is no functionality to restore the data after migration. Currently we use this class for implementing the TIP agents.

The class `MobileAgent` adds the migration functionality to `LocalAgent`. There are methods to move the agent and restore the transient data structures after migration. The KQML, KIF and knowledge base objects are transient, so the data of these objects, namely the knowledge base has to be serialized by the agent. The objects are then newly created after migration. Furthermore the classes for these objects are distributed to all nodes of the agent system, so they don't have to be transferred during migration. The agents AgentManager, ProxyAgent and TrafficInformationAgent inherit from the MobileAgent class.

4.4 Performance Results

In the following we present some performance results we obtained using our prototype implementation. Table 1 shows the different sizes of our agents, after serialization using the common Java object serialization mechanism and the amount of data which has to be transferred when the agent classes (this includes all necessary classes) are not locally available at the target node. Table 2 shows different times for the migration of the PA and the TIAs. The time `moveTO` is conducted for the Voyager-Method `moveTO` of the class `Agent`. The time represents only the overhead for transferring the particular agent over the network. The time `move` measures the time for migrating the agent with the method `move` of our class `MobileAgent`. It includes re-registering at the new location and re-initializing the agent's knowledge base. We conducted our measurements

agent type	size in bytes		
	agent	classes (jar)	classes (jar,compressed)
PA	3815	254548	124148
TIA	3391	212410	103231

Table 1. The size of the serialized agents and necessary classes.

for 100VG AnyLAN on two Pentium Pro 200MHz, 64MB RAM Workstations running WindowsNT and for Ethernet and GSM 1800 on a ThinkPad 760D (Pentium 166MHz, 64MB RAM) running Windows95 and on one of the workstations mentioned. The results show the average of 500 runs. In our scenario TIA and PA never migrate using a GSM connection, the measurements are just for completeness. Of more interest for the comparison between client/server and agent approach is the reduction of the number of messages sent. The measured average size of an KQML-message, including information about a traffic incident in our prototype implementation is 164 bytes. The average (out of 500 repetitions) transfer times are shown in table 2. The relatively high transfer times emphasize measurements of other sources like [1] and reflect the rather poor performance of current Java and RMI implementations. Assuming a client/server-like traffic

	PA		TIA		Messages
	moveTO	move	moveTO	move	
AnyLAN	347.7	2117.5	258.8	1666.5	88
Ethernet	377.2	4137.9	366.1	2548	249
GSM 1800	7776.8	13279.7	7748.5	11854.2	2190

Table 2. Measured agent and message transfer times in ms.

information system, we have to poll for information about our intended route or the system sends information about congestions in an specified interval. Assuming the latter and an observation interval of one hour, a message about a 3 km congestion from Jilhava to Bratislava may be sent every 5 minutes, 12 times a hour. Our TIA sends this message only once. In this case our model consumes 3 messages (send TIA, TIA sends one message, kill TIA) so we save 9 Messages, neglecting the consumed amount of bandwidth for the agent transfer. This reduction in the number of interactions facilitates the efficient use of the scarce resource bandwidth. We wont keep a GSM connection alive for listening to a traffic information provider because of the high cost and limited number of channels per cell. A problem may arise resulting from the current implementation of the GSM data transfer mechanisms. A data transfer requires the establishment of a channel. This may result in resource scarcity, when many drivers receive information about a congestion simultaneously. Future enhancements of the GSM standard (GSM Phase II+) will incorporate packet oriented facilities for data transmission (General Packet Radio Service (GPRS), see [13]), so this problem vanishes.

5 Conclusion and further work

We have shown the feasibility and applicability of an integrated approach of mobile computing and mobile agent technology for application partitioning in a traffic telematics scenario. Applications in the area of traffic telematics have to deal with the inherently dynamic system configuration, changing user requirements and non-predictable traffic peaks. Agent technology facilitates the fast creation of flexible and personalized applications and services. Mobile agents let us model the real world in a more realistic way. Users install proxies in the wired infrastructure which act on their behalf, migrate along their path and contact them in case of predefined events.

Today configurability and adaptability are the driving force for agent applications, but as measurements show, the performance still cannot compete with traditional client/server mechanisms. The benefit of the agent approach is the reduction in the number of necessary interactions between the system and the client application. Our approach combines asynchronous operation (PA and TIAs), data filtering and scheduling in a user specific manner.

Our solution is not limited to this example, but rather an approach for a particular application domain. The separation into an application component on the mobile host, a Proxy Agent and specialized Subagents seems to be appropriate for the application domain of traffic telematics. It is still a first attempt at generalized questions like: When and where should we split an application? How and where should we place the resulting components? Consequently questions such as – Which possibilities exist for the extraction of generic functionality for a particular application domain, enabling the distribution in advance of agent functionality to all or probably often visited agent locations for preserving bandwidth? – are still open.

References

1. Voyager and RMI Comparison. Technical report, ObjectSpace Inc., December 1997.
2. *Voyager Core Technology User Guide, Version 2.0 Beta 1*, 1997.
3. Andrew Athan and Daniel Duchamp. Agent-Mediated Message Passing for Constrained Environments. In USENIX Association, editor, *Proceedings of the USENIX Mobile and Location-Independent Computing Symposium: August 2–3, 1993, Cambridge, Massachusetts, USA*, pages 103–107, Berkeley, CA, USA, August 1993. USENIX.
4. A. Aziz and W. Diffie. Privacy and Authentication for Wireless Local Area Networks. *IEEE Personal Communications*, 1:25–31, 1994.
5. M. Baldi, S. Gai, and G. Picco. Exploiting Code Mobility in Decentralized and Flexible Network Management. *Lecture Notes in Computer Science*, 1219:13–26, 1997.
6. Amotz Bar-Noy and Ilan Kessler. Tracking Mobile Users in Wireless Communication Networks. Technical Report RC 18276, IBM Research Center, Yorktown Heights, NY, 1992.
7. Joachim Baumann, Fritz Hohl, and Kurt Rothermel. Mole - Concepts of a Mobile Agent System. Technical Report TR-1997-15, Universität Stuttgart, Fakultät Informatik, Germany, August 1997.
8. D. Chess, B. Grosof, C. Harrison, D. Levine, C. Parris, and G. Tsudik. Itinerant Agents for Mobile Computing. *IEEE Personal Communication*, 2(5):34–49, October 1995.
9. N. Davies, G. Blair, and S. Pink. Services to Support Distributed Applications in a Mobile Environment. In *IEEE Computer Society First International Workshop on Services in Distributed and Networked Environments (SDNE94)*, pages 84–89, June 1994.
10. M. R. Genesreth, R. E. Fikes, et al. Knowledge Interchange Format, Version 3.0 Reference Manual. Technical Report Logic-92-1, Computer Science Department, Stanford University, 1992.
11. James Gosling and Henry McGilton. The Java Language Environment – A Whitepaper. Technical report, Sun Microsystems, October 1995.
12. Robert S. Gray, David Kotz, Saurab Nog, Daniela Rus, and George Cybenko. Mobile agents for mobile computing. Technical Report TR96-285, Dartmouth College, Computer Science, May 1996.
13. Jari Hämäläinen and Hannu H. Kari. Packet Radio Service for the GSM Network. In *The Second International Workshop on Mobile Multimedia Communications*, April 1995.

14. A.D. Joseph, J.A. Tauber, and M.F. Kaashoek. Mobile Computing with the Rover Toolkit. *IEEE Transactions on Computers: Special issue on Mobile Computing*, 46(3):337–352, March 1997.

15. J. J. Kistler and M. Satyanarayanan. Disconnected Operation in the Coda File System. *ACM Transactions on Computer Systems*, 10(1):3–25, February 1992.

16. D. Kotz et al. Agent TCL: Targeting the Needs of Mobile Computers. *IEEE Internet Computing*, 1(4):58–67, July/August 1997.

17. Y. Labrou and T. Finin. A Proposal for an new KQML Specification. Technical Report TR CS-97-03, Computer Science and Electrical Engineering Department, University of Maryland, Baltimore, Maryland, 1997.

18. D. B. Lange and M. Oshima. Programming Mobile Agents in Java – With the Java Aglet API, 1997.

19. George Y. Liu. *The Effectiveness of a Full-Mobility Architecture for Wireless Mobile Computing and Personal Communications*. PhD thesis, Royal Institute of Technology, Department of Teleinformatics, Sweden, March 1996.

20. Sun Microsystems. The Java Developers Kit, Version 1.1.1. http://java.sun.com/products/jdk/1.1/index.html, 1996.

21. D. S. Milojicic, D. Bolinger, M. Zurko, and M. Mazer. Mobile Objects and Agents. Technical Report TR CS-97-03, The Open Group Research Institute, November 1996.

22. Michel Mouly and Marie-Bernadette Pautet. *The GSM System for Mobile Communications*. Cell & Sys, 1992.

23. M. Nakamura, H. Tsunomachi, and R. Fukui. Road Vehicle Communication System for Vehicle Control Using Leaky Coaxial Cable. *IEEE Communications Magazine*, 34(10):84–89, October 1996.

24. J. K. Ousterhout. *Tcl and the Tk Toolkit*. Addison Wesley, Reading Massachusetts, 4 edition, 1994.

25. C. Perkins. IP Mobility Support, October 1996.

26. Apostolis K. Salkintzis and Christidoulos Chamzas. Mobile Packet Data Technology: An Insight into MOBITEX Architecture. *IEEE Personal Communications*, 4(1):10–18, 1997.

27. Alexander Schill, Sascha Kümmel, and Thomas Ziegert. Mobility aware Multimedia X.400 email: A Sample Application Based on a Support Platform for Distributed Mobile Computing. In *Proceedings of IMC 96 Workshop on Information Visualization and Mobile Computing*. Zentrum für graphische Datenverarbeitung, February 1996.

28. Yorgos J. Stephanedes, Christos Douligeris, and Sadao Takaba. Communications for the Intelligent Transportation System. *IEEE Communications Magazine*, 34(10):24,26,28,30, October 1996.

29. J. E. White. Telescript Technology: The Foundation for the Electronic Marketplace. White paper, General Magic, Inc., 2465 Latham Street, Mountain View, CA 94040, 1994.

30. Bruce Zenel and Daniel Duchamp. Intelligent Communication Filtering for Limited Bandwith Environments. In *Workshop on Hot Topics in Operating Systems (HotOS-V)*, May 1995.

Stationary vs. Mobile User Agents in Future Mobile Telecommunication Networks[1]

Axel Küpper and Anthony S. Park

Department of Computer Science (Communication Systems)
Aachen University of Technology, Ahornstraße 55, 52056 Aachen, Germany
[kuepper|park]@informatik.rwth-aachen.de

Abstract. Third generation mobile networks will be characterized by service variety and multi-provider-scenarios, requiring new concepts for service control and location management. Mobile agents seem to be appropriate for service customization and user localization. However, it is very unclear whether or not their migration costs lead to an overload of the underlying signaling network. This paper answers the question whether the use of mobile agents in telecommunication systems makes sense at all, by analytically comparing a conventional stationary concept with mobile agents. These analyses are based on various call and movement behavior patterns of mobile customers, and on measurement results achieved in the mobile agent system JAE.

1 Introduction

Current research and standardization activities in the field of mobile telecommunication focus on the development of new antennas, coding schemes, and frameworks for controlling and administering the underlying networks. These emerging technologies will lead to services enabling communication anywhere any time, with QoS features comparable to those available in fixed networks. In Europe, activities relating to the *Universal Mobile Telecommunication System* (UMTS) are carried out by various ACTS-projects and the *European Telecommunication Standardization Institute* (ETSI).

Whereas UMTS focuses on the use of *Intelligent Networks* (IN) for service control and mobility management, an international collaboration of telecommunication providers and manufacturers is working on the definition of the *Telecommunication Information Networking Architecture* (TINA) that is based on distributed computing and object orientation [1]. Unfortunately, TINA ignores certain questions that arise in the context of 3rd generation mobile systems, especially those concerning location management related aspects and terminal mobility [2].

This paper addresses these issues by examining how concepts of the TINA Service Architecture may be applied in a mobility context, and provides an approach for an

---

[1] This work is partly funded by the Deutsche Forschungsgemeinschaft under grant no. Sp. 230/12-1.

integrated service and location management. Customers are represented by so-called *user agents* in the fixed network part which contain the customers' current geographical position and service profile, thus allowing the customization of communication services and the use of *tailored services*. Mobile agents may be appropriate to realize these user agents. First approaches have been proposed by [3]. However, current research mainly concentrates on the development of architectures for mobile agents. Up to now, there is a lack of analytical research that compares mobile agents and their potentially considerable migration costs with conventional stationary concepts. This paper answers the question whether the use of mobile agents in telecommunication systems makes sense at all, by analytically comparing a conventional stationary concept with mobile agents.

The paper is structured as follows: first, user agents' main principles are explained and it is shown, how stationary and mobile agents may interwork in a UMTS network when performing session setup and location update operations. In order to analyze both strategies, we have assumed service rates achieved by measurements in the mobile agent system JAE which is presented in the third section. Finally, both approaches are analyzed in the final section.

2   Realizing Stationary and Mobile User Agents in UMTS

The UMTS architecture comprises several *access networks*, a *core network*, and an *intelligent network*. An access network is the link between a certain number of *base stations* (BS), each of which covers a geographical region (*cell*), and the core network. In the access network, signaling information is separated from the user data and forwarded to the local *Mobile Switching Control Point* (MSCP) which, in turn, is interconnected to a local *Mobile Switching Data Point* (MSDP). The MSCPs and MSDPs of all access networks and further centrally arranged components are linked via the *Signaling System No. 7* (SS7). Our approach assumes that either the entire MSCP/MSDP-component, or parts thereof, are realized as TINA objects.

TINA models all resources as objects, thus enabling rapid service creation, scalability, fault tolerance, and software reuse. Each service, even each service component, is represented by a *Computational Object* (CO) sitting on top of a common middleware architecture. A CO has a fixed set of interfaces over which its functionality can be invoked by other COs. The *Common Object Request Broker Architecture* (CORBA) has been identified as the main candidate for being applied as TINA's middleware architecture. The standardizing body, the *Object Management Group* (OMG), has recognized the significance of its CORBA framework for the telecommunication domain and has recently launched a dedicated Task Force. The two most promising assignments of this Task Force are the specification of CORBA for INs [4] and the adaptation of CORBA to mobile terminals [5].

The most frequently operations used by the service logic of mobile networks are the *call* or *session setup* and the *location update* (LU). In the following, we consider a TINA-compliant session setup and present a concept for a TINA-compliant LU, which has not been standardized so far.

Establishing a service session is the most expensive task in the signaling network. As can be seen in figure 1, four COs in the signaling network are involved in the setup process with the remaining ones, the *User Application* (UAP) and the *Provider Agent* (PA), located in the mobile terminal. The *User Agent* (UA) plays the central role in the setup. Each customer subscribed to a mobile terminal is represented by one UA in the fixed network part. The UA contains its user profile and may allocate resources according to this profile. Each exchange of signaling information between mobile terminal and fixed network part passes through the UA where it is checked against the user profile. The customer may configure this profile, and he may even manipulate the behavior of his UA by adding, removing or exchanging code modules. To some degree, the UA is then able to act autonomously on behalf of the customer in the network. In this way, individual communication environments and tailored services can be realized.

The setup is subdivided into three parts. The first part, *Starting a new Service Session*, launches a *Service Session Manager* (SSM) by the *Service Factory* (SF). Both components are arranged in the respective access network. The SSM represents the main service control object; it starts, administers, and terminates sessions, manages the participating parties, and always holds the current state of a session. The second part is called *Inviting a User to Join an Existing Service Session*. Having received this invitation, the called customer can refuse participation, or he can accept it in the third step *Joining an Existing Service Session*. Figure 1 shows that the UAs of both the calling and the called party are involved in all three steps.

A UA is always aware of its customer's current geographical position. A provider subdivides his coverage area into many *location areas* (LA). An LA (which in turn comprises several cells) is the smallest unit for which the provider maintains the current position of a customer. [6] provides a comprehensive survey of location management methods in third generation mobile systems. The *location area identifier* (LAI), holding a customer's current LA, is supposed to be stored in an MSDP-component somewhere in the network. However, we suggest to store the LAI in the UA. In case of an incoming call, the UA may then initialize the *paging* procedure at all BSs of the respective LA to determine the cell of the called customer.

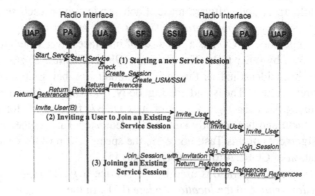

Fig. 1. Service Session Setup

The LU procedure works as follows: each mobile terminal is equipped with a *Location Manager in the Terminal* (LMT), which is a CO that permanently listens a channel for the LAI regularly broadcasted by the BS to all terminals of that cell. When a customer enters a new LA, the LMT receives a different LAI than before. Upon receipt of that new LAI, it initializes the LU and thus informs the UA about the new geographical position.

There is a high amount of signaling traffic between a UA and the remaining COs for both service provision and location management. Our approach aims at keeping this signaling traffic as small as possible. To fulfil the strong time constraints of mobile networks it is further intended to reduce the signaling delay. To do so, we consider the strategies of *Stationary User Agents* (SUA) and *Mobile User Agents* (MUA). For both approaches we assume a hierarchical core network with access networks at its leaf nodes, as depicted in figure 2. Each leaf node represents the access point for signaling information and user data for several LAs.

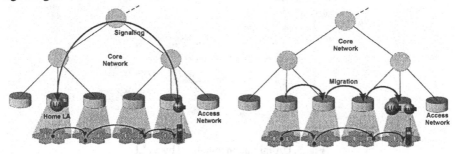

Fig. 2. Stationary and Mobile User Agents

Stationary User Agents: SUAs permanently remain in the access network of the customer's home LA. Since SF and SSM have to be allocated in the access network covering the customer's current position the entire signaling traffic caused by session setups has to traverse the network between home LA and current location. The same applies for an LU: when the LMT receives a new LAI, the LU is invoked at the UA. First, this invocation is sent to the current access network over the radio interface. It is then forwarded to the UA residing in the remote home access network of the mobile user.

Mobile User Agents: With this approach the UA follows the movement of the user through the fixed network. Each time the user enters the coverage area of another access network, the UA has to migrate from the previous to the new access network. Thus, the UA always stays as close as possible to the user and at the same time resides in the same local network as SF, SSM (in the case of outgoing calls), and other resources. It is expected, that in this way signaling costs can be reduced in comparison to the SUA strategy.

Realizing mobile agents require the availability of a mobile agent system in each access network that provides the core technology for security, and the management of services and mobility. The *Java Agent Environment* (JAE), which is presented in the next section, is such a mobile agent system. The OMG also addresses this need by specifying the *Mobile Agents System Interoperability Facility* (MASIF) [7]. Together with OMG's activities in the Telecom Domain Task Force, as mentioned above, MASIF might be a good candidate for being applied in future mobile networks.

However, MUAs lead to the problem of migration costs. If the customer is moving between LAs within the coverage area of an access network, the UA is already available and the LU can be performed as usual. However, if the customer crosses the boundaries of an access network, the LU initializes the *Request_UA* operation according to figure 3. The migration process is then initialized on the previous node and the UA is moved to the new access network. Here, the agent is launched again and the successful migration is confirmed. Subsequently, the LU can be performed and confirmed to the LMT.

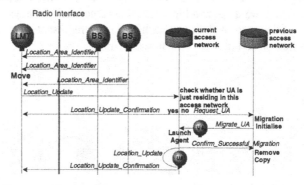

Fig. 3. UA migration initialized by an LU

Given this complex process, it may be probable that the migration costs exceed the saved signaling costs in case of frequent migration. This paper compares these costs and answers the question whether or not the deployment of mobile agents in cellular mobile networks makes sense or whether conventional strategies, for example SUA, work more efficiently. Before performing an analysis of response times for LUs and session setups, we have done measurements in order to obtain realistic service rates concerning the migration of mobile agents.

3 Testbed measurements

In this section we give a brief description of the mobile agent system, *Java Agent Environment* (JAE) [8], and the testbed that supplied us with the measurement values. The mobile agent system has been developed as a case study to check the usability of mobile agents against the requirements of mobile clients. This testbed has been developed at the Department of Computer Science at Aachen University of Technology [9]. JAE is a framework for developing and deploying both mobile and stationary agents. It contains the core technology for security, services and mobility and allows easy implementation of user-created agents. Experiences gained during the implementation relate to the easy realization of agent based distributed applications and the flexibility that the mobile agent concept offers to programmers. Once the set of service agents has been defined and established, the combination of these services to fulfil tasks via mobile agents is very simple. The measurements of the prototype implementation serve as a basis for the analytical computation for UMTS.

Figure 4 depicts the simplified distributed JAE testbed, showing only four host machines, each running an agent engine and an agent directory server providing yellow pages functionalities. The hosts *Q42*, *Worf* and the directory server are SUN Ultra 1 workstations (167 MHz) equipped with 128 MB RAM. *Frontera* and *Carolus* are Pentium 133 and 200 MHz PCs respectively, with 64 MB RAM each. Mobile agents can be executed in each of the JAE engines.

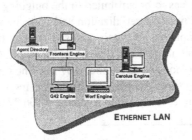

Fig. 4. JAE measurement testbed

Within this testbed we measured the service rates required for the performance analysis of the TINA session setup and LU. Obviously, the future UMTS will have other data transmission characteristics than the local area network in the testbed, but the TINA-nodes will have capacities similar to e.g. a workstation. Therefore, the measurement of the internal management of the agent engine with serialization, initialization and registration remains valuable for the calculation. Service rates of interest that can be retrieved from the mobile agent system include:

- initializing of a migration and its subsequent migration
- registration and de-registration of mobile agents
- retrieving of mobile agents (on a new node) and their execution

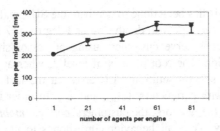

Fig. 5. Migration time depending on the number of mobile agents

The measurement has been repeated 200 times to smooth the emerging deviations caused by the network or the background processes of the host machines. Figure 5 and 6 reflect the measurements that have been done on a SUN Ultra machine.

As expected, it turned out that the process time for initializing and (de)registration of mobile agents is constant, only depending on the load of the machine and the number of mobile agents served by the agent engine. The migration time depends on the number of mobile agents per engine and increases linearly (see figure 5) with a maximum deviation of about 35 ms. Other measurements have shown that the average migration time of a mobile agent for a local loop back is about 190 ms. Evidently, the serialization of the mobile code is varying heavily depending on its size and the number of global variables. Figure 6 shows that the time for receiving and sending of the smallest and simplest mobile agent class (3.288 bytes) differs by about 80 ms (similar results were achieved with desktop PCs). The time discrepancy between sending and receiving of mobile code has to be attributed to the outgoing buffer of the TCP stack and the different process time for serialization and de-serialization. Nevertheless, the process times can be employed to obtain realistic service times. The average time measured with JAE to initiate and serialize an agent is 24,96 ms. Finally, removing this agent from the engine/node costs another 0,47 ms. The migration time depends on the network and will therefore be obtained from the requirements of UMTS. The average receive process time, as shown in figure 6, is 106,27 ms.

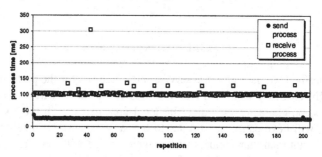

Fig. 6. Send and receive process time of an agent engine

4   Performance Analysis

A performance analysis has been done to compare the SUA and MUA strategies. The hierarchical signaling network with depth $d=4$ and degree $g=7$ is modeled as a queuing system whose nodes serve customers using processor sharing with a general service time distribution. The root node is of level 1, whereas the leaf nodes are of level d. Requests for session setup and LU arrive at the leaf nodes according to a Poisson distribution with parameters $\lambda_{Session}$ and λ_{LU}. In order to describe the path a request takes through the network, the customers' *call* and *mobility behavior* must be modeled appropriately. The call behavior corresponds to the distance between the access network of the calling party and the access network containing the UA of the called party. The mobility behavior is determined accordingly; in the case of SUA the distance refers to the access network through which an LU-operation is directed and the customer's home access network. Applying the MUA-strategy, the UA of a customer is either already located in the current access network, or it must be requested from the node visited previously. The distance corresponds to a level L up to which a request ascends in the hierarchy before it descends towards the appropriate leaf node. According to [10], the probability to reach a certain level, the *level probability*, can be described as follows:

$$P(L_x = i) = e^{-\alpha_x(d-i)} \frac{1 - e^{-\alpha_x}}{1 - e^{-i\alpha_x}} \text{ with } 1 \le i \le d \text{ and } x \in \{SetUp, LU\}. \tag{1}$$

It must be stressed that we assume a rather local user behavior, i.e. customers predominantly move within one certain geographical region and mainly make calls to persons nearby. This has an impact on the operations' distance in the network hierarchy, and consequently on the level to which they ascend. Since the user behavior is hard to predict, it can be varied using the *locality parameter* α_x; the higher α_x the lower the probability that a request ascends to the next higher level. Since call and mobility behavior are independent, two parameters α_x with $x \in \{Setup, LU\}$ are considered in the following.

Sign	Operation	Value [1/ms]
μ_D	Dereference an operation	2.0
μ_{Ex}	Execute an operation at a CO	1.0
μ_R	Return from an operation	2.0
μ_T	Transmission rate between two nodes	1.0
μ_I	Initializing a migration and subsequent migration	0.09
μ_L	Launching an agent on a new node	0.3
μ_{RA}	Removing an agent	2.0
μ_M	Migration of an agent	1.0

Table 1. Service Rates.

Sign	Operation	Value [1/ms]
λ_{LU}	Arrival rate of LUs per leaf node and hour	10000
λ_{Setup}	Arrival rate of set-ups per leaf node and hour	$C/M * \lambda_{LU}$

Table 2. Arrival Rates.

Before calculating each node's load and the response times, the arrival and service rates for the required operations have to be established. The service rates are partly based on investigations of the RACE MONET projects and partly - as far as mobile agents and migration costs are concerned - on results achieved with the JAE measurement testbed described in the previous section. The main problem when determining these rates is the fact that measurement results achieved with the JAE testbed cannot easily be applied to future telecommunication networks. These networks will show a tremendous increase of performance characteristics in comparison with today's switching and service logic equipment, which itself is many times faster than a Java-based testbed. However, the JAE testbed allows us to adapt the measurement results by relating all costs for mobile agents and their migration to the costs of database operations estimated in various RACE MONET projects. The resulting service rates are shown in table 1. Table 2 shows the arrival rates for session setups and LUs per leaf node and hour.

Using these service and arrival rates, the load of each node in the signaling network can be determined. First, the calculation is done separately for each operation. The load of a node depends on its level in the hierarchy. In the following, the load equations for an LU are given as an example for other operations, i.e. the session setup. In the case of an SUA, the load of a leaf node caused by LUs is yielded by

$$\rho_{SUA,LU} = \frac{\lambda_{LU}}{g^{d-1}} \left(P(L_{LU} < d) \left(\frac{1}{\mu_D} + \frac{1}{\mu_R} \right) + \frac{1}{\mu_{Ex}} \right). \tag{2}$$

Performing the LU operation at the UA is represented by the service rate for the *Execute* operation μ_{Ex}. This operation is performed in the access network of the customer's home LA whenever the LU is initiated by a terminal. However, the *Dereference* and the *Return* operations are only executed when the corresponding UA does not stay in the current access network (i.e., the customer is roaming outside his home LA), which is why the service times must be weighted with a level probability according to (1). In the case of an MUA strategy the calculation is a little more complex since the migration of a UA must be considered appropriately:

$$\rho_{MUA,LU} = \frac{\lambda_{LU}}{g^{d-1}} \left(P(L_{LU} < d) \left(\frac{2}{\mu_D} + \frac{1}{\mu_I} + \frac{1}{\mu_L} + \frac{1}{\mu_{RA}} \right) + \frac{1}{\mu_{Ex}} \right). \tag{3}$$

Again, the LU is performed with rate μ_{Ex}, when the UA is already staying in the current access network or after its migration to this access network. The load caused by the migration process itself is represented by the term weighted with the level probability. It can be interpreted by means of figure 3. Figure 7 depicts the load of a node depending on its level using SUA (left) and MUA (right), respectively.

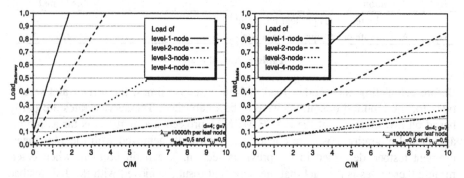

Fig. 7. Load of a node in dependence on its level for SUA (left) and MUA (right) and for $\alpha_{LU}=0,5$ and $\alpha_{Setup}=0,5$.

The load is determined by the *Call to Mobility Ratio* (C/M) that relates the arrival rate of session setups to the arrival rate of LUs fixed with 10000 LUs per leaf node and hour. A node becomes overloaded or overburdened if its load exceeds 1. Figure 7 demonstrates that networks applying the MUA-strategy become overloaded of higher C/M ratios than networks using the SUA-strategy. This applies to all nodes of level 1, 2, and 3. Level 4 nodes (i.e. the access networks) show a slightly increased load in comparison to SUA which is due to the expensive costs of performing the UA-migration. However, nodes of this type are far from becoming overloaded in case of the arrival rates assumed here. It can generally be noticed that the bottlenecks of the signaling infrastructure are not the access networks, but the nodes of level 1 and 2. The reason for this is that seven nodes of level 2 and one node of level 1 are responsible for forwarding traffic from 343 access networks. However, it must again be stressed that our scenario is based on the assumption that the user behavior is predominantly local and therefore a considerable amount of traffic does not even reach nodes of these levels.

Each LU and each session setup are composed of a sequence of single operations, listed in table 1. In order to determine average service times for these operations when executed on different nodes of the network, waiting times at each node must be considered which in turn depend on the respective load. As mentioned above, we assume a processor sharing strategy to be realized on each node, with requests being executed in a round robin fashion. According to the BCMP theorem [11], the probability that n customers are served in a node of a certain level is then given by:

$$p(n) = (1 - \rho_{x,total})\rho_{x,total} \text{ with } x \in \{SUA, MUA\}. \tag{4}$$

The average number of jobs in a node can be calculated with

$$E(N_x) = \frac{\rho_{x,total}^2}{1 - \rho_{x,total}}. \tag{5}$$

The mean waiting time can then be derived from the average number of jobs with

$$E(W_x) = \frac{E(N_x)}{\lambda_{total}(e_{x,LU} + e_{x,Setup})}. \tag{6}$$

In this term, $e_{x,LU}$ and $e_{x,Setup}$ represent visit rates which can be derived from (1) and the C/M ratio. Having determined these values, both the average LU and setup times can be obtained by adding the respective service and waiting times and weighting them with the appropriate level probabilities. Figure 8 shows the resulting average LU times for SUA (left) and MUA (right) and for different locality parameters α_{LU}.

The heavy increase at a certain C/M ratio is caused by network overload. For $\alpha_{LU} = 0,5$ the point of overload corresponds to the C/M rate in figure 7 where the root node becomes overloaded. The results also demonstrate the impact of the locality parameter α_{LU} on response times and the point of overload. The higher α_{LU}, i.e. the more local the movement behavior, the lower the load and consequently the lower the mean response times. It can further be noticed that LU costs are considerable higher in the case of MUA which is mainly due to migration costs in the leaf nodes. Figure 9 compares the average response times for session setups.

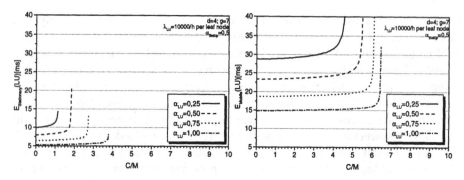

Fig. 8. Average LU response times for SUA (left) and MUA (right)

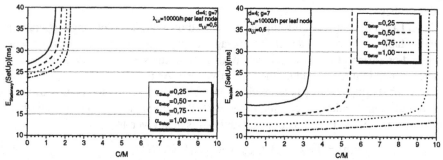

Fig. 9. Average session setup response times for SUA (left) and MUA (right)

Since the UAs always stay in the current access network, the signaling can mainly be performed locally leading to reduced response times. The higher the ratio of session setups compared to LUs, the higher the gain achieved with the MUA-strategy. The difference between both strategies regarding LUs and setups together is depicted in figure 10.

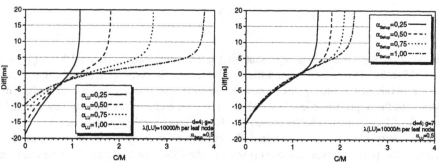

Fig. 10. Average difference of response times between SUA and MUA

This difference is calculated considering the response times of both operations weighted with the respective arrival rates. It can be seen in figure 10 that the difference between SUA and MUA becomes positive at a C/M ratio of about 1. Thus, on average the MUA-strategy leads to decreased response times provided that the customers' call behavior exceeds the average movement behavior.

5 Conclusions

Finally, one can conclude that the MUA strategy really seems to be suitable to reduce signaling traffic and keep the network stable for higher arrival rates than the SUA strategy. However, it must be stressed that the efficiency of mobile agents strongly depend on the user behavior. Although it seems that even a compensated relation between calls and LUs is favorable for mobile agents, there remains a factor of uncertainty. Therefore, ongoing research concentrates on extended strategies using adaptive and replication mechanisms [12]. Furthermore, it is intended to develop a broker network that enables flat and provider independent addressing in order to localize agents.

References

1. TINA-C: Overall Concepts and Principles of TINA. Version 1.0 (1995)
   http://www.tinac.com/deliverable/deliverable.htm
2. TINA-C: Service Architecture. Version 5.0 (1997)
   http://www.tinac.com/deliverable/deliverable.htm
3. Ramjee, R., LaPorta, T. F., Veeraragahvan, M.: The Use of Network-Based Migrating User Agents for Personal Communication Services. IEEE Personal Communications, Vol. 2 No. 6 (1995) 62-68
4. The Object Management Group, Telecom Domain Task Force: Interworking between CORBA and Intelligent Networks Systems, Request for Proposal. telecom/97-12-06 (1997) http://www.omg/library/schedule/CORBA_Intelligent_Networks_RFP.htm
5. The Object Management Group, Telecom Domain Task Force: Supporting Wireless Access and Terminal Mobility in CORBA, Request for Information, telecom/98-05-xx
6. Tabbane, S.: Location Management Methods for Third-Generation Mobile Systems. IEEE Communications Magazine, Vol. 35 No. 8 (1997) 72-78
7. Milojicic, D. et al: MASIF, The OMG Mobile Agent System Interoperability Facility. To appear in: Proceeding of Mobile Agent '98, Lecture Notes in Computer Science, Springer Verlag (1998)
8. Park, A. S., Küpper, A., Leuker, S.: JAE - A MULTI-Agent System with Internet Services Access. Fourth International Conference on Intelligence in Services and Networks "Technology for Cooperative Competition", Como, Al Mullery et al. (Eds.) Lecture Notes in Computer Science 1238, Springer Verlag (1997)
9. Park, A. S., Reichl, P.: Personal Disconnected Operations with Mobile Agents. 3rd Workshop on Personal Wireless Communication, PWC '98, Tokyo (1998)
10. Hoff, S.: Mobility Management in Open Systems - Performance Analysis of Directory Services. Dissertation, Aachen University of Technology (in German)
11. King, P.: Computer and Communication System Performance Modeling. New York, Prentice Hall, 1990
12. Küpper, A.: User Agents - An Approach for Service Provision and Location Management in 3rd Generation Mobile Networks. Proceedings of International Conference on Telecommunications '98, Greece (1998)

Integrating Mobile Agents into the Mobile Middleware

Ernö Kovacs[1], Klaus Röhrle[1], Matthias Reich[2]

[1]Sony International (Europe) GmbH, Telecommunication Research, Fellbach, Germany
[2]Siemens AG, Corporate Technology, Munich, Germany
e-mail: kovacs@fb.sony.de

Abstract. Mobile agents are a new paradigm for distributed computing that is especially well suited for mobile computing over global wireless networks. This paper describes the approach taken in the ACTS OnTheMove[1] project to integrate a mobile agent system into the Mobile Application Support Environment (MASE), a middleware for mobile computing. In this project, an existing mobile agent system was adapted for the requirement of mobile computing. We present the changes that had to be made to the agent system to adapt it to the wireless communication. We also present some of the application areas where a mobile agent system is suitable for mobile communication. We describe an agent based pre-fetcher application where an agent operates disconnected from the user on the fixed network and prepares web pages for the anticipated next connection of the user using the Quality-of-Service trading functions available in MASE.

1   Introduction

Data services provided by today's global wireless networks (like GSM) are only available at a very high cost with limited bandwidth, long connection setup times, and high latency. The upcoming third generation of wireless networks - currently developed in the ETSI's *Universal Mobile Telecommunication System (UMTS)* standardisation initiative - will provide much higher data rates (up to 2 Mbit for the stationary user and 144 Kbit for the user travelling in a car) with better *Quality-of-Service (QoS)*. Nevertheless, mobile communication will remain costly, unreliable, and different from communication over fixed networks.

The mobile agent approach is a new paradigm for structuring distributed applications that has gained a lot of research interest in the last years. This approach has some very promising properties for mobile users. It inherently enables disconnected operations

---

[1] The ACTS OnTheMove [5] project is sponsored partially by the European Commission in the Advanced Communication Technologies and Services program under contract AC034. The project participants are Ericsson Radio Systems AB, Deutsche Telekom MobilNet GmbH, Ericsson Eurolab GmbH, Siemens AG, RWTH Aachen, IBM France, Tecsi, BT, Bonnier Business Press, Royal Institute of Technology - KTH Sweden, Sony International (Europe) GmbH, Swedish Institute of Computer Science - SICS, Burda Com Media Solutions GmbH, Centre for Wireless Communications – CWC and Iona Ltd.

that allow shutting down the costly wireless connections while the agent is executing. Applications developed for mobile users can be stored in the fixed networks. They can be broken into pieces, downloaded to the mobile device and then executed. They can easily be adapted to the scare resources available on the mobile device and the wireless networks.

The ACTS project *OnTheMove* (OTM) [1] has developed a mobile middleware that provides useful services to a wide range of mobile applications. This middleware is called the *Mobile Application Support Environment (MASE) [2]*. In the second phase of the OTM project, an existing mobile agent system was adapted for the requirements of mobile communication and integrated with the MASE services. This paper describes the required changes of the agent system and the application provided for the mobile user.

The next section explains the overall system architecture of the MASE system and its physical distribution. After that we summarize the changes to the mobile agent system SWARM to adapt it for wireless communication. We then describe the integration into the MASE system and some of the applications developed for the integrated system. At the end, we give some performance figures for mobile agents migrating over different networks. We conclude with a summary and an outlook on open problems.

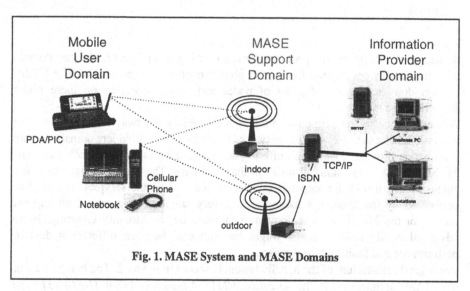

Fig. 1. MASE System and MASE Domains

2 Mobile Application Support Environment (MASE)

The *Mobile Application Support Environment (MASE)* is a distributed system that provides middleware functionality required by mobile users. The MASE is divided into three logical domains: the *mobile user domain*, the *MASE support services*

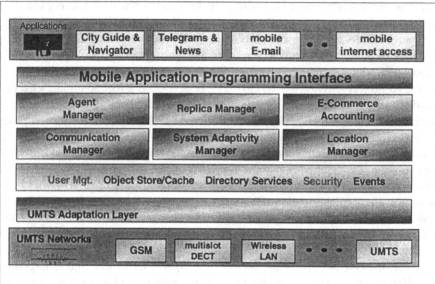

Fig. 2. MASE Architecture

domain, and the *information provider* domain (see Figure 1). Users in the user domain have mobile devices ranging from smart phones over PDA to notebooks. The MASE support domain consists of a set of nodes and server processes on these nodes supporting the mobile users.

A special node in the support domain is the Mobility Gateway that possesses the network interfaces to the wireless network. The information providers domain contain information providers, which are offering dedicated services for the mobile user. The MASE itself is installed on all nodes in these domains. The actual configuration of a single MASE installation depends on the domain and on the services requested or performed by the node. For example, in a very simple configuration, all support servers of the MASE support domain are located on the Mobility Gateway. In an advanced configuration, servers might be replicated between different nodes for performance and fault-tolerance reasons.

The logical architecture of the MASE system is shown in Figure 2. The bottom part of the MASE architecture is the so-called *UMTS Adaptation Layer (UAL) [3]*. The UAL's main task is to abstract from the underlying network bearer and to provide a universal interface to different networks. It hides different connection set-up and control interfaces, monitors the status of the connected networks and provides Quality-of-Service information to the upper layers. Wherever it is possible and supported by the attached networks (or the available network drivers), TCP/IP is used as the transport layer protocol. As shown in the picture, the UAL adapts to networks like GSM, multi-slot DECT, WaveLan, Ethernet, and more. It also provides interfaces to the anticipated upcoming UMTS data services.

On top of the UAL, a *General Support Layer (GSL)* provides functionality generally required in a middleware system for distributed computing. A LDAP-based directory system enables the lookup of objects and their attributes located somewhere in the system. User and Security Management Functions (working closely with the directory function) are required to authenticate MASE users, to protect the data exchange and to provide information for mapping between different network addresses, device names and logical addresses (e.g. the telephone numbers, IP addresses, current WaveLan cell identification, and more). An Object Store and Caching module manages different kind of data objects persistently on the different nodes of the system. An Event Management collects event messages (e.g. about a sudden bearer change, a drop in the QoS, or a loss of connectivity) and forwards them to interested components of the MASE system.

On top of these two layers, a set of manager components provides different services. The set of available components depends on the current configuration of the MASE installation. This is used to tailor the MASE installation to the available resources of the device (in the case of mobile devices) or to the functionality it should provide (in the case of a support server).

The Communication Manager implements application protocols for reading E-Mails (using the IMAP4 protocol), accessing Web pages (using HTTP1.1), asynchronous message queues, alerts, sending of GSM SMS messages, or a real-time multimedia data stream. The protocol processing is adapted to the mobility aspects. For example, a multimedia object contained in one of the applications protocols (e.g. as an attachment to an e-mail or an image referenced by a Web-page) can be automatically adapted to the QoS provided by the current network bearer by using media-conversion routines provided by the System Adaptivity Manager. The Location Manager accesses different sources of location information (e.g. an installed GPS device [4], the WaveLan cell id) and maps this information to a common data format. The Replication Manager keeps track of replicated files in the system and controls the task of re-synchronising the different replicas. The Accounting Manager does the bookkeeping about the cost for the current network usage and provides a Mobile-SET (Secure Electronic Transaction) protocol. Using the Mobile-SET protocol a SET transaction is started on the mobile device, but the communication steps required by the normal SET protocol are performed by one of the support servers in the MASE support domain. This reduces the communication required over the wireless link.

All MASE services are offered to MASE-aware applications through the so-called Mobile-API. The Mobile-API is intended for standardisation.

3 Agent Management

The Agent Management component of the MASE enables the use of mobile agents for mobile communication. There are several reasons for integrating the Agent Management into the MASE architecture:

- **Dynamic Distribution of Functionality**
  Mobile agents are used to dynamically enhance the functionality installed on the mobile device. The mobile agents migrate to the devices and stay here until their tasks are finished. After that the resources required by the agents are set free again.
- **Bandwidth and Air-Time Conservation**
  Giving the current wireless networks, bandwidth is very limited and air time is very costly. Using mobile agent helps to reduce the required network bandwidth and will reduce the overall connection time.
- **Resource Management**
  With the very limited set of resources available on the mobile device, mobile agents are also a good unit to move currently not required functionality from the mobile device to a support server in the MASE support domain.
- **Start Processes in the Support or Information Provider domain**
  Mobile agents can be used to perform (distributed) processes in the MASE support domain. Using an agent repository installed in the MASE support domain or in the Information Provider domain, an agent application can be started from the mobile device without having a special client application installed locally.
- **Disconnected Operations**
  The MASE contains a messaging facility based on asynchronous message queues (based on the product MQSeries from IBM). Through its reliable transaction concepts, applications are shielded from the effects of sudden disconnections. These applications require the application code to be installed in advance, thus occupying valuable resources on the mobile device. Furthermore, writing such application in such a way that they can deal meaningful with all kind of disconnection is a very complex task. Mobile agents usually deal with communication problems on the language level or in the service primitives of the migration command, so that the handling of disconnection fits better into the programming model.

3.1   Integration with MASE

The OnTheMove project [5] selected the Siemens SWARM system for integration with the MASE system. The SWARM system is a JAVA-based [6] system for mobile agents ([7], [8]). It is a descendant of the MOLE [9] system developed by the University of Stuttgart.
The SWARM system had to be adapted to fit to the mobile communication situation. The following changes had to be made:

- **Dynamic Management of available Agent Places**
  The original system had assumed that all agent places were known in advanced and kept in a static configuration database. For the purpose of OnTheMove, the SWARM system now maintains a list of available agent places and allows to dynamically add new agent places to this list of possible communication partners.

- **Communication Channel**

  In the original system a static communication channel was established and kept open for all agent places. For the purpose of mobile communication, the agent system now opens a communication channel and keeps this open for a certain time (short-hold mode). It closes the channel so that the MASE system might disconnect from the fixed network to save money.

- **Trader**

  A trader component was added to dynamically locate available services in the network.

- **Class Server**

  The SWARM system has a class server concept. JAVA classes required to execute a mobile agent can be loaded from the class server. Instead of transmitting the required classes together with the agent state, they can be fetched from a class server. This is especially useful when an agent migrates from a mobile device to the fixed network. In this way, the class server system was used to minimize the amount of data transferred over the low-bandwidth wireless link.

3.2   Integration of SWARM into MASE

The MASE system consists of several managers each performing a dedicated task. To integrate the SWARM system into the MASE, a new Agent Manager was created. The agent manager performs the necessary steps to integrate the agent system into the MASE.

1. At system start-up, the agent manager checks whether the SWARM system is installed on the local system. It then loads the SWARM JAVA classes for an agent place and starts the execution engine in its own JAVA thread.
2. It further creates some system agents in the agent places that offer the MASE services to mobile agents.
3. It loads a set of persistently stored agents and made them available in the agent place.
4. On a mobile device, upon connection to the network, the agent manager informs the agent manager on the mobility gateway about the new connection and inserts its own address into the list of available places at the mobility gateway.

After performing these steps, the basic configuration of the agent system within MASE is established.

3.3   MASE System Agents

The MASE system agents offer a subset of the Mobile-API to the mobile agents. A system agent is a fixed agent started in the agent place. The agent place usually prevents agents from calling methods outside of its own classes. System agents are equipped with access rights to the MASE API and are allowed to offer these services to other agents. Which parts of the Mobile-API are offered to which mobile agent depends on the security policy active on this particular node. The system agents enforce this security policy by maintaining an access control list and by checking the credentials of the agent against the access lists of the MASE service.

4   Agent Applications

The OnTheMove project has developed several example applications based on mobile agents.

4.1   Http Pre-Fetching

Today's wireless networks offer only low bandwidth to the mobile users. In order to improve the response time of applications like Web-Browsing and Multimedia E-Mail, the MASE system trades the quality of the requested multimedia objects against the time required for downloading. It does this by applying multimedia conversion routines reducing the size and quality of the multimedia object. This is done transparently at access time by a server running in the MASE support domain on the fixed network. To select a suitable reduction method the QoS trader uses information about the current network QoS as well as end terminal properties and the user's preferences. This information is stored in profiles managed by the MASE profile manager (a part of the System Adaptivity Manager).

In order to improve the downloading time and to reduce connection time, it is useful to access and convert interesting web pages while the mobile user is off-line. A traditional system would offer the user a range of options to indicat when to download which page. Other options could include for example, whether the pre-fetcher should also fetch pages linked to this page and also the depth of links to be followed. Using the available options, a user might be able to define a list of Web pages that he will access later and also add when these pages should be downloaded.

The problem of that approach is that the options offered are usually pre-programmed and fixed, so that a user might only select between the offered choices. If the process of downloading and converting the Web-pages could be controlled by a mobile agent, the options of which page to download at what time are not limited to the ones offered by the provider of the pre-fetching service. Instead, other parties can extend and modify the pre-fetching agent according to their needs. For example, an information service provider might offer a specialised agent specifically prepared for the information offered by this provider. Instead of simply following all links contained in a page, the agent knows which links are important and which might have changed recently. So, instead of pre-fetching all pages referenced, a specialised mobile agent will only access pages really required by the user.

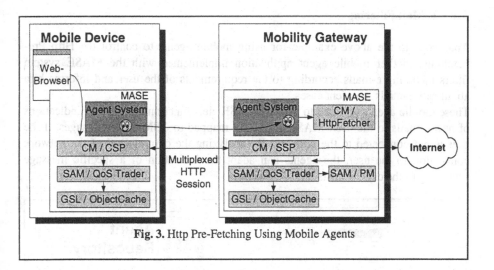

Fig. 3. Http Pre-Fetching Using Mobile Agents

Other specialised agents might not wait for a specific time upon which to fetch the pages, but for a certain event. For example, the agent might monitor a wireless LAN and start the pre-fetching when the user connects to the LAN.

In order to allow a mobile agent to control the pre-fetching and conversion process, a special MASE *HttpFetch* system agent was written, that offers an interface by which agents could request Web-pages (see Fig. 4). The HttpFetch agent will fetch the web-page, store the page in the MASE cache, and use the MASE service to compress it. It will furthermore fetch all multimedia object contained in the page and convert them according to the user preferences and the anticipated network over which the user will connect.

A mobile agent using the HttpFetch service, is furthermore able to parse the Web-page contained in the cache in order to follow links on the page according to its own requirements.

This example illustrates some important advantages of using mobile agents. Traditional client-server systems trend to provide complex server interfaces in order to minimize the amount on interactions between the client and the server. Using the mobile agent concept, the server interface can be much simpler relying on the fact that the agent can interact with the server at relatively low cost. If complex operations are required they can be encapsulated into the mobile agent. It also shows that a generic functionality (i.e. the http-fetching and the qos trading) can designed in such a way that it can be augmented with very specific functionality (i.e. the logic when to access which page).

4.2 E-Mail Filtering

Analogous to the above example for using mobile agents to control the Http Pre-Fetching, another mobile agent application implemented with the MASE system filters incoming e-mails according to the requirements of the user and informs him about new e-mails in urgent cases.

These mobile agents are able to use the MASE alert function for sending indications of new e-mails to the user. MASE Alerts are mapped to GSM SMS messages, if the user is not connected to the network. By analyzing the current QoS of the network connection to the user, the agents can adapt the indication of a specific message according to the current costs and bandwidth.

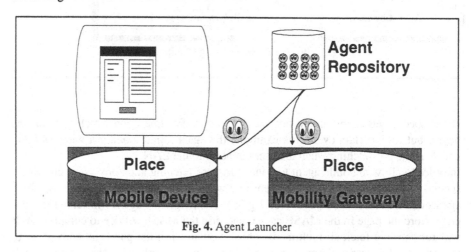

Fig. 4. Agent Launcher

4.3 Agent Launcher

An important possibility offered by mobile agents is the ability to install an application in the network and to offer the user the ability to start and access this application without having to install software on his device. Furthermore, the application can be started directly on the fixed network. This is especially important when considering the small amount of resources available on today's mobile devices which might range in the area of only a few thousand bytes of permanent storage (e.g. on a Smart card or static RAM).

For the MASE system a special application was written which allows installing a mobile agent based application in the fixed network. The user is able to browse through the available application servers in the mobility support domain and start a application directly.

The SWARM agent system uses the concept of class servers from which the JAVA classes required to run a mobile agent are loaded. Applications are installed in the MASE support domain by loading the required agent code into the provided class servers. A description file is provided which describes the application and also additional parameters, e.g. where to start the agent. An agent could start on the mobile device, the mobility gateway, any server of the MASE support domain equipped with an agent place, or directly at an agent place located in the information provider domain. In order to do so, the agent launcher application (see Fig.4) requests a list of available services from the MASE support domain, and presents them to the user. The list also contains options where to start the agent. The user might then start the agent, which will execute on the fixed network or on the mobile device.

5   Performance

The following Table 1 will give some performance figures to understand the implication of using a mobile agent over different kind of wireless networks. The measurements are done using a notebook and a PC-based server. Both were equipped with the MASE agent system. Measurements were taken for Ethernet (100Mbit/s), a wireless LAN (WaveLAN, 2 Mbit/s) and a GSM connection (9600 Bit/s). The measurements were done several time and an average was computed. The agent was a simple agent just moving from one place to the other and back. The class code was 1.9 Kbyte. The times shown are the round trip times – the agent move from the MASE support domain to the mobile device and back again. We compare the time for a local class load (the classes are already locally installed, but must be loaded into the JAVA virtual machine), with the time required to load the classes remotely (from the original site). We also provide the time when the classes were already loaded and only the state of the agent had to be moved. It was ensured that during measurement no DNS lookup was performed.

Ethernet (Round Trip)	
Local Class loading	827 ms
Remote Class loading	1252 ms
Class already loaded	578 ms
WaveLAN (Round Trip)	
Local Class loading	1602 ms
Remote Class loading	2114 ms
Class already loaded	658 ms
GSM (round trip)	
Local Class loading	9.237 ms
Remote Class loading	15.307 ms
Class already loaded	5942ms

Table 1. Migration Times

The figures in Table 1 show that not only the network speed but also the effects the class loading effects the migration time. Comparing the time for class loading with the theoretical maximum possible over the different networks also shows that the protocol used for determining which class has to be loaded seems to have an effect on the performance. Especially the long latencies over GSM connections seems to cause problems.

The currently implemented protocol is best suited for a scenario where a restricted set of agents (usually provided by the MASE itself, or by some service providers) is used several times. This is achieved by triggering the network transfer of agent classes by the receiving site, in case the respective class is not yet available locally.

A scenario with lots of user-defined special purpose agents would demand for a distinct protocol where the sender site transfers agent classes in advance, i.e. without knowing whether the respective classes are really missing at the receiver site.

6   Conclusion

This paper described the integration of a mobile agent system into the mobile middleware developed by the OnTheMove project. We described the Mobile Application Support Environment system and gave some motivation why to integrate a mobile agent system into it.

We showed how an existing mobile agent system had to be adapted in order to better fit to the wireless communication. We then described the way to integrate the mobile agent system into the middleware and to offer the middleware services to the mobile agents.

Some example applications were discussed in detail. The main concern of these applications was to use the flexibility provided by mobile agents to enhance the current features of the middleware. It should be quite clear that mobile agents could be used for completely different applications useful for the mobile user.

At the end we gave some performance measurements for mobile agents migrating over different kind of networks. A brief analysis of these results showed that there is still room for improving the protocols used by the agent system. We can also conclude that for a system using GSM we might design the agent application in such a way, that only a small agent performing the user interactions will migrate to the device and that the application logic will be executed by a different set of agents. It is our opinion, that there is still a lot of research issues involved on how to structure and design a mobile agent based application which should be accessed over GSM.

7   References

[1] Birgit Kreller, Anthony Sang-Bum Park, Jens Meggers, Gunnar Forsgren, Ernö Kovacs, Michael Rosinus, *UMTS: A Middleware and Mobile-API Approach*, to appear in: IEEE Personal Communications Magazine, volume 2, April 1998

[2] Anthony Sang-Bum Park, Jens Meggers, Vera Travnicek. Gunnar Forsgren, Ernö Kovacs, Michael Rosinus, *Mobile Application Support Environment - MASE*. 4rd International Workshop on Mobile Multimedia Communications (MoMuC'97), Seoule, South Korea, September 1997.

[3] Jens Meggers, Anthony Sang-Bum Park, Reiner Ludwig: Roaming between GSM and wireless LAN. ACTS Mobile Communication Summit, Granada, November 1996.

[4] U.S.Coast Guard Navigation Centre: GPS, DGPS, LORAN, OMEGA, LNM. http://www.navcen.uscg.mil/gps/gps.htm.

[5] OnTheMove Homepage: http://www.sics.se/~onthemove.

[6] D. Flanagan: Java in a Nutshell, O'Reilly, Bonn, 1996.

[7] General Magic Inc., Magic Cap Developer Resources, 1996, Technical Documentation, Accessed from [http://www.genmagic.com/Develop/MagicCap/Docs/index.html at 97/02/04 14:03].

[8] Crystalize, Inc., General Magic, Inc., GMD Fokus, International Business Machine Corporation, *Mobile Agent Facility Specification,* June 1997.

[9] Joachim Baumann, Fritz Hohl, Nikolaos Radouniklis, Kurt Rothermel, Markus Straßer: *Communication Concepts for Mobile Agent Systems,* Pages 123-135, Proceedings of the First International Workshop on Mobile Agents (MA '97), Rothermel, Kurt; Popescu-Zeletin, Radu (Eds.), Lecture Notes in Comuter Science 1219, Springer Verlag, Berlin, Germany, April 1997.

A Mobile Object Workbench

Michael Bursell, Richard Hayton, Douglas Donaldson, Andrew Herbert

APM Ltd Poseidon House, Castle Park, Cambridge CB3 0RD United Kingdom

Email: apm@ansa.co.uk Fax: +44 1223 359779

Abstract: Existing mobile agent systems are often constructed with a focus on intelligence and autonomy issues. We have approached mobility from a different direction. The area of distributed systems research is quite mature, and has developed mechanisms for implementing a "sea of objects" abstraction. We have used this as our starting point, and added to this the ability for objects to move from host to host, whilst maintaining location-transparent references to each other. This provides a powerful and straight-forward programming paradigm which embraces programming language semantics such as strong typing, method invocation and encapsulation. We have built a Mobile Object Workbench on top of a flexible Java middleware platform, which can be used as a the basis for a Mobile Agent System. In this paper we examine the philosophy and design of the Mobile Object Workbench, and describe how this is being extended to provide a security framework oriented towards agents.

1 Introduction

Software agents, and in particular mobile agents, are currently an active area within both the research community and the commercial sector [1], [2]. However, despite obvious interest, the commercial take up of mobile agent technology has been slow, and the search for a 'killer app' continues. We believe that one of the reasons for this caution is that the mobile agents approach has been billed as an alternative to the traditional distributed systems paradigm. Typically, the transition to agent based programming requires a programmer to learn a new programming language, and discard existing programming tools and network services.

This sets up a chicken and egg situation for agent systems: until they can provide all the services and integration capabilities of current middleware such as CORBA [3] and DCOM [4], developers will be reluctant to build large systems using them.

We believe that the correct approach is to extend existing programming paradigms by adding autonomy and mobility facilities. This will allow developers to use these facilities where appropriate, and standard distributed systems techniques elsewhere.

We therefore present 'agent facilities' as a natural extension to the programming environment used for existing distributed system development.

This approach has many additional advantages when coupled to a network-oriented object programming language such as Java: method invocation extends naturally to remote method invocation, and strong typing support offers greater safety over ad-hoc messaging found in some current agent systems. Java has specific features that benefit our approach. *Interfaces* may be considered as the published access points for services, and *objects* as the means by which these services are implemented. This separation is important, as it allows some other object to act as a *proxy* for a real service object - by implementing the same interface, and providing the same semantics by communicating with the remote service. The construction and use of proxy objects can be made transparent to the application programmer, and it is easy to imagine how proxies may be used to represent services that are themselves mobile.

The notions of object and interface are fundamental to the design of distributed systems, and is formalized in the ODP reference model [5]. RM-ODP defines a number of *distribution transparencies*. Existing platforms such as CORBA provide *access* and *location* transparencies - the ability to communicate with an object regardless of its location or network address. The Mobile Object Workbench that we have constructed adds two additional transparencies: *relocation* transparency - a client need not be aware that a service has moved - and *migration* transparency - a service need not be aware that it itself has moved. Together these form a basis for the construction of mobile agents. The other ODP transparencies are replication, persistence, transactions and security. These are being addressed within the wider context of our project.

The mobile object workbench described in this paper is an implemented system that provides objects with access, location, relocation and migration transparency within the Java object model. It is not in itself an agent system; however it provides many of the basis facilities required by a mobile agent framework, and provides an easy transition path for programmers wishing to incorporate agent behaviour within the context of a larger distributed system. The work on the Mobile Object Workbench has been undertaken as part of the FollowMe ESPRIT project (No. 25,338) on support for mobile users. Other partners within the project are designing a fuller agent system on top of our Mobile Object Workbench [6].

1.1 Related Work

Many existing agent systems have been built from scratch, and have had to contend with both agency and distribution issues. This division of effort has led to general weaknesses in distribution abstractions: for example untyped message passing is common (e.g. [7]).

Many agent system designers have tackled the problem of implementing mobile code by basing their systems on scripted languages, simplifying the mobility of code across heterogeneous systems, and allowing control of its execution (e.g. suspension and resumption) (e.g. [8]). The disadvantage of this approach is that introduces new programming languages, which currently have no tool support, and no integration with other services.

Java solves many of the problems of agent system designers. Code mobility is relatively straightforward, although there remain problems of controlling execution. This has prompted some designers to port and upgrade their systems to make use of the new facilities (e.g. [9]), but few have taken the approach of using Java as the agent programming language, and adding to it facilities for object movement and remote method invocation.

An exception to this is Voyager [10] which takes an approach similar to ours. However this makes use of the Java RMI service [11] which add its own restrictions. RMI divides objects into two categories, service objects and data objects. Data objects may be copied in a remote method invocation, but service objects may not. This precludes the possibility of a service object moving - effectively ruling out the most natural approach for mobile agents. Voyager overcomes this with some complex wrapping of service objects, we avoid the problem entirely by using our own remote invocation and binding mechanisms [12].

The OMG's Mobile Agent Facility [13] is an important piece of standardization work being done in the area of mobile agents. Whilst we see the Mobile Object Workbench as providing basic facilities to be extended by an agent implementation, in practice we provide the majority of the MAF facilities, and extension of the Mobile Object Workbench to provide a MAF-compliant platform is one possible option for future work.

2 Principles

In this section, we describe the basic principles which we have adopted in the design and implementation of the Mobile Object Workbench. Throughout, we have striven to extend rather than replace our base language, Java, at both the language level and the distributed systems level. This principle, we believe, makes for ease of use (as we build on abstractions which are already familiar).

Where possible, we have also aimed for "selective transparency", particularly of engineering mechanism, so that application programmers need not concern themselves with the details of the implementation or design in order to use the system, although they retain the ability to set policy and respond to errors.

2.1 Clusters

Language level objects are typically too small to be a useful unit for mobility. For example, it would not generally be useful to provide mobility for a simple string. A mobile agent is more likely to consist of several language level objects, with a single object as its 'root'. It is neither helpful or useful to move the constituent objects individually, and instead we need a grouping mechanism or policy for deciding which parts of a program should move together.

We introduce the notion of a *cluster* as both a grouping and encapsulating construct to address this issue. A cluster is an encapsulated set of objects in the sense that references that pass across a cluster boundary are treated differently from those entirely internal or external to it. In particular, when resolving an external reference, the system may have to locate a cluster on a remote machine (possibly after it has moved) and may have to perform security checks, such as access control and auditing. Even when two clusters are located on the same host, they still communicate through the encapsulation boundary via system-provided mechanisms, although the base transport can be via local memory rather than the network. This allows clusters to protect themselves from each other, and gives them some degree of autonomy.

Clustering is not a new concept. The notion of clusters was present in ANSAware [14] and RM-ODP [5]. In Java, each applet is effectively a cluster, and programming using clusters is no more complex than applet programming. As clusters provide units of encapsulation for mobility, security and other functions, each mobile agent would normally be constructed within its own cluster.

2.2 Encapsulation

The cluster boundary provides a strong encapsulation boundary between clusters. Access to objects within one cluster from threads in another is restricted to interfaces that have been passed (directly or indirectly) between the clusters. Clusters cannot examine the internals of each other, nor may arbitrary methods on objects in one cluster be called from another. We can (and do) take this approach even further. When a thread in one cluster invokes a method on an exported interface from another cluster, we de-couple the threads so that the callee and caller cannot adversely affect one another by blocking or thread termination. In addition each cluster may effectively be given a separate Java security manager, and class loader. Effectively, each cluster is a 'virtual process' that is de-coupled from other clusters in terms of privileges, code base and management. Although one cluster may crash the entire process or starve it of resources, clusters are isolated from each other as effectively as possible, making them suitable vessels for storing wandering agents.

2.3 Location Transparent Communications

In order to maintain transparency of use of interfaces, some mechanism must be provided to allow communications between clusters which are remote from one another. Like other distributed object systems, the Mobile Object Workbench makes use of local *stubs* to represent interfaces to object in remote clusters. This means that there is no special API for communications in the Mobile Object Workbench; communications is as close to the pure language semantics as possible, and transparency is to a large extent preserved. The Mobile Object Workbench API is entirely related to the life cycle and movement of clusters.

Unlike RMI or CORBA we do not require an off-line stub generator. Instead we allow the generation of stubs on demand, whilst allowing caching of previously

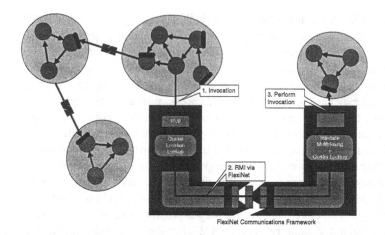

FlexiNet Communications Framework

Fig. 1. Clusters, showing internal and external communications.

generated code for performance. The generation of stubs on demand has the important benefit that since stubs are locally generated they may be treated as trusted, rather than potentially hostile, code.

It has long been a point of contention in distributed systems research as to whether distribution transparency is achievable, or indeed desirable. In FlexiNet, the approach taken is for *selective transparency*. Ordinarily, remote communication is transparent. However, the application or middleware programmer can link in "binding objects" which describe special action to be taken when resolving inter-cluster interface references; for example an application programmer may provide code for ruling on access control policy, or for explicitly choosing a communications protocol. These binding objects are invoked when interface references are initially bound, rebound after Mobile Object migration, or when failures occur.

3 Implementation

Figure 1 shows an example set of objects and clusters, and how the engineering framework provides the transparency of remote references. One of the communications bindings between clusters is expanded to show that invocation of an external interface reference is achieved using a proxy (stub) with a communications stack.

In order to encapsulate clusters, we must distinguish references between objects within the same cluster, and references between objects in different clusters. As objects within a cluster share the same privileges, and are always collocated, these references can be ordinary language level references. References that cross the encapsulation boundary appear to the programmer to be the same, but in fact are implemented via interface proxies and (potentially) remote communication. Each cluster is created with a reflexive communications stack, and all references to external clusters or services are bound to the communications stack. We ensure that any references passed or returned in method invocations using proxied interfaces are also treated in a similar way. This ensures that a cluster remains encapsulated. Any objects created within a cluster become part of the same cluster as the object performing the creation, and a special mechanism is used to create new clusters. Objects and data may be passed in method invocations over the encapsulation boundary, and are passed by copying.

3.1   Location transparent communications

All references to interfaces within the Mobile Object Workbench are treated identically by the programmer, that is, the application/agent performs the same action, whether a reference is to an interface on a local or remote cluster, or whether it is to a cluster that is currently in transit. A call to a remote cluster may result in an exception if the cluster is unreachable within a pre-set interval (or if the access is disallowed after access controls). These exceptions may be caught, or may be ignored and allowed to propagate through the client code.

When an interface reference is returned from a remote call, a local stub is transparently constructed on-the-fly from the interface definition using Java introspection. This contains references to a communication stack, and the name of the remote interface. When a call is made on the interface, we first attempt to locate the remote interface using the last known location. If the remote interface happens to be on a mobile cluster that has moved, the remote host will raise an exception. This is caught within the infrastructure on the client machine, and a secondary mechanism is then used to relocate the cluster. We are constructing a robust directory-based distributed location service to perform this task, though the architecture is flexible, and other approaches could be employed. This is an advantage over other systems which 'hard-wire' protocols such as forwarding tombstones - which are inappropriate for highly mobile long-lived objects.

When a cluster is to move, we must carefully orchestrate the behavior of its threads, and any calls made to it, to ensure that a consistent version of the cluster is moved, and that the move is atomic with respect to calls made from other clusters. As we have built our system on top of the Java virtual machine, we have little control over thread execution, and in particular it is not possible to serialize a thread during execution in order to move it. This is the price we have had to pay for using a standard language implementation, rather than providing our own interpreter. However, in practice the price is not high: a cluster must close down any internal threads prior to movement, and restart them after movement. The infrastructure monitors thread activity and ensures that the move is atomic. This is described in detail in [15].

```
public abstract class MobileObject
{
  void pendMove(Place dest) throws MoveFailedException;
  void syncMove(Place dest) throws MoveFailedException;
  Object copy(Place dest)    throws MoveFailedException;
  abstract Object init(...) throws
InstantiationException;
  abstract void restart(Exception reason);
}

public interface Place
{
  public Tagged newCluster(Class cls,Object[] init_args)
      throws InstantiationException;
  public Object getProperty(String propertyname);
}
```

Fig. 2. Mobile Object Workbench API.

3.2   Mobile Object Workbench API

The Mobile Object Workbench API (figure 2) is wholly concerned with the lifecycle and management of clusters. Communication between object in clusters takes place using application level remote method invocation and is therefore not specified in the API. An abstract class MobileObject gives a 'hook' on which the implementation of a particular mobile object may hang (in much the same way as the class Applet). Each subclass may provide instance initialization by providing an init method, which allows arbitrary arguments to be passed to the mobile object upon creation. The restart method is called on completion of a move, in order to allow a mobile object to restart threads. The Tagged type represents a most general interface reference type (whereas the Java Object type represents the most general object reference type). The interface Place is exported by system provided objects that represent execution environments for mobile objects. Mobile objects are created in places, and may move between them. Places also provide properties which mobile objects can use to interrogate their environment.

3.3   Location-transparent naming service

When a call is made on a cluster, the encapsulation layer at the called host will determine whether the cluster (still) exists at this host. If it does not, then the host will raise an exception which is passed back to the callee and caught by the infrastructure in the callee's cluster. This then contacts the name relocation service to determine the new location of the object. The relocation service is a federation of a number of directories. Each directory contains a mapping from old to new cluster addresses. Our naming service was developed with five key properties:

1. We control what entities are able to update the directories - only hosts from which a cluster is moving may update the record for the cluster. This is possible as cluster names (transparently to the applications programmer) contain information about their current network host. This prevents fraudulent changing of naming records by "spoof" hosts or clusters.
2. We provide a hierarchy of directories, for scale and robustness. This means that an instance of the relocation service may decide to copy the naming record for a cluster up the hierarchy to increase its stability, or to reduce the load placed upon it.
3. We allow naming records to be moved between directories so that an optimal directory location can be chosen for the record (e.g. following the movement of a cluster around the network).
4. We allow caching for performance. A naming record can be kept at a previous directory, as well as being passed up the hierarchy, to reduce look-up time.
5. We arrange that a client can locate the appropriate directory for a cluster rapidly, without having to search other directories.

4 Support for Agents

As described so far, the Workbench is does not provide a suitable platform for mobile agents; two additional capabilities are required. First, agents are generally considered as autonomous. Support is therefore required to ensure that a cluster's movement is under its own control. Second, unlike a single application with mobile parts, a mobile agent system typically consists of agents with mutual distrust between each other, and with complex trust relationships between agents and hosts. Security covers a whole range of issues from data protection to code integrity, and a mobile agent system must deal with these if it is to be viable in the wider network.

4.1 Autonomy of movement

We have stated that a basic facility is for clusters to be able to be moved from one host to another. An important issue is who is at liberty to decide when a cluster should move. We note that a cluster cannot move at an arbitrary point in time - it may have to release resources cleanly, and it is therefore not reasonable to command a cluster's movement externally - rather, the process should be within the cluster. This does not, of course, preclude a *request* for movement being made from an external entity. As agents may be malicious or erroneous, it is essential that a cluster can be *destroyed* by an external signal, and this is provided. Thus our Mobile Objects are autonomous, as might be expected to meet the needs of agent-based applications.

The standard encapsulation mechanism is all that is required to enforce the autonomy of movement. If a cluster never exports the interface containing the *move* method, then this is not accessible outside its encapsulation boundary. Of course a malicious host can always circumvent this (or any other) mechanism, which is why we employ cryptographic security measures so that we can detect if a cluster has been tampered with, or if a malicious host is attempting to impersonate a trusted one.

4.2 Security

We have found that the approach of designing and engineering from the point of view of a mobile object system allowed us build on established security principles [16]. In particular we identify six basic areas of security concern within the Mobile Object Workbench:

1. **Host integrity** - protecting the integrity of a hosting machine and data it contains from possible malicious acts by visiting objects.
2. **Cluster integrity** - it should be possible to determine if a cluster has been tampered with, either in transit or by a host at which it was previously located. We may wish to allow hosts to modify parts of a cluster (e.g. data) but not others (e.g. code).
3. **Cluster confidentiality** - a cluster may wish to carry with it information that should not be readable by other clusters, or by (some of) the hosts which it visits.
4. **Cluster authority** - a cluster should be able to carry authority with it, for example a user's privileges, or credit card details. To provide this we need both cluster integrity and cluster confidentiality.
5. **Access control** - a host should be able to impose different access privileges on different clusters that move to it. Clusters and hosts should also be able to enforce access control on exported methods.
6. **Secure communications** - clusters and hosts should be able to communicate using confidential and/or authenticated communication. Some applications may also require other security communication features, such as non-repudiation.

We believe that unless all of these aspects of security are addressed, any mobile object system will not prove secure enough for real world applications, and we have therefore adopted the principle of including security issues from the outset, rather than as an "add-on", bolted on at a later date. Recent Java releases provide a number of cryptographic capabilities which have aided this work.

4.2.1 History and provenance

Within a mobile object context, issues of trust take on a different slant to non-mobile systems. In both mobile and non-mobile systems, questions of how much trust is placed in an object must be based on the provenance of that object - where it originated, and its history. In a non-mobile object oriented system, such as the base Java implementation, objects are typically instantiated from class files, having no other state. In Java, object capabilities are controlled within a Security Manager [17], and policies are typically granted based on the provenance of these classes. Classes may be signed to provide extra confidence of provenance, and a JVM may assign policies to instantiations of these classes based on this signing.

However, in a mobile object context, an object arriving from a remote host has a history that is not captured by the signature on the class file. Class signatures alone do not provide sufficient information on which to assign security policy, as they can solely give information about the initial "birthplace" of a set of classes, and not about the history of a particular instantiation.

For this reason, we have designed and implemented a Security Manager which extends Java's model by allowing policies to be assigned to instances of objects, rather than just their class. This has been possible because of the strong thread encapsulation we have employed within the Mobile Object Workbench, which gives each cluster its own thread group. As Java allows checking of the thread performing a particular operation, we may determine the cluster from which an invocation originated, and hence enforce the appropriate policies.

This security policy allows hosts to restrict operations allowed by particular clusters, thereby protecting their own integrity. It also provides a good base from which to extend cluster-to-cluster access restrictions.

4.2.2 Integrity and confidentiality concerns

Cluster integrity and confidentiality are enforced by encrypting and/or signing certain objects within a cluster. This prevents a host without sufficient access privileges from examining a cluster's state, and allows one host to detect if a cluster has been modified by a host which it visited earlier. In addition to this, we must ensure that clusters are not dissected, as otherwise a malicious host could 'steal' parts of the cluster that represented encrypted passwords and use them to build its own clusters. To do this, we require a mechanism for specifying and validating integrity statements. For example we may annotate a cluster's definition to indicate that a particular field may only be modified by certain hosts. We may then use digital signature techniques to ensure that whenever the field is modified it obtains a signature from the current host, and when other hosts attempt to read this field we can throw an exception if the signature is incorrect.

We are currently developing a system to allow integrity policy statements to be specified. Once specified, the use of secure fields or objects can be made almost transparent to the programmer. All that is required is that they use accessor functions to access the protected fields.

Cluster authority can be implemented by leveraging cluster integrity and confidentiality. Together these allow a cluster to carry with it a password or other secret information, without the concern that this secret can be read at any host which is visited. Clearly, once the secret *is* revealed to a host, there is nothing that can be done to prevent the host from misusing it. For this reason we have a model that the mobile object moves into a secure environment before revealing a secret. Figure 3 gives an example; a cluster may move between several hosts before eventually arriving at a 'Bank' host. At this host, it may reveal a password to allow it access to a bank account. However, as the Bank host already knew the password, revealing it has not

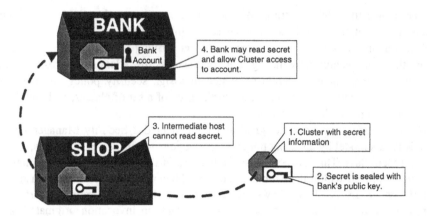

Fig. 3. Clusters with secrets.

given the bank any additional privileges, and the security of the password has not been weakened.

4.2.3 Method access and communications

Method access control and secure communications may be implemented using standard techniques. We use FlexiNet's reflective binding system to allow a cluster to receive notification of an invocation immediately prior to its execution, so that it may implement its own security policy, and throw an access control exception if appropriate. Secure communication between places may take place using a FlexiNet binder that supports SSL [18]. Secure communication between mobile clusters may also take place using SSL, but requires that clusters reveal the information used to prove their identity to the host from which they are communicating. This is reasonable in some circumstances, but should be used with caution.

5 Status

The FollowMe project, and the design of the Mobile Object Workbench, started in October 1997. We now have a fully functioning mobile object system written using 100% pure Java. The limitations of this system are primarily an incomplete implementation of the security infrastructure described, and limited scalability within the relocation service. We are concentrating our efforts in these directions. Other FollowMe project members are working on an agent system, pilot applications and other services underpinned by the mobile object system.

Although relatively young, the Mobile Object Workbench has undergone three releases, and has been in used by FollowMe project members and the ANSA consortium for the past six months.

6 Summary

The Mobile Object Workbench has shown how to add mobility to an existing object language. The key principle has been strong encapsulation of both state and threads, which has meant that the addition of mobility has not been too difficult. With our simple computational model of passing all interfaces by reference and all objects by copy, we have provided transparency of remote communications, and by providing a robust directory-based location service, we have ensured location-transparency for communications as well.

References

1. MA 97: First International Workshop on Mobile Agents 97, Berlin, April 7-8, 1997. http://www.informatik.uni-stuttgart.de/ipvr/vs/ws/ma97/ma97.html
2. The Agent Society: Agent Product and Research Activities http://www.agent.org/pub/activity.html
3. Object Management Group: CORBA/IIOP 2.1 Specification. Aug. 1997. http://www.omg.org/corba/corbiiop.htm
4. Brown, N. and Kindel, C.: Distributed Component Object Model Protocol - DCOM/1.0 - Network Working Group INTERNET-DRAFT. *Microsoft Corporation*, Jan. 1998. http://www.microsoft.com/oledev/olecom/draft-brown-dcom-v1-spec-02.txt
5. International Standards Organisation : Open Distributed Processing - Reference Model. Sep. 1995. http://www.iso.ch:8000/RM-ODP/
6. FAST e.V.: FollowMe project overview. http://hyperwav.fast.de/generalprojectinformation
7. Lange, D.B. and Chang, D.T. : IBM Aglets Workbench - Programming Mobile Agents in Java, A White Paper (Draft). IBM Corp.. Sept. 1996. http://www.trl.ibm.co.jp/aglets/
8. General Magic Inc:Telescript Language Reference. 1995
9. General Magic Inc: Agent Technology http://www.genmagic.com/agents/
10. ObjectSpace: ObjectSpace Voyager Core Technology. http://www.objectspace.com/Voyager
11. Sun Microsystems: Java Remote Method Invocation (RMI) Specification. *http://www.sun.com/products/jdk/1.1/docs/guide/rmi/* 1996
12. Hayton, R.J. and Herbert, A.J.: A flexible component oriented middleware system. SIGOPS European Workshop 1998
13. Crystaliz, GMD FOKUS, General Magic, IBM, The Open Group: Mobile Agent Facility. http://www.genmagic.com/agents/MAF/
14. O'Connell, J. Edwards, N. and Cole, R. A review of four distribution infrastructures. Distributed Systems Engineering 1 (1994) 202-211
15. Hayton, R.J. Bursell, M.H., Donaldson, D.I. and Herbert, A.J. : Mobile Java Objects Middleware 1998.
16. Wallach, D.S., Balfanz, D., Dean,D. and Felten, E.W.: Extensible Security Architectures for Java. Proceedings of the Sixteenth ACM Symposium on Operating Systems Principles 31,5, Dec. 1997, pp. 116-128.
17. Erdos, M., Hartman, B. and Mueller, M.: Security Reference Model for the Java Developer's Kit 1.0.2. Sun Microsystems. Nov. 1996. http://java.sun.com/security/SRM.html
18. Netscape Inc.: The SSL Protocol. http://home.netscape.com/newsr ef/std/SSL.html

An Overview of AgentSpace:
A Next-Generation Mobile Agent System

Alberto Silva, Miguel Mira da Silva[1] and José Delgado

{Alberto.Silva, Jose.Delgado}@inesc.pt, [1]mira-da-silva@p.pt
INESC & IST (Technical University of Lisbon)
Rua Alves Redol, nº 9, 1000 LISBOA, PORTUGAL

Abstract. This paper gives an overall overview of the AgentSpace framework, a next-generation Java mobile agent system developed on top of the ObjectSpace Voyager system. We first introduce the notion of dynamic and distributed agent-based applications and argue that the AgentSpace features are suitable to support them. The AgentSpace novelties include: flexible and dynamic association between agents, security policies and users; transparency of agent location through the use of views; and easy and clean way to create agents through the use of abstract classes and method factories.

1 Introduction

Nowadays, there are many Mobile Agent Systems (MAS) proposals – such as Aglets [1], Agent-Tcl [2], Odyssey [3] or Tacoma [4] – that have roughly the same purpose and present a common set of functionalities. Nevertheless, they also present some important technical and even conceptual differences.

For instance, Telescript [5] used to be the usual reference for MAS with a very high technological level. However it is (or it was) a proprietary system, with a difficult-to-learn programming language, and badly suitable to a dynamic and open environment such as the Internet. On the other hand, a system such as ffMAIN [6] is language and system independent. However, it shows severe limitations on the overall performance and difficulties in developing complex applications. The Aglets Workbench – today the reference Java-based MAS – lacks an elaborate object model, e.g., without the notion of execution places hierarchically organized; without management operation on agent families and clusters. It also lacks some technical capabilities, e.g., just two ACLs (access control levels); without the notion of an agent class manager, without the "open channel" capability [16], or even without the notion of users transparently associated to agents. We expect that, in the future, these MASs will be improved in order to support the development and execution of more flexible, reliable, secure and efficient agent-based applications (ABA).

In a recent paper [7] we have proposed a conceptual MAS architecture composed by three complementary components: AES, for Agent Execution System; ACS, for Agent Class System; and AEE, for Agent Execution Environment. We argue these components should be the "building blocks" of a next-generation MAS. We have also identified other related components needed to develop, manage and monitor agent-based applications. Based on that preliminary work, a Java-based framework was implemented. This framework – called *AgentSpace* – was developed on the top of Voyager [11] from ObjectSpace.

In this paper we overview the main aspects of AgentSpace from a developer's point of view, namely its exported API (Java interfaces and classes). AgentSpace will be further improved to be used in the ESPRIT COSMOS project [12].

The paper is organized as follows. In Section 2 we present our own definition of agent and agent-based application, and also introduce the main aspects of Voyager. In Section 3 we overview the AgentSpace architecture and object model. In Section 4 the AgentSpace API is described. Finally, Section 5 summarizes the contributions with a small discussion of agent-based applications that will be consider in the future.

2 Agents and Agent-Based Applications

Due to the proliferation of agent definitions with different point of views, scopes and possible applications – see for example [13, 14, 15] – we start this paper by defining the meaning of an agent in our work context.

2.1 Agents and Mobile Agent Systems

In this paper, an *agent* is a software entity with a well-known identity, state and behavior, with autonomy to somehow represent its user. The agent's user might be a human or an organization (enterprise, community, etc.) as well as another agent.

From a more technical point of view, an agent can be implemented as an active object of medium granularity. This means that an agent is an instance of some defined class – with its own group of threads, state and code – identified by a unique global identity.

From yet another perspective – the human-computer interaction perspective – agents may be viewed as a new interface paradigm to help end-users access future Internet applications, including electronic commerce. In this world, end-users change the way they interact with the computer, from direct manipulation (e.g., word processors, web browsers, and so on) to indirect management (e.g., information search). Using agents, users can delegate a set of tasks to be done by agents, instead of doing these tasks themselves directly. This new paradigm is especially attractive to help users in complex, tedious or repetitive tasks in open, dynamic, vast and unstructured information sources such as those found on the Internet.

2.2 Agent-based Applications

We define an *agent-based application* (or ABA for short) as a dynamic, potentially large-scale distributed application in an open and heterogeneous context such as the

Internet. The basic conceptual unit for designing and building ABAs is the agent as defined above.

The notion of ABA is quite novel by itself. An ABA is not a typical application that is owned and managed by some people or some organization. Instead, an ABA is best understood as: a web of agents each owned and managed by a number of entities with different (and possibly conflicting) goals and attitudes, hosted in different computing platforms, such as workstations and mobile phones.

ABA applications have a number of characteristics and requirements that have been dealt with independently in the past. It is their combination that poses problems.

- *Autonomous*: Each user creates and maintains their own agents using their own resources and/or using resources from others.
- *Heterogeneous*: Each user has bought, got used to and used different interfaces, machine architectures, programming languages, database systems, communication packages, operating systems and so on.
- *Open*: Some agents may depend on other agents and applications, even from external organizations. This means agents will have to inter-operate with other (legacy) information systems (applications, databases and so on).
- *Dynamic*: Agents will be added, updated and removed at any time without previous notice. They will have to cope with unavailability, new interfaces, oscillating bandwidths, and other variable characteristics.
- *Robust*: Agents will have to tolerate different kinds of failures on machines, networks or at any level of software. For example, agents cannot stop executing just because a company is rebooting their gateway to the outside world.
- *Secure*: The system should provide different levels of security depending on each particular part of the whole application. There will be public, place-specific and administrative access control lists.

All these characteristics make ABA potentially very difficult to implement and use. However, we believe MAS, and in particular AgentSpace, will help developers build and manage them.

2.3 An Overview of Voyager

ObjectSpace's Voyager [11] is a commercial product to support the development of distributed Java applications. Amongst other features, Voyager provides a "100% Java" ORB (remote method invocation) well designed and integrated with the JDK 1.1 class interfaces. Voyager can be seen as a traditional CORBA object request broker (ORB) with extended features such as object mobility and life spans.

Despite Voyager's powerful capabilities and overall elegance, *Voyager offers only limited support* to the kind of applications described in Section 2.2 above. These applications have requirements regarding openness, dynamicity, and access control mechanisms that are (at least currently) lacking in Voyager. Voyager's "agents" are not truly software agents as we defined in Section 2.1 above because they are just objects with mobility support and a given life-span. For example, these objects don't keep any specific information regarding their owner or their native and current execution place.

The conclusion is that a higher-level agent-based framework should be designed and built in order to develop the new kind of agent-based applications. In this paper we propose AgentSpace as such a framework that is being built on the top of Voyager. As a consequence, AgentSpace is able not only to provide the majority of Voyager's features but also new ones to properly support software agents.

3 An Introduction to AgentSpace

3.1 Architecture

AgentSpace's main goals are the support, development and management of ABAs as described in Section 2. These goals are provided through three separated but well-integrated components as depicted in Fig. 1.

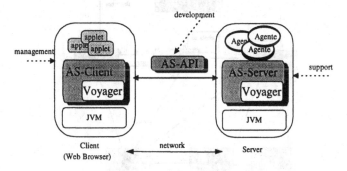

Fig. 1. AgentSpace architecture

Both server and client components run on top of Voyagerand Java Virtual Machine (JVM), and they can execute in the same or in different machines. Agents run always on some AS-Server's context. On the other hand, they interact with their end-user through (specific or generic) applets running in some Web browser's context.

The *AgentSpace server* (*AS-Server*) is a Java multithreaded process in which agents can be executed. The AS-Server provides several services, namely: (1) agent and place creation; (2) agent execution; (3) access control; (4) agent persistency; (5) agent mobility; (6) generation of unique identities (UID); (7) support for agent communication; and (8) optionally a simple interface to manage/monitor itself.

The *AgentSpace client* (*AS-Client*) supports – depending on the corresponding user access level – the management and monitoring of agents and related resources. The AS-Client is a set of Java applets stored on an AS-Server's machine in order to provide an adequate integration with the Web, offering Internet users the possibility to easily manage their own agents remotely. Furthermore, the AS-Client should be able to access several AS-Servers, providing a convenient trade-off between integration and independence between these two components.

The *AgentSpace application programming interface* (*AS-API*) is a package of Java interfaces and classes that defines the rules to build agents. In particular, the AS-API supports the programmer when building: (1) agent classes and their instances (agents) that are created and stored in the AS-Server's database for later use; and (2) client applets (that are stored in the AS-Server's file system or in the AS-Server's database) in order to provide an interface to agents.

These clients/applets can be either generic mini-applications – such as the AS-Client itself, see above – or specific to some particular agent, for example, to input data or present a report.

3.2 Object Model

AgentSpace involves the support, development and management of several related objects: contexts, places, agents, users, groups of users, permissions, ACLs (access control lists), security managers, tickets, messages, and identities. Fig. 2 shows the relationships between these objects through an UML [18] class diagram.

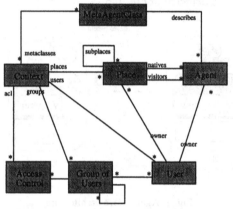

Fig. 2. UML class diagram of AgentSpace

The *context* is the most important and critical object of the AS-Server, as each AS-Server is represented by one context. The context contains the major data structures and code to support the AS-Server, such as lists of places, users, groups of users, meta-agent classes and access control lists.

Each context has a number of places. The *execution place*, or simply *place*, has mainly two objectives. First, to provide a conceptual and programming metaphor where agents are executed and meet other agents. Second, to provide a consistent way to define and control access levels, and to control computational resources.

The place has a unique global identity and knows the identification of its owner/manager. It also maintains a keyword/value list that allows an informal characterization. Optionally, places can be hierarchically organized. The place can also contain the maximum and current number of agents allowed in order to support some resource management. In order to keep track of its agents, the place keeps a list containing its visitant agents and another with its native agents. The place also knows in which place its native agents are executing at a given point of time.

The *agent* is the basic element of the system. Agents are identified by a unique global identity. Agents have two parts: (1) a visible component, that should be developed, or specialized, by programmers (more on this later on); and (2) an invisible component, called "internal-agent", kept by AgentSpace. Agents are active objects that execute in some AS-Server, but from a conceptual perspective, they are currently in some place. Agents can navigate to other (local or remote) place if they have permission to do it.

Just one user owns an agent. Nevertheless, other users (or even agents from other users) might interact with it, if this is granted by the agent' security policy.

The AS-Server also maintains lists of *users, groups of users* and *acl* to implement the permission and access control mechanism. A user may belong to one or more groups. Groups may be hierarchically organized to simplify permission management. This means that all users of some specialized group have implicitly all the permissions they inherit from the more general groups. By default, every AS-Server defines four groups of users and establish a convenient security access policy, based on them: anonymous group; end-users group; place owners group; and AS-Server's administrators group.

4 AgentSpace API

In the previous section we introduced the main concepts related to the AgentSpace design. Nevertheless, the objects that implements these concepts cannot be used directly by ABA programmers. This is not possible in order to provide a flexible security policy and to hide several complexities from the developer (such as those related to distribution, persistence, mobility, and so on).

In this section we concentrate on the main aspects of the interface offered by AgentSpace. There are two complementary uses of this API: to develop agents and AgentSpace-based applets; and to develop generic client tools, such as the AS-Client as mentioned in Section 3.1.

These interface elements (Java objects, classes and interfaces) are organized together as the `inesc.as.agentspace` package, that basically defines the public AS-API.

4.1 Identities

Each element of the AS-Server that is potentially accessible has a unique global identity, namely the `ASId`, `PlaceId` and `AgentId` types identify respectively an AS-Server's context, a place and an agent.

4.2 Users

The user is identified by a unique identity – represented by the `User` class – which contains: user's name; a public key; a set of certificates; the organization and country the user belongs to; and user's e-mail. In spite of all these attributes, the name is the single mandatory field. `Identity` and `Principal` types belong to the `java.security` Sun's package.

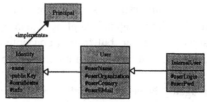

Fig. 3. User classes handled by AgentSpace

Moreover, the user may have different identifiers depending on the context the user belongs to. This specific identity is represented by the `InternalUser` class as depicted in Fig. 3, which contains, in addition to all referred fields authentication attributes (e.g., login and password).

4.3 Views and Security Policies

Together with the factory methods (see Section 4.4 below), views are an important design pattern to support the dynamicity of the agent-based application as referred in Section 2.2.

We have adapted the *Proxy* design pattern [17] at different levels of the AgentSpace design, namely, at the context, place and agent level. This design pattern, which we call *"View"*, is very suitable to support transparent and secure access to these different types of objects.

- `ContextView` provides controlled access to the AS-Server's context. Depending on the user's authentication, the `ContextView` object enables, or not, a set of general operations. Namely, operations to manage users, groups of users, permissions, and execution places. Examples of these operations are `createPlace`, `groups`, `createUser`, `removePlace`, `getPlaceOf`, etc.
- `PlaceView` provides a controlled access interface to a specific place. Examples of operations protected through place views are: `createAgent`, `removeAgent`, `save`, `flush`, etc. For example, an user can create an agent in some place only if that operation is allowed by that place's security manager.
- `AgentView` provides access to agents independently of their current place. This access goes indirectly through views in order to protect agents and to hide their current localization. Additionally, the `AgentView` class avoids the need to create and manage network-based classes (e.g., virtual objects in the Voyager system). Examples of operations protected through agent views are `getCurrentPlace`, `sendMessage`, `getClassName`, `start`,and `moveTo`.

AgentSpace provides three distinct levels to define security policies, namely at the context, place, and agent level. These different policies are defined and managed dinamically and in a independent way amongst themselves. For example, a security policy defined to some context might be liberal, while the security policy to some place, in this same context, might be extremely restrictive.

The actual policy at the *context level* is based on the existence of four groups of users associated to four distinct profiles, namely: administrators; execution places managers; recorded users; and anonymous users. The access to the context is established through some `ContextView` instance, based on which the execution of some operation is, or is not, allowed.

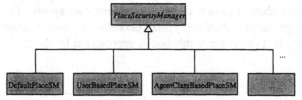

Fig. 4. Possible hierarchy of place's security managers

On the other hand, the security policies at the *place and agent levels* are defined through the dynamic association of specific classes. These classes (respectively, specialization of the `PlaceSecurityManager` and `AgentSecurityManager` abstract classes) may be developed by ABA's programmers in an easy way and are associated to places and agents at their creation time. In that way, it is possible the definition of different security managers, for example, some of them based on user information, other based on agent classes information, etc. Fig. 4 presents a class diagram depicting a possible hierarchy related to place's security managers.

4.4 Factories

AgentSpace provides design patterns to allow the dynamic creation of the following objects: instances of agents and places, and references (views) to agents, places, and contexts. Namely, the *abstract factories* and *method factories* design patterns [17].

Table 1. Factories Methods in AgentSpace

Purpose	Factory method		Result object
	Base Class	**Method**	
Context:			
- reference generation	*AgentSpace*	*getContextView*	*ContextView*
	AgentView	*getCurrentContext*	
Execution Place:			
- creation	*ContextView*	*createPlace*	*PlaceView*
- reference generation	*ContextView*	*getPlaceOf, places,*	
	AgentView	*myPlaces*	
		getCurrentPlace	
Agents:			
- creation	*PlaceView*	*createAgent*	*AgentView*
	Agent	*clone*	
- reference generation	*ContextView*	*getAgentOf*	
	PlaceView	*getNatives, getVisitors,*	
		queryAgents	

Table 1 summarizes the main classes of the AS-API involved with the creation and generation of references to the main involved objects. It is particularly important to note that the access and manipulation of these specific methods (e.g., `createAgent` and `createPlace`) is controlled by their respective views.

4.5 Agents

Agents are the extensible elements of AgentSpace. Basically, programmers should derive the `Agent` abstract class in order to build their own agents. The `Agent` class has three main groups of methods: (1) final; (2) callbacks; and (3) helper methods, as depicted in Fig. 5. (The `Agent` subclass is represented by the `ConcreteAgent` class.)

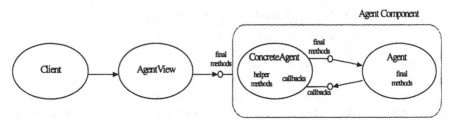

Fig. 5. Agent's main groups of methods in AgentSpace

- *Final methods* are pre-defined operations provided to all agents that cannot be changed by the programmer. Examples of these final methods are: `moveTo`, `save`, `die`, `backHome`, `clone`, `getId`, `sendMessage`, etc.
- On the other hand, *callbacks* are methods to be customized by specific agent classes, and are usually invoked transparently as the result of some event. Events are trigged by some action started by the agent itself or by other related entity, such as another agent, an end-user (via same applet), a time service, etc. The callback mechanism provides the desired extensibility of the agent component. Examples of callbacks are: `run`, `onCreation`, `beforeDie` and `handleMessage`.
- Finally, agent classes also have *helper methods* (usually with private or protected access modifiers) in order to support specific functions of that class/object.

Helper methods should be defined in concrete agent classes and are used internally by callback methods. On the other hand, callbacks should be specialized in concrete agent classes, and final methods can only be used/invoked either directly by concrete agent classes or indirectly through `AgentView` interfaces. Additionally, some callbacks may be defined in order to be called after the navigation operations. These methods are referred explicitly as a parameter in `moveTo` methods.

The final methods of the `Agent` class can be analyzed following two main groups: management methods; and get/set methods.

The first group concerns on methods associated with life cycle, navigation, user interaction, and communication operations. The execution of these methods involve, in general, the invocation of a correspondent callback as summarized in Table 2.

Final methods defined in the `Agent` class can be invoked directly in their subclasses without the utilization of any `AgentView` instance. This means that in some concrete agent class it is possible to specify autonomous behaviors, for example, an agent may decide to move itself to another place (`moveTo`) or to its native place (`backHome`), or suspend itself (`flush`), etc.

Table 2. Events and methods associated to the agent execution

Operation/Event	Final Method	Correspond Callback
Life cycle:		
- Creation	*createAgent*[1]	*onCreation*
- Activation	*start*[1]	*run*
- Clone	*clone*	*beforeCloning; run*
- Memory Management	*flush*	*beforeFlush; afterLoaded*
- Persistence	*save*	-
- Delete	*die*	*beforeDie*
End-user interaction:		
	getUserInterface[1]	*doUserInterface*
Navigation:		
	moveTo	*run; or atPlaceX*[2]
	backHome	*afterBackHome*
Communication:		
- Asynchronous (by default)	*sendMessage*[1]	*handleMessage*
- Synchronous (by default)	*doOperation*[1]	*handleOperation*

(1) These methods are invoked only through the `AgentView` interface

(2) Callback not predefined – defined by the programmer at concrete classes

The second group of final methods doesn't imply the execution of any type of callback. These methods (see Table 3) just allow the getting and setting of information associated to each specific agent.

Table 3. Get and Set final methods of the `Agent` class

Purpose	Final Method	Result Type
Get/Set the agent's informal description	*getDescription*	*String*
	setDescription	-
Get agent's identifier	*getId*	*AgentId*
Get the agent's native place identifier	*getNativePlaceId*	*PlaceId*
Get the agent's current place identifier	*getCurrentPlaceId*	*PlaceId*
Get a reference to the agent's current place	*getCurrentPlace*	*PlaceView*
Get a reference to the agent's current context	*getCurrentContext*	*ContextView*
Get the agent's class name	*getClassName*	*String*
Get the agent's class	*getAgentClass*	*Class*
Get the agent's meta agent class	*getMetaAgentClass*	*MetaAgentClass*
Get the agent's owner	*getOwner*	*InternalUser*
Get/Set the agent's properties	*getProperty*	*String*
	getProperties	*Enumeration*
	setProperty	-

The `getMetaAgentClass` method returns a particular type – the `MetaAgentClass` class –, which provides a flexible mechanism to handle agent classes existent in every AS-Server's context.

4.6 Other Classes

It is not the goal of this paper to describe fully all the details of the AS-API. Nevertheless, the AS-API also provides other related types that will not be further described in this paper:

- `Message` – to provide inter-agent communication;
- `Ticket` – to provide agent mobility with an access control mechanism;
- `AgentSpace` – to provide a context view factory;
- The `inesc.as.security.acl` package that includes classes such as: `GroupImpl`, `PermissionImpl`, `AclEntryImpl`, `AclImpl`, and so on – to provide access control management.

5 Conclusions

In this paper we presented the AgentSpace mobile agent system as a new Java framework to support, manage and develop future agent-based applications. The focus of this paper was to present an overview to the main components of AgentSpace, its exported object model and programmer's API.

It is important to note how suitable, to support dynamic and distributed applications, can be the process of creating agents as well as places. Firstly, there is no use or explicit reference to network-enable classes (like virtual objects in the Voyager framework, or like stubs and skeletons classes in RMI). Secondly, all agents are created through the `createAgent` method in a transparent, clean and easy process. Additionally we provide a very extensible and elegant way to handle security policies related to the access and interactions between agent and end-users, and between agents themselves. Basically, one security manager is attached to the agent (or place) object just in the moment of its creation.

Other novel aspect of AgentSpace is the well integrated association between users and agents/places. This mechanism, intrinsic by default in AgentSpace, provides a simpler way to develop and manage this class of applications.

One important reason of the AgentSpace's abilities is due necessarily to Voyager, with its very well suitable features, namely support for object mobility and persistence. Due to Voyager, AgentSpace agents may be accessed from applets running on Web browsers, or easily support the communication in the open-channel situation (i.e., agents can communicate transparently even if one has been moved to another place). Another important reason is obviously due to Java itself with its recent features (JDK 1.1), namely reflection, dynamic class loaders and object serialization.

For the interested reader, we have some recent papers that describe complementary aspects of AgentSpace. In [9] we proposed the *Agent* pattern design, which is suitable to support dynamic and distributed applications. In [10] we describe an electronic-commerce ABA which was developed both on top of AgentSpace and the Aglets Workbench. Based on these prototypes we present some preliminary performance figures comparing AgentSpace with Aglets. We also discuss the advantages of

AgentSpace from the programmer's point of view. For a detailed and complete discussion of these (and other) aspects the reader is referred to [8].

We have also put some source code and related information available for download at the following address: http://berlin.inesc.pt/~agentspc/.

References

1. IBM Tokyo Research Laboratory. The Aglets Workbench: Programming Mobile Agents in Java (1997).
   http://www.ibm.co.jp/trl/aglets
2. Gray, R.: Agent Tcl: A transportable agent system. In Proceedings of the CIKM'95 Workshop On Intelligent Information Agents (1995).
3. General Magic, Inc. Odyssey Product Information (1996).
   http://www.genmagic.com/agents/odyssey.html
4. Hohansen, D., Renesse, R., Schneider, F.: An Introduction to the TACOMA Distributed System. Computer Science Technical Report 95-23. University of Tromso, Norway (1995).
5. White, J.: General Magic, Inc. Mobile Agents White Paper (1994)
   http://www.genmagic.com/agents/Whitepaper/whitepaper.html
6. Lingnau, A., Drobnik, O., Domel, P.: An HTTP-Based Infrastructure for Mobile Agents. In Proceedings of the Fourth Int'l WWW Conference (1995).
7. Rodrigues da Silva, A., Mira da Silva, M., Delgado, J.: Improving Current Agent Support Systems: Focus on the Agent Execution System. Presented to the *Java Mobile Agents Workshop of the OOPSLA'97* (1997).
8. Rodrigues da Silva, A.: AgentSpace: Support, Development and Management of Agent-based Dynamic and Distributed Applications. PhD Thesis (in Portuguese), Technical University of Lisbon (1998).
9. Rodrigues da Silva, A., Delgado, J.: The Agent Pattern: A Design Pattern for Dynamic and Distributed Applications. Proceedings of the EuroPLoP'98, Third European Conference on Pattern Languages of Programming and Computing, Irsee, Germany (1998).
10. Rodrigues da Silva, A., Delgado, J.: AgentSpace versus Aglets: Agent Infrastructures for the Future Internet Applications (in Portuguese). Proceedings of the SBC'98, Congresso da Sociedade Brasileira de Computação, Belo Horizonte, Brasil (1998).
11. ObjectSpace: Voyager Core Package Technical Overview (1997)
12. Ponton, COGEFO/CEFRIEL, Hamburg University, INESC, Interzone Music Publishing, Oracle UK, and SIA: COSMOS – Common Open Service Market for SMEs, ESPRIT Research Project Proposal (1997)
13. Riecken, D., editor: Special Issue: Intelligent Agents. Communications of the ACM (1994), 37(7)
14. M. Wooldridge, N. Jennings. Intelligent Agents: Theory and Practice. *Knowledge Engineering Review*, 10(2), Cambridge University Press (1995)
15. J. Baumann, C. Tschudin, J. Vitek, editors. Proceedings of the 2nd ECOOP Workshop on Mobile Object Systems (Linz, Austria), Dpunkt (1996)
16. Milojicic, D. et al.: Concurrency, a Case Study in Remote Tasking and Distributed IPC. Proceedings of the 29th Annual Hawaii International Conference on System Sciences (1996)
17. Gamma, E., Helm, R., Johnson, R., Vlissides, J.: Design Patterns – Elements of Reusable Object-Oriented Software. Addison-Wesley Longman (1995)
18. Rational Software Corp: UML – Unified Modeling Language, version 1.0 (1997)
    http://www.rational.com/uml

μCODE: A Lightweight and Flexible Mobile Code Toolkit

Gian Pietro Picco

Dip. Automatica e Informatica, Politecnico di Torino
C.so Duca degli Abruzzi 24, 10129 Torino, Italy
Phone: +39-11-5647091, Fax: +39-11-5647099
E-mail: picco@polito.it, Web: http://www.polito.it/~picco

Abstract. Although a thorough evaluation of mobile code technology does not exist yet, some studies already evidenced that the powerful (and often heavyweight) abstractions and mechanisms proposed so far are not always flexible enough to fully exploit the benefits of migrating code. μCODE is a new mobile code toolkit designed to be flexible, extensible, and lightweight. Its small set of abstractions and mechanisms can be used directly by the programmer or composed in higher-level abstractions— mobile agents included. This paper discusses the fundamental concepts and features of μCODE, together with its rationale and motivation.

1 Introduction

Code mobility is becoming increasingly popular among researchers and practitioners due to its expected benefits and to the huge interest revolving around the Java language and the Internet world in general. However, the only pervasive mobile code application is nowadays the execution of *applets* in a Web browser— a rather limited exploitation of the mobile code potential. Most researchers are in fact focusing on the proposal of new technologies, and only very few studies [3, 10] focused on building applications and identifying the benefits and tradeoffs involved. As a consequence, a wider acceptance of code mobility is presently hampered by the fact that the soundness of the abstractions and mechanisms proposed are not verified by quantitative evaluations and experimental evidence.

The goal of this work is to propose a different perspective on the design of language support for mobile code. This is achieved by leveraging off of previous work done by the author in evaluating qualitatively and quantitatively the benefits of mobile code [2, 3], exploiting mobile code in applications [4], and building a conceptual framework for code mobility [6]. The outcome is a proof-of-concept system called μCODE, a mobile code toolkit for Java conceived to overcome some of the drawbacks of existing mobile code systems (MCS).

The paper is structured as follows. Section 2 analyzes the rationale and motivations for the development of μCODE, discussing the principles underlying its design. Section 3 illustrates the basic concepts of the toolkit, and Section 4 describes in greater detail its features. Finally, Section 5 provides some implementation details and concluding remarks, and discusses options for future work.

2 Rationale and Motivation

μCODE[1] has been designed after research done by the author aimed at identifying precisely the benefits brought by mobile code in the design and implementation of distributed applications. To ground the conclusions in the real world rather than in toy examples, these studies focused on the application domain of network management, adopting both a qualitative [2] and quantitative [3] style of analysis. In particular, the latter defined an analytical model of a management task and derived criteria to compare the effectiveness of client-server and mobile code in reducing the network traffic generated by management. The theoretical findings were verified by measuring the performance of a SNMPv1 [5] implementation against several mobile code alternatives implemented with the Java Aglets API [9]. We chose this platform because it is considered by many researchers as one of the most reliable, supported, and complete. However, the aforementioned studies and the mobile code application described in [4] evidenced the drawbacks discussed in the following[2], and gave rationale to the development of μCODE.

	C $\notin$ CLASSPATH	C $\in$ CLASSPATH
C $\in$ AGLET_EXPORT_PATH	C cannot be shipped, but can be fetched	C can be shipped and can be fetched
C $\notin$ AGLET_EXPORT_PATH	C can be neither shipped nor fetched	C can be shipped but cannot be fetched

Table 1. How to constrain migration of classes with Java Aglets.

Lack of flexibility in the strategies for code relocation. According to the taxonomy for code mobility presented in [6], Java Aglets support weak mobility by enabling shipping and fetching of stand-alone code—the *aglets*. Since the API relies on Java, Aglets support also fetching of code fragments—the aglet classes. However, the strategies that rule class relocation are not completely under the control of the programmer. When an aglet must be migrated, its class must satisfy the constraints illustrated in Table 1. These constraints are specified at setup time by setting the environment variables CLASSPATH and AGLET_EXPORT_PATH, and cannot be easily changed dynamically. Moreover, there is no means to relocate all the classes needed by an aglet in a single operation—missing classes are retrieved remotely and linked dynamically using the class loader mechanism. An example can clarify why this may be a problem. As discussed by many researchers and confirmed by the aforementioned studies, among the benefits of mobile code and particularly mobile agents is the capability to minimize communication over high-cost links, cost being for instance availability of bandwidth, security concerns, or the money paid to use the link. Mobile agents allow for performing a

---

[1] μ is the Greek letter for m, initial of *mobile*, thus μCODE is short for *mobile code*. However, μ is also the symbol for *micro*, suggesting that the toolkit is lightweight and small. Along this line, our toolkit can be regarded as the *microcode* for systems providing higher levels of abstraction, much like the microcode in a processor.

[2] Although focused on Java Aglets, most of the remarks apply also to many other Java-based MCSs, like Mole [12] or Odyssey [8].

task remotely in a disconnected fashion, without keeping the client connected during task execution. For instance, on a GSM connection at 9,600 baud it is meaningful to send in one shot all the classes for an aglet to minimize communication on the expensive link and leverage off of disconnected operations. If, in the context of the same application, we are now traversing a local Ethernet, it can be also meaningful to send only the aglet class to minimize the computational overload at loading time on the remote node and exploit the fast link for remote dynamic linking. In other words, *the strategy adopted for the relocation of code is determined by the environment and is not necessarily a property of the code being relocated.* The impossibility to specify dynamically the constraints on relocation of classes and to limit dynamic linking hampers a full exploitation of the mobile agent paradigm.

Level of abstraction. The Java Aglets API is nicely centered around a single, fundamental abstraction: mobile agents. However, an application exploiting mobile code does not necessarily need all the power contained in this abstraction. If this is the case, the semantic richness of the agent concept can backfire on the programmer, who is forced to express lower level concepts in a higher level framework. For instance, imagine a scenario where a site must be upgraded with new classes *proactively* rather than *reactively* as enabled by the Java class loading mechanism. A scheme dispatching an agent on the destination site to install the classes is convenient if several sites must be upgraded at the same time, because the agent can perform the task autonomously. However, this scheme becomes artificial if only a site must be upgraded; using lower level primitives that deal directly with the relocation of classes is more natural. Similar considerations hold for the implementation of a remote evaluation paradigm [11, 6]. In many Java-based systems, the only means to realize it is to create locally and dispatch to destination a mobile agent that has been coded explicitly to handle communication of the remote evaluation results. Again, a different set of primitives may be appropriate, even if they are characterized by a lower level of abstraction.

Communication performance. As evidenced in [3], the size of the code being moved is a key factor in determining the threshold after which code mobility becomes useful in reducing network traffic—another motivation to avoid abstractions enforcing unnecessary verbosity. However, a key factor affecting performance is also the overhead introduced by communication protocols. Network and transport level protocols are usually part of the system requirements, but the language designer retains control on the application level protocol used to transfer mobile code. Existing systems exploit different solutions that range from the direct use of the Java serialization protocol [14] to the use of protocols for distributed objects [8]. Java Aglets employ an Agent Transfer Protocol (ATP) that, as characterized quantitatively in [3], increases significantly the communication overhead under given conditions. Clearly, the overhead of application protocols should be minimized, and in this respect Java serialization provides a good tradeoff between compactness of the encoding and ease of programming and customizability.

Hence, our toolkit is designed around the following principles:

1. *Flexibility.* This has in turn different facets:
   (a) *Control over code relocation.* For the same mobile code, different strategies must be available to cope with different situations.
   (b) *Access to different levels of abstractions.* Although high-level constructs are provided by the toolkit, lower-level constructs must be accessible when some particular or customized functionality is needed.
   (c) *Control over the run-time support.* The run-time support can be controlled directly by programs, and is not an external, opaque program.
2. *Minimality.* The set of concepts and mechanisms must strive for minimality, thus fostering composability and ease of understanding.
3. *Non-invasiveness.* Code mobility is just another option for the programmer, for whom the effort to deal with mobility must be minimized and design freedom maximized. As an example, the programmer should not be forced to subclass from particular classes to use mobile threads. Mobility should be applicable directly to Java threads, thus fostering exploitation of mobile code even in applications that were not initially designed for it.
4. *Extensibility.* μCODE is a thin layer providing core mobile code functionality on top of the Java Virtual Machine (VM). Its design must be open, such that its basic primitives can be composed in higher-level abstractions, or specialized run-time supports can be built.
5. *Portability.* The toolkit must be fully compatible with Java, in order to run seamlessly on all the platforms supported by this language.

Notably, security is missing. Although security is often a major concern in applications exploiting mobile code, this does not hold in general. An example is constituted by network management. The vast majority of organizations still rely on SNMPv1, whose security model is limited to a "community name" transmitted unencrypted along with each SNMP request. In this case, performing local SNMP interactions with mobile code does not provide additional breaches in the management system, because this untrusted code contains the same information exchanged remotely by SNMP, whose rather trivial authentication protocol can be implemented at the application level for mobile code. In this cases the overhead imposed on the run-time support by security is undesirable. For similar reasons, our system does not provide any special abstraction for communication among migrating units. Security and communication mechanisms can be implemented in μCODE either at the application level or by a higher-level mobile code layer, whose development is actually the subject of on-going work.

3 Fundamental Concepts

The basic operations provided by μCODE enable creation and copy of thread objects on a remote μServer, and class relocation among μServers. A μServer is an abstraction of the run-time support and represents a computational environment for mobile threads. Upon migration, thread objects retain their data state and lose their execution state. Thus, only weak mobility is supported, through all the mechanisms identified in the taxonomy [6]; μCODE supports code shipping and fetching of both code fragments and stand-alone code, with both synchronous and asynchronous invocation, as well as deferred and immediate execution of mobile code. As for data space management, no mechanism for resource sharing is in place besides those provided by Java, as this issue is orthogonal to the relocation of code and threads addressed by μCODE. However, a package providing the appropriate mechanisms on top of μCODE is currently under development.

In μCODE, the unit of migration is the *group*. A group is simply a container for classes and objects. This abstraction is reminiscent of TACOMA briefcases [7] or, more closely, of the object-group abstraction found in Sumatra [1]. However, there at least two significant differences:

- In Sumatra, the classes needed by objects in an object-group are not transferred along with the group, and must be shipped explicitly with a separate downloadClass operation. The rationale behind this choice is to provide the programmer with finer control on which classes must be provided by the sender and which are already available at destination. This is in accordance with the design principles of μCODE, although it provides a similar operation shipClass and its complementary fetchClass, but also the capability to insert classes needed at destination directly into the group. The added value coming from this choice is improved atomicity. In the decoupled approach, connectivity may be lost in between class shipping and group transmission. In our approach, either the whole group is reconstructed correctly, or none of its components are available at destination.
- In Sumatra, object-groups cannot contain thread objects. Sumatra designers modified the Java VM to support strong mobility and enable threads to retain their execution state across migration; including threads in an object-group would pose significant semantic problems. μCODE supports only weak mobility to preserve full compatibility with the Java VM. The problems above do not arise because thread objects stored in a group lose their control flow and then become akin to conventional objects.

Classes can be added to a group either individually or collectively by computing the closure of a given class. The *class closure* C^* of a class C is such that:

1. $C \in C^*$;
2. $C' \in C^*$ if $\exists \gamma \in C^*$ such that C' is either: the superclass of γ; the class of a field declared by γ; the class of an exception, parameter, or return value for a method or constructor declared by γ; an inner class declared by γ.

Thus, for example, in the fragment

```
public MyClass extends MySuper implements MyInterface {
  public MyField f;
  public MyReturn myMethod(MyPar p) throws MyException {
    MyVar v = new MyVar();
    class MyInnerClass {...}
  }
}
```

the classes and interfaces MyClass, MySuper, MyInterface, MyField, MyReturn, MyPar, MyException, and MyInnerClass belong to the class closure of MyClass, but MyVar does not. If MyVar must be transferred as well, it must be added explicitly to the group. Differently from class serialization, managed directly by μCODE, object serialization relies on Java mechanisms and thus requires the class of the object being inserted in a group to implement the appropriate interfaces defined in [14]; an exception is raised otherwise. Java serialization relies on the notion of *object closure*. The object closure of an object o is constituted by o, by all the objects that are fields of o, by all the objects that are fields of the objects above, and so on, recursively. The amount of the closure being serialized can be constrained by declaring a field as `transient`, which prevents serialization of the corresponding object even when this is possible.

The actions taken by a μServer when it receives a group are ruled by two classes associated with the group: the handler and the root. The *handler* class is used to instantiate an object responsible for "unpacking" the group and manipulating its contents. μCODE defines a default handler that implements the basic operations provided by the toolkit. However, programmers can define their own specialized group handlers and, doing so, even define their own relocation primitives. The *root* class provides additional information for handling a group by specifying the class on which the relocation operation must be performed, e.g., to specify which class must be used to spawn a new thread in the destination μServer. The handler and root classes can be any classes and even coincide, and it is not necessary to transmit them along with the group, although in this case it is up to the programmer to ensure that they are found at destination.

After the group has been handled, possibly spawning one or more threads, the corresponding classes are kept into a *private class space*, a name space for classes. The presence of a separate class space avoids name clashes among classes belonging to different mobile threads and guarantees that a mobile thread actually uses the classes shipped with its group rather than some other class with the same name already present on the μServer. However, μCODE provides operations that enable a thread to "publish" classes in the *shared class space* associated with a μServer. There, they become available to every thread hosted by the μServer and can also be accessed by operations shipping or fetching classes performed by threads on remote μServers. Class spaces guide the resolution of class names at loading time. When a class C needs to be resolved during execution of a thread t managed by a μServer S, the μCODE customized version of the Java class loader is invoked and performs the following steps:

1. Check whether C is a *ubiquitous class*, i.e. a class available on every μServer. The set of ubiquitous classes can be changed dynamically. Classes belonging to the Java API and μCODE are ubiquitous by default. Checking ubiquitous classes first prevents redefinition of their behavior.
2. Search for C in the private class space[3] associated with t in S.
3. Search for C in the shared class space associated with S.
4. If t is allowed to perform dynamic download, C is retrieved from the remote site specified by the user at migration time, and loaded.
5. If C cannot be found, throw a `java.lang.ClassNotFoundException`.

---

[3] Threads created directly by applications and not as a consequence of migration are all associated with the same class space, managed by the default Java class loader.

```
public final class Group {
  public void addClass(String className)
  public void addClassClosure(String className)
  public void addObject(String label, Object obj)
  public Object getObject(String label)
  public void addMobile(Mobile threadObj)
  public Mobile getMobile()
  public int ship(String destination, String dynLink, boolean synch)
}
public interface GroupHandler {
  public abstract Runnable unpack(Group group, MuServer server)
}
public interface Mobile extends Runnable, Serializable {
}
```

Fig. 1. The class Group and the interfaces GroupHandler and Mobile.

4 Programming with μCODE

μCODE is structured along three layers of abstraction. All the abstractions and mechanisms provided by μCODE are built using the implementation of the concepts described in the previous section, i.e., groups and their handling, and class spaces. Thus, the core of μCODE are the classes Group and ClassSpace, and the interfaces GroupHandler and Mobile, described in the following. This first layer of core functionality, although still available to the programmer, is used to compose operations that handle relocation of classes and threads at a more convenient level of abstraction. These are the operations made available by the MuServer class, that also provides access to the underlying run-time support. Finally, a third layer is constituted by user abstractions composed using those provided by the other layers; the mobile agent abstraction is an example. This section gives a brief description of the API provided by μCODE.

The Class Group and the Interfaces GroupHandler and Mobile The methods of Group are shown[4] in Fig. 1. addClass inserts in the Group instance the class corresponding to the given className, specified with the usual Java convention for packages. Already existing classes are overwritten. addClassClosure inserts the whole class closure rooted at className. addObject inserts a given object in the group. The parameter label provides a way to tag objects for later retrieval on the remote μServer, using the complementary method getObject. The methods addMobile and getMobile are a variant of the above that insert and retrieve an object implementing the interface Mobile, shown in Fig. 1. Mobile extends Runnable and Serializable, and thus represents an object that can contain a thread of control and yet be transferred on a different μServer. The aforementioned methods are just a more convenient way to manage the common case where a single thread object is moved. In fact, although a group can contain more than one Mobile object, only the one inserted with addMobile is handled automatically by the system; a customized handler is required for the others. The handler class can be any class implementing the interface GroupHandler, shown in Fig. 1. This interface defines a single method unpack called automatically by the run-time support when the group is received. This method returns

---

[4] The declarations of exceptions are omitted for the sake of clarity.

```
public final class ClassSpace {
  public boolean containsClass(String className)
  public Class getClass(String className)
  public void removeClass(String className)
  public void copyClassTo(String className, ClassSpace classSpace)
  public void copyClassFrom(String className, ClassSpace classSpace)
  public void moveClassTo(String className, ClassSpace classSpace)
  public void moveClassFrom(String className, ClassSpace classSpace)
}
```

Fig. 2. The class ClassSpace.

an object implementing the interface Runnable defined by Java, i.e. an object that can be used to spawn a new thread of execution. However, a null object can be returned when group handling does not require a new thread, e.g., to provide new class relocation primitives. Finally, the ship method provides relocation of the Group on the μServer specified by destination, identified by a pair hostname:port. The dynLink parameter enables dynamic linking of classes from a remote μServer, thus providing direct support for a code on demand paradigm [6]. This way, the group is allowed to provide just a subset of the classes required for its handling and the execution of the associated thread objects, if any. If and when additional classes are needed, they will be downloaded from the location specified by the dynLink parameter and linked by the remote class loader. A null value for this parameter prevents remote dynamic linking. All the classes that are not transmitted along with the group but are indeed needed for group handling must be present at destination or, in alternative, remote dynamic linking must be enabled. In any other case, an exception java.lang.ClassNotFoundException is raised on the destination μServer, as described in the previous section. The synch parameter determines whether the ship operation is performed synchronously or asynchronously. If synch is true, the operation is blocking for the caller, that is suspended until a return value is received after group handling on the remote μServer. If synch is false, the method returns immediately after group transmission is completed.

The Class ClassSpace The methods of ClassSpace, in Fig. 2, enable management of the contents of a class space by testing the presence of a class in a class space, getting the class object of a class belonging to the class space, removing the class from the class space, as well as moving and copying a class across different class spaces. These features are useful when performing group handling, and in general to modify the set of classes that are available either to a given thread or to all the threads sharing a class space in a μServer.

The Class MuServer This class provides the abstraction of a μServer, and collects methods that provide code mobility on top of the classes described so far. The first three methods in Fig. 3 support remote cloning and creation of threads, and rSpawnGroup is the most general operation. The contents of the group parameter transferred on the remote μServer are completely up to the programmer. When the group is received at destination, if no custom handler is specified, the default handler looks into the received group for a thread object by performing a getMobile, and spawns a new thread of control for it. If

```
public final class MuServer implements Runnable {
  public static final int NONE
  public static final int ROOT
  public static final int FULL
  public int rSpawnGroup(String destination, Group group,
                         String dynLink, boolean synch)
  public int rSpawnThread(String destination, String className,
                          int classClosure, String dynLink,
                          boolean synch)
  public int rCopyThread(String destination, Mobile threadObj,
                         int classClosure, String dynLink,
                         boolean synch)
  public int fetchClass(String destination, String className,
                        int classClosure, boolean synch)
  public int shipClass(String destination, String className,
                       int classClosure, boolean synch)
  public static MuServer getServer()
  public ClassSpace getPrivateClassSpace()
  public ClassSpace getSharedClassSpace()
  public Group createGroup(String rootClass, String handlerClass)
  public void boot(int port)
  public void shutDown()
}
```

Fig. 3. The class `MuServer`.

the thread object is not found, it is created using the root class. The parameters `destination`, `dynLink`, and `synch` retain the meaning defined for the `ship` method in `Group`. The creation of a `Group` object must be requested to a specific μServer, through a `createGroup` operation; in fact, resolution of the handler and root classes depend on the contents of the class spaces associated to a particular μServer. `rSpawnThread` creates a new thread at the specified μServer and makes it easier to build the corresponding group, by enabling the programmer to specify just the `className` of the object for which a thread is going to be spawned. This class actually constitutes the root class of the group being sent by μCODE. In addition, the class closure rooted at `className` can be included. The parameter `classClosure` can assume the values `NONE` if no class should actually be transmitted, `ROOT` if only the `className` class should be transmitted, and `FULL` if the full class closure should be transmitted. Finally, `rCopyThread` clones the `Mobile` object `threadObj` on a remote μServer, discarding the execution state. By default, the classes being transferred as a consequence of the invocation of the three operations above are cached on the destination μServer in the private class space associated with the resulting thread. These classes can be moved to the shared class space using the methods provided by `ClassSpace`; a reference to these spaces is acquired using the methods `getPrivateClassSpace` and `getSharedClassSpace`. Also, a reference to the `MuServer` object hosting the thread can be acquired with the `getServer` method; the result is `null` for threads that have not been created as a consequence of migration.

The methods `shipClass` and `fetchClass` enable relocation of classes across different μServers. Both operations can access only the shared space of the destination μServer, as required by the semantics of private class spaces. In any case, since no built-in naming scheme to identify threads is present in μCODE, there are no means to fetch or ship a class directly to the private class space of a thread running on a remote μServer. If needed, this kind of mechanism

```
public abstract class MuAgent implements Mobile, GroupHandler {
  private transient MuServer server = MuServer.getServer();
  public MuAgent(MuServer server) {this.server = server;}
  public final int go(String destination, int classClosure,
                      String dynLink, boolean synch) {
    String className = this.getClass().getName();
    Group group = server.createGroup(className, className);
    group.addMobile(this);
    switch (classClosure) {
    case MuServer.NONE:
      break;
    case MuServer.ROOT:
      group.addClass(className);
      break;
    case MuServer.FULL:
      group.addClassClosure(className);
      break;
    }
    server.rSpawnGroup(destination, group, dynLink, synch);
    Thread.currentThread().stop();
  }
  public final Runnable unpack(Group group, MuServer server) {
    MuAgent agent = (MuAgent) group.getMobile();
    agent.server = server;
    return agent;
  }
}
```

Fig. 4. The implementation of the class MuAgent.

can be built on top of μCODE. shipClass copies one or more classes from the current μServer to the shared class space of the remote μServer. Analogously, fetchClass copies one or more classes from the shared class space of the remote μServer to the one of the μServer hosting the thread requesting the operation. In both cases, the class(es) remain available at their source μServer. As before, the amount of code transferred is determined by the classClosure parameter, although the value NONE now raises a MuCodeException because the semantics of the operations prescribe that at least one class must always be transferred.

The method boot activates the run-time support listening for incoming mobile code on the specified port; multiple μServers can co-exist on the same machine and even in the same Java VM. Nevertheless, this is needed only if the application needs to receive and execute incoming mobile code. In the case where the application only needs to send mobile code, *no additional run-time support is needed* besides the Java VM and the classes in the μCODE package. Additional methods of MuServer, not shown in Fig. 3, allow for specifying ubiquitous classes and setting properties like compression and communication timeout.

The Class MuAgent The class MuAgent provides a natural abstraction for implementing a mobile agent paradigm with a technology providing weak mobility. Movement is reduced to a single instruction, the go method, with parameters similar to the ones in MuServer methods. In particular, a MuAgent instance can perform dynamic linking from a remote μServer. MuAgent exemplifies how the abstractions provided by μCODE can be composed in higher-level abstractions. Figure 4 shows the whole implementation of class MuAgent, except for minor details. The interesting part is the go method body. It retrieves first the class name of the MuAgent subclass for the object the method is actually bound to. The information about the class name is then used to create an instance of Group. The method body adds to it the thread object to which the go is bound, using addMobile as described earlier. When the group is received at destination, the run-time support present at that node calls the implementation of the method unpack, shown in Fig. 4, that retrieves the thread object using the complementary method getMobile and returns it to the run-time support, that spawns a new thread of execution for it. After adding itself to the group, the method go adds the amount of the class closure requested by the user. Then, it uses rSpawnGroup to actually send the group on the remote μServer. Finally, it stops the current thread, that will be eventually garbage collected.

5 Discussion and Future Work

This paper presented μCODE, a mobile code toolkit designed and developed entirely by the author to provide flexible, extensible, and lightweight support for code mobility in distributed applications developed using Java. The rationale for μCODE comes from research developed by the author and his colleagues in evaluating the benefits of mobile code in real world application domains. μCODE is being effectively used to implement applications for active networks [4] and network management. The current implementation of μCODE consists of less than a thousand non-commented source statements, which generate approximately 40Kbytes of bytecode. Additional figures are not yet available, but the use on the field of μCODE showed that it provides adequate flexibility and a reduction in communication overhead.

The implementation of μCODE leverages off of some advanced features provided by the Java language. The computation of the class closure employs the reflective features provided by Java [13] to retrieve information about the members of a class. However, the Java reflection mechanism cannot detect the need for classes that are declared in method bodies, as exemplified in Section 3. To work around this limitation would involve on-the-fly inspection of the class bytecode—a major endeavor with respect to the benefits achievable. The object serialization mechanism provided by Java has been redefined to provide a specialized handling of classes during serialization and customized class loading during deserialization. Class loading is fundamental to the provision of class spaces. Each μServer contains at least two class loaders: a default class loader servicing requests for classes present on the system and one servicing requests for the shared class space. When the μServer is handling a group, a new class loader is created for it. Due to the semantics of class loading in Java, every subsequent class loading triggered by the classes resolved through this class loader will go again through it, thus preserving a separate class space.

The notion of class space plays a key role in improving flexibility. Through the shared class space, the set of classes that are visible to other μServers can be redefined dynamically by the applications rather than being hard-wired in some configuration file. Furthermore, the distinction between the shared and private class spaces enables the definition of mechanisms for class "caching" on remote μServers, leaving the control in the programmer's hands rather than to some predefined policy of the system. The idea of class space is reminiscent of the *dictionary* concept found in MO [15], in that it provides direct access to the name space of an executing unit. The coincidence is not by chance. Like MO, μCODE aims at providing a set of basic abstractions and mechanisms to build higher-level systems. Unlike MO, however, these features rely directly and completely on the Java language, rather than on a complicate Postscript-like notation.

On-going work on μCODE is developing extensions providing higher-level abstractions and mechanisms, addressing in particular resource sharing, communication, and security. At the same time, the toolkit is being used in several project and its performance is being characterized quantitatively and compared to that of other systems.

Acknowledgments The author wishes to thank Gianpaolo Cugola and Giovanni Vigna for their precious comments on an early draft of this work.

References

1. A. Acharya, M. Ranganathan, and J. Saltz. Sumatra: A Language for Resource-aware Mobile Programs. In *Mobile Object Systems: Towards the Programmable Internet*, volume 1222 of *LNCS*, pages 111–130. Springer, April 1997.
2. M. Baldi, S. Gai, and G.P. Picco. Exploiting Code Mobility in Decentralized and Flexible Network Management. In *Mobile Agents: 1st International Workshop MA'97*, volume 1219 of *LNCS*, pages 13–26. Springer, April 1997.
3. M. Baldi and G.P. Picco. Evaluating the Tradeoffs of Mobile Code Design Paradigms in Network Management Applications. In *Proc. of the 20th Int. Conf. on Software Engineering*, pages 146–155, April 1998.
4. M. Baldi, G.P. Picco, and F. Risso. Designing a Videoconference System for Active Networks. In this proceedings.
5. J.D. Case et al. Simple Network Management Protocol. RFC 1157, May 1990.
6. A. Fuggetta, G.P. Picco, and G. Vigna. Understanding Code Mobility. *IEEE Trans. on Software Engineering*, 24(5):342–361, May 1998.
7. D. Johansen, R. van Renesse, and F. B. Schneider. An Introduction to the TACOMA Distributed System—Version 1.0. Technical Report 95-23, Tromsø and Cornell Univ., June 1995.
8. J. Kiniry and D. Zimmerman. A Hands-On Look at Java Mobile Agents. *IEEE Internet Computing*, 1(4):21–30, 1997.
9. D.B. Lange. Java Aglets Application Programming Interface (J-AAPI). IBM Corp. White Paper, February 1997.
10. M. Ranganathan et al. Network-Aware Mobile Programs. In *Proc. of the USENIX 1997 Annual Technical Conf.*, January 1997.
11. J.W. Stamos and D.K. Gifford. Remote Evaluation. *ACM Trans. on Programming Languages and Systems*, 12(4):537–565, October 1990.
12. M. Straßer, J. Baumann, and F. Hohl. Mole—A Java Based Mobile Agent System. In *Special Issues in Object-Oriented Programming: Workshop Reader of the 10th European Conf. on Object-Oriented Programming ECOOP'96*, pages 327–334. dpunkt, July 1996.
13. Sun Microsystems. *Java Core Reflection*, January 1997.
14. Sun Microsystems. *Java Object Serialization Specification*, February 1997.
15. C. Tschudin. *An Introduction to the MO Messenger Language.* Univ. of Geneva, Switzerland, 1994.

Mobile Agents and Intellectual Property Protection

Stephane G. Belmon* and Bennet S. Yee**

Department of Computer Science and Engineering
University of California, San Diego
La Jolla, CA 92093-0114

Abstract. Technical enforcement of intellectual property (IP) rights often conflicts with the ability to use the IP. This is especially true when the IP is data, which may easily be copied while it is being accessed. As electronic commerce of data becomes more widespread, traditional approaches will prove increasingly problematic. In this paper, we show that the mobile agent architecture is an ideal solution to this dilemma: by providing full access to the data but charging for the transmission of results back to the user — *results-based billing* — we resolve the access versus protection conflict. We define new requirements for agent frameworks to implement results-based billing: "data-aware accounting" and "data-tight sandboxing", which, along with the common requirements such as authentication, authorization, agent self-monitoring, and efficiency, provide the mechanisms by which database owners can effectively grant users access to their intellectual property.

1 Introduction

The concept of intellectual property (IP) protection is usually viewed as necessary for innovation. It protects the IP creators from seeing their work used without remuneration, economically motivating research and development of new ideas and technologies. Unfortunately, it also often conflicts with freedom of use. Unlike academic circles where the only remuneration is "giving proper credit", IP protection in a commercial setting often means controlling all forms of access, especially when legal protection (copyright and patent laws) alone is deemed unsatisfactory. This tension between accessibility and protection is especially acute when the IP is in electronic form.

To use a simple bookstore analogy, the IP protection problem originates in the difficulty of electronically allowing "free, in-store, full-text browsing" while retaining the "buy-it-to-read-it" model. Traditionally, data is either made available or not to a customer's computer, and further use is beyond the provider's control. The usual solution is defensive, and the data is not made available in its entirety, but only by fragments supposed to be sufficient for the customers'

---

* sbelmon@cs.ucsd.edu
** bsy@cs.ucsd.edu

purposes (the table of contents, for example, hopefully enough to whet the customers' appetite so they will pay for physical goods, e.g., a CD-ROM or a book). While this solution might work for books, it severely limits usefulness. Furthermore, we will show that there are other common scenarios where it simply does not fit the customer's needs.

In this paper, we describe a solution to this conflict called *results-based billing* based on mobile agent technology. It allows a maximum freedom for the customer, retains strong intellectual property protection, and most important of all, charges a fair cost to the customer for almost any possible use.

In the next section, we present some application scenarios which can be readily solved by our agent-based IP protection scheme, motivating its use. In Section 3, we present "traditional", non-agent-based approaches to these IP protection applications, and discuss the limitations of these approaches. In Section 4, we provide a more detailed description of our vision of how an agent system can be used for IP protection. In Section 5, we compare our scheme with watermarking and fingerprinting, two methods also being developed for IP protection. Next, in Section 6, we examine the agent system infrastructure requirements needed to support our IP protection scheme. Finally, in Section 7, we make some concluding remarks.

2 Intellectual Property Applications of Agents

In this section we present a few application scenarios that involve intellectual property of data. The point of view adopted throughout this section is intentionally an end-user one. In other words, we are not as much concerned about *how* the system solves the problem as we are about *what* end-users see. By end-users, we refer to the customer and some individuals at the company providing the service — mostly, the accountants and the content-providing departments, hence, the tendency to emphasize billing and copyright issues.

We believe that these scenarios are typical, and we will later show the common pattern underlying them. However, it should be noted that we do not present any solution in this section. These cases can be solved in many ways, and though the choice of cases is arguably biased towards agent-based solutions, we hope that the way we express the problems themselves here is fair.

Our first application is a multimedia database, whose content is the whole set of films, videos, and sound-tracks owned by a major motion picture company. The company wants to let customers access this database as conveniently as possible while charging them in a manner consistent with their actual needs. The company also wants to keep the information systems costs under control. Let us give some examples of these customer needs:

– Basic video-on-demand, with advanced search for the cast, plot, etc. The cost to the user should be comparable to the purchase of a videotape with the film on it through a store. The resolution and sound quality are user-specified and should have an impact on cost.

- Clip retrieval. Given some rough lines of the script, the user wants to retrieve a specific clip in a film. The film and even the actors may be unknown to the user. The cost should mostly be a function of the clip duration and should be definitely less than that of the whole film containing the clip. More advanced searches could involve some pattern recognition or other advanced techniques.
- Poster editing. Maybe through the previous example, the user retrieves some clips and/or still images in low resolution. She mixes, blends and otherwise edits those to form a custom image, using an image editing tool. After having finished the work, the original, very high quality source images are used to build a final high resolution image. The cost should be comparable to that of a single high quality picture (and definitely less than that of the whole set of high quality images used in the process). The company might also charge for some computation costs, should the chosen solution involve significant calculations.

Our second application is a DNA database containing the complete sequencing of several species. This database is owned by a company trying to amortize the sequencing costs. The billing is primarily based on the length of the extracted sequences and the effort required for the search in terms of company resources (users are free to post-process the results at will). Beyond the usual pattern matching and regular expressions search, the company wants customers to be able to test new theories. The company wants to allow them to use the database with a freedom comparable to that of the case where they would actually have total access, and still be able to bill them in a fair manner.

An example is the search for the gene encoding for a protein in all known DNA sequences given some clues about its structure. This could involve inferring some information about the sequence, in order to restrict the search to a small subset, and then computing a likely structure for these remaining few sequences. The structure prediction process should be user-specified, as the field is still evolving (and as the general problem is likely to remain unsolved for some time). The cost should not be that of extracting the whole set of sequences from the database, but that of the computations required in addition to the price of the final answer (which could be mostly length-dependent) [9].

Other examples include the computation of various new metrics to measure the evolutionary distance between all species in the database. The fair cost for this computation should be reasonable, and very small compared to the price listed by the sequencing company to give total freedom of access to the whole database.

3 Traditional Solutions

In this section, we present the traditional solutions for the applications discussed. By "traditional", we refer to those implementations that do not involve the use of agents, for example systems utilizing a client-server or remote procedure call computation model. The solutions discussed here are what we believe to be representative of reasonable choices of implementation.

For the first set of applications involving services provided by a multimedia database, a traditional system configuration is that of a client-server model. The server is a multimedia database that serves the information contents to clients through the use of a querying service. Based on this model, possible implementations of the three applications in this domain discussed previously are described below.

- Basic video-on-demand: This service can be provided by a relational database server that can be queried using a database query language such as the Structured Query Language (SQL) [6]. The query language chosen must provide enough expressive power to allow the clients to specify various aspects of the desired data such as the resolution levels, compression, and formats (i.e. audio, video, etc). It must also be flexible enough to adapt to changes in technology, such as new compression techniques or data formats, so that it can continue to provide the services after the changes take place. In addition, an advanced accounting system must be provided so that appropriate fees can be charged, for example, for the price of the films and the queries.
- Clip retrieval: A similar configuration as described above can be used to provide a clip retrieval service. The video format must support an efficient retrieval of a specific clip, preferably without the needs to decompress the data before executing the queries. Other advanced search capabilities must be included in the database query language. In addition, the accounting system must be modified accordingly.
- Poster editing: We see two possible approaches for this application:
  - The first approach is to design a language that can describe sequence of actions performed on an image. This language will describe video editing actions in the same way a language such as Postscript describes a page description of a document. A sophisticated accounting system must also be designed to calculate the fees. Furthermore, both the language and the accounting system must be upgradable as the format and the set of possible actions change.
  - The second approach is to allow the client to download all the data needed to produce the final result. Since it will be more fair to charge the client only for the final result, care must be taken to ensure that the client will not be able to obtain unrestricted access to any part of the retrieved data. The client must be allowed to apply a certain set of actions to the data and to obtain only the final result. To fully satisfy the security requirements, the data must be encrypted and downloaded to secure hardware in the client's machine [11]. The encryption prevents the client from "understanding" the data. The secure hardware is the only component that can decrypt the data, perform the sequence of actions as requested by the client, and yield the final results. The accounting system in this approach will be responsible for monitoring the secure conversation between the server and the secure hardware.

We now consider a possible solution to the DNA database search and structure prediction problems. A relatively straight-forward implementation of the DNA database for searching can be realized by utilizing a search engine-type setup along with a language for the definition of DNA "regular expressions.[9]" Advantages of the use of a remote search engine system include the provision for a fair amount of flexibility limited only by the DNA expression language and the low bandwidth usage requirements for sending out the initial query. However, since this is an intellectual property application, the major drawback of this system is that the client has to be charged for whatever results are returned. The cost to the client is the charge for the total amount of data returned, regardless of whether or not the sequences were actually useful.

Protein and RNA structure prediction involves the search for a protein exhibiting a given spatial form. In order for the client to be able to give queries to the DNA database server, a special purpose language must be created to express these spatial representations. Similar to the general DNA sequence search application, this language must provide query expressions (in this case, expression of spatial orientations) that will allow the server to return a subset of sequences that exhibit a comparable spatial form. This query language must allow for additional specifications to be added at a later time to account for advances in structure prediction technology. Under this type of system, the queries will be large because of the large amounts of data needed to encode the spatial information. Again, the client must pay for all sequences returned by the search.

4 Agent-Based Systems

In this section, we will describe an IP protection solution based on mobile agents.

In an agent system with *results-based billing*, users pay for the answers that they receive back from the agent. By using agents in this way, we achieve simple, natural, and elegant solutions for IP protection.

Here is how we use agents. To the first approximation, users of a results-based billing system may send agents into a server to access the intellectual property arbitrarily. Once within the server, there are no access restrictions on the data or other server-side resources, and the agent may use whatever algorithms it needs to process it. The only restriction is in sending messages off the server — the agent must pay in order to send results back to the user. (Clearly, our first approximation is imperfect. Resource limits and nominal usage charges must exist, or the servers will be abused. We will see later in more detail what should be done in practice.)

Results-based billing is natural in many ways. The user learns only what is communicated back to him. The user's agent may chose to compress or otherwise pre-process the data in order to make the message size as small as possible, but even with perfect compression schemes the information theoretic limits provide a nice measure of the amount of IP disclosure. Furthermore, as noted for agent systems in general, unlike other systems such as RPCs or per-item billing such a scheme will provide a very flexible interface to the users and yet retain strong IP protection guarantees.

While results-based billing has great appeal, note that it should not be used when data of wildly varying values are available on a server. For example, a geographical database which contains both the exact latitude and longitude of Stuttgart, Germany and the latitude and longitude of an otherwise-undiscovered, gold laden sunken Spanish galleon should price the information differently.

Let's see how this scheme will work for our examples. For the video-on-demand and clip retrieval applications, a full featured database management system is not strictly necessary because an agent may choose to perform a brute-force scan of the data itself. This data scan incurs no network bandwidth costs since it is executing locally on the data server. The agent can process the data into any format it chooses, thus relieving the server of providing several specific video formats. An agent-based system provides accurate accounting costs because charges are only applied for the hardware resources used and for the data returned to the client. The poster editing application requires a similar agent-based solution with perhaps additional basic image editing primitives usable by the agent.

An agent-based implementation of the DNA database can be realized either by allowing a brute-force search or by providing some regular expression search mechanism for the agent. This search mechanism would be used just to reduce the brute force search to a manageable subset. The protein structure prediction is performed by the user code perhaps with the assistance of some basic blocks provided by a library. This library may be provided by a third party so that the server can simply link it to the agent when needed. Advantages of such an approach are that the server is not required to have any knowledge of the library implementation (libraries may be updated without any change to the server code) and the library itself may exist as compiled native machine code for improved efficiency.

5 Watermarking and Fingerprinting

The solutions discussed so far tried to forbid any kind of uncontrolled use of data. Another relatively new approach is to try to deter users from misusing the data by embedded identifying information in it.

One simple idea is to hide some information, such as the provider's and user's names, within images, e.g., the low-order bits of the image pixel values. This is known as *watermarks* and *fingerprints*, respectively. Simply using low-order bits is not very secure, in that such an encoding can easily be removed without significantly affecting the image quality, even when the exact encoding scheme is unknown to the attacker. Other approaches [3], however, embeds information more securely: the data is placed in perceptually significant components of the data, and attempts to remove the information should significantly degrade the image — while the difference between the original image and the protected one will still be "invisible" to the naked eye. With watermarking (and fingerprinting), if the user claims the data as being his (or if he spreads numerous copies of it), the provider can prove the offense; and users, even while colluding in a group, have no way of removing the watermarks (fingerprints) without damaging the image.

Watermarking and fingerprinting are orthogonal to our proposal.

Fingerprinting cannot prevent uncontrolled private use. It relies on the assumption that the user will make and spread enough unauthorized copies to let the IP owner discover the misuse. Unfortunately, this assumption is not always true, such as our poster-editing example or limited redistributions to "close friends". Furthermore, there are media for which any modification is unacceptable or impossible — many forms of text and our DNA example are in this category. Fingerprinting and watermarking is also very media-specific. While agents do not provide complete control over private use, they give a much better level of control than traditional solutions.

On the other hand, fingerprinting can protect data in ways that are not possible in our framework. It can let users view a film and still deter them from making many copies of it, or from broadcasting it. In this respect, fingerprinting is clearly very useful. The two approaches can be used together to provide even more security, and still give maximum convenience to the users.

6 Requirements

In the previous sections we argued that our results-based billing scheme is an ideal solution to the IP protection problem. However, to utilize it, certain requirements must be met by the underlying agent system, and we will now present these specific requirements. We will only discuss those that are pertinent to our applications. The requirements that are applicable to agent-based systems in general can be found in [4].

6.1 Accounting

IP owners want to charge for access to their IP. To do this, the agent infrastructure must provide the mechanisms to monitor resource usage.

In our IP usage metering scheme, the central idea is that we charge the agent-owners for answers received. This implies that agent network communications must be measured and charged on a per-byte or per-bit basis.

Unfortunately, the scheme is necessarily more complex than just charging for data transmissions. Because an agent can chose to trade CPU time for communications by employing data compression, usage of the CPU should also be charged. By requiring payment for CPU time, we also limit frivolous or inefficient squandering of server-side resources. Similar to CPU time, memory usage should be monitored and "rented out" to the agents. In typical situations, the resource usage costs will be small compared to the data costs.

One might try to charge data transfers differently, depending on what is transmitted – such as a low price for images and a higher one for texts, arguing that text has "more information" per byte than images have. As shown in [1], it is extremely difficult to make sure that agents are not using the available channels to communicate "hidden" information. This means that one should use an uniform rate, charging "by the byte".

However, the price charged an agent may depend on the agent's execution history: if the agent has only read from the "public knowledge" portion of a server, it would be charged a low fee; if, on the other hand, the agent has accessed the "cutting-edge research data" portion of a server, the data transmission charges would be concomitantly higher. Similarly, other access controls may be placed on the IP data; for example, a medical database may allow full read and certain kinds of append access for patient records (and genetic information) to the patient and the patient's doctors, but only provide restricted views for medical researchers who should only have access to aggregate information.

Mobility and agent migration, including that of transferring per-thread invocation stacks[5], implies message transfers for which an agent would be charged. If an agent has accessed "cutting edge" data, the server would have to charge a high fee for migration as well. For many IP protection problems, the agents can send back (compressed) results rather than migrating home from the server, so the initial migration to the IP-providing server is a one-way trip. This also implies that greater resource co-location is needed; the agent must have everything it needs to compute its result, since migrating to external resources from the IP-containing server is expensive.

6.2 Secure and Data-Tight Sandboxing

The service provider must be able to prevent agents from bypassing the accounting system discussed in Section 6.1. As expected in any agent-oriented application, an agent must not be able to "harm" the server. Furthermore, it should not be able to gain access to data it is not entitled to. By *data-tight*, we mean that it is impossible for the agent to bypass the accounting system when exporting data.

As research on multi-level security systems have demonstrated, processes in different security domains do not have to only use the system-provided communication mechanisms to send messages to each other: they can use unintentionally provided mechanisms, or "covert channels" [7], to communicate with each other. When the server can run several agents simultaneously and variable pricing is used[1], covert channels between agents should be eliminated or bandwidth-restricted.

While complete elimination of covert channels is extremely difficult if not impossible, a simple pragmatic solution exists: as long as we can estimate the maximum bandwidth achievable for a given amount of computation, we can charge enough for the CPU or other resource usage to compensate for the data

---

[1] If uniform pricing is used and there are no other access controls on the data, then covert channels between agents are not an issue: as long as we can meter outgoing data transmissions, these covert channels do not benefit the agents.

leaked over any potential covert channels. The system needs only to be reasonably data-tight.

In contrast to preventing agents from harming the server or leaking information, another desirable property would be the protection of agents from hosts: ensuring that their computations and communications are not tampered with, and private data are kept confidential [12]. This is difficult to achieve, and may require the use of secure hardware [11], but may be important for proving that the paid-for solution is actually correct.

6.3 Authentication and Authorization

The service provider must be able to authenticate the agent using its service. It must ensure that the agent is who it claims to be so that the fees can be charged to the appropriate party. This authentication mechanism must also prevent a replay attack where a network eavesdropper obtains a packet that has been used by a legitimate agent to identify itself, and simply retransmits it some time later. This attack will cause a fee to be charged to the legitimate agent's account even though it has neither requested nor received a service.

Some service providers may want an agent to agree to a contract, such as a non-disclosure agreement, before providing services for it. An agent is said to have obtained an "authorization" for the service once it agrees to the contract. The service provider must be able to keep track of and only provide services for authorized parties. Furthermore, some agents may have more privileges than others. The company providing the service may have a contract with some other parties to disclose information that would normally be otherwise inaccessible.

6.4 Agent Self-Monitoring

An agent must be able to monitor its own spending to keep its expense under a limit allocated for it. In other words, it should know its "financial status" at any point in time to be able to make an informed decision whether to continue consuming resources. Knowing in advance the cost of certain operations might be useful, but not generally feasible — for example it would be difficult to predict the cost of executing a non trivial procedure. An agent should be allowed to stop before its expenditure exceeds a certain limit [10]. In this case, it is the agent's responsibility to keep track of its own expenses, whether by explicitly arranging with the server for usage limits and warning notifications (interrupts), or by periodic checks (polling) on the resource billing. Obviously, servers cannot charge for resource usage without providing a mechanism by which agents can determine resource costs and current charges.

Resource monitoring may have to be coarse-grained: it would be disastrous if, by making the metering and billing mechanisms fine grained, the cost of these mechanisms became a significant fraction of the cost of the agent's execution.

In addition, the server must be able to monitor and perhaps inform the agent just before it has exhausted its given limit so that it will have time to either migrate to a server with less expensive resources or ask its home site for more "money." This notification is analogous to the situation with the soft CPU time and filesystem usage limits in Unix, which causes the delivery of the SIGXCPU and SIGXFSZ signals [8]. The messages sent for this purpose must be pre-defined, and the fees, if any, for such notifications should be comparatively low compared to data transfer charges.

6.5 Efficiency

While the need for an efficient agent system for the IP protection application may not appear to differ much from that of a "normal" agent system, we believe that it places greater stress on the efficiency of the system.

In general, uses of mobile software agents for IP protection will be more resource intensive than other applications. IP is of value when it is difficult to re-create, and agents are most useful when index pre-computation is difficult or impossible — otherwise standard database techniques may be applied. Large scale searches through unstructured or minimally structured data — for example, DNA database searches where no pre-computed indices exist because searches are wildly different — will necessarily be data and computationally intensive: the searching agent may have to scan through vast amounts of data and build for itself indices or other auxiliary data structures.

7 Conclusion

Intellectual property protection requires balancing usability, accessibility, and data security. In this paper, we explored an hitherto unexplored region of the design space and presented a scheme that strikes a new balance: in lieu of fine-grained metering of data accesses, we proposed using mobile agent systems for *results-based billing*, i.e., where the user's agent is charged not for accessing the data, but for sending the data (or the result of some computation thereof) back to the user. We showed that such a system would be highly flexible, easy to administer, and very secure.

To optimally support results-based billing, the importance of some existing design criteria increases and new criteria arises. We discussed the needs for *data-tight sandboxing* and greater *resource co-location* compared to "conventional" mobile agent systems. Additionally, we contrasted results-based billing with several traditional intellectual property protection schemes, and discussed their relative strengths and shortcomings.

Acknowledgments

Portions of this paper are based on an earlier survey [2] written for Keith Marzullo's operating systems course. In that paper, the authors evaluated several agent systems for their ability to protect intellectual property using results-based billing, and it provided the impetus to finally write up our ideas here; without that work, this paper would likely still remain on the back burner. We would also like to thank Keith for his invaluable input and advice on the earlier paper.

References

[1] Ross Anderson. Stretching the limits of steganography. *Lecture Notes in Computer Science*, 1174:39–48, 1996.

[2] Stephane Belmon, Chanathip Namprempre, Kenji Onishi, Sule Ozev, and John Seng. Mobile agents and the intellectual property of data. Technical Report CS98-573, Computer Science and Engineering Department, University of California at San Diego, La Jolla, CA, February 1998.

[3] Ingemar J. Cox, Joe Killian, Tom Leighton, and Talal Shamoon. A secure, robust watermark for multimedia. In *International Workshop on Information Hiding*. Newton Institute, University of Cambridge, May 1996.

[4] Colin G. Harrison, David M. Chess, and Aaron Kershenbaum. Mobile agents: Are they a good idea? *Lecture Notes in Computer Science*, 1222:25–47, 1997.

[5] Matthew Hohlfeld and Bennet S. Yee. How to migrate agents. Technical Report CS98-588, Computer Science and Engineering Department, University of California at San Diego, La Jolla, CA, June 1998.

[6] C. J. Hursch and J. L. Hursch. *SQL: The Structured Query Language*. Tab Books; ACM CR 8812-0907, 1988.

[7] B. Lampson. A note on the confinement problem. In *Communications of the ACM*, pages 613–615. ACM, October 1973.

[8] Marshall K. McKusick, Keith Bostic, and Michael J. Karels. *The Design and Implementation of the 4.4 BSD UNIX Operating System*. Addison-Wesley, 1996.

[9] Joao Meidanis and Joao Carlos Setubal. *Introduction to Computational Molecular Biology*, chapter 8. PWS Publishing Co., 1996.

[10] J. E. White. Mobile agents. In J. Bradshaw, editor, *Software Agents*. AAAI Press and MIT Press, 1996.

[11] Bennet S. Yee. *Using Secure Coprocessors*. PhD thesis, School of Computer Science, Carnegie Mellon University, May 1994. CMU-CS-94-149.

[12] Bennet S. Yee. A sanctuary for mobile agents. Technical Report CS97-537, Computer Science and Engineering Department, University of California at San Diego, La Jolla, CA, April 1997.

Ensuring the Integrity of Agent–Based Computations by Short Proofs

Ingrid Biehl[1], Bernd Meyer[2] and Susanne Wetzel [*][3]

[1] Technische Universität Darmstadt, Fachbereich Informatik, Alexanderstraße 10, D–64283 Darmstadt, Germany, email: ingi@cdc.informatik.tu-darmstadt.de
[2] Siemens Corporate Technology, Otto-Hahn-Ring 6, D–81730 München, Germany, email: bernd.meyer@mchp.siemens.de
[3] Daimler Benz AG, FTK/A, HPC 0507, D–70546 Stuttgart, Germany, email: swetzel@acm.org

Abstract. Mobile code technology is gaining growing importance for example for electronic commerce applications. To come to a widespread use of mobile agents a lot of security aspects have to be seriously considered and security problems have to be solved to convince potential users of this technology. So far, most work concerning security in the area of mobile code was done to protect hosts from malicious agents. However, in the very recent literature approaches are discussed which lead to different levels of security for the mobile agent against attacks by dishonest hosts. A central problem consists in the *integrity of computation*: In order to profit from mobile agent technology, techniques have to be used which guarantee the correctness of the results returned by a mobile agent to its originator. In this paper we explain a general approach to cope with the integrity problem by supplementing computation results with very short proofs of correctness which can a posteriori be checked by the originator of the mobile code to verify whether the result is reliable or not.

1 Introduction

Mobile code technology is considered to play a central role for example in the future development of electronic commerce. Obviously, a lot of security aspects have to be seriously considered to guarantee the reliability and trustworthiness of this technology which is essential for its widespread use.

A mobile agent consists of (static) code and its current configuration, including global data structures, stack, heap and control information as the program counter, and is expected to migrate between different hosts which offer environments in which the code can be executed. Moreover, each host may be asked

---

[*] This work was done while the author was a member of the Graduiertenkolleg Informatik at the University of Saarbrücken, a fellowship program of the DFG (Deutsche Forschungsgemeinschaft).

to deliver some input for the mobile agent. Lots of scenarios are conceivable in which the task of a mobile agent consists in travelling along a line of several hosts, collecting some input and computing step by step a result determined by these inputs.

Obviously, there are a lot of security risks involved in allowing a mobile agent migrating into one's own host machine and being executed. A lot of successful research is done to cope with this security aspect of *protecting hosts from malicious agents*. Techniques proposed are for example proof-carrying codes (see [7], [17], and [13]), packet filters (see [14]), type safe languages (see [4] and [11]) and Java archives (see [8]).

The other side of the problem consists in the necessity to protect the mobile agent from malicious hosts. The issues considered here are *privacy of computation* and the *integrity of computation*. Both areas are still in their infancies.

Privacy of computation means that the malicious host learns as little information as possible about the mobile agent's code and configuration during its execution. Well-founded research in the area of theoretical cryptography (secure multiparty computation, see for example [3], remote function evaluation with information hiding, see for example [1]) may help to solve this problem if one allows the agent to have more or less communication with its originator or if one allows families of related agents to do their job on different machines and work as (hopefully) trustworthy databases to each other. This approach is hardly considered so far, probably since it seems to be very costly.

The problem gets to be much more striking if the mobile agent is expected to do its job without interaction with its originator or other trustworthy agents. To guarantee privacy of computation in this case, a general approach is proposed by Sander and Tschudin (see [18]): The code of the mobile agent is a kind of encrypted program which can be executed on encrypted data without decryption of code and data at all. Although this idea is amazing there are a lot of problems to be solved both in theory (so far the class of programs to be protected is seriously restricted) and in practice to profit from this approach. On the other hand more practical solutions are proposed as for example by F. Hohl in [9] and [10] which use code obfuscation techniques to confuse the malicious host. The disadvantage of these techniques consists in the fact that there seems to be no way to quantify and estimate their strengths. Thus, privacy of computation is considered the most expensive and hard to reach goal among the discussed security goals for mobile agents.

Fortunately, privacy of computation is not a necessary demand for all kinds of applications of mobile agents. The problem of *integrity of computations* has to be considered to be even more critical, i.e. techniques have to be found by which the originator of a mobile agent can check at the end of the agent's journey or from time to time the correctness of the executions of the agent's code on the different hosts visited so far. Please notice that the following techniques (including our proposal) cannot prevent a malicious host from executing the agent's computation several times independently on different inputs, choosing the best result for his purposes and proving only the integrity of this computation.

In the approach of G. Vigna in [20] the host creates a trace of the agent's execution, computes some short hash value of this trace by means of a one-way hash function and sends this value in signed form to the originator. In case the originator mistrusts this host he can ask for the whole trace. Since the host signed the hash value of the trace he is urged to send the trace he hashed and signed before.

In Yee's paper "A Sanctuary for Mobile Agents" (see [22]) a similar technique, called *proof verification* is presented. The idea is that the host has to forward a proof of the correctness of the execution to the originator. Yee gives hints how to do this: Recent results in cryptography and complexity theory prove the existence of so–called *holographic proofs* for NP–languages, i.e. certificates for the correctness of some statement which can be checked by investigating only constantly many bits of the holographic proof by use of logarithmically many random bits. Apart from the fact that there is a long way from these theoretical results to practical implementations, Yee points out the following problem of this approach: The fact that the originator has to check only constantly many bits of the proof does not mean that the host has to send only constantly many bits, but the host has to send the whole long proof since the originator must be able to randomly choose the bits he wants to check. Thus, the use of these sophisticated proof strings seems not to save bandwidth.

In this paper we present a method which overcomes this problem: By means of recent results about *private information retrieval* (see [12] and [6]) we augment Yee's method such that only proofs of sublinear size have to be sent by the host to the originator to convince the originator about the correct execution of his mobile agent's code. Using the most efficient methods known in the theory of private information retrieval one can construct implementations in which the size for the correctness proofs is sublinearly resp. polylogarithmically bounded in the length of the execution trace depending on the private information retrieval method used. Thus, indeed major savings of bandwidth are possible!

2   The Model

We consider a mobile agent consisting of static information like its program code and dynamic information like its current configuration including global data structures, heap, stack and program counter. Thus the configuration may contain especially information collected while visiting some hosts. The mobile agent migrates from one host to another. The sequence of visited hosts might be determined by the originator or might be influenced by the computations done on the host machines visited so far. We suppose that the mobile agent sends after a while a message containing its computation results to its originator. It is not necessary that the mobile agent sends a message each time it finishes its execution at some host. We propose to augment the computation results with some *proof of integrity* which is a certificate for a correct execution of the agent's code on this host. (Please notice that our approach cannot prevent a malicious host from restarting the agent on different inputs and choosing the best for his purposes.) A naive proof of integrity might consist of the mobile agent's code and configuration as it arrived and the execution trace of the mobile agent. Moreover, this set of data has to be signed by the current host in order to guarantee its authenticity and the possibility to hold the host responsible for incorrect manipulations.

The disadvantage of this method consists in the length of the execution trace which might be much too large to be tolerable under bandwidth considerations. Moreover, verifying the whole execution trace is as costly for the originator as performing the execution by himself. Thus, it makes no sense to launch a complex mobile agent if the originator has to redo each computation step after the arrival of the results.

We consider hosts and originators as probabilistic (universal) Turing machines and the code of mobile agents as a polynomial-time bounded interactive program (description of a Turing machine which can be simulated by universal Turing machines). Since an agent is an interactive Turing machine it can communicate with other processes residing on the host and thus cause side effects while being executed. For this purpose the model of an interactive Turing machine possesses a tape containing the messages received from other processes (comprising all kinds of inputs), a tape with the messages sent to other processes, an unerasable coin-toss tape recording all random choices made by the Turing machine and a write-only output tape. The content of the communication tapes is expected to be not erased by the interactive Turing machine (i.e. by the mobile agent). Thus the configurations of a mobile agent contain the messages sent and received by other processes (i.e. especially they contain the inputs by the host).

Let t be the configuration at the beginning of the execution of the mobile agent on the current host and s its final configuration at the end of its execution. Then s may contain information which is not necessary or even not intended for further computations on subsequent hosts or for the originator. Thus we expect that there are two functions f and g and that the host extracts $t' = f(s)$ as the new starting configuration for the execution of the agent on the next host and $r' = g(s)$ as the information for the originator about the agent's computation result on this host. Usually t' will neither include the messages exchanged between the mobile agent and the processes residing on the host nor the list of random choices made so far by the agent. Please notice: Depending on the application r' may contain information about side-effect (as messages sent and received while communicating with other processes on the host) as well as computation results (accordingly to a functional view of the agent's behaviour).

Moreover, to protect this information r' from being read by following hosts it can be encrypted by means of the originator's (public-key) encryption scheme thus being readable only for the originator. Delivering r' instead of s to the originator permits to get rid of useless information and so to increase efficiency (for example by sending less information). On the other hand s contains the full information about inputs delivered by processes on the host. Thus sending r' instead of s to the originator guarantees that the originator learns no more information about these inputs by the host than the information which can be derived from r'. Thus the originator has to ensure by the choice of the function g, that the information contained in $g(s)$ is sufficient to learn which result (i.e. function value and side effects) was computed by the agent on this host and the host has to check whether $g(s)$ discloses no information to the originator which should be private to the host. (Of course, it depends on the specific agent whether this is possible or not and has to be supported by techniques different from those discused in this paper.)

We consider the functions f and g to be elements of the static part c of the mobile agent which includes its program code, too. Let h be a cryptographic hash function, i.e. h maps inputs of arbitrary length to outputs of constant length and it is infeasible to compute two different input values a, b with $h(a) = h(b)$ (see [16] for an introduction to cryptographic hash functions).

Then, the set $\text{TE} = \{(c, t, t', h(s), r')\}$ forms a language in NP, i.e. for each triple $(c, t, t', w', r') \in \text{TE}$ there is a proof of polynomial length which proves that there is a configuration s with $h(s) = w'$ such that the mobile agent with static part c started in t finishes its execution in configuration s with $t' = f(s)$ and $r' = g(s)$. The correctness of such a proof string can be checked in polynomial time. Examples for such a proof are the execution trace or s itself since s contains all messages sent and received by the agent as well as the agent's random choices made while execution. Thus, one can reconstruct the whole computation done by the agent given s.

We expect an agent to migrate from one host to the next as a triple (c, t', a') where c is its static part, containing the program code, f and g and some additional information q which will be explained in Section 5 (c has to be signed by the originator), t' is the starting configuration for the next host and a' is some additional, possibly encrypted information for the originator not necessary for the execution of the agent on other hosts. Especially, a' contains $c, t, t', h(s), r'$, is signed by the last host and is part of the integrity proof by this host. By including $h(s)$ this host is committed to the value s as the final configuration and so to all inputs made while executing the agent's code. Therefore, he cannot change his mind afterwards. (Committing to $h(s)$ instead of committing to s is more efficient since $h(s)$ has constant length depending only on some predetermined security factor.) This is guaranteed by the use of the cryptographic hash function h.

3 Probabilistically Checkable Proof Systems

As stated above it is much too costly to send as proof of integrity the execution trace of the mobile agent's execution. Fortunately, the task of correctness proving can be formulated as the NP language TE as explained in the last section. Thus we can use recent, very involved results from complexity theory: the theory of *probabilistically checkable proofs*. The idea is that a verifier Turing machine gets as input some x and has to check whether x belongs to some NP language L (as for example TE) or not. Since L is a NP language there is a polynomial-size certificate for x which convinces the verifier if and only if $x \in L$. In [2] it was shown that there exist certificates of some special form, sometimes called *holographic* or *transparent proofs*, such that the verifier only needs random access to the certificate string and to read constantly many randomly chosen bits of the certificate in order to check the correctness of the proof. To do so, only logarithmically many random coin tosses are needed. This is a casual formulation of the famous theorem:

Theorem 1. *(Arora, Lund, Motwani, Sudan, Szegedy, [2])*

$$NP=PCP(O(\log n), O(1))$$

This means in our application: Given $y = (c, t, t', w', r')$ and s there is a transformation which computes in polynomial time some holographic proof $p(s)$ of polynomial size in the length ℓ of the representation of s (i.e. its length is bounded by ℓ^d for some constant $d > 0$) and a verifier machine V' with the following properties:

Let k be the security parameter. (We will see below its meaning.) The verifier has to generate $O(k \log \ell)$ coin tosses $b \in \{0,1\}^{O(k \log \ell)}$ and computes a list $q = Q(\ell, b)$ of j ($j \in O(k)$) bit positions in $p(s)$ he wants to see. Notice, that this list depends only on b and ℓ. Then, if $y \in$ TE the verifier will accept y with probability 1 if he gets the bit values in $p(s)$ at the positions in q. If $y \notin$ TE no matter which string p' is presented by the malicious host to cheat the verifier, the verifier will detect the betrayal with probability $1 - 1/2^k$. Thus, the security parameter k determines the error probability for the verifier to be cheated in case $y \notin$ TE.

This idea is sketched by Yee in [22], too. Since the verifier, i.e. the originator of the mobile agent needs random access to all bits in $p(s)$, Yee points out that the host has to send the whole string $p(s)$ and thus this method does not save bandwidth compared to sending s itself. Its advantage consists in the faster verification process for the originator given $p(s)$. We extend this construction in the following and come to a method by which the host has to send only a string of sublinear length in ℓ that is a string of length $\ell^{1/d}$ or even $\log^d \ell$ for some constant d which means major savings both of bandwidth and time needed for verification.

4 Private Information Retrieval Techniques

To improve the approach by Yee we benefit from some very recent results about efficient *private information retrieval*. In [12] and [6] techniques are presented which allow a user of a database with t information blocks $p_1, \ldots, p_t$ to get the information p_i while keeping the choice of the index i secret from the database.

Suppose that each information block consists of one bit. Then the user has to compute some kind of encrypted database query q, called *hidden (database) query* in the following, and to send q to the database to get p_i. The database has to compute in polynomial time an answer string $z = F(q, p_1, \ldots, p_t)$ accordingly to some predetermined function F and sends z to the user. In this string, called *hidden answer* in the sequel, the value p_i is encrypted. One can interpret z as an encryption of p_i which hides the index i from the database and which can be decrypted by the user to p_i. The length of the queries and the answer string is sublinear resp. polylogarithmic in the size of the database content depending on the method one uses:

Theorem 2. *(Kushilevitz, Ostrovsky, [12])*
Let $c \in \mathbb{R}_{>0}$ be some arbitrary constant. If the quadratic residue problem is infeasible then there is a system for private information retrieval which uses query and answer strings of length $O(t^c)$ where t is the size of the database (in case the information blocks are single bit blocks).

Theorem 3. *(Cachin, Stadler, [6])*
If factorization (of integers of some special form, see [6]) is infeasible there is a constant $c \in \mathbb{N}$ and a system for private information retrieval which uses query and answer strings of length $O(\log^c(t))$ where t is the size of the database (in case the information blocks are single bit blocks).

5 Construction of Sublinear Proofs of Integrity

In our application consider the database to be the host, the database content to be the holographic proof $p(s)$ of size ℓ^d, and the user to be the originator of the mobile agent. Thus, the originator can encode in advance which bits of the holographic proof he would like to check, encrypt the corresponding indices as a set of constantly many hidden database queries and send these along with the mobile agent. The host now computes the corresponding answers to the hidden queries applied on $p(s)$ and sends these answer strings to the originator which can decrypt them in polynomial time and use these constantly many bits as stated above to check the correctness of $p(s)$ and thus the correctness of the execution trace of the mobile agent on this host.

We explain the steps to be done in the following in more details: Let k be the security parameter.

Initialisation of the mobile agent

The originator chooses j $(= O(k))$ bit positions, he wants to check in the (holographic) proofs of integrity to be created by the hosts. Let q_i $(i = 1, \ldots, j)$ be the hidden queries according to the chosen private information retrieval protocol and q be the set of all q_i. The mobile agent's description is supplemented by these hidden queries. We consider it to be included in the static part c of the mobile agent which is signed by the originator. Then the agent is sent to the first host as (c, t, a) with "empty" starting configuration t and empty string a.

Please notice that the hidden database query strings created by the originator before starting the mobile agent can be reused for all hosts. Thus the number of visited hosts has not to be known in advance.

Computation by hosts

The host gets (c, t, a) and has to execute the code of the mobile agent starting in t. Let s be the final configuration. Then the host does the following steps:

1. He computes $t' = f(s)$ and $r' = g(s)$ and a holographic proof $p(s)$ for $(c, t, t', h(s), r') \in$ TE.
2. The host computes the hidden answers to the hidden queries q in the static part c and gets constantly many strings of short size (sublinear resp. polylogarithmic depending on the used private information retrieval method) as a short proof of integrity z.
3. The host signs and (possibly) encrypts with the encryption scheme of the originator $(c, t, a, t', h(s), r', z)$ and sets a' to this value. Then he signs and sends (c, t', a') to the next host or to the originator.

To guarantee the authenticity of the data sent from host to host they have to be signed by each host before the mobile agents migrates to the next host. Thus, at the end of its journey the originator has to check the correctness and authenticity of the computations done in reverse order, i.e. he starts with checking the correctness of the last host's computations.

We illustrate the modification of the agent's description caused by some host in the following figure:

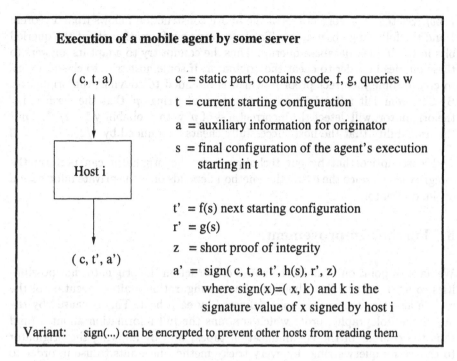

Execution of a mobile agent by some server

(c, t, a)

c = static part, contains code, f, g, queries w

t = current starting configuration

a = auxiliary information for originator

s = final configuration of the agent's execution starting in t

Host i

t' = f(s) next starting configuration

r' = g(s)

(c, t', a')

z = short proof of integrity

a' = sign(c, t, a, t', h(s), r', z)

where sign(x)=(x, k) and k is the signature value of x signed by host i

Variant: sign(...) can be encrypted to prevent other hosts from reading them

Finally, we have to explain the computations done by the originator to extract the result of the mobile agent's computations and to check the integrity and authenticity of this result.

Result extraction and integrity check by the originator

The originator collects the values r' in a and recursively checks the computation results computed while visiting host $H_1, \dots, H_t$. He starts with the last host H_t: He checks the authenticity of the last result (i.e. he verifies H_t's signature) and the short proof of integrity by extracting the queried bits of z and applying the verification algorithm derived from the proof of Theorem 1 to these bits. Moreover, he has to check whether each host correctly started the agent in the starting configuration t sent to him. This has to be done repeatedly for all hosts. If some check fails, the host under consideration deviated from the stipulated procedure.

We summarize the above construction in the following theorem.

Theorem 4. *If the quadratic residue problem resp. factorization (of integers of some special form, see [6]) is infeasible, each mobile agent system can be converted into a system which guarantees the integrity of computations done on untrustworthy servers which causes sublinear resp. polylogarithmic overhead compared to the unprotected system.*

Proof. Sketch: The correctness of the above construction follows from Theorem 1 and the following observation: The host gets no information about the queried bits in the hidden database queries. Thus, he cannot try to adapt its answers to these queries in order to cheat the originator. If some host tries to cheat, he has to create some incorrect proof p' which is intended to convince the originator. By Theorem 1 it follows for all incorrect proof strings p' that the verifier, i.e. the originator, will detect the incorrectness of p' with probability $1 - 1/2^k$. Thus the probability that the host successfully cheats is bounded by $1/2^k$. □

Please notice that by our technique only the originator can perform the integrity check since the extraction method depends on some private information of the originator.

6 Further Improvements

We have to point out that in the above construction the originator has possibilities to learn information about the final configuration s after execution of the mobile agent and thus the input delivered by each host. This is caused by the use of the holographic proof which contains the full information about s (and thus the content of the communication tapes) and by allowing the originator to choose its query strings by every tricky method he wants to use in order to catch information about s. The latter involves for example the possibility for the originator to learn relations between bits of the database entries instead of learning bits themselves. One can see this by looking into the details of the private information retrieval construction (see [12] and [6]). This can be prevented by techniques from the theory of zero-knowledge proofs: The originator has to send a non-interactive zero-knowledge proof along with his queries which convinces the hosts that the query strings are of the correct form. In case the query strings are of polylogarithmic size the non-interactive zero-knowledge proof for their correctness is of polylogarithmic size, too (see for example [5]). The prominent property of a non-interactive zero-knowledge proof consists in being a certificate which convinces the host about the correctness of the queries without giving him information especially about the indices which are encrypted in the queries. Nevertheless, even correctly queried bits of $p(s)$ may contain information. To prevent this seems to be a difficult problem.

Please notice that the size of a grows considerably from host to host. Using hash values of c, t, t' instead of these values themselves and extending the holographic proof appropriately can improve this.

Another problem consists in the fact that a malicious host can erase results (i.e. parts of the a string) computed formerly on previously visited hosts. Thus the originator never gets these results. To cope with this problem there are several possibilities: Either the mobile agent follows some predetermined route and the originator can check whether results computed in the correct order are included and correctly signed by these hosts or the mobile agent sends to the originator a short message signed by the current host each time the mobile agent migrates to the next host.

7 Discussion and Conclusion

Integrity of computation is a central requirement in secure mobile agent technology. As proposed by Yee in [22] the use of holographic proofs or similar techniques may be a valuable approach for the construction of efficient proofs of integrity. We overcome a major problem in Yee's construction which leads to prohibitive long proof strings by presenting a method to come to proofs of integrity of sublinear resp. polylogarithmic length. Our construction and analysis follows the methodology of cryptographic research and is not based on heuristics. The security of our method depends only on generally accepted cryptographic assumptions. Our result proves that there exist short proofs of correct execution of a mobile agent by a host where short means that they are of size sublinear resp. polylogarithmic in the size of the mobile agent's running time. To extend a mobile agent's program with the necessary control information, i.e. the query strings, creates costs of size sublinear resp. polylogarithmic in the size of the original mobile agent's running time.

Unfortunately, following the literature about the construction of holographic proofs will lead to very costly constructions. Nevertheless, we suppose that there are more direct constructions for holographic proofs for concrete examples of mobile agents and thus practical implementations of the above approach. Indeed, techniques from the area of efficient checking of polynomials and programs which underly the construction of holographic proofs might be a good starting point for the search for efficient practical implementations.

Acknowledgements
The first author would like to thank Fritz Hohl for bringing the problem of malicious hosts in mobile computing to her attention. Moreover, the authors thank two anonymous reviewers for accurate proof-reading and very helpful comments concerning possible attacks and the necessity to clarify the computation model.

References

1. M. Abadi, J. Feigenbaum, J. Kilian, *On Hiding Information from an Oracle*, Journal of Computer and System Science, vol. 39, n. 1, pp. 21–50, 1989.
2. S. Arora, C. Lund, R. Motwani, M. Sudan, M. Szegedy, *Proof Verification and Hardness of Approximation Problems*, Proc. of the 33rd IEEE FOCS, pp. 14–23, 1992.
3. D. Beaver, *Secure Multiparty Computation Protocols and Zero-Knowledge Proof Systems Tolerating a Faulty Minority*, Journal of Cryptology, Springer, pp. 75–122, 1991.

4. B. N. Bershad, S. Savage, P. Pardyak, E. G. Sirer, M. E. Fiuczynski, D. Becker, C. Chambers, S. Eggers, *Extensibility, Safety and Performance in the Spin Operating System*, Proc. of the 15th Symposium on Operating Systems Principles, 1995.

5. M. Blum, P. Feldman, S. Micali, *Non-Interactive Zero-Knowledge and Its Application (Extended Abstract)*, Proc. of the 20th ACM STOC, pp. 103–112, 1988.

6. C. Cachin, M. Stadler, *Efficient Private Information Retrieval and Oblivious Transfer*, unpublished, 1997.

7. J. Feigenbaum, P. Lee, *Trust Management and Proof-Carrying Code in Secure Mobile-Code Applications*, DARPA Workshop on Foundations for Secure Mobile Code, Monterey, CA, USA, 1997, Position Paper.

8. J. S. Fritzinger, M. Müller, *Java Security*, httpwwwjavasoftcom securitywhitepaperps, 1996.

9. F. Hohl, *An Approach to Solve the Problem of Malicious Hosts*, Universität Stuttgart, Fakultät Informatik, Fakultätsbericht Nr. 1997/03.

10. F. Hohl, *Time Limited Blackbox Security: Protecting Mobile Agents From Malicious Hosts*, in: Giovanni Vigna (Ed.), *Mobile Agents and Security*, Lecture Notes in Computer Science, Springer, 1997.

11. W. C. Hsieh, M. E. Fiuczynski, C. Garrett, D. Becker, B. N. Bershad, *Language Support for Extensible Operating Systems*, Proc. of the Workshop on Compiler Support for System Software, 1996.

12. E. Kushilevitz, R. Ostrovsky, *Replication is Not Needed: Single Database, Computationally-Private Information Retrieval*, Proc. of the 29th ACM STOC, 1997.

13. P. Lee, G. Necula, *Research on Proof-Carrying Code For Mobile-Code Security*, DARPA Workshop on Foundations for Secure Mobile Code, Monterey, CA, USA, 1997, Position Paper.

14. S. McCanne, V. Jacobson, *The bsd Packet Filter: A New Architecture for User-level Packet Capture*, Proc. of the USENIX Technical Conference, pp. 259–269, 1993.

15. C. Meadows, *Detecting Attacks on Mobile Agents*, DARPA Workshop on Foundations for Secure Mobile Code, Monterey, CA, USA, 1997, Position Paper.

16. A. J. Menezes, P. C. van Oorschot, S. A. Vanstone, *Handbook of Applied Cryptography*, CRC Press Inc., 1997.

17. G. Necula, *Proof Carrying Code*, Proc. of the 24th Annual Symposium on Principles of Programming Languages, 1997.

18. T. Sander, C. T. Tschudin, *Protecting Mobile Agents Against Malicious Hosts*, in: Giovanni Vigna (Ed.), *Mobile Agents and Security*, Lecture Notes in Computer Science, Springer, 1997.

19. A. Polishchuk, D. A. Spielman, *Nearly-linear Size Holographic Proofs*, Proc. of the 26th ACM STOC, 1994.

20. G. Vigna, *Protecting Mobile Agents through Tracing*, to appear in the Proc. of the ECOOP Workshop on Mobile Object Systems'97.

21. R. Wahbe, S. Lucco, T. E. Anderson, S. L. Graham, *Efficient Software-based Fault Isolation*, Proc. ACM SIGCOMM Symposium 1996, 1996.

22. B. S. Yee, *A Sanctuary for Mobile Agents*, DARPA Workshop on Foundations for Secure Mobile Code, Monterey, CA, USA, 1997, Position Paper.

Protecting the Computation Results
of Free-Roaming Agents

G. Karjoth, N. Asokan, C. Gülcü

IBM Research Division
Zurich Research Laboratory
{gka|aso|cgu}zurich.ibm.com

Abstract. When mobile agents do comparison shopping for their owners, they are subject to attacks of malicious hosts executing the agents. We present a family of protocols that protect the computation results established by free-roaming mobile agents. Our protocols enable the owner of the agent to detect upon its return whether a visited host has maliciously altered the state of the agent, thus providing forward integrity and truncation resilience. In an environment without public-key infrastructure, the protocols are based only on a secret hash chain. With a public-key infrastructure, the protocols also guarantee non-repudiability.

1 Introduction

Mobile agents are software programs that live in computer networks, performing their computations and moving from host to host as necessary to fulfill their goals. In [8], White envisions mobile agents that make and keep appointments for their owners; provide useful information such as television schedules, traffic conditions, restaurant menus, and stock market results, and help them carry out financial transactions, from booking theater tickets, to ordering flowers, to buying and selling stock.

Electronic commerce appears to be a particularly interesting application for agents (BargainFinder, ShopBot [3], Kasbah [1], Bazaar, etc.). BargainFinder, for example, is an intelligent agent that comparison shops among Internet stores to find the best price for a compact disc, and thus has demonstrated the potential impact of agents on virtual retailing. Although all of the above agents are stationary, comparison shopping has been proposed for mobile agents as well. The principal scheme for comparison shopping, described for example in [8, 5, 7], is the following:

1. The agent owner sets up the agent with a description of the good he wishes to purchase.
2. The agent travels from the owner's site to the directory in the electronic marketplace, where it obtains the locations of all retailers that offer the good.
3. The agent visits the electronic store-front of each retailer in turn. Each store-front is a different location in the electronic marketplace. The agent gives the description of the good to the store-front and is quoted a price.

4. The agent eventually returns to its owner's location and delivers a report of its findings.

However, mobile agents are exposed to a very serious security threat: malicious hosts might endanger agents passing by. In terms of the above scenario, servers might have an incentive to subvert the computation of a visiting agent, for example by removing cheaper offers. Although denial-of-service attacks cannot be prevented, the following policy might be a strong incentive even for a malicious server to let the agent pass: *In order to submit his own offer a merchant must at least also preserve the offers of all merchants the agent has visited before it arrived at the merchant's server.* However, to enforce this policy it is necessary to be able to tell whether an agent has been changed at any server on its itinerary.

In [9], Yee proposed schemes using cryptographic hashing and digital signatures that offer practical solutions to protect the integrity of results collected by mobile agents. In particular, Yee defines the notion of *forward integrity*, which states if a mobile agent visits a sequence of servers $S_1, S_2, \ldots, S_n$, and the first malicious server is S_k, then none of the partial results generated at servers S_i, where $i < k$, can be forged. In this paper, we incorporate and extend Yee's work. We define a set of security properties that are more general and thus address a conspiracy of servers. Our protocols prevent a shop from being able to modify offers collected later by the agent, including its own offer. There are also fewer possibilities to truncate a chain of collected offers without being detectable by the agent originator. The comparison shopping application is used throughout the paper. In the rest of this paper we omit the directory and simply assume that an agent finds its way to the shops of interest.

The paper is organized as follows. In Section 2, we describe our trust model, give the definitions and notation used in the paper, and formalize our goals. Section 3 describes two protocols usable in an environment where a public-key infrastructure exists. In Section 4, we describe two protocols that assume only that the originator's public key is known. Finally, conclusions are drawn in Section 5.

2 Trust Model

The purpose of the system is to let agents travel from server to server, collecting intermediate results. We do not care how much work had been done on a server prior to finding the result and whether the computation ran correctly as long as the computation is independent of any input from previous servers. Comparison shopping is an example application, as the intermediate result, the price, being independent of previous price quotes.[1] The primary goal, however, is to guarantee that the partial results collected by the agent and returned to the originator are not undetectably tampered with.

---

[1] Offers of previous shops are kept confidential in order not to influence future price quotes. We do not consider the possibility that a server may learn about the prices of competitors by querying them directly.

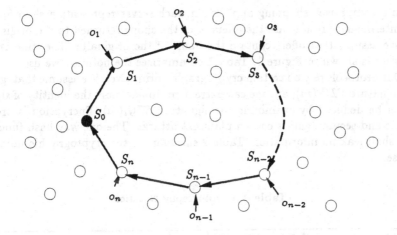

Fig. 1. Agent itinerary to collect offers o_1 to o_n

In the case of a fixed itinerary, i.e. at agent departure all servers are known as well as the order in which the agent will visit them, there are mechanisms to ensure that all intermediate results will be received and no result will have been tampered with. However, the following classes of itineraries make it more difficult to preserve the integrity of the intermediate results:

- the nodes to be visited are predetermined but the agent is free to select the next node;
- all nodes are known but the agent is free to decide which m out of n nodes to visit and in what order;
- the agent might visit nodes not known at departure.

In this paper we address in particular the latter two classes; the itinerary of the agent is not (completely) fixed when the agent leaves the originator's site. This means that any place that will host the agent can determine the next hop or hops of the agent. The actual decision process is beyond the scope of this paper.

Table 1. Model Notation

$S_0 = S_{n+1}$	Originator.
$S_i, 1 \leq i \leq n$	Shops.
o_0	A token issued by S_0 to identify the agent instance on return.
$o_i, 1 \leq i \leq n$	Offer from S_i.
$O_i, 1 \leq i \leq n$	Encapsulated offer (o_i with protective encapsulation) from S_i.
$h_i, 1 \leq i \leq n$	Integrity check value associated with O_i
$O_0, O_1, O_2, \ldots, O_n$	The chain of encapsulated offers from shops $S_1, S_2, \ldots, S_n$.

In a comparison shopping application, each server represents a shop S_i and the intermediate results are the offers o_i of the shops returned to the originator S_0. We assume that offers contain the name of the originator. The itinerary of an agent is shown in Figure 1. Table 1 summarizes the notation we use.

Our protocols rely on certain cryptographic primitives. We assume that, given the signature $SIG_i(m)$, anyone can extract m. In addition, the identity of signer S_i can be deduced by examining the signature $SIG_i(m)$. Encryption is probabilistic and secure against chosen plaintext attacks. The one-way hash function used shall leak no information. Table 2 summarizes the cryptographic notation we use.

Table 2. Cryptography Notation

r_i	A nonce generated by S_i.
$\mathcal{ENC}_0(m)$	Message m encrypted with the public encryption key of S_0.
$SIG_i(m)$	Signature of S_i on a message m.
$\mathcal{H}(m)$	A one-way, collision-free hash function (e.g., SHA-1[4]).
$\mathcal{MAC}_k(m)$	Message Authentication Code generated with secret k.
$[m]$	A message m sent via a confidential channel.
$Alice \rightarrow Bob$: m	Alice sending message m to Bob.

A chain $O_0, O_1, O_2, \ldots, O_n$ is an ordered sequence of encapsulated offers such that each entry of the chain depends on the previous and/or the next members. This dependency is specified by a *chaining relation*. We say that a chain is *valid at* O_k if the chaining relation holds at each link up to and including O_k. A chain is *valid* if the chain is valid at its last element. If defined properly, any modification of the chain, including deletion or insertion of elements, will invalidate the link for all members dependent on the altered element.

If two or more malicious servers conspire, they might control all data established between the first and the last conspirator on the itinerary. The same situation arises when an agent visits the same shop twice. We say that two servers conspire if they exchange secrets used in building the chaining relation.

2.1 Attacks

After capturing an agent holding a chain of offers $O_0, O_1, \ldots, O_m$, the attacker might (1) *modify* existing encapsulated offers by changing the purported sender S_i or by altering the offer o_i for any i, $1 \leq i \leq m$; (2) *insert* offers that would not have been included without the intervention of the attacker; or (3) *delete* any of the existing offers. The particular attack where all offers after the ith offer are deleted is called *truncation* at i. The combined attack where the attacker simultaneously truncates at i and appends fake offers is referred to as *growing a fake stem* at i.

As an agent might visit the same shop twice or as shops might conspire, a malicious shop might modify an agent before, at, or after its own node. This might lead to a stem (add), truncation (delete), or other misrouted itinerary.

2.2 Security Properties

Below we define a number of properties that are defined with respect to an attacker that captured a mobile agent holding a chain of encapsulated offers $O_0, O_1, \ldots, O_m$. Thus, the agent has visited an undetermined number m of shops, $m \leq n$; some shops, but not shop S_m, may conspire with the attacker, possibly being shop S_{m+1}. Let i range over $1, \ldots, m$.

- *Data Confidentiality:* Only the originator can extract the offer o_i of shop S_i.
- *Non-repudiability:* Shop S_i cannot repudiate its offer o_i once it has been received by originator S_0.
- *Forward Privacy:* None of the identities of the creator of offer o_i can be extracted.
- *Strong Forward Integrity:* None of the encapsulated offers O_k, where $k < m$, can be modified.
- *Publicly Verifiable Forward Integrity:* Anyone can verify the offer o_i by checking whether the chain is valid at O_i. Thus, any intermediate server or the agent itself can verify the partial results already collected by the agent and abort the agent's itinerary if necessary.
- *Insertion resilience:* No offer can be inserted at i unless explicitly allowed; i.e. the attacker is actually shop S_{m+1}.
- *Truncation Resilience:* The chain can only be truncated at i if shop S_i colludes with the attacker.

By relaxing Yee's assumption of the "honest prefix" of the agent's route, our definition ensures that it is impossible to forge an offer, even when it was made by oneself or by a colluding server. Therefore, we will also refer to Yee's definition as weak forward integrity. Correspondingly, we speak of weak truncation resilience when a chain can be truncated at i if shop S_j, where $j < i$, colludes with the attacker.

Note that forward integrity is defined with respect to O_m, assuming that O_m cannot be changed or removed. Therefore, strong forward integrity does not imply resistance against a truncation attack at O_k with $k < m$. Moreover, truncation resilience does not preclude a denial-of-service attack in which all offers are removed (i.e. $k = 0$), but it would be detected by originator S_0.

3 Per-server Digital Signatures

We assume that a public-key infrastructure exists. Each entity, be it the originator or a shop, has a distinguished name and a public signature verification key bound to the name via a certificate issued by a certification authority. There is a directory service from which certificates can be retrieved.

For clarification and reference, we formalize Yee's original per-server digital signature protocol [9] where each shop signs its offer using its own key, so the result is non-repudiable and unforgeable. Optionally, the offer may be encrypted by the originator's public key to ensure data confidentiality.

- *Encapsulated Offer*
    - $O_i = \mathcal{SIG}_i(\mathcal{ENC}_0(o_i)),\ 0 \leq i \leq n$
- *Protocol*
    - $S_i \rightarrow S_{i+1}: \{O_k \mid 1 \leq k \leq i\},\ 0 \leq i \leq n$

However, to detect the removal of offers, Yee's protocol requires that the agent originator knows at least the length of the agent's itinerary. Furthermore, if a server catches the agent again later, it is able to modify its own previous result.

The two protocols presented next provide strong forward integrity and truncation resilience. Protocol P1 allows anyone to authenticate the shops involved, whereas protocol P2 hides the identity of the involved shops to everybody except the originator.

3.1 Publicly Verifiable Chained Digital Signature Protocol (P1)

Protocol P1 extends Yee's per-server digital signature protocol [9] with a hash chain that links the offer of the previous shop with the identity of the next shop. This disables a shop from modifying its own offer later, and thus strong forward integrity is achieved.

Description

- *Encapsulated Offer*:
    - $O_i = \mathcal{SIG}_i(\mathcal{ENC}_0(o_i, r_i), h_i),\ 0 \leq i \leq n$
- *Chaining Relation*
    - $h_0 = \mathcal{H}(r_0, S_1)$
    - $h_i = \mathcal{H}(O_{i-1}, S_{i+1}),\ 1 \leq i \leq n$
- *Protocol*
    - $S_i \rightarrow S_{i+1}: \{O_k \mid 0 \leq k \leq i\},\ 0 \leq i \leq n$

To begin the protocol, the originator S_0 picks a random number r_0. Next, it computes the hash value h_0, the anchor value of the chaining relation, by applying $\mathcal{H}()$ over r_0 and the identity of the first shop S_1. Then it encrypts the token o_0 and the random value r_0 with its own public key. Finally, it constructs a dummy encapsulated offer O_0 by signing the encryption and h_0, which is sent to the first shop S_1.

When the agent arrives at shop S_i, it contains the set of previously collected encapsulated offers, including encapsulated offer O_{i-1} from which the next hash value h_i can be computed. In general, an encapsulated offer o_i $(i > 0)$ contains the following two items:

- the offer o_i probabilistically encrypted so that only S_0 can retrieve it, and

- a hash of the previous offer O_{i-1} concatenated with the identity of the next shop S_{i+1}.

The second item serves two purposes. First, it links the previous offer with the current offer: O_{i-1} cannot be modified without modifying O_i as well. In fact, even shop S_{i-1} cannot modify its own offer later without invalidating the chain at O_i. Second, the inclusion of the identity of the next shop guarantees that no one other than S_{i+1} can append the next offer. Figure 2 illustrates the protocol, where the dashed lines show the linkage of information.

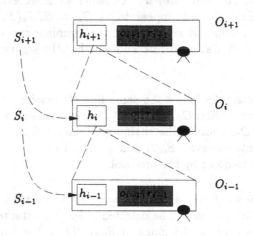

Fig. 2. Chaining in P1

Goals

Data Confidentiality. If the encryption scheme is secure, no one other than S_0 can decrypt $\mathcal{ENC}_0(o_i, r_i)$ to extract o_i. As the encryption is probabilistic, no one other than S_0 and S_i will get any[2] information about o_i given $\mathcal{ENC}_0(o_i, r_0)$.

Non-repudiability. The encapsulated offer O_i contains a signature by shop S_i. If the signature scheme is secure, S_i cannot repudiate O_i.

Strong Forward Integrity. Suppose the attacker leaves O_m intact but changes the kth ($k < m$) offer. Assume that $k = m - 1$ and that the attacker replaced O_{m-1}

---

[2] We assume that the encryption scheme is secure against chosen plaintext attacks. We also include the random factor r_i in the encryption. Both together imply that even when an attacker knows one or more encryptions of a given plaintext, he has no better chance of recognizing yet another encryption of the *same* plaintext than he would have had without those encryptions.

by O'_{m-1}. As O_m was not changed, the chaining relationship at m must still hold. O_m is of the form $\mathcal{SIG}_m(\mathcal{ENC}_0(o_m, r_m), h_m)$, where $h_m = \mathcal{H}(O_{m-1}, S_{m+1})$. In order for the chaining relation to hold, $\mathcal{H}(O'_{m-1}, S_{m+1}) = \mathcal{H}(O_{m-1}, S_{m+1})$. But this violates our assumption that the hash function $\mathcal{H}()$ is collision-free. Hence as long as $\mathcal{H}()$ is collision-free, it is not possible to modify O_{m-1} without modifying O_m and still maintain the chaining relation at O_m. Similarly, it is not possible to modify any O_k, $k < m - 1$ without modifying O_{k+1} and still maintain the chaining relation at O_{k+1}. The property follows by induction.

Publicly Verifiable Forward Integrity. Consider someone examining the chain $O_0, O_1, \ldots, O_i$. Each O_k will appear to be $O_k = \mathcal{SIG}_k(X_k, h_k)$, where only X_k is an uninterpretable bit string. Thus the examiner can verify whether the chaining relation holds at each link and whether the signature on each O_i is valid.

Insertion Resilience. We follow the same line of reasoning as above. Given a chain of encapsulated offers $O_0, O_1, \ldots, O_m$, no one can insert an offer anywhere between O_1 and O_m because the chaining relation will not be respected after the insertion point. However, S_{m+1} can insert an offer after S_m because it is explicitly allowed to do so by the protocol.

Truncation Resilience. Given a chain of encapsulated offers $O_0, O_1, \ldots, O_m$, any truncation at k with $k < m$ will be detected unless the attacker is able to insert simultaneously an offer in the name of S_{k+1}. Thus, the truncation resilience property is fulfilled. However, because any shop in the chain can truncate all offers following its own, the protocol allows the attacker to insert other fake offers before the agent is sent back to the originator.

3.2 Chained Digital Signature Protocol with Forward Privacy (P2)

By changing the order of signing and encrypting an offer, it is possible to hide the identity of the shops that provided offers.

Description

- *Encapsulated Offer:*
  - $O_i = \mathcal{ENC}_0(\mathcal{SIG}_i(o_i), r_i), h_i,\ 0 \le i \le n$
- *Chaining Relation*
  - $h_0 = \mathcal{H}(r_0, S_1)$
  - $h_i = \mathcal{H}(O_{i-1}, r_i, S_{i+1}),\ 1 \le i \le n$
- *Protocol*
  - $S_i \to S_{i+1}: \{O_k \mid 0 \le k \le i\}$

Thus, the shop signature is encrypted and can only be revealed by the originator.

Goals

Instead of publicly verifiable forward integrity, protocol P2 achieves forward privacy. The other properties of protocol P1 are still satisfied. The proofs in Section 3.1 apply to these cases with no modifications.

Forward Privacy. If the encryption scheme is secure, no one other than S_0 can decrypt a sealed offer O_i. As the components of O_i (encryption and hashing) are randomized, they will leak no information about their contents, and will resist dictionary attacks as well. Thus, no one other than originator S_0 can determine the creator of the sealed offer.

4   Hash Chains

Now we assume that there is no public-key infrastructure. However, each shop knows the public key of the originator. Let us first examine why this assumption is realistic. An example scenario is when a big company solicits bids from small subcontractors to carry out a project (invitation of tenders). All subcontractors know the public key of the big company. There is no need for a non-repudiable contract offer. The big company can examine all the offers collected by the agent, pick the offer(s) of interest, and contact the subcontractors directly.

Yee's Partial Result Authentication Code demonstrates the authenticity of an intermediate agent state or partial result that resulted from having run on a server [9]. With each server, there is an associated secret key used to compute an authentication tag on this data. After a tag is computed, the agent/server takes care to erase the secret key associated with the current server prior to migrating to the next server. For efficiency, Yee uses a secure hash function to generate the secret keys from a single secret h_0.

- *Encapsulated Offer*
  - $O_i = o_i, \mathcal{MAC}_{h_i}(o_i),\ 0 \leq i \leq n$
- *Chaining Relation*
  - $h_{i+1} = \mathcal{H}(h_i),\ 1 \leq i \leq n$
- *Protocol*
  - $S_i \rightarrow S_{i+1}\colon \{O_j \mid 0 \leq j \leq i\}, [h_{i+1}],\ 0 \leq i \leq n$

The erasure step ensures weak forward integrity. The protocol also satifies insertion and weak truncation resilience. If selected, data confidentiality and forward privacy can be realized.

4.1   Chained MAC Protocol (P3)

Protocol P3 extends Yee's message authentication code protocol. Each shop S_i generates a random number r_i and encrypts it together with the offer and the identifier of the next shop under the originator's public key. The value r_i, being part of the encapsulated offer, is an input to the computation of the next hash key h_{i+1} and thus prevents shops from modifying their own offers later. More importantly, it prevents a shop S_i from being able to modify the offers of shop S_j, where $j > i$.

The protocol requires that each pair of shops be connected via a confidential channel.

Description

- *Encapsulated Offer*:
  - $O_i = \mathcal{ENC}_0(r_i, o_i, S_{i+1}),\ 0 \leq i \leq n$
- *Chaining Relation*:
  - $h_1 = \mathcal{ENC}_0(r_0, o_0, S_1)$
  - $h_{i+1} = \mathcal{H}(h_i, r_i, o_i, S_{i+1}),\ 1 \leq i \leq n$
- *Protocol*:
  - $S_i \to S_{i+1}\colon \{O_k \mid 0 \leq k \leq i\}, [h_{i+1}],\ 0 \leq i \leq n$

Figure 3 depicts the chaining procedure for this protocol. The term h_i serves to link all the previous encapsulated offers to the current offer. The term r_i prevents a shop $S_k (k < i)$ from being able to replace any encapsulated offer O_j that comes *after* O_i $(j > i)$ in the chain because S_k does not know (and cannot predict) the chaining factor h_j that must be embedded into O_j.

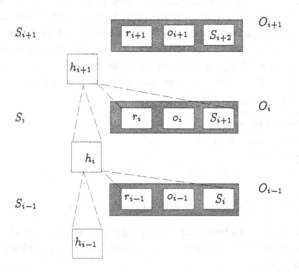

Fig. 3. Chaining in P3

Embedding of S_{i+1} provides no authentication as in the previous protocols. It can merely help S_0 make a sanity check. If h_i is embedded in the encrypted offer O_i, the originator can determine at which shop the chaining relation broke.

Goals

The proof for insertion and truncation resilience is identical to that in Section 3.1.

Data Confidentiality. If the encryption scheme is secure, no one other than originator S_0 can decrypt $O_i = \mathcal{ENC}_0(r_i, o_i, S_{i+1})$ to extract offer o_i. The random component r_i renders the encryption probabilistic. Therefore, given O_i, no one other than S_0 can infer any information about o_i.

Strong Forward Integrity. Assume that an attacker can leave O_m, h_{m+1} (i.e., the quantities added to the state of the agent by S_m) intact and still change O_k, $0 \leq k < m$ without being detected by S_0. Assume that $k = m - 1$ and that the attacker replaced O_{m-1} by O'_{m-1}. We can assume that O'_{m-1} is of the form $\mathcal{ENC}_0(r'_i, o'_i, S_{i+1})$, otherwise S_0 will reject the chain as malformed, thereby violating our assumption. As h_{m+1} and O_m were not changed, the chaining relationship at m must still hold. Suppose $\mathcal{H}(h'_{m-1}, r'_{m-1}, o'_{m-1}, S_m)$ evaluates to h'_m. As the chaining relationship at O_m must be preserved, it must be the case that $\mathcal{H}(h'_m, r_m, o_m, S_{m+1}) = h_{m+1}$. But the attacker (who is by definition not the same as S_m) does not know r_m and o_m. Therefore, the only way he can satisfy the above relationship is to make sure that $h'_m = h_m$. This implies that $\mathcal{H}(h'_{m-1}, r'_{m-1}, o'_{m-1}, S_m) = \mathcal{H}(h_{m-1}, r_{m-1}, o_{m-1}, S_m)$. But this violates our assumption that the hash function $\mathcal{H}()$ is collision-free. Hence as long as $\mathcal{H}()$ is collision-free, it is not possible to modify O_{m-1} without modifying O_m, h_{m+1} and still maintain the chaining relation at O_m. Similarly, it is not possible to modify any O_k, $k < m - 1$ without modifying O_{k+1}, h_{k+1} and still maintain the chaining relation at O_{k+1}. The property follows by induction.

Forward Privacy. If the encryption scheme is secure, no one other than S_0 can decrypt a given sealed offer O_i. The random salt r_i makes O_i a randomized encryption, thereby ensuring that it will leak no information about its contents. Thus, no one other than originator S_0 can determine the creator of the given sealed offer.

4.2 Publicly Verifiable Chained Signatures (P4)

Yee also introduces a scheme that makes PRACs publicly verifiable, i.e. any intermediate server not sharing the secret key with the originator can itself verify the partial results already collected by the agent. For this purpose, each server provides its successor with a secret signature function and certifies the corresponding verification predicate. With the received signature/verification function pair, a server signs its partial result and certifies a new verification function to be used by the next server. The originator provides the agent with the initial secret signature function and a certified verification predicate. Each server destroys the signature function received but adds the new verification function generated itself to the list of certified verification predicates carried by the agent.

With the above scheme, the originator must not precalculate the signature function/verification pairs, and the list of certified verification functions grows linearly with the number of shops visited. One-time digital signatures as well as public-key digital signatures can be used to implement the digital signature system. Let $SIG_{\overline{y_i}}(m)$ denote the (one-time) signature of shop S_i on a message m generated with the secret key $\overline{y_i}$.

Protocol P4 uses only the public key of the originator to set up the signature chain. The originator includes the initial public key of the signature chain in the encapsulated offer O_0 signed with its public key-based digital signature. The corresponding secret key $\overline{y_1}$ is then sent together with the encapsulated offer to shop S_1. Each shop S_i generates a secret/public key pair $\overline{y_{i+1}}/y_{i+1}$ and includes the public key y_{i+1} in the encapsulated offer O_i. The encapsulated offer is signed with the secret key $\overline{y_i}$ received from the previous shop.

Description

- Encapsulated Offer:
  - $O_0 = SIG_0(\mathcal{ENC}_0(o_0, r_0), h_0, y_1)$
  - $O_i = SIG_{\overline{y_i}}(\mathcal{ENC}_0(o_i, r_i), h_i, y_{i+1}), 1 \leq i \leq n$
- Chaining Relation
  - $h_0 = \mathcal{H}(r_0, S_1)$
  - $h_i = \mathcal{H}(O_{i-1}, S_{i+1}), 1 \leq i \leq n$
- Protocol
  - $S_i \rightarrow S_{i+1}: \{O_k \mid 0 \leq k \leq i\}, [\overline{y_{i+1}}], 0 \leq i \leq n$

Applying above signature chain to protocol P2, it is even feasible to achieve forward privacy together with publicly verifiable forward integrity.

5 Conclusion

We developed a number of protocols that protect the results established by free-roaming mobile agents. All protocols, even if relying only on a secret hash chain and the public key of the originator, achieve strong forward integrity, truncation resilience, and data confidentiality. In addition, publicly verifiable forward integrity and forward privacy can be achieved. With a public-key infrastructure in place, non-repudiability of offers is added. By having disabled a shop from modifying even its own offer later, our protocols tolerate collusion among shops. Application areas of these protocols include comparison shopping, bidding, and network routing [2].

Our definition of forward integrity has the constraint that the attacker does not change the last element O_m in the chain of encapsulated offers. Lifting this restriction, only protocols where the originator can authenticate shop offers still satisfy the strengthened definition. Otherwise, the attacker has always the possibility to truncate the chain and to grow a fake stem.

Truncation is the most difficult problem to tackle in preserving the state of the offer chains. To achieve even stronger resistance against truncation, we see the following three possibilities:

1. Whenever an agent obtains addresses of new shops to be visited, these names could be stored in the agent, for example by embedding the partially precomputed itinerary $S_{i+1}, S_{i+2}, \ldots, S_{i+k}$ into O_i. Thus it would be possible to check after returning home whether the agent had been at all shops listed. Of course, this implies that a shop must also express the fact that it does not desire or is not able to give an offer.

2. Originator S_0 broadcasts or publishes an itinerary after the fact, allowing victim shops to complain [6].

3. If the forward or next-hop function is verifiable, the originator could recompute the itinerary.

If shops were anonymous, it would be more difficult for them to conspire. For example, assume that the agent first visits a trader that provides it with a list of anonymous shops. Whenever the agent moves to another shop, it reshuffles the collected data to make it impossible to track the agent. Even conspiring shops would not be able to identify each other or the moving agent.

Acknowledgments

The authors thank Michael Steiner, Gene Tsudik, and Michael Waidner for their many helpful suggestions.

References

[1] A. Chavez and P. Maes. Kasbah: An agent marketplace for buying and selling goods. In *First International Conference on the Practical Application of Intelligent Agents and Multi-Agent Technology*, pages 75–90, 1996.

[2] G. Di Caro and M. Dorigo. Mobile agents for adaptive routing. In *31st Hawaii International Conference on System Science (HICSS-31)*, Big Island of Hawaii, January 6–9,1998.

[3] B. Doorenbos, O. Etzioni, and D. Weld. A scalable comparison-shopping agent for the world-wide web. In *AGENTS-97*, 1997.

[4] NIST National Institute of Standards and Technology (Computer Systems Laboratory). Secure hash standard. Federal Information Processing Standards Publication FIPS PUB 180-1, April 1995.

[5] D. Rus, R. Gray, and D. Kotz. Transportable information agents. In M. Huhns and M. Singh, editors, *Readings in Agents*. Morgan Kaufmann Publishers, 1997.

[6] G. Tsudik. Personal communication.

[7] G. Vigna. Protecting mobile agents through tracing. In *Third Workshop on Mobile Object Systems*, June 1997.

[8] J.E. White. Mobile agents. In J. Bradshaw, editor, *Software Agents*. AAAI Press and MIT Press, 1996.

[9] B.S. Yee. A sanctuary for mobile agents. Technical Report CS97-537, UC San Diego, Department of Computer Science and Engineering, April 1997.

Wide-Area Languages

Luca Cardelli

Microsoft Research
EMail:luca@luca.demon.co.uk

1 Abstract

I discuss the implications of programmable wide-area networks on programming language features and design. Wide-area networks (WANs) provide a fundamentally different computational infrastructure than local-area networks (LANs). As with the switch from mainframes to LANs, the semantic difference of WANs will eventually be reflected in programming language features. The spread of LANs in the 70's and 80's produced client-server computing and distributed object-oriented programming. The spread of WANs demands new advances including, for example, mobile secure computing.

2 About the Speaker

Luca Cardelli was born in Montecatini Terme, Italy, studied at the University of Pisa (until 1979), and has a Ph.D. in computer science from the University of Edinburgh (1982). He worked at Bell Labs, Murray Hill, from 1982 to 1985, and at Digital Equipment Corporation, Systems Research Center in Palo Alto, from 1985 to 1997, before assuming his current position at Microsoft Research Ltd, in Cambridge UK.

His main interests are in theory of programming languages, for applications to language design, semantics, and implementation. He implemented the first compiler for ML (the most popular typed functional language) and one of the earliest direct-manipulation user-interface editors. He was a member of the Modula-3 design committee, and has designed a few experimental languages, of which the latest is Obliq: a distributed higher-order language. His more protracted research activity has been in establishing the semantic and type-theoretic foundations of object-oriented languages, resulting in the recent book "A Theory of Objects" with Martin Abadi. Currently, he is interested in global and mobile computation.

Agent-User Communications:
Requests, Results, Interaction

Anselm Lingnau and Oswald Drobnik

Fachbereich Informatik (ABVS),
Johann-Wolfgang-Goethe-Universität
60054 Frankfurt
{lingnau, drobnik}@tm.informatik.uni-frankfurt.de

Abstract. Communication between mobile agents and their users is an interesting but largely unresearched topic with important applications. We investigate the various types of interaction required and propose a versatile, easy-to-implement and secure WWW-based method to allow mobile agents to interact with arbitrary users.

1 Introduction

1.1 Why Communicate?

Mobile agents are programs that do things on behalf of people. They must know what to do, where to go and what resources to use. They must be able to interact with other agents (or even people) elsewhere to obtain the information they need to carry out their missions. They need to be able to access databases, WWW servers and other sources of information. Finally, they must be able to return the results of their work to their owners. In short, mobile agents need to communicate.

Agent-to-agent communication has been a "hot topic" for a while. It is surprising that its counterpart, the communication between mobile agents and people (agent "owners" and others) has not received nearly as much study. In this paper, we examine requirements and methods for communication between mobile agents and people, and outline a prototypical implementation based on the ffMAIN infrastructure and common World-Wide Web technology.

1.2 Related Work

A reasonable amount of research has gone into agent communication. While much of this pertains to topics which are not strictly within the scope of this paper, some of the results must be mentioned here. The AI community has been working on communicating agents for quite some time (see, e. g., [1]) and this has even led to standards efforts in the area of agent communication languages (KQML, [2]), standardized representation formats (KIF, [3]) and ontologies. Much of this work is based on Austin's speech act theory [4]. As far as mobile agents are concerned, communication between agents is often reduced to inter-agent method calls [5, 6]; an area which, although offering flexibility and speed, is fraught with naming and security problems. We have proposed an alternate approach involving the decoupling of different agents through a shared communication medium called the *information space* [7] and demonstrated its usability both for various kinds of agent interaction patterns [8] and the integration of different types of mobile agent frameworks [9].

By comparison, the area of agent-to-user communication has remained virtually untilled at least from a mobile-agent point of view. Here as well, the AI community has laid some groundwork through the study of "helper"-type agents (see, e.g., [10, 11]) that aid a user in performing certain tasks involving communication. In a mobile-agents context, security considerations are much more important than in a classical AI approach. Telescript [12] presumes an interaction facility based on a system that is essentially closed and centrally controlled; if mobile agents are to be considered a technology for general adoption such control cannot be taken for granted.

2 Types of Communication

2.1 An Overview

From \ To	User	Agent
User	outside scope of this paper	− Initial mission − Control (status requests, additional info, ...) − Query replies
Agent	− Results (intermediate, final) − Queries − Error messages	− Publication of facts/services − Queries/requests for services − Replies/results

Table 1. Various types of mobile-agent communication

In a mobile-agent system, four different kinds of communication among users and agents can be considered (see Table 1). Obviously, communication between users is not of prime importance in a paper about mobile agents, and thus will not be discussed here. On the other hand, agent-agent communication has been the subject of various papers. Therefore it will only be mentioned in passing to say that every mobile-agent infrastructure contains some means for agents to communicate among one another. After all, the point of a system based on mobile agents is to have the agents interact on behalf of their owners. The "interesting" types of interactions from the point of view of this paper include user-to-agent and agent-to-user communication.

2.2 The Initial Mission

Before a mobile agent can begin to carry out a task, the agent's "owner" – the person on whose behalf the agent is to work – must specify exactly what the agent is supposed to do, its "initial mission".

Of course, part of the initial mission is already specified through the particular agent that the user selects for the task. There is a trade-off between *general-purpose agents* which are suitable for a wide variety of tasks and *special-purpose agents* that are geared towards performing a particular task; in general, the former will need more configuration prior to every mission, while the latter may get by with very little setup because its field of application is already quite narrow. For example, an agent performing a literature search could be written as a very general program accepting as configuration inputs the field of endeavour to be searched, the names of authors of interest and a number of relevant keywords which are likely to occur in the titles of papers. On the other hand, one could have a search agent which is preconfigured to search biochemistry journals and only needs an area such as "recombinant DNA" to retrieve everything published on the topic during the last three months. Evidently, both types of agents have their merits; the general-purpose agents can support many diverse types of queries, while the specialized agents perform a particular query more efficiently, both from the point of view of the user (who does not need to spend much time setting up the agent) and from a systems point of view, since it does not need to carry around extraneous code which is unnecessary for the currently ongoing query.

Besides the specification of an agent's task, the initial mission also describes various kinds of *resources* which are available to the mobile agent during its mission. For instance, the agent's owner may want to specify a "search horizon" or a maximal lifetime for the agent on the grounds of cost (an agent that traverses half the Internet over a period of weeks is likely to incur huge costs – at least once access to databases etc. is supposed to be paid for, which is not an unlikely prospect) or usefulness of the result (it may be important to obtain a result within three hours, so if the agent has not carried out its mission within this period it might as well stop altogether). Another resource which is likely to gain importance in the future is "money" (either "real" money – such as electronic cash – or Monopoly-type money used, e.g., to pay for memory and/or CPU time consumed). The route, or set of hosts to be visited, can be specified either explicitly, or the agent can be given some leeway to select "interesting" places of its own accord; there is also a possibility of using *semantic routers* that suggest destinations to mobile agents based on their actual mission [13].

Finally, the user must specify how he wants the agent to return the result of its task. Should the agent confine itself to returning a single end result, or should it report its progress by sending intermediate results to the owner at suitable points in its lifetime? We will examine the question of how to actually return results later in this paper.

2.3 Controlling an Agent

Once a mobile agent has begun to carry out its mission, its owner may want to monitor its status or interact with the agent in various ways. In the first instance, an agent owner should be able to query the agent infrastructure about the current status of the agent, e. g., its current whereabouts, its execution status (is it running, waiting for some resource or has it crashed?) and the amount of resources such as remaining CPU time or "money". If feasible, such a status report could also include an indication of how far the agent has progressed in the solution of its task. Another important operation which should be available to the agent owner is to "kill" the agent if it is no longer needed. This is usually straightforward to implement. More difficult, but very useful when debugging, is the ability to obtain a picture of the internal state of an agent (a "brain dump") in order to locate errors in the programming. In some cases it may be possible to "freeze" an agent while it is in transit between two hosts and inspect the externalized representation of the agent's state using appropriate tools; in other cases, languages such as Tcl which contain sophisticated introspection mechanisms make it feasible to obtain a comprehensive picture of an agent's state at any time.

If the agent infrastructure uses a method of limiting the resources available to an agent, a desirable feature would be for an agent that is running low to send a request for a larger allowance to its owner before falling into "stasis". The owner can then decide whether he wants to concur with the request, add to the relevant quota of resources and reactivate the agent.

All these operations can be supported by the agent infrastructure without detailed knowledge of or support by the mobile agent in question. Of course, there are other possible types of interaction which involve cooperation by the author of the agent code. For instance, it may be feasible to amend an agent's mission while the agent is underway, e. g., because the owner has found out something interesting in the meantime that is relevant to the ongoing task.

2.4 Returning Results

Another interesting topic is how the results of a mobile agent's mission are to be returned to the agent's owner. We can distinguish between methods that are realized "internally" – within the agent infrastructure – and methods that rely on transport media and software tools which are not part of the actual agent infrastructure. In this context, it is important to consider one of the major advantages of mobile agents, namely that they can go about their tasks while their owner is busy doing something else. In a networked environment involving,

e. g., PDAs with wireless links, the owner of an agent may not even be on-line at any given time, and so any scheme must involve the possibility of storing a result until the owner sees fit to look at it.

An obvious way of returning the result of a query would be for the mobile agent to come back to the place of its origin, carrying the result with it. The agent infrastructure then needs some way of presenting this result (stored within the agent) to the agent owner. While this method makes it possible to include the perusal of results with the rest of the agent user interface, it is inefficient if a big agent is supposed to return a very small result (part of the advantage of mobile agents, namely the reduced network load obtained by carrying out most of the interaction locally at the remote end, may be neutralized). Also, the approach does not allow for intermediate results other than by the agent returning to its "home" several times while its mission is still being carried out. These problems could partly be alleviated by allowing the agent to dispatch separate (small) result-carrying agents instead of returning "in person". Another "internal" method could have the agent send back results instead for storage and presentation within the agent infrastructure, through the user interface otherwise used for submitting and controlling agents.

A possible problem with these approaches is the fact that the agent system must be "misused" to perform a task that has been approached from lots of different angles, namely to store some information and present it to the user in a convenient fashion. It would be inconvenient to have to reinvent much of the functionality already existing in different contexts for the purposes of a mobile agent infrastructure. Therefore it is interesting to examine alternative ways of returning results outside the agent infrastructure itself.

One obvious approach to take is to have the mobile agent send results by way of electronic mail. This is a very well-established and convenient method of bringing things to the notice of people, and it works fine even if the destination party is not available for direct communication. Another advantage in the case of small machines such as PDAs is that they are very likely to feature e-mail software since this is what many PDA users would want to have, anyway. Therefore the software demands on the part of an agent owner are not too big. An obvious disadvantage of the approach is that usually e-mail is dealt with through a different user interface than the one used for sending and controlling agents, namely the e-mail reader. If this is perceived as a problem, one could institute a "mail filter" in order to divert agent-related mail out of the generic mailbox into an area accessible to the agent software, and have the agent UI present these messages instead. This brings the e-mail approach more in line with the "internal" methods discussed above, while keeping the advantages of e-mail transport over a (different) method of returning results via the agent infrastructure. This saves some overhead on the part of additional protocol suites.

The final method to be mentioned here, which combines advantages from both areas discussed above, involves use of the World-Wide Web [14] for returning results. One obvious plus is that most users will want WWW access (in addition to agent services) anyway, and so the necessary infrastructure such as a browser and HTTP protocol stack are likely to exist even on PDAs. It also allows the agent system to be tightly integrated with other WWW-based services—in fact, in an infrastructure such as ffMAIN, a WWW browser can serve as the user interface for all of the agent services provided by the system. Furthermore, there is very active research going on in the areas of authentication and encryption for WWW contents. The results arising from this are directly applicable to WWW-based agent communication, and thus there is the very real possibility of obtaining, e. g., authenticated and confidential access to WWW-presented agent results essentially for free by virtue of software already integrated in many WWW browsers. With dedicated agent UI software, the required code would need to be adapted and deployed as part of the infrastructure.

2.5 Communicating with Other People

The final consideration is whether agents should be allowed to communicate with users other than their owners. This would open up possible application areas such as interactive questionnaires, voting, appointment scheduling, workflow management or even advertising, which presently need the support of special user interface software. A method for allowing this in a convenient way will be discussed in the next section.

This broader view of agent-user communication involves important security considerations. In general, mobile agents need to be prevented from damaging their hosts through, say, formatting a disk, and from obtaining information they are not entitled to have (such as a system's password file). If agent-to-arbitrary-user communication is allowed, the security mechanisms must extend to keeping mobile agents from annoying users or spying on their actions (which in the case of several popular GUI systems is altogether quite easy to do once a program controls a window on the user's display). The best solution appears to be not to allow the mobile agent to interact with the user's GUI directly in the first place.

3 Implementing WWW-Based Agent-User Communication

3.1 The ffMAIN Agent Infrastructure

At the Johann Wolfgang Goethe-Universität we have developed an experimental mobile agent infrastructure called ffMAIN [7]. This infrastructure relies on *agent servers* which accept, execute and forward mobile agents written in different languages such as Tcl [15] or Perl [16]. The current canonical agent server is written in Tcl and runs as an extension of a general-purpose HTTP server implemented by Brent Welch and Stephen Uhler [17]. HTTP is used as the protocol basis for the submission and control of mobile agents as well as for agent communication. Figure 1 shows the architecture of ffMAIN.

One of the key advantages of ffMAIN is the fact that it makes use of ubiquitous World-Wide Web software to let users submit and control mobile agents. This

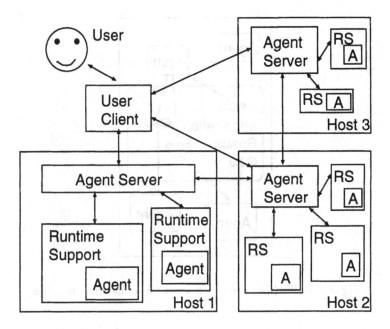

Fig. 1. The architecture of the ffMAIN agent infrastructure

brings mobile agent technology to mobile computers or even hand-held PDAs with a wireless link to the Internet. The prototypical implementation of agent-user communication explained in this section exploits this fact to make mobile agents even more appealing under the circumstances.

3.2 The Information Space

The basic abstraction for agent-agent communication in ffMAIN is the *information space*. This conceptual device (Figure 2) is based on a parallelization concept called Linda [18]. Each agent server maintains its own information space which is accessible to all mobile agents executing under the control of that server. In this information space, agents can deposit triples (k, a, v) called *items*, where k is the *key* (or "name") of the item, a is an *access control list* and v is the *value* of the item—in the general case just an unstructured sequence of bytes. Through the agent server, mobile agents can atomically store and read individual items, and they can also retrieve an item while removing it from the information space. Additionally, a mobile agent can also "subscribe" to a key or range of keys to be notified asynchronously if the items in question change. This capability is not strictly necessary but makes it easier to implement communication paradigms such as RPC in an efficient manner.

The agent server also allows access to the information space from non-agents (e. g., a user's WWW browser). This is subject to suitable authentication schemes

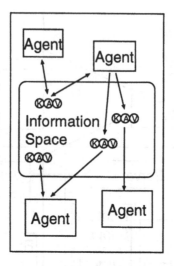

Fig. 2. The ffMAIN information space for agent communication

such as "Basic" HTTP authentication[1]. In this context, the stipulation that an item's value is an unstructured byte sequence is not strong enough to be versatile. Therefore it is possible to associate a MIME type (such as `text/html`, see [19]) with a value when the item in question is written. This MIME type is then forwarded to the browser when the item is accessed, and allows the browser to render the item's value in an appropriate form.

As far as enabling WWW-based agent-user communication is concerned, this has several important advantages: First of all, agents can present information through any appropriate technique available to WWW browsers. Besides HTML, it is possible to use inline graphics or even Java applets. It is trivial to construct links between different information space items. An agent can deposit an HTML form that a user can fill in using his favourite WWW browser and put into the information space for the agent's subsequent perusal. Finally, this mechanism is available to agents written in any programming language that ffMAIN supports.

3.3 An "Inbox" Agent

An interesting partial problem in agent-user communication is how a person finds out that there is an agent waiting to contact him or her. While it would be tedious to require somebody to do periodic checks on the off-chance that this might be the case, it would be annoying or even dangerous if arbitrary agents were allowed to interact with users when- and however they wanted. Some form of mediation is evidently called for.

---

[1] It would be straightforward to use a stronger authentication/encryption scheme such as SSL, but this has not yet been implemented

In our prototype, we have decided to interpose an entity called an *inbox agent* between the user and incoming mobile agents. This is a stationary agent which is started by the user, and which is in charge of all inquiries by mobile agents. If some mobile agent wants to interact with the user, it must apply to the inbox agent first, giving the URL that it wants to present. The inbox agent disposes of the mobile agent's request according to the user's preferences and the properties of the requesting agent. For example, the user may want to keep a "blacklist" of mobile agents (or mobile agent senders) who have been bothering her with unsolicited advertising, and have her inbox agent summarily turn these agents away. On the other hand, if the daily agent collecting the lunch orders comes around, she may want to have the inbox agent notify her immediately. In its inactive state, our implementation of a simple inbox agent displays a "letterbox" icon similar to the one used by e-mail notification programs such as "xbiff". When a mobile agent has asked for a user notification and is not refused outright, the flag on the letterbox is raised and a bell sounds. The user can then click on the icon to view a list of outstanding requests by mobile agents. Given a suitably sophisticated WWW browser, it is possible to click on any of the requests in the list in order to look at the WWW page in question.

There is considerable scope here for inbox agents to be customized according to each user's preferences. In fact, such an agent might constitute an "intelligent agent" in the AI sense of the word (see [10]) and be able to observe the user's disposal of incoming agent requests in order to take the correct course of action when it is acting independently on the user's behalf. On a less sophisticated note, it is of course possible to make the agent configurable through the same information-space based mechanism that is used for communication with arbitrary agents as detailed earlier on.

Another legitimate question in this context is why one would want to have a separate inbox agent for notifications if the same function might more efficiently be performed by the agent server. After all, the agent server handles all accesses to the information space and could easily and (probably) efficiently take care of the user notification as well. One possible answer to this is that a separate inbox agent is more easily customized according to the user's preferences or replaced if its methods do not suit altogether. Furthermore, it allows for a separation of concerns between the server and the inbox agent. It is quite possible that many agent servers will not have to deal with user notifications at all (e. g., servers for agent-enabled databases, digital libraries or large WWW sites) and therefore it does not seem necessary to burden the general agent server with the notification code.

3.4 An Agent-User Communication Scenario

Figure 3 shows a typical scenario for a mobile agent communicating with an arbitrary user. Assume that the mobile agent (lower left) wants the user (upper left) to fill in an HTML form (e. g., a document which is part of a work-flow). It places the form in the information space (step 1) as the value of an information space item with type `text/html`. Then the mobile agent makes a request to the

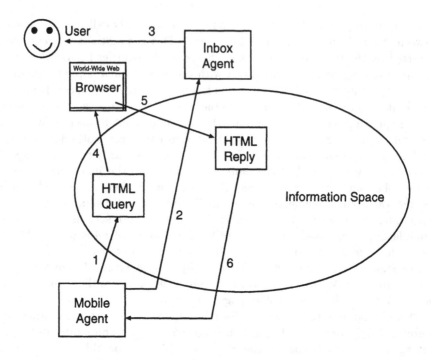

Fig. 3. A typical scenario for agent-to-user communication

inbox agent using the canonical protocol [8] (step 2) and citing the key of the item written in step 1. to have it notify the user on the mobile agent's behalf. The inbox agent disposes of this request according to the preferences of the user; in this example the request is forwarded to the user (step 3) together with the URL of the HTML form, which can be constructed from its information space key. The user can then retrieve the form (step 4) and peruse it in his WWW browser. The filled-in form is placed in the information space (step 5) where the mobile agent can pick it up (step 6).

At first glance, this method may seem unnecessarily roundabout. However, its advantage is that the user is protected from obnoxious mobile agents because all interaction is channeled through the information space. It is not possible for an arbitrary mobile agent to interact directly with the user. The interaction takes place *off-line* in the sense that the user need not be available at the moment the communication request comes in—it would perfectly possible for the inbox agent to send a notification by e-mail in this case, and for the mobile agent to wait until the filled-in form finally comes back. On the other hand, the mobile agent may well decide after a while that further delays are unwanted, and it can withdraw both the form and the notification request.

In ffMAIN, high-level agent support such as the one provided by its Tcl run-time environment makes communicating with users according to the scheme

```
set user {bill}                      ;# Name of the target user
set myID [agent attrib Local-ID]     ;# the mobile agent's own ID
set htmlForm {...<FORM ACTION="/info/$myID:reply">...}
proc replyCallback {key} { ... process the returned FORM ... }

# Put the HTML form into the information space
agent put $myID:form $htmlForm -contentType text/html

# Arrange for 'replyCallback' to be invoked when form comes back
agent subscribe $myID:reply replyCallback

# Find and notify $user's inbox agent
set inboxAgentID [agent find -info inbox-$user/1.0]
set reply [agent request $inboxAgentID $myID:form]
# 'reply' is now one of 'Forwarded', 'Refused', ... according to
# the disposal of the notification by the inbox agent
```

Fig. 4. Excerpt from a mobile agent (written in Tcl) that communicates with user bill. The "agent ..." commands are part of the ffMAIN runtime support.

outlined above fairly convenient. Figure 4 shows an excerpt from a program that implements the mobile agent discussed in the scenario.

3.5 A Case for Standardized Communication Support

As we have seen, the agent infrastructure which supports the communication patterns does not make assumptions about the specific programming languages or protocols used or the contents of a communication. However, the implementation of agents and services based on this approach can be considerably simplified when the language-specific agent runtime environment provides library support, e.g., for higher-level communication constructs. Common requests such as "extension of lifetime" could be provided as part of the local infrastructure, as could support for a KQML front-end that agents could use. In general, if agents can rely on standardized communication libraries which are provided by the infrastructure, the amount of code that must be moved can be decreased considerably. Of course there is a trade-off involved between the flexibility gained by being able to include arbitrary code in mobile agents and the efficiency obtainable by using local libraries. This is an interesting topic that merits further research.

4 Conclusions and Future Work

We have discussed the importance of allowing, within a mobile agent infrastructure, a convenient means of communication between agents and users. One reasonable approach which is both straightforward to implement and to use as well as quite secure makes use of the World-Wide Web and its associated software to provide this communication. This approach has been implemented within the ffMAIN agent infrastructure, where it supports expressive communication for mobile agents written in various languages.

By off-loading the actual interaction to a WWW browser (a piece of software which is virtually guaranteed to exist on any reasonable system) mobile agents have no need for direct access to a user's graphics display. This prevents snooping as well as denial-of-service attacks – e.g., by constantly opening up lots of large windows –, whose aversion would otherwise require extra mechanism within the graphics toolkit or display infrastructure. In a similar fashion, an "inbox agent" makes it unnecessary for mobile agents to have an immediate means of obtaining a users' attention. Security mechanisms researched in the context of the World-Wide Web are directly applicable to the agent system and provide well-understood ways of authentication and encryption.

In the area of user-to-agent communications, various questions remain open. While the mechanism discussed in this paper would be adequate for the initial configuration of an agent from the point of view of the agent infrastructure (including specification of the task it is to perform), it is by no means clear that there are no more efficient or convenient methods to do this. There is considerable room for research in exactly *how* an agent's task is to be specified.

Finally, within the context of the method discussed here, it is obvious that there needs to be a way of limiting, e.g., the amount of space an agent's data may occupy in the information space and the number of requests for user notification an agent may have open simultaneously. This is necessary to prevent several classes of denial-of-service attacks that a hostile agent could mount on the communication mechanism itself. This problem also needs further investigation.

References

1. Shoham, Y.: Agent-oriented programming. Artificial Intelligence 60 (1993) 51–92
2. Finin, T., Fritzson, R., McKay, D., McEntire, R.: KQML as an Agent Communication Language. In: Proc. of the 3rd International Conference on Information and Knowledge Management (CIKM '94). ACM Press (Nov. 1994)
3. Genesereth, M. R., Fikes, R. E., et al.: Knowledge Interchange Format Version 3 Reference Manual. Logic-92-1, Stanford University Logic Group (Jan. 1992)
4. Austin, J. L.: How to Do Things With Words. Oxford University Press (1962)
5. Straßer, M., Baumann, J., Hohl, F.: Mole–A Java-Based Mobile Agent System. In: Proc. ECOOP'96 Workshop on Mobile Object Systems (Oct. 1996)
6. White, J. E.: Telescript Technology: An Introduction to the Language. General Magic White Paper GM-M-TSWP3-0495-V1, General Magic, Inc., 420 North Mary Avenue, Sunnyvale, CA 94086 (1995)
7. Lingnau, A., Drobnik, O., Dömel, P.: An HTTP-based Infrastructure for Mobile Agents. In: Fourth International World Wide Web Conference Proceedings, no. 1 in World Wide Web Journal. W3C, O'Reilly and Associates, Sebastopol, CA (Dec. 1995) 461–471
8. Lingnau, A., Drobnik, O.: Making Mobile Agents Communicate: A Flexible Approach. In: The First Annual Conference on Emerging Technologies and Applications in Communications (etaCOM'96). IEEE (May 1996) 180–183

9. Dömel, P., Lingnau, A., Drobnik, O.: Mobile Agent Interaction in Heterogeneous Environments. In: Proc. of the 1st International Workshop on Mobile Agents (MA'97), Lecture Notes in Computer Science. Springer (Jan. 1997) 136–148
10. Genesereth, M. R., Ketchpel, S. P.: Software Agents. Commun. ACM 37 (1994) 48–53, 147
11. Kautz, H., Milewski, A., Selman, B.: Agent Amplified Communication. In: AAAI-95 Spring Symposium on Information Gathering from Heterogeneous, Distributed Environments (Mar. 1995)
12. White, J. E.: Telescript Technology: The Foundation for the Electronic Marketplace. General Magic White Paper GM-M-TSWP1-1293-V1, General Magic, Inc., 2465 Latham Street, Mountain View, CA 94040 (1994)
13. Moritz, T.: Entwurf und Implementierung eines Agenten für inhaltsgesteuerte Zielsuche. Diplomarbeit, Johann Wolfgang Goethe-Universität Frankfurt am Main (Jan. 1997)
14. Berners-Lee, T., Cailliau, R., Luotonen, A., Frystyk Nielsen, H., Secret, A.: The World-Wide Web. Commun. ACM 37 (1994) 76–82
15. Ousterhout, J. K.: Tcl and the Tk Toolkit. Addison-Wesley, Reading, MA (1994)
16. Wall, L., Schwartz, R. L.: Programming Perl. O'Reilly & Associates, Sebastopol, CA (1990)
17. Welch, B., Uhler, S.: Web Enabling Applications. In: Proc. 5th Annual Tcl/Tk Workshop. USENIX (Jul. 1997)
18. Gelernter, D.: Generative Communication in Linda. ACM Trans. Prog. Lang. Syst. 7 (1985) 80–112
19. Freed, N., Borenstein, N.: Multipurpose Internet Mail Extensions (MIME) Part Two: Media Types. RFC 2046, Network Working Group (Nov. 1996)

A Plug-in Architecture Providing Dynamic Negotiation Capabilities for Mobile Agents

M.T. Tu, F. Griffel, M. Merz, and W. Lamersdorf

Distributed Systems Group, Computer Science Department,
University of Hamburg
Vogt–Kölln–Str. 30, D–22527 Hamburg
{tu, griffel, merz, lamersd}@informatik.uni-hamburg.de
http://vsys-www.informatik.uni-hamburg.de

Abstract. The diversity of research and development work on agent technology has led to a strong distinction between *mobile* and *intelligent* agents. This paper presents an architecture aiming at providing a step towards the *integration* of these two aspects, concretely by providing an approach of dynamically embedding *negotiation capabilities* into mobile agents. In particular, the requirements for enabling automated negotiations including negotiation protocols and strategies, a plug-in component architecture for realizing such requirements on mobile agents, and the design of negotiation support building blocks as components of this architecture are presented.

1 Introduction

In recent years, the development of agent technology has drawn particularly great attention of people working in very different fields of computer science such as distributed systems, artificial intelligence, system management and electronic commerce. This at a first glance quite surprising fact is essentially based on the appealing general supposition that agents are *autonomous* entities which can perform tasks assigned to them independently, i.e. completely without user intervention. Thus, even if there is no universally accepted definition of software agents, autonomy is commonly considered one of the most important features of agenthood. Due to this growing interest, the agent programming paradigm has made considerable progress and is going to be well established, especially through agent systems based on Java and WWW technologies such as [7, 12, 17, 9] etc..

However, a consequence of the diversity of research and development work on agent technology is that a strong distinction between "mobile" and "intelligent agents" has emerged which can also be regarded as a distinction between *location autonomy* and *decision autonomy*. This simple de-facto classification of agents at present seems unfortunately inaccurate because the features of mobility and intelligence are obviously by no means mutually exclusive or even only contrary. And although the integration of these two qualities is certainly desired in order to face the challenging requirements of *realistic* agent application fields such as mobile/asynchronous computing, information retrieval, electronic commerce etc., there have been up to now very few concrete approaches in this direction. This paper presents an architecture aiming at providing a step towards such an integration, concretely by providing an approach of dynamically embedding negotiation capabilities into mobile agents. Before going into this approach, some general requirements arising from the integration problem should be mentioned: One of the main difficulties a practical approach has to deal with is that the incorporation of "intelligent" capabilities into mobile software agents can become very expensive because reasoning mechanisms, for instance, are usually much more complex than a few "go" and "select" commands coded in simple agents roaming the network nowadays, i.e. the agents can become literally too "fat" and consequently, their mobility is reduced. This problem is even more severe if the concrete purpose or task of the agent is not known ahead (at compilation time), in which case either many agents for different tasks or very general-purpose agents, which are likely even bigger in size, have to be built. In order to cope with this problem, some important requirements have to be imposed on a corresponding system design:

- Role-specific functionality: A mobile agent should not be loaded with every kind of available functionality or intelligent capability at the same time (as it is usually the case with complex AI systems or human beings), but should rather carry with him only the functionality required to fill out the actual *role(s)* assigned to him at a given time, for instance "seller" or "notary" in the context of electronic commerce.
- On-the-fly loading: Moreover, the functionality of an agent should be able to be loaded "on demand", i.e. at (or short before) the moment it is really needed.
- Flexible configuration: The agent's functionality should also be flexibly and dynamically configurable so that it can be reused in many similar, but differently constrained situations without having to replace its corresponding implementation.

In order to satisfy these requirements, a flexible *plug-in* component architecture has been designed and is being implemented in the DYNAMICS project at University of Hamburg. It is used as the framework to dynamically embed the negotiation capabilities for mobile agents presented in this paper, the rest of which is organized as follows: In section 2, the requirements for enabling automatic negotiations, especially those concerning negotiation protocols and strategies, are identified. Section 3 then outlines the plug-in architecture of DYNAMICS. Next, the building blocks to support automated negotiations are described in section 4. Implementation issues are discussed in section 5 and finally, the paper is concluded by section 6.

2 Requirements for Enabling Automated Negotiations

One of the most obvious motivations for developing agent technology is to provide agents which are able to perform commercial transactions on behalf of the people launching them (see, e.g., [4]). Using mobile agents in electronic commerce is attractive for several reasons: disburdening people from routine transactions, handling (gathering, selecting) great amounts of information in a given time, supporting mobile device users by asynchronous communication etc. (see [1]). Such agents would be even more useful if they could autonomously negotiate a deal in case the default assumptions of the participants about the desired transaction do not exactly match, much analogous to the way people carry out business negotiations. Indeed, with negotiating agents, the possible benefit of negotiations, i.e. finding the best possible options for a transaction, would likely be employed much more frequently because of the low cost the agents raise in comparison to the cost of human negotiators. However, in order to enable software agents to carry out automatic negotiations, the process of negotiation must first be formally specified by a respective *protocol* and, for each agent, a *strategy* of producing the proper negotiation actions needs to be implemented. In the following, we will discuss the requirements for formal negotiation protocols and strategies.

2.1 Negotiation Protocols

To make software agents interact in a meaningful way with the purpose of reaching an agreement, a set of rules must be defined which constrain the possible interactions between the participating agents. The formal specification of the rules applying to the interactions during a negotiation is usually called a negotiation *protocol*. Even in most conventional negotiations, a set of more or less explicit rules has to be followed to maintain a meaningful course of the negotiation process. More explicit rules apply, for example, in case of an auction or an advertised bidding, less explicit ones in case of a car purchase. Concerning automated negotiations, the protocol has to be precise and extensive enough to cope with all situations that may occur during a negotiation, even with those that are not expected in human interactions. Furthermore, it has been shown that the design of negotiation protocols may have quite sophisticated influence on the strategic behavior of participants (see, e.g., [15]) and is also therefore worth to be investigated thoroughly.

In order to develop a general approach to implement negotiation protocols, the first question to be raised is which aspects of a negotiation can be regulated or constrained by a protocol. Indeed, these aspects are manifold and can refer to:

– *Issue*: A negotiation can have one or more issues, each of which is associated with a set of fixed or negotiable attributes.
– *Participants*: Constraints applying to participants concern following subaspects
  – Roles: In many negotiation types, participants have fixed roles which determine their type of relationship to the issues, e.g., customer, and therefore which actions they can take.

- Quantity: For each role, it is to specify how many instances need to (at minimum) or can (at maximum) be involved.
- Admission and exclusion: Conditions of when to admit and to exclude participants need to be specified, e.g., whether it is possible for additional parties to enter an on-going negotiation.
- *Validation*: The validity of the actions taken by the participants is to be checked, particularly with regard to the syntactical and semantical correctness of offers submitted.
- *Proceeding*: Constraints applying to the proceeding of a negotiation include following sub-aspects
  - Round definition and number: A negotiation process can be specified in terms of rounds, i.e. periodical phases of exchanging offers and counter-offers, in which case it must be precisely specified what constitutes a round as well as the min. and max. number of rounds to be performed.
  - Voting method: In order to determine the agreement of the involved parties, some voting method has to be applied which is to be specified by the protocol.
  - Timeout: In general, every action of the participants needs to be assigned a timeout period and timeout handling measures are to be specified.
  - Truncation condition: The protocol has to specify when the negotiation process is terminated, in case of success as well as in case of failure.
- *Bindingness*: In case of success, the result of a negotiation is not always binding to all participants, e.g., in case of an auction. On the other hand, the negotiation result could also apply to participants who have not voted for it, as in case of a shareholders' meeting, for example. Therefore, the bindingness of negotiation results needs to be specified precisely.

There exist some formal mathematical treatments of negotiation protocols which can serve as a nice theoretical basis to understand some formal aspects of negotiation protocols (see, e.g., [11]). However, such models usually do not consider several aspects listed above such as admission and exclusion of participants, round definition and number, timeout and bindingness. In general, this kind of *static* modeling alone does not seem appropriate to capture the dynamic aspects of a negotiation process. Therefore, we have chosen a Petri-net based workflow management approach to handle negotiation protocols in the DYNAMICS project described below.

2.2 Negotiation Strategies

Although negotiation protocols have the purpose of restricting the possible courses of negotiation, they must obviously leave alternatives for participating parties to choose from. In choosing between or proposing protocol-compliant alternatives, each participant follows its own negotiation *strategy* which is normally not disclosed to other parties. Thus, in order to enable automated negotiations using agents, it is neccessary to equip each agent with a formalized strategy to compute actions and offers corresponding to the role it takes in the negotiation.

Formalization Criteria In order to design a general framework to implement such negotiation strategies, it is necessary to examine the criteria that are relevant for their development first. (In 4.3 we will see how such criteria are used to specify the interfaces of a strategy component.)

- *Utility function*: Intuitively, the goal of a negotiation strategy is achieving "good" results, which is achieved mainly by producing good offers. Therefore, *utility functions* are required to evaluate offers according to many possible criteria, for example price or quality of goods, time to negotiate etc.. Usually, a combination of such criteria has to be taken into account which leads to an optimization problem.
- *Knowledge base*: Then, in order to produce offers that are likely to fit a given utility function best, some kind of knowledge base is often employed which can contain either *domain knowledge* such as information about market values or *specific knowledge* about concrete negotiators obtained from previous encounters such as the result of the last negotiation on the same issue.
- *Protocol conformity*: There is a very close relationship between negotiation protocols and strategies. First of all, it is a necessary condition for every concrete strategy to compute offers or actions that conform with a given protocol.[1] Secondly, the protocol may have great influence on the efficiency of a strategy. For example, exploiting the *timeout* for a negotiation action specified by the protocol can be essential when negotiating with several parties, as shown in [16].

Classification Criteria In principle, a negotiation strategy can be realized by any algorithm that computes proper actions for a participant during the negotiation. And since a wide variety of possible algorithms, most of which are dedicated to some specific negotiation problem, has been proposed, it is not easy to classify them in an exhausting way. However, they can be grossly classified according to the following criteria:

- *mathematical/analytical*: are those strategies using some analytical method to compute negotiation actions.
- *heuristic/evolutionary*: are most strategies using some kind of *evolutionary programming* techniques.
- *local*: are strategies which do not depend on cooperation with other negotiators.
- *distributed*: On the contrary, distributed strategies make use of cooperation between negotiators.

The two pairs of contrasting criteria, i.e., analytical/evolutionary and local/distributed, thus yield two dimensions to characterize the strategies. In the next section, the differences between analytical and evolutionary strategies are briefly discussed.

---

[1] This condition does not apply, however, to meta-strategies (see 4.4).

Analytical versus Evolutionary Strategies Analytical and evolutionary strategies have both been often proposed, but are based on very different computing paradigms, each of which has some advantages as well as disadvantages in comparison to the other. Whereas the first employ some kind of relatively *static* mathematical model to compute negotiation actions, the latter make use of very *dynamic* computing techniques which are based on evolution principles such as selection, recombination and mutation (see [8] for an extensive treatment of evolutionary programming techniques).

Regarding analytical strategies, there already exist quite sophisticated and elaborated strategies for specific negotiation problems. For example, in [19], a technique of guessing the acceptance threshold of the other party (in a bilateral negotiation) based on the Bayesian method is presented. This technique also demonstrates that although the computing method is static, a learning effect can be achieved by using some knowledge base that is updated dynamically during the negotiation, so that every negotiation can take a different course. Analytical strategies have some advantages: They are immediately ready for operation and have a stable, reliable behavior. The main disadvantage is the potential predictability due to the underlying static model.

With evolutionary strategies, the learning effect is generally greater and also has a different dimension, since not only the data basis can evolve, but also the algorithms operating on these data themselves (which is called evolution based program induction). Thus, evolutionary strategies are principally much more creative and self-adaptable than those based on analytic models. However, there only exist a few implementations of simple, data oriented evolutionary negotiation strategies [13]. The main disadvantage of the evolutionary approach is that the resulting mechanisms always need a certain inititial phase to adapt so that they are not immediately ready for (effective) operation.

3 The DYNAMICS Architecture

The general goal of the DYNAMICS (DYNAMIcally Configurable Software) project is the design and implementation of highly configurable software components [6] which can be used as building blocks to assemble ready-to-use applications in a dynamic manner. With regard to mobile agents, this means that the functionality of an agent can be composed of several independently developed components which are plugged together. Especially, the agents should satisfy the requirements of role-specific functionality, on-the-fly loading and flexible configuration mentioned in section 1. In the following, some concrete components for building negotiating agents are introduced, which will then be described in more detail in section 4.

3.1 Components for Building Negotiating Agents

From an external point of view, negotiating agents are opaque entities which are just discernible by their exchange of negotiation messages. Different message exchange mechanisms can be used to distribute a message to one (unicast) or many (multicast) agents simultaneously, depending on the underlying negotiation protocol.

As illustrated in Figure 1, however, a negotiation enabled agent in the DYNAMICS architecture is internally structured into the following main components:

- *Communication module (C)*: This component is concerned with the delivery and processing of any kind of messages exchanged between the agents (see 4.1). When a message is recognized as a negotiation message, its content is passed to the protocol module.
- *Protocol module (P)*: This is the component responsible for the protocol compliance of an agent, which implies that the content of each incoming and outgoing negotiation message is inspected by the protocol module. It can be implemented either as an independent entity or as a front-end of a central protocol engine which seems more appropriate in case of protocols with complex semantics (see 4.2).
- *Strategy module (S)*: This is the component that implements a negotiation strategy which is responsible for producing proper negotiation actions as required by the protocol module. This module can also directly call the communication module, as in case of distributed strategies (see 4.3).

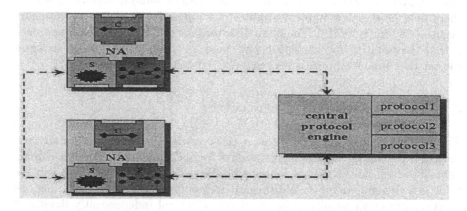

Fig. 1. Main components of negotiation enabled agents

This modular structuring has some obvious advantages: The functionality of each module is clearly defined by interfaces so that it can be developed independently using very different implementation methods or algorithms, as in case of the strategy module. Moreover, a component such as the protocol module can be provided and/or certified by a third-party instance in order to prove the correct behavior of an agent with respect to a protocol. In this way, a clear separation of "private" (strategy) and "public" (protocol) matters is achieved.

3.2 Plug-in Types

In the DYNAMICS architecture, most of the application semantics of mobile agents is realized by *plug-ins* which are components that can be added to and removed from agents at run-time. This means that in the first place, these agents can be seen as plug-in containers which provide a minimal, orthogonal functionality of mobile agents, i.e. mobility and persistence. Plug-in components, which can be dynamically incorporated into agents to provide application semantics, are classified into the following types:

- *Roles*: Roles are plug-ins that introduce new functionality into agents or entities which serve as role containers. Intuitively, the functionality associated with a role represents the semantics of some business entity such as "seller", "buyer" or "notary". Adding a role to a plug-in container object means providing this object both with a new (or additional) interface and a corresponding implementation (which may be loaded on demand).
- *Substitutes*: A substitute is a plug-in that is used to provide a new or replace an existing implementation for some interface, i.e. the interface remains unchanged.
- *Configurations*: A configuration plug-in is used to reconfigure an application component dynamically. That means, both the interface and implementation of the reconfigured component remain unchanged. Typical of a configuration plug-in is the rule module (R) (see 4.4) which can be used to impose a constraint, for example, about the total budget available for the negotiation, on the strategy module. Adding such a rule module results in the plug-in structure of negotiation enabled agents depicted in Figure 2.

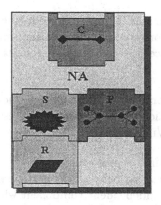

Fig. 2. Completed plug-in structure of a negotiation enabled agent

4 Negotiation Support Building Blocks

In this section, we describe the functionality and outline the design of the main modules serving as building blocks for negotiation enabled agents.

4.1 Communication Module

The communication module is a role plug-in that provides an agent with the capability of using a communication language, or to put it figuratively, it transmutes a (basic) agent into a "speaking" agent. In order to be interoperable with other agent systems as much as possible, we have chosen to use KQML [3] for the communication module. KQML, which was developed as part of the DARPA Knowledge Sharing Effort [14], offers the following advantages:

- Commonly recognized standard for agent communication.
- Enabling flexible, asynchronous exchange of informations and action requests.
- Applicable for many different application fields by introducing an *ontology* for each field (e.g., medicine).

The communication module is itself a plug-in container in which several *message interpreters* can be dynamically embedded to deal with different ontologies. In order to identify negotiation messages, a new ontology *negotiation* has been introduced. That means, when an incoming message is recognized as belonging to the ontology negotiation, its *content* field is passed to the corresponding interpreter which performs a syntax check and then passes it further to the protocol module.

4.2 Protocol Module

The protocol module is a substitute plug-in called by the communication module, or more precisely, by the corresponding interpreter embedded in the communication module. The interface between these modules is basically determined by the following parameters:

- *In*: Incoming negotiation message content and sender of message.
- *Out*: Outgoing negotiation message content, addressee(s) of message and/or sending mode (unicast/multicast).

In case of simple negotiation protocols, which do not require any essential coordination and synchronization between the participants, the protocol module can be implemented as an independent component which is completely loaded into the agent. For example, an agent participating as a prospective buyer in an auction needs with regard to the protocol only to determine whether he is treated correctly by the auctioneer, i.e. make sure that he is sold the good if he made the highest last bid.

However, in case of protocols with complex semantics (see, e.g., the 3-peer scenario described in [5]), it is more appropriate to provide the protocol module as a front-end to a central protocol engine (as depicted in Figure 1). Such a central engine is a specialized workflow engine executing protocols specified in a Petri-net based workflow description language (see [10]) which is suitable to express the dynamic aspects of a negotiation process described in section 2.1.

4.3 Strategy Module

The strategy module is a substitute plug-in called by the protocol module. The strong protocol dependence described in 2.2 entails that the interface between the strategy and the protocol module cannot be statically specified, i.e. using static data types, but has to allow dynamically typed parameters:

- *In*: The current negotiation state is passed from the protocol to the strategy module. What constitutes the negotiation state is mainly dependent on the protocol.[2] Optionally, the protocol module can pass the set of all protocol compliant actions, from which the strategy module can choose one to proceed with, as in case of the contract net protocol ([2]).
- *Out*: The negotiation action computed by the strategy module, for example, a counter-offer to the last offer. Which offers are valid is also dependent on the protocol.

Optionally, the strategy module can have interfaces to additional components such as a knowledge base (see 2.2) or it can make use of the communication module to interwork with other strategy modules in case of distributed strategies.

4.4 Rule Module

The rule module is a configuration plug-in for the strategy module. Generally, rules can be seen as objects that do not provide an external functionality for the components they are plugged into through call interfaces, but rather (re-)configure or constrain these components. The configuration effect can be achieved by performing actions which manipulate the (external) properties of the configured component, as shown in [18].

Rule Types Rules in the DYNAMICS architecture are classified into the following types:

- *Invariants*: An invariant is a condition that must hold true at any time with regard to the entity it is assigned to, which can be an agent or a group of (cooperating) agents. For example, the invariant (**budget** > 0) $\wedge$ (**size** $\leq$ **100**) can be interpreted as: The budget the agent may use to negotiate must be always positive and its total size must not exceed 100 units.

---

[2] In an auction, for instance, it could be just the last bid, but for another protocol, it might be a vector containing the negotiation states of all participants.

- *Policies*: A policy consists of a condition, called *goal*, and an action which leads to the goal, when it does not (longer) hold. For example, the policy
  P1: (budget $\geq$ 100) $\leftarrow^3$ deposit(1000)
  specifies that the action deposit(1000) is to be performed when the budget becomes less than 100 units.
- *Action rules*: An action rule consists of a condition, called *trigger*, and an action to be performed when the trigger holds. For example, the action rule
  A1: (budget $<$ 100) $\rightarrow$ deposit(10)
  specifies that the action deposit(10) is to be performed when the budget becomes less than 100 units.[4]

Thus, invariants can be seen as *passive* rules, whereas policies and action rules are *active* ones. See [18] for a detailed description of mechanisms to formalize, evaluate, unify, compare and activate policies, most of which are applicable to the other rule types as well.

Using Rules to Implement Meta-Strategies Using rules to configure the strategy module can achieve the effect of *general* strategies, i.e. those that are applicable for many negotiation types and in particular are not dependent on a concrete negotiation protocol. For example, the space between two price offers can be specified by a policy which is manually specified or computed by a *meta-strategy* component which is protocol independent. In this way, simple general behavior patterns expressed in terms of "cautious/patient" or "risky/fast-paced" can be easily imposed on the strategy module and such a meta-strategy component can be reused for different negotiation protocols and strategies.

5 Implementation Issues

An implementation which is so "dynamic" that it allows for the compositional substitution as required by the concept of roles outlined above is quite demanding on the system technology's capabilities. Separating interfaces from their implementations, the possibility to substitute both of them at run–time as well as representing and evaluating domain knowledge supporting an agent's strategic decisions are the main challenges.

Choosing typical object–oriented, class–based "production" languages such as C++ or Java for realizing the required plug–in architecture leads to the

---

[3] Please note that in this context, "$\leftarrow$" and "$\rightarrow$" do not denote *logical implication*, but rather serve as symbols for the "causal" relationship between a condition on the one hand and an action on the other hand.

[4] Although policies and action rules seem to have similar semantics, they are not interchangeable, since the action of a policy must lead to the goal (otherwise, an exception will be thrown), whereas the action in an action rule can be any arbitrary one. To give another example, the expression A2: (budget $<$ 100) $\rightarrow$ dieNow() represents a correct action rule, whereas P2: (budget $\geq$ 100) $\leftarrow$ dieNow() does not represent its policy counterpart.

well–known problem of *class evolution* of systems which treat classes as (static) compile–time concepts. On the other hand choosing possibly more appropriate environments like typical interpreted AI languages as Scheme or CLOS which allow for more dynamic, (self–) modifiable systems as well as proven knowledge representation techniques lacks the ubiquitous availability required by a mobile agent system.

Therefore, the "pragmatic" decision for the DYNAMICS project was to build the whole architecture on top of the widespread Java–Technology available with minimal effort as an ubiquitous networked infrastructure. The first prototype of the here presented *pluggable agents* architecture has been implemented on top of Objectspace's Java–based *Voyager* system[5] [12], which provides the basic functionality for building mobile agents in a very efficient manner. The decision has been not to choose one of the "main" agent systems like Odyssey [4] or Aglets [7] but an infrastructure that provides a small, clear concept of movable objects, thus keeping unnecessary overhead small, but nevertheless having a solid base to build the specially required agent containers on. Also, Voyager's small footprint is well suited for ubiquitous network distribution.

The dynamic pluggability of the components which can be used to assemble a role-specific agent is based on the generic concept of a *Pluggable* which is implemented using the *MessageEvent* mechanism of Voyager to delegate method calls to the right target(s). The design of the main interfaces and classes implementing this plug-in mechanism is depicted in Figure 3.

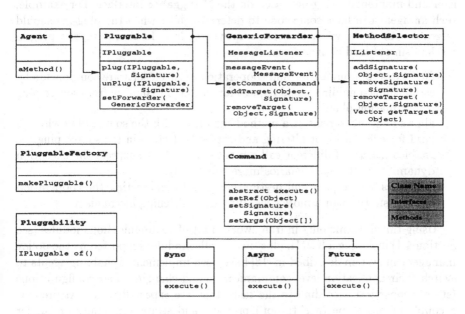

Fig. 3. Class diagram for plug-in mechanism

---

[5] The version currently being used for our prototype implementation is 2.0 Beta 2

IPluggable is the interface common to all objects that can act as a plug-in container by providing the methods plug and unPlug to add a plug-in (called *destination plug*) into or remove it from the container object (or *source plug*). Pluggable is one implementation of the IPluggable interface using a generic forwarder, which can be dynamically set by the method setForwarder, to delegate method calls to their target objects. The GenericForwarder implements Voyager's MessageListener interface, defines methods for adding and removing targets of requests (addTarget and removeTarget), provides the forwarding mechanism through the method messageEvent and enables different call semantics through the method setCommand. To handle the message events, the generic forwarder makes use of the class MethodSelector which defines methods for filtering message events based on signatures (methods addSignature, removeSignature, select) and for determining the targets of the signatures (methods getTargets, removeTarget). The abstract class Command provides a generic DII mechanism for executing method calls on targets (through execute) and defines methods for dynamically changing targets, method name and parameters to method calls. Sync, Async and Future are implementations of Command corresponding to the call semantics *synchronous, asynchronous* and *future* in Voyager, respectively. The PluggableFactory class provides static factory methods in order to construct plug-ins at run-time. Pluggability provides a static method (of) in order to add the plug-in capability to an object dynamically. Finally, Agent is a plain Voyager agent inheriting from Pluggable to serve as a plug-in container and containing some (application-specific) code to administer and manipulate plug-ins based on the IPluggable interface. For example, such an agent can have some code to determine if or when the plug-ins should migrate with it (or when to move somewhere else). In summary, the plug-in mechanism outlined above

- facilitates communication and cooperation between software components by establishing a unidirectional request forwarding mechanism from source plug to destination plug.
- allows plug-ins to register a method signature with the source plug which is used for efficient event filtering and method selection in the source plug.
- enables the use of different call semantics in order to express the execution dynamics of different scenarios more adaquately.
- decouples source plug and destination plug by indirecting the cooperation mechanism through a more general message listening mechanism.

Using this dynamic plug-in framework, a set of communication modules (see Section 4.1) including a KQML plug–in and rule modules supported by the policy management system described in [18] have been implemented enabling agents to switch their application level communication and changing their configurations (state, properties) according to the tasks they are expected to do. At present, a couple of prototype (negotiation) protocol and strategy modules are under development giving the agents the possibilty to act in different "market scenarios" like auctions, wholesaling, black–boards and flea–markets adapting to the varying behavior and strategies found in these scenarios.

6   Summary and Outlook

In this paper, we have presented an approach of dynamically embedding negotiation capabilities into mobile agents. First, it was shown that the requirements for enabling automatic negotiations, with respect to both negotiation protocols and strategies, are manifold, the main consequence of which is that a framework of corresponding building blocks has to be generic and flexible enough to be able to support a wide variety of protocols and strategies. Then, a plug-in architecture for mobile agents consisting of four main negotiation support modules and the corresponding plug-in types required to implement them was proposed. Next, the design of the concrete modules was presented and finally, some relevant implementation issues were described.

However, there are some issues which have not been addressed in this paper. The first one concerns the question of how the agents can find appropriate partners to start a negotiation in an open environment such as the Internet without being given prior knowledge. Related to this is the question of how to establish a group or consortium of partners which can participate in a negotiation as one role. Another issue is how to provide as much support as possible for the execution of a negotiated result or contract. These are some questions which we are currently examining in the context of a generic contracting service for electronic commerce applications.

Acknowledgement This work is supported, in part, by grant no. La1061/1-1 from the German Research Council (Deutsche Forschungsgemeinschaft, DFG).

References

1. D. Chess, B. Grosof, C. Harrison, D. Levine, C. Parris, and G. Tsudik. Itinerant agents for mobile computing. Technical Report RC 20010, IBM Research Division, T.J. Watson Research Center, 1995.
2. R. Davis and R.G. Smith. Negotiation as a Metaphor for Distributed Problem Solving. *Artificial Intelligence*, (20):63–109, 1983.
3. T. Finin, R. Fritzson, D. McKay, and R. McEntire. KQML as an Agent Communication Language. In *Proceedings of the Third International Conference on Information and Knowledge Management (CIKM'94)*. ACM Press, November 1994.
4. General Magic. Odyssey, 1997. www.genmagic.com/agents/.
5. F. Griffel, T. Tu, M. Mnke, M. Merz, W. Lamersdorf, and M. M. da Silva. Electronic Contract Negotiation as an Application Niche for Mobile Agents. In *Proceedings of the First International Wokshop on Enterprise Distributed Object Computing, EDOC'97, Australia*, pages 354–365. IEEE, Oktober 1997.
6. Frank Griffel. *Componentware*. dpunkt-Verlag, 1998. (In German).
7. IBM. Aglets, 1997. www.tri.ibm.co.jp/aglets/.
8. C. Jacob. *Principia Evolvica : Simulierte Evolution mit Mathematica*. dpunkt-Verlag, 1997. (In German).
9. Boris Liberman, Frank Griffel, Michael Merz, and Winfried Lamersdorf. Java-Based Mobile Agents — How to Migrate, Persist, and Interact on Electronic Service

Markets. In Kurt Rothermel and Radu Popescu-Zeletin, editors, *Proceedings of the First International Workshop on Mobile Agents, MA '97, Berlin, Germany*, number 1219 in LNCS, pages 27–38. Springer, April 1997.

10. K. Müller–Jones, M. Merz, and W. Lamersdorf. Realisierung von Kooperationsanwendungen auf der Basis erweiterter Diensttypbeschreibungen. In H. Krumm, editor, *Entwicklung und Management verteilter Anwendungssysteme — Tagungsband des 2. Arbeitstreffens der GI/ITG Fachgruppe 'Kommunikation und verteilte Systeme' und der GI Fachgruppe 'Betriebssysteme'*, pages 20–30. Universität Dortmund, Oktober 1995. (In German).

11. J.P. Müller. A Cooperation Model for Autonomous Agents. In J.P. Müller, M.J. Wooldridge, and N.R. Jennings, editors, *Intelligent Agents III: Agent Theories, Architectures, and Languages (Proceedings of ECAI'96)*, LNCS. Springer, August 1996.

12. ObjectSpace. Voyager — core technology user guide, Dezember 1997. www.objectspace.com/voyager/documentation.html.

13. Jim R. Oliver. *On Artificial Agents for Negotiation in Electronic Commerce*. PhD thesis, Wharton, 1996. wharton.upenn.edu/~oliver27/dissertation/diss.zip.

14. R. Patil, R. Fikes, P. Patel-Schneider, D. McKay, T. Finin, T. Gruber, and R. Neches. The DARPA Knowledge Sharing Effort: Progress report. In B. Nebel, C. Rich, and W. Swartout, editors, *Principles of Knowledge Representation and Reasoning: Proc. of the Third International Conference (KR'92)*. Morgan Kaufmann, November 1992.

15. J. Rosenschein and G. Zlotkin. *Rules of Encounter: Designing Conventions for Automated Negotiations among Computers*. MIT Press, 1994.

16. T. Sandholm and V. Lesser. Issues in Automated Negotiation and Electronic Commerce: Extending the Contract Net Framework. In V. Lesser, editor, *Proceedings of the First International Conference on Multi-Agent Systems (ICMAS'95)*, pages 328–335, San Francisco, June 1995. AAAI / MIT Press.

17. M. Straβer, J. Baumann, and F. Hohl. Mole - A Java Based Mobile Agent System. In *Special Issues in Object-Oriented Programming, Workshop Reader ECOOP'96*, pages 327–334. dpunkt–Verlag, 1996.

18. M.T. Tu, F. Griffel, M. Merz, and W. Lamersdorf. Generic Policy Management for Open Service Markets. In H. König and K. Geihs, editors, *Proc. of the Int. Working Conference on Distributed Applications and Interoperable Systems (DAIS'97), Cottbus, Germany*. Chapman & Hall, September 1997.

19. D. Zeng and K. Sycara. How Can an Agent Learn to Negotiate? In J.P. Müller, M.J. Wooldridge, and N.R. Jennings, editors, *Intelligent Agents III: Agent Theories, Architectures, and Languages (Proceedings of ECAI'96)*, LNCS. Springer, August 1996.

Reactive Tuple Spaces for Mobile Agent Coordination*

Giacomo Cabri, Letizia Leonardi, Franco Zambonelli

Dipartimento di Scienze dell'Ingegneria – Università di Modena
Via Campi 213/b – 41100 Modena – ITALY
E-mail: {giacomo.cabri, letizia.leonardi, franco.zambonelli}@unimo.it

Abstract. The paper surveys several coordination models for mobile agent applications and outlines the advantages of uncoupled coordination models based on reactive blackboards. On this base, the paper presents the design and the implementation of the MARS system, a coordination tool for Java-based mobile agents. MARS defines Linda-like tuple spaces that can be programmed to react with specific actions to the accesses made by mobile agents.

1 Introduction

Traditional distributed applications are designed as a set of processes assigned to given **execution environments** (from now on **EE**s) and cooperating in a (mostly) network-unaware fashion. The **mobile agent** paradigm, instead, defines applications composed by network-aware entities (*agents*) capable of changing their EE by transferring themselves while executing (*mobility*) [9]. The shift to the mobile agent paradigm is broadly justified by the advantages it provides over traditional approaches in widely distributed applications: *(i)* mobile agents can significantly save bandwidth, by moving locally to the resources they need, instead of requiring the transfer of possibly large amounts of data; *(ii)* mobile agents can carry the code to manage remote resources without needing the remote availability of a specific server and thus leading to a more flexible application scenario; *(iii)* mobile agents do not require continuous network connection, because interacting entities can be moved to the same EE when the connection is available and interact without requiring further network connection; as a consequence *(iv)* the mobile agent paradigm intrinsically suits mobile computing systems.

In the last few years, several systems and programming environments have appeared to support the development of distributed applications based on mobile agents [15, 17]. Nevertheless, there are still several open research issues to make the mobile agent technology widely accepted: appropriate programming languages and coordination models, security, efficiency and standardisation [9].

In mobile agent applications, one of the fundamental activities is coordination between the agents and the entities they encounter during execution, being them **other**

---

* This work has been supported by the Italian Ministero dell'Università e della Ricerca Scientifica e Tecnologica (MURST) in the framework of the Project "Design Methodologies and Tools of High Performance Systems for Distributed Applications".

agents or **resources** on the hosting EEs. However, mobility and openness of the scenario imply different problems than traditional distributed systems [1,10]. The paper introduces, in section 2, a simple taxonomy of the coordination models that can be adopted by mobile agent systems, and shows that coupled coordination models do not suit mobile agent applications and force complex design choices. Instead, fully uncoupled (Linda-like) coordination models have the necessary adaptivity to suit a wide and heterogeneous networked scenario and lead to simpler application design. Further flexibility and safety stem from reactive coordination models [7], in which the semantics of the interactions can be programmed to meet specific needs, as shown in section 3.

The above considerations motivate the design and the implementation of the **MARS (Mobile Agent Reactive Spaces)** system, described in section 4. MARS is based on the definition of a Linda-like tuple space associated to each EE. An agent arriving to a site can use the tuple space both to coordinate itself with other application agents and to access to local resources. Differently from raw Linda-like tuple spaces, MARS tuple spaces can be programmed (either by the local administrator or by the agents themselves) to react with specific actions to the accesses made to them by agents. This characteristic of MARS grants flexibility in mobile agent applications, allowing to define specific and stateful coordination policies and to enforce secure agent execution. In section 5, reaction examples for a testbed application show the effectiveness of the MARS approach.

2 Coordination Models for Mobile Agent Applications

During its nomadic life, an agent needs to coordinate with other entities, let them be other agents or resources on hosting EEs. In particular:

- an application is composed of several mobile agents that cooperatively perform a task and, then, in need of coordinating their activities;
- a mobile agent is usually in need to roam across remote EEs to access to resources and services there allocated.

	Temporal	
	Coupled	Uncoupled
Coupled	Direct *Odissey, Agent-TCL*	Blackboard-Based *Ambit, ffMain*
Uncoupled	Meeting-Oriented *Ara, Mole*	Linda-like *Jada, MARS, TuCSoN*

Spatial (Name)

Fig. 1. Coordination Models for Mobile Agents

While coordination models have been extensively studied in the past [1,10], mobility and the openness of the Internet scenario introduce new problems and needs. In this section, we define a taxonomy of the coordination models for mobile agent applications, together with a brief survey of several mobile agent proposals [3]. Two main characteristics distinguish different coordination models: spatial and temporal coupling. In particular:

- spatially (or name) coupled models require the involved entities to share a common name space; spatially uncoupled models enforce anonymous interactions;
- temporally coupled models imply synchronisation of the involved entities; temporally uncoupled models achieve asynchronous interactions.

Therefore, four categories of coordination models can be derived (see figure 1).

2.1 Direct Coordination

In **direct** coordination models, agents initiate a communication by explicitly naming the involved partners (spatial coupling). This usually implies their synchronisation (temporal coupling). In the case of inter-agent coordination, two agents must agree on a communication protocol, typically a **peer-to-peer** one. In the case of the access to the hosting EE resources, coordination usually occurs in a **client-server** way [1].

The general adoption of direct coordination models in mobile agent applications is not suitable. Repeated interactions require stable network connections, making communication highly dependent on network reliability. In addition, wide-area communications between mobile entities require complex and highly informed routing protocols. Finally, because mobile agent applications are intrinsically dynamic (through dynamic agent creation and dynamic migration), it may be difficult to adopt a spatially coupled model in which the communication partners must be identified. Therefore, direct coordination can be effectively exploited only for accessing to local EE resources: a local server can be provided and agents interact with it in a client-server way.

Most of the Java-based agent-systems – like *Odyssey* [11] – adopt the client-server style typical of object systems, and can also exploit low-level message-passing via TCP/IP. *Agent Tcl* [12] provides direct communication between two agents, based on message-passing, and also provides asynchronous communication modes.

2.2 Meeting-Oriented Coordination

In **meeting-oriented** coordination, agents can interact with no need of explicitly naming the involved partners (spatial uncoupling). Interactions occur in the context of known meeting points that agents join, either explicitly or implicitly, to communicate and synchronise (temporal coupling) with each other. Apart from always-opened meetings – that can abstract the role of servers in an EE – an active entity must assume the role of initiator to open a meeting point. Often, meetings are locally constrained: to avoid the problems related to non-local communications (i.e., unpredictable delay and unreliability), a meeting takes place at a given EE and only local agents can participate in it. Clearly, because agents must share the common knowledge either of the meeting names or of the events that force them in joining a meeting, full spatial uncoupling is not achieved.

The meeting model solves only partially the problem of exactly identifying the involved partners, and it has also the drawback of enforcing a strict synchronisation between agents. Because in many applications, the schedule and the position of agents cannot be predicted, the risk of missing interactions is very high. In addition, to let a meeting agent remain on one EE, as it can be required for many kinds of interactions, is not safe: a malicious agent can exploit the time it is on a EE to furnish information to the external.

Meeting-oriented coordination is implemented in *Ara* [20]: an agent can assume the role of meeting server announcing a meeting point at one hosting EE; incoming agents can enter the meeting to coordinate each other. The concept of event-based communication and synchronisation, defined by the OMG group [18] and applied to mobile agents in *Mole* [2], can be categorised as a meeting-oriented coordination model.

2.3 Blackboard-Based Coordination

In **blackboard-based** coordination, interactions occur via shared data spaces, local to each hosting EE, used by agents as common repositories to store and retrieve messages. As far as agents must agree on a common message identifier to communicate and exchange data via a blackboard, they are spatially coupled.

The most significant **advantage** of this coordination model derives from fully temporal uncoupling: messages can be left on blackboards without needing to know, neither where the corresponding receivers are nor when they will read the messages. This clearly suits a mobile scenario in which the position and the schedules of the agents can be neither monitored nor granted easily. In addition, being any inter-agent interaction forced to be performed via a blackboard, hosting EEs can easily control all interactions, enforcing security. The **drawback** of this model is that the sender and the receiver have to agree on a common message name to interact.

Several systems propose and implement blackboard-based coordination models for mobile agent applications. In *Ambit* [4], a recently proposed formal model for mobile computations, agents can attach and read messages on the blackboard local to each EE. The *ffMAIN* agent system [8] defines mobile agents that interact – both with other agents and with the local resources of the hosting EEs – via an information space accessed through the HTTP protocol, where data can be stored, read and extracted.

2.4 Linda-like Coordination

In Linda-like coordination, the accesses to the local blackboards are based on **associative mechanisms** [10]: information is organised in tuples, retrieved in an associative way via a pattern-matching mechanism. Associative blackboards (i.e., tuple spaces) enforce full uncoupling, requiring neither temporal nor spatial coupling.

Associative coordination suits well mobile agent applications. In a wide and dynamic environment, as Internet, having a complete and updated knowledge of hosting EEs and of other application agents may be difficult or even impossible. Then, because agents would somehow require pattern-matching mechanisms to adaptively deal with uncertainty, dynamicity and heterogeneity, it is worthwhile to integrate these mechanisms directly in the coordination model, to simplify agent programming and to reduce application complexity.

The *Jada* system [6] implements the concept of associative blackboards, to be used by mobile agents to store and associatively retrieve object references on a EE.

3 Adding Reactivity to Tuple Spaces

In the tuple space coordination model, reactivity stems from embodying computational capacity within the tuple space itself, to let it issue specific programmable reactions that can influence the access behaviour [7]. The tuple space is no longer a mere tuple repository with a built-in and stateless associative mechanism, as in Linda. Instead, it can also have its own state and react with specific actions to the accesses made by mobile agents. Reactions can access the tuple space, change its content and influence the semantics of the agents' accesses.

A reactive tuple space can provide several advantages. Reactions can be used to implement specific local policies for the interactions between the agents and the hosting EEs, to achieve better control and to defend the integrity of the EEs from malicious agents. In addition, reactions can adapt the semantics of the interactions to the specific characteristics of the hosting EE, thus simplifying the agent programming task much more than the fixed pattern-matching mechanism of Linda. Furthermore, the reactive space can allow the specification of inter-agent coordination rules as high-level directives, achieving a separation of concerns between algorithmic and coordination issues [10]

While the necessity of adding reactivity to the raw Linda model has been already recognised [7], a few proposals apply this concept to mobile agents. The *TuCSoN* model [19] defines programmable logic tuple centres for the coordination of knowledge-oriented mobile agents: reactions are programmed as first-order logic tuples. Another interesting effort, although not currently supporting mobile agents, is the *PageSpace* project [5], that defines an enriched Linda-like coordination model for distributed Web applications. Special-purpose agents can change the content of the tuple space to influence the interactions of the application agents.

Reactivity can be integrated also in different coordination models. For example, in the OMG event-based communication model [2,18], synchronisation objects can embody specific policies to influence the interactions between agents.

4 The MARS System

The **MARS** (Mobile Agent Reactive Spaces) system, developed at the University of Modena in the context of the MOON research project [16], implements a portable reactive Linda-like coordination architecture for Java-based mobile agents.

4.1 The MARS Architecture

The MARS system is conceived for the coordination of **Java-based mobile agent** applications in a wide heterogeneous network (as Internet). We assume that each node of the network hosts a **mobile agent server** in charge of accepting and executing incoming autonomous Java agents. The mobile agent server keeps a reference to a local tuple space: as an agent arrives on a node (step *a* of figure 2), the local server provides it this reference (step *b*).

We stress that our aim is not to build a new engine for the execution of Java-agents. Instead, the goal is to develop a general and portable coordination architecture for Java agents. The MARS tuple space is only loosely coupled to the agent server and it is not bound to any specific server implementation. In fact, it may be associated to different Java-based mobile agent systems, as IBM *Aglets* [14] or *Odyssey* [11], with only a slight extension (i.e., the execution engine must keep the reference to the local space and provide it to incoming agents). The mobile agent server adopted for the first prototype is the **Java-to-go** package [13], a well documented environment, developed at the University of California at Berkeley (CA).

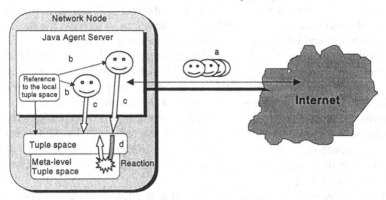

Fig. 2. The MARS Architecture (smiles represent mobile agents)

As an agent is bound to the local tuple space, it can access to it for reading, extracting and putting tuples (step *c* in figure 2). Then, an agent associatively retrieves from the tuple space primitive data items and references to objects that represent EE resources. For these reason, the problem of dynamically binding local references to mobile entities [9] is solved in MARS by dynamically extracting references from the local tuple space. In addition, the tuple space can be exploited for inter-agent communication.

MARS defines a **reactive tuple space** model in which the effects of the operations on the tuple space can be dynamically modified. Agents access to the tuple space always with the same basic set of operations (Linda-like). Specific reactions can be associated to the accesses to the tuple space made by mobile agents (step *d* in figure 2), as described in section 3. A meta-level tuple space is introduced to associatively manage reactions.

4.2 The MARS Interface

Each tuple space is a Java object, instance of the **Space** class, that implements the interface with which agents can access to the tuple space. The MARS interface (figure 3) extends the one of the SUN *JavaSpace* specification[1] [21], that is likely to become the *de facto* standard tuple space interface for Java.

MARS tuples are objects that represent ordered sets of typed fields. To define a tuple type, one must derive a class from the **Entry** class (that define the basic tuple properties) and define, as instance variables, the specific tuple fields. The order of the

---

[1] Since the first prototype of MARS was developed, a new JavaSpace specification has been released. However this does not affect our proposal significantly, because it implies only a slight change (in progress at the time of writing) in the MARS interface.

field values passed as parameters to the class constructor defines their ordering. Each field of the tuple refers to an object that can also represent primitive data (*wrapper* objects in the Java terminology).

```
public interface MARS extends JavaSpace
{// method interface inherited from JavaSpace
// void write(Entry tup, Transaction txn, Identity who);
// put a tuple into the space
// Entry read(Entry req, Transaction txn, Identity who);
// read a tuple from the space
// Entry take(Entry req, Transaction txn, Identity who);
// extract a tuple from the space
// methods added by MARS
Vector  readAll(Entry req, Transaction txn, Identity who);
Vector takeAll(Entry req, Transaction txn, Identity who);}
```

Fig. 3. The MARS interface

The JavaSpace interface defines three operations to access to the tuple space:
- write, to put a tuple, supplied as parameter, in the space;
- read, to retrieve a tuple from the space, on the basis of a request tuple supplied as parameter and to be used as pattern for the matching mechanism;
- take, which works as the read operation but extracts the matching tuple from the space.

In addition to the tuple parameter, the *transaction* parameter specifies the characteristics of the operation; in MARS, it is used to specify whether a read or take operation must be blocking or not: a non-blocking operation that finds no matching tuple returns *null*. The *identity* parameter specifies who asks for the operation and it is used for identification and security purposes.

The MARS interface adds two operations (readAll and takeAll), to give the capability of retrieving *all* the tuples that match with the tuple supplied as parameter.

The request tuple supplied by reading and taking operations can have both actual (defined) and formal (null) values. Because in JavaSpace (as in MARS) tuples are objects and because the elements of a tuple can be non-primitive objects, the matching rules must take into account the presence of objects. A request tuple R and a tuple T match if and only if all the following conditions are verified:
- R is an instance of either the T's class or of one of its superclass; in this sense, JavaSpace extends the Linda model by permitting a match also between two tuples of different type, provided they belong to the same class hierarchy;
- the actual fields of R that represent primitive types (integer, character, boolean, etc.) have the same value of the respective fields in T;
- the actual non-primitive fields (i.e., objects) of R are equal – in their serialised form – to the respective ones of T (we recall that two Java objects assume the same serialised form only if each of their instance variables have equals values, recursively including enclosed objects);
- a null value in T corresponds to a null value in R.

Once a tuple is obtained from the space, its actual field objects can be accessed as any other Java object.

As an example, let us suppose that a file of the local file system is represented by a tuple of this type (String PathName, String Extension, Date ModificationTime, File ActualFile). Then, a request tuple (null, "html", null, null) matches with the tuple ("/usr/local/htdocs/index", "html", 02/01/98:17.34.20, File@[12a34]) and also with ("/home/j2go-server/mobile_agents", "html", 01/10/97:14.12.54, File@[b6c52]); a request tuple ("/home/j2go-server/mobile_agents", "html", null, null) matches only with the second tuple.

4.3 The Reactive Model

Unlike JavaSpace, MARS permits to associate programmable **reactions** to the tuple space accesses performed by agents. Reactions are stateful objects with a method that can access the tuple space itself, change its content, and influence the semantics of the operations performed by agents.

There are four components to be considered when associating reactions: *reaction (Rct), tuple item (T), operation type (O)* and *agent identity (I)*. The association of a reaction to an access is represented via a 4-*ple (Rct, T, O, I)*: the reaction (i.e., the method of the reaction object *Rct*) is executed when an agent with identity *I* invokes the operation *O* on a tuple matching *T*. Therefore, the association of reactions to tuples is dealt with **meta-level tuples** that can be considered enclosed in a meta-level tuple space which follows the same associative mechanisms of the base-level tuple space. Putting and extracting tuples from the meta-level tuple space provide to install and de-install reactions associated to events at the base-level tuple space. A 4-*ple* (possibly with some non-defined values) associates the reaction to all the accesses that matches the 4-*ple*. A match in the meta-level triggers the corresponding reaction. In case of multiple matches, all corresponding reactions are triggered in the same order in which matches occurs.

For example, a 4-*ple* (ReactionObj, null, read, null) specifies to associate the reaction of ReactionObj to all read operations, disregarding both the peculiar tuple type and content and the agent identity. Analogously, one can associate reactions to a specific tuple, to all tuples, or to the tuples of a given class.

In the meta-level tuple space the pattern-matching mechanism is activated for any access to the "base-level" tuple space to check for the presence of reactions to be executed. When an agent with identity *I* invokes a retrieving (i.e., read or take) operation *O* supplying a request tuple *R*, the MARS system executes the following steps:

1. it issues the pattern matching mechanism in the base-level tuple space to identify the tuples that match with *R*;
2. for each matching tuple *T*, it executes a read in the meta-level tuple space by providing the request tuple (null, T, O, I); this issues a matching mechanism in the meta-level tuple space, to check for the presence of matching 4-*ples*;
3. if a matching 4-*ple* in the meta-level is found, the corresponding reaction is executed and its result is returned to the invoking agent.

In case of a write operation, a similar search is performed in the meta-level tuple space, but no result has to return to the invoking agent.

A reaction has access to the base-level tuple space and can perform any kind of operation on it (operations on the base-level tuple space performed within the code of a reaction do not issue any reaction, to avoid endlessly recursions). This can be used to exploit the base-level tuple space as repository of reaction state information, in addition to the intrinsic reaction object state. As a consequence, the behaviour of the reaction can depend both on the actual content of the tuple space and on past access events. Also, the reaction, as it is executed, has the availability of the result of the matching mechanism issued by the associated operation. Then, the reaction can also influence the semantics of operations and, for example, can return to the invoking agents different tuples than the ones resulting from the raw, stateless and less flexible, Linda-like matching mechanisms. The above characteristics distinguish the MARS approach form the *notify* mechanism of JavaSpace, which is simply a way to make external entities aware of matches in the tuple space and influences neither the built-in pattern-matching mechanism nor the semantic of the operations.

An aspect of our model that we have not fully investigated yet relates to agent authentication and tuple space access grants. The JavaSpace specification defines a simple identification mechanism (based on access control lists) to enforce control in the accesses to the space. In MARS, the capability of programming the tuple space and the possibility for reactions to access and modify the tuple space itself introduce different security issues. In particular, we are currently evaluating how and to which extent agents can be allowed to install reactions into remote servers.

5 How to Use MARS: A Case Study Application

In this section we show how to exploit the MARS system to implement reactions. As an example, let us consider a simple WWW information retrieval application, which will be used as a case study. An explorer agent is sent to a remote site to analyse WWW pages and to come back with the URLs of the pages that contain a specific keyword. The agent clones itself for any remote link found in the pages of interest and clones move to the found sites, to recursively continue the search.

In this application, coordination of an agent with one EE means to define a precise protocol to **access and retrieve information** (i.e., HTML pages) on a site. Coordination between agents is needed to avoid **multiple visits** of different agents on the same site (since it is common to find cross-references in HTML pages).

A local EEs can provide access to the HTML pages via tuples that identify file general characteristics, such as pathname, extension, dimension and modification time, and that contain a reference to a File object to be used to access the content of the file. In MARS, each of these tuples is an instance of the FileEntry class (figure 4). Agents looking for HTML pages on a site have to obtain references to them by accessing the tuple space. The explorer agents of our application retrieve all HTML files on the node by invoking the readAll operation in a non-blocking mode (to avoid indefinite block in case the local site does not provide any HTML tuple). The readAll operation supplies a request FileEntry tuple in which only the Extension field is defined (with the "html" value) and returns all matching tuples (i.e., those which represent HTML documents) in a vector. For each element of the vector, the explorer agent accesses the HTML page via the File object, to search for the keyword of interest in its content: a list of files containing the keyword is returned to the user. For each remote link in the HTML document, the agent clones to continue the work on a different site. A fragment of the Java code of the explorer agent is shown in figure 5.

```
class FileEntry extends Entry { // Entry: generic tuple
  // object fields
  String PathName;        // pathname of the file
  String Extension;       // representative of the file type
  Date ModificationTime; // date of last update of the file
  File ActualFile;        // to access the content of the file }
```

Fig. 4. The FileEntry class for the tuples representing files in the tuple space

```
  ...
FileEntry FilePattern = new FileEntry(null, "html", null,
null);  // creation of the request tuple
Vector HTMLFiles = LocalSpace.readAll(FilePattern, NO_BLOCK,
myIdentity);
// read all matching tuples and return a vector of tuples
if (HTMLFiles.isEmpty()) // no matching tuple is found
    terminate();     // nothing to return to user
else
{   for (int i = 0; i < HTMLFiles.size(); i++)
        // for each matching tuple
    { FileEntry Hfile = (FileEntry)HTMLFiles.elementAt(i);
        // Hfile is the tuple representing the file
        if (this.SearchKeyword(keyword, Hfile))
        // search for the keyword in the file
            { FoundFiles.addElements(LocalHost, Hfile);}
        // store the file in a private vector
        // to be returned to the user
        this.SearchLink_and_Clone(Hfile);
        // search for remote links and clones itself
        // clones are sent to remote sites
    }
    go_to(home); //return to the user site
}...
```

Fig. 5. Code of the explorer agent (fragment)

5.1 Enforcing the Safety

Let us suppose that the local tuple space, as the file system, is managed by a local system manager – with full access rights – that has decided to deny foreign agents the extraction of the tuples representing local files. It is possible that a malicious or bad-programmed agent tries to perform take operations on these tuples. In this case, the system administrator can decide not to raise any exception to these unauthorized operations but, instead, to let the agent read the content of the matching tuples without deleting them. To this purpose, the administrator can install a simple stateless reaction that provides to transform any take operation on the FileEntry tuples, performed by a foreign agent, into a read one (figure 6).

5.2 Avoiding Duplicated Searches

To avoid multiple visits on the same site, inter-agent coordination is needed. Let us suppose that agents are allowed to install reactions. Then, the application agents can install a stateful reaction that does not simply avoid the retrieving of duplicated information, but also takes into account the updating of HTML pages. When an agent accesses to the tuple space to retrieve the references to the HTML pages, the reaction checks – for any matching FileEntry tuple – whether the corresponding file has been modified or not since the last visit of another application agent. If the file has not been modified, the corresponding tuple is not returned to the agent. Figure 7 shows the reaction class for this case. In this case, the state of the reaction is stored in an instance variable of the reaction object. However, as already stated, the reaction could also store it as a tuple in the tuple space.

```
class TransformTake implements Reactivity {
public Entry reaction(Space s, FileEntry Fe, Operation O,
Identity I) {
// the parameters represent the reference to the local
// tuple space, the reference to the matching tuple,
// the operation type and the identity of the agent
  if (I.equals(SysAdmId)) return s.take(Fe, NO_BLOCK, I);
      // the tuple is deleted from the space
      // because the administrator has full rights
  else return Fe; // the tuple is returned but not deleted }}
```

Fig. 6. The TransformTake reaction class

```
class IncrementalVisit implements Reactivity {
   private Date visit;      // date of the last visit
   public IncrementalVisit()      // constructor
   { visit = new Date(); } // when the reaction is installed
   // by an agent, the date of last visit is automatically set
public Entry reaction(Space s,Entry Fe,
                        Operation O,Identity I)
   { if ((FileEntry)Fe.ModificationTime.before(visit))
     // was the document modified before last visit?
       return null;    // if not, no tuple has to be returned
     else
     { visit = new Date(); // set the time of the last visit
       return Fe; } // return the tuple of the updated page}}
```

Fig. 7. The IncrementalVisit reaction class

6 Conclusions and Work in Progress

The paper describes the design and implementation of the MARS system, whose aim is to define a general coordination architecture based on reactive tuple spaces for Java-based mobile agents. The capability of embodying programmable reactivity into the coordination media permits to tune the semantics of the interactions and to lead to more flexible and secure coordination model.

Currently, we are extending MARS for integration into the WWW: the MARS tuple space is going to be encapsulated in a HTTP proxy, with the goal of defining a general framework for the execution of distributed interactive WWW applications based on mobile agents [5].

References

[1] R. M. Adler, 'Distributed Coordination Models for Client-Server Computing', IEEE Computer, Vol. 29, No. 4, April 1995, pp. 14-22.

[2] J. Baumann, F. Hohl, N. Radouniklis, K. Rothermel, M. Strasser, "Communication Concepts for Mobile Agents", in [15], pp. 123-135.

[2] G. Cabri, L. Leonardi, F. Zambonelli, "How to Coordinate Internet Applications based on Mobile Agents", 7th IEEE Workshops on Enabling Technologies: Infrastructures for Collaborative Enterprises, Stanford (CA), June 1998.

[4] L. Cardelli, D. Gordon, "Mobile Ambients", Foundations of Software Science and Computational Structures, LNCS, No. 1378, Springer-Verlag (D), 1998, pp. 140-155.

[5] P. Ciancarini et al., "Redesigning the Web: From Passive Pages to Coordinated Agents in PageSpaces", 3rd Symp. on Autonomous Decentralized Systems, pp. 377-384, 1997.

[6] P. Ciancarini, D. Rossi, "Jada - Coordination and Communication for Java Agents", in [17], pp. 213-226.

[7] E. Denti, A. Natali, A. Omicini, "On the Expressive Power of a Language for Programmable Coordination Media", ACM Symp. on Applied Computing, Feb. 1998.

[8] P. Domel, A. Lingnau, O. Drobnik, "Mobile Agent Interaction in Heterogeneous Environment", in [15], pp. 136-148.

[9] A. Fuggetta, G. Picco, G. Vigna, "Understanding Code Mobility", IEEE Transactions on Software Engineering, 1998, to appear.

[10] D. Gelernter, N. Carriero, "Coordination Languages and Their Significance", Communications of the ACM, Vol. 35, No. 2, Feb. 1992, pp. 96-107.

[11] General Magic, http://www.generalmagic.com/technology/odyssey.html.

[12] R. Gray, "Agent Tcl: A flexible and secure mobile-agent system", in Mark Diekhans Mark Roseman editor, 4th Annual Tcl/Tk Workshop, Monterey (CA), July 1996.

[13] W. Li, D.G. Messerschmitt, "Itinerative Computing Using Java", http://ptolemy.eecs.berkeley.edu/dgm/javatools/java-to-go.

[14] D. B. Lange, D. T. Chang, IBM Aglets Workbench - Programming Mobile Agents in Java", IBM Corporation White Paper, September 1996.

[15] "Proceedings of the 1st International Workshop on Mobile Agents", Berlin (D), LNCS, No. 1219, Springer-Verlag (D), April 1997.

[16] The MOON Home Page, University of Modena, http://sirio.dsi.unimo.it/MOON.

[17] "Mobile Object Systems", LNCS, No. 1222, Springer Verlag (D), February 1997.

[18] Object Management Group, "Common Object Services Specification", Volume 1, March 1994, http://www.omg.com.

[19] A. Omicini, F. Zambonelli, "TuCSoN: a Coordination Model for Mobile Agents", 1st Workshop on Innovative Internet Information Systems, Pisa (I), June 1998.

[20] H. Peine, T. Stolpmann, "The Architecture of the Ara Platform for Mobile Agents", in [15], pp. 50-61.

[21] "The JavaSpace Specifications", Sun Microsystems, June 1997.

Enabling a Mobile Network Manager (MNM)
Through Mobile Agents

Akhil Sahai, Christine Morin

IRISA-INRIA,
Campus Universitaire de Beaulieu
35042 Rennes Cedex (France)
{asahai, cmorin }@irisa.fr

Abstract. Network management comprises of monitoring and control of a network. Ideally a network management system should be able to provide the facility of managing the network from any site and from any system and network. However the present network management systems are centralized and tied to particular systems. We introduce the unique concept of a Mobile Network Manager (MNM) to provide network administrators a system and location independent network manager which will be useful under a variety of circumstances. In order to enable the MNM mobile agents have been used. The mobile agents are furnished by the mobile agent environment MAGENTA (Mobile AGENT environment for distributed Applications) which provides autonomous, reactive, proactive and communicative mobile agents. MAGENTA has been designed and implemented to support mobile user aware applications. The mobile agents are used not only to facilitate the disconnected mode of functioning of the MNM but also to decentralize network management functionalities. The applicability and usefulness of mobile agents in implementing the functionalities of MNM has been compared with the client-server mechanism.

1   Introduction

Network management plays an important role in the configuration, proper functioning, and maintenance of a network. The task of network management relies heavily on the competence of the administrator to discern the large amount of available data. It is thus necessary for the administrator to be available in the proximity of a Network Management Station (NMS). However, the nature of network faults being random it is often not the case. In case of an unforeseen and untimely emergency an administrator away from office can utilize the MNM from the present location without wasting precious time. In the existent network management systems the administrator receives a cryptic pager message in case of an emergency and one of the recourse left to the administrator is to rush to the management station. Administrators absent from their office (due to work meetings, travelling etc) may also intend to perform some amount of their duties and may avail of the MNM. The MNM would also be useful when mobility of the administrator comes as a part of job description. In case of administrators managing large intranets the administrator may be obliged to move from one site to another(e.g, because of some network upgrade being carried out). The administrator however should be able to perform his/her duties normally in spite of being mobile. The usage of MNM can be envisaged during installation and upgrade of networks. The field personnel installing a network component may wish to study the components behaviour in the context of larger network and may wish to utilize an MNM to continuously study and modify the component characteristics. The MNM has thus been designed to be a system and location independent manager which can be utilized by the administrator from whichever system or site he/she is present on. The MNM executes on a portable computer and thus is constrained by the minimal resource available to it and also by the fallible and costly link which the mobile computer utilizes to connect to the wired network. In order to overcome the resource constraints and also to provide for disconnected computing the MNM is enabled through mobile agents.

The agent-based computing has been found to be more effective than the client-server paradigm in certain application domains [6] and specially in the case of partially connected computing. Of late mobile agents have evoked lot of interest [2][5] [4][3]. The mobile agents used by the MNM are furnished by MAGENTA. The MAGENTA (Mobile AGENT environment for Administration) agents are autonomous, they perform according to predefined goals, react to changes in the environment and communicate with other mobile agents and thus satisfy the weaker notion of agency [1]. MAGENTA provides for extensible and modifiable functionalities of the agents, fault-tolerance, dynamic adaptability to changes in the environment, flexibility in choice of location of agent code, simultaneous and fast execution of agents, true system independence along with access to system functions and the facility of remote execution.

In this paper, we present the motivations, design and implementation of the MNM. We also present the MAGENTA environment and describe, how it is utilized to enable the functioning of the MNM. The rest of the paper is structured as follows. The subsequent section provides a background on mobile agents followed by a brief overview of network management systems. Section 4 presents the design of MNM. The MAGENTA environment is then presented in Section 5. The next section describes the functioning of MNM followed by performance measures of the MNM before concluding.

2 Overview of Network Management

A typical network management system contains four types of components: Network Management Stations (NMSs), agents[1] running on managed nodes, management protocols, and management information. A typical NMS is depicted in

---

[1] These are network management programs executing at the network elements, not to be confused with mobile agents

Figure 1. A NMS uses the management protocol to communicate with agents running on the managed nodes. The information communicated between the NMS and agents is defined by a Management Information Base (MIB). The management standards that have emerged are the Simple Network Management Protocol (SNMP)[8] and the OSI management system which utilizes the Common Management Information Protocol (CMIP)[8]. The SNMP protocol provides *get, set, trap* primitives for interaction between the NMS and SNMP agents.

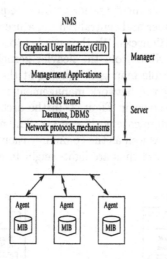

Fig. 1. A typical Network Management System

Each resource to be managed at the SNMP agent is represented by an object and MIB is a structured collection of such objects. The MIB is defined in terms of a tree structure. Each object is assigned an object identifier (oid). These objects are placed under different groups. Some of the important groups in the commonly used MIB-2 are system, interfaces, at, ip, icmp, tcp, udp, egp etc. These groups consists of large number of variables. The group system for example, comprises of *sysDescr, sysObjectID, sysUpTime, sysContact, sysName, sysLocation* and *sysServices*. These variables describe a system, for example, sysUpTime describes the time since the network management portion of the system was last reinitialized and sysName refers to an administratively assigned name for the managed node. The NMS requests the SNMP agent from time to time the values of these variables by referring to them by their oids. The SNMP agents send a trap to the NMS in case there is an alarming change in the SNMP variables. The NMS also typically utilizes client-server mechanism to access the SNMP values.

3 Design of the MNM

In order to implement the MNM we made some design choices. These design choices were guided by the special nature of the environment of execution of the MNM and also by the nature of tasks to be performed by it. Following are some of the design choices we made.

3.1 Design choices

Distribution of the network management system

We intended to build a light-weight and portable network manager, however the existent Network Management Stations (NMS) require a large amount of resource are limited in number and centralized in nature which leads to scalability problem and network bottlenecks. We thus needed to separate the management applications part of the NMS from the heavier kernel part. This enabled the possibility of having multiple managers existing at the same time and thus the possibility of distributing the network management system. We thus came up with an architecture as shown in Figure2. In the architecture there are multiple managers which communicate with a server. The manager comprises of the GUI and the applications as well as the communication mechanism to access the server and SNMP agents and thus are light-weight in nature.

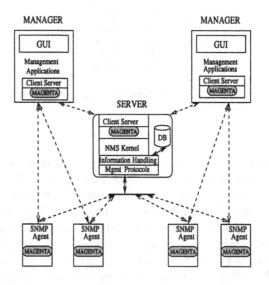

Fig. 2. The utilized network management architecture

Location independence

We also intended to have a location independent manager i.e MNM needed to operate from any site. In case of absence of wired network, the MNM is obliged to use the telephone line or use the wireless link. In the network management system we have provided mechanisms to the managers so as to access the server and SNMP agents from a remote site using different types of connections and possibly simultaneously, irrespective of the location of the site.

System independence
The existent network management systems are normally tied to a particular system and have dedicated machines for their operation. We distributed the network management system in order to provide for a uniform and simple interface, irrespective of system. Java being architecturally neutral provides the facility of a uniform interface on different platforms. Our network management systems being written in Java is also cost-effective.

Overcoming resource constraints
The MNM was to execute from a portable computer operating either in the tethered mode (using telephone lines) or in the wireless mode. Both types of connections are characterized by a limited bandwidth availability, high cost and fallibility. In addition the portable computer has limited battery power and resources. Thus, it could not be connected for a long time to the network. In order to get around these problems, mobile agent technology has been used to enable the functioning of the MNM.

3.2 Agent based network management system

Our network management system comprises of managers, a server and SNMP agents. The managers are dual mode in nature. In static mode the manager executes on a wired computer while in the mobile mode it operates on a mobile computer. The manager communicates with the server and the SNMP agents using either the client-server mechanism or the mobile agent mechanism. The mobile agents are furnished by the MAGENTA (Mobile AGENT environment for distributed Applications) environment. All the management components namely, managers, server and SNMP agents as shown in Figure 2 are integrated with the MAGENTA environment. The managers also are provided with the client-server mechanism and can perform get, get-next and set operations on the SNMP agents directly.

4 MAGENTA Environment

MAGENTA is a mobile agent environment available over a large range of systems as it is written in Java. The MAGENTA environment essentially comprises of the *lieus* and *agents*. A lieu is a program that implements support services for reception, execution, storage and moving of incoming agents, and services to maintain information about other lieus and agents in the environment. The lieu also facilitates communication between agents allowing the agents to reside on it. Every lieu has a globally unique name and can appear and disappear dynamically. The

MAGENTA agents are programs that move between the lieus, following a travel itinerary and performing a predefined task. Each agent is provided with a *purpose* which defines its type behaves autonomously to achieve its purpose. The agent executes a *perform* primitive which comprises of code of execution. Each agent is also provided with a *permit* in order to determine its suitability for execution on a lieu; an agent that arrives on a lieu is first authenticated and after, if it passes the security requirements, it is allowed to access the services available on the lieu. The agents also detect changes in the environment and store the information in their variable *knowledge*. In MAGENTA, the agents have the ability to operate autonomously, to react to changes in the environment by changing their itinerary, to *meet* other agents in order to communicate and exchange *notes* with them. MAGENTA in addition to general features provides mechanisms of support for mobile computing. Following are some of the important features of the environment:

4.1 Different types of agent mobility

MAGENTA provides for weak migration of agents i.e it provides for retention of the data state of the agent while on the move. However, it also provides for remote execution, remote evaluation and code on demand. In remote execution an agent can be initialized and sent to a remote site where it executes. Remote evaluation is more suitable for extremely resource constrained devices like PDA which can not either execute a lieu or do not support the Java environment. Such devices can request a remote lieu to initialize and launch an agent on its behalf and can collect the results of the computation once the agent's execution has terminated. Code on demand is a variant of agent mobility paradigm where a site requests another to send an agent to it with the desired code.

4.2 Naming Scheme

In MAGENTA each lieu has a globally unique name. This name can be either chosen at the time of commencement of the lieu or can be automatically assigned. For a lieu on a mobile computer the lieu name is so chosen so as to remain constant over different sessions. This renders the network transparent to the applications using MAGENTA. Even if the IP address changes from one session to another the lieu name remains constant. Once the lieu reconnects with a new address, the information is passed off to other lieus which update their references. The agents thus do not perceive any apparent change and can identify the correct lieu to return to.

4.3 Appearance and disappearance of lieus

The mobile computers are likely to connect intermittently. The disconnections could be preplanned or unplanned. MAGENTA provides for such likelihoods. In MAGENTA the lieus can appear dynamically and disappear dynamically. This disappearance can be foreseen or unforeseen. In case of planned disappearance a mechanism of *exit* is provided to the lieus. The lieu informs all the other lieus about its imminent disappearance and then quits gracefully. When the lieu reappears subsequently all the lieus in the environment are informed about the appearance of the new lieu. A distributed update of information is thus carried out. In case of abrupt disappearance of the lieu, fault-tolerance mechanisms are provided for detecting such disappearances.

The abrupt disappearances of lieus are detected by the following mechanism. Each agent, moving from a lieu to another avoids the unavailable lieus found during its travel, dynamically altering its itinerary and keeping track of the failed lieus in its variable *knowledge*. When the agent arrives at the last destination of its itinerary, it provides the lieu information about the unavailable lieus, if there are such failed lieus, then the destination lieu informs all other lieus about the disappeared lieus. On receiving this information, all other lieus update their local information. So the failure of a lieu running on a mobile computer which disconnects abruptly can be discovered by an agent not launched by it but having it in its itinerary.

A lieu executing on a portable computer might disappear abruptly after launching an agent. The agent after finishing its itinerary moves to the last destination lieu on the wired network. It tries to move to the mobile lieu but it fails in its attempt. It informs the lieu of residence about its failure which in turn informs all other present lieus about the abrupt disappearance of the mobile lieu. Thus a failed lieu is also discovered by the agents launched by it when they try to come back to it at the end of itinerary. The agent in this case waits on the last static lieu for the mobile lieu to connect back. Once the mobile computer lieu appears again, the other static lieus are informed and the agents waiting for the mobile lieu at different lieus come back to the mobile lieu.

4.4 Tolerating faults

The agents because of their very nature of execution are prone to falling prey to numerous accidents. The lieus are also liable to disappear because of abrupt disconnection of portable computers or system crashes. Fault tolerance schemes have been provided to minimize the overheads associated in detection and recovery from such site failures.

In MAGENTA we provide for disappearance and recreation of agents from a single fault at a time. We maintain backup copies of the agents in order to take care of abrupt disappearance of an agent. In order to reduce the number of backup copies and to reduce the communication which results in case of disappearance of an agent we employ a scheme to maintain judicious number of copies. A lieu before sending an agent to the next lieu saves a copy of it and takes the temporary responsibility of detecting the failure of the next lieu. The next lieu after sending the agent to another lieu informs the lieu with the backup to remove the backup. The lieu with the backup periodically performs checks on the next lieu until it receives a message from the next lieu to destroy the backup. In case such a message is not received by the lieu with the backup within timeout and if it detects that the next lieu has crashed it recreates the agent from the backup copy.

This is explained with an example as shown in Figure3. Before an agent moves from a lieu, lets call it a lieu A to the next lieu, say lieu B it makes a copy of itself on lieu A. Lieu B processes this agent and makes a copy of it before moving it to the next lieu, say lieu C. As soon as the agent is successfully moved to the lieu C, lieu B requests lieu A to delete the copy of the agent. In case lieu B discovers that it is not possible to move the agent to lieu C because of some problem, it tries to reach lieu D. In case this operation is successfully carried out it asks lieu A to delete the copy. Lieu B after successfully moving the agent to the next lieu waits for a message from the next lieu, say lieu C. In case, the lieu C fails to send message to lieu B, lieu B understands that lieu C has not been able to move the agent to the next site in the itinerary because of some problems. It thus first does its own check to find out the problem. In case lieu C has crashed the backup copy of the agent on lieu B is used to create the agent and is passed to the next alive lieu. This scheme thus takes care of single fault and regeneration of agent by keeping the messages to a bare minimum.

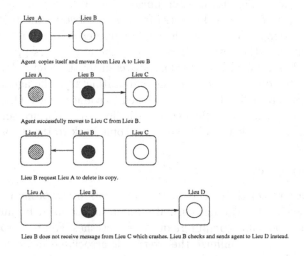

Fig. 3. The implementation of fault-tolerance scheme

4.5   Tracability of agents

In **MAGENTA** a directory service has been provided so as to trace the agents. Every lieu can request all the other lieu about the latest information about the agents present on them and launched by them. This comes in handy to any lieu to determine the status of execution of agents sent by it.

4.6 Flexibility of location of code

The agent can either bring the code to be executed along with it or can execute code present at a remote site. The choice of the location of the code to be executed thus can be made depending on the resources available and the frequency of usage of the code. If the code needs to be used over a long period of time it can be placed at the remote site however if the code is to evolve over time the code is brought by the agent.

4.7 System independence

MAGENTA is implemented using Java programming language, in order to have a system independent implementation. It was envisaged that for some applications for example MNM it was necessary to access system information. Different systems use a different path separator and also need different native method implementations. So an effort was made to satisfy the requirement and at the same time maintain the system independence of MAGENTA. Dynamic class loaders were written for a lieu. The Native method implementations are thus loaded on the fly in case they exist. In the absence of such implementations and error is provided to the agent. A dot-notation has also been used to take care of the different path separators available on different separator.

5 Functionalities of the MNM

The MNM has been provided a variety of mobile agent based functionalities. These functionalities range from performance study of network components to installation of software at multiple remote sites. Following are some of the functionalities.

Performance

The MNM can either obtain the values of the SNMP variables from a remote SNMP agent by using client server technique or can use mobile agents for the same. In case of client server mechanism the get, get-next, set request primitives are used to interact with the network components.

While using mobile agents, the agent is given a number of samples, multiple oids (Object identifiers) and component's lieu name. The agent moves to the network component studies the oid values for a given number of samples and comes back to the MNM carrying it's results in its folder. The studied values can be displayed in charts namely histograms, bar, pie and line charts. This is also useful for studying behaviour of network components over a long time.

Install

The agent is provided a software, the directory where to install the software and a list of network components. The agent moves from one component to another installing the software and returns with the results in its folder. MAGENTA uses a dot notation to overcome the problem of different path separators in different operating systems. These dots are replaced by local class path separators.

In case the desired directory is not found the mobile agent installs the software in a default directory provided by the lieu. The folder of the agent contains the information about which components have the software installed and on which of them the agent was unable to install the software. The same agent is also used for software upgrade.

Audit

The agent is provided a list of parameters to look into e.g disk usage, system and application configuration, users using the machine etc and a list of network components. The agent moves from one host to another finding all the required information and comes back to the MNM with all these results in its folder.

Retrieve

The agent is told to retrieve the desired information from one or more components. It is used to query the server for large quanta of informations, especially to study the archives.

Net checker

The agent moves to the lieu on the server and performs get on all the SNMP variables from a list of SNMP agents provided by the MNM. This is useful to test the status of the health of the network.

6 Performance Evaluation

In order to compare the usefulness and applicability of mobile agents in implementing the basic network management functionalities we have compared it with the client server mechanism. The MNM was executed on *Cezembre* IBM ThinkPad 760 EL, a Pentium PC, 133 MHz, having 16Mo memory, executing windows 95 connected onto a 10Mbps Ethernet. The server was run on *Astrolog* an IBM Power PC executing AIX 4.1 and connected on the same Ethernet. SNMP agents were run on a variety of machines. The results so obtained are depicted in the following figures.

The comparison of bandwidth utilization is done as follows. In the case of client-server mechanism a SNMP get requests are sent continuously from cezembre to Astrolog for the desired number of samples and the response packets are received continuously at Cezembre. In the case of mobile agents, the agent is sent from Cezembre to Astrolog where it collects locally the required number of samples and comes back to Cezembre. The packet sizes of the SNMP get query and that of the response were noted and the size of the agent sent and received were noted and the bandwidth utilization comparison is depicted in Figure 4.The comparison is pessimistic in approach because even a small amount of data as is the case in client-server might require a large UDP packet. The curve for the mobile agent starts at 20K bytes as the size of the agent sent is 10K bytes. The increase in size of the agent results from the data collected at Astrolog. The packet size of the SNMP get request was measured to be 40 bytes and the response packet size was measured to be 31 bytes at the application level. A similar comparison for retrieval of samples of 5 SNMP variables is shown in Figure 5. In terms of bandwidth utilization thus client-server is beneficial to a threshold of

300 samples after which the mobile agent technique becomes more effective. In the latter case this threshold reduces to 60 samples. Thus mobile agent approach is suitable for long term monitoring of network components.

In Figure 6 the comparison of bandwidth utilization, when a single agent is sent in a itinerary to retrieve 400 samples of a single SNMP variable from multiple machines and client-server technique is shown. The client-server mechanism is used from the manager machine to the SNMP agent machines separately and the requests are made in parallel. We observe that for this particular case an itinerary of no more than 23 machines is desirable. Thus after this threshold either the agent should return to the launching lieu or empty its load before moving on to new lieus which will reduce its size and thus the bandwidth usage. In Figure 7 the response times between client-server and the mobile-agent technology are compared. From the manager machine the time (in millisecs) it took for both the agents and the client-server technique to retrieve the given number of samples were noted and plotted as shown. The response time in retrieving the samples were initially found better in client-server technique. But for larger number of samples the response time was better in sending an agent to retrieve the values than using client-server technique to continuously query and obtain the values of the SNMP variable from the SNMP agent.

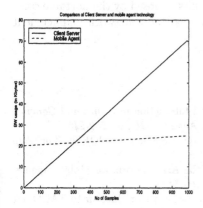
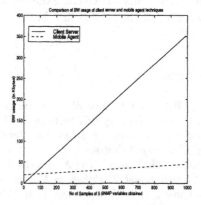

Figure 4:Comparison of bandwidth utilization

Figure 5:Comparison of bandwidth ut ilization

7 Conclusion

In this paper we have presented the design and implementations details of the unique idea of a Mobile Network Manager which we think would be of great importance in the realm of distributed system management. In this context we

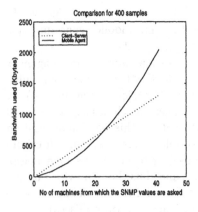

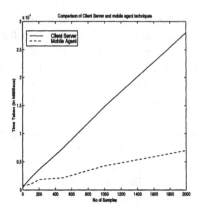

Figure 6:Comparison of bandwidth utilization

Figure 7:Comparison of response tim es

have designed and implemented the MAGENTA environment which is highly generic in nature. It provides autonomous, reactive, proactive and communicative mobile agents. We enable the MNM through the utilization of mobile agents which we use not only to overcome the constraints imposed by the portable computer and that of the fallible link but also to distribute network management functionalities.

References

1. Russell Beale and Andrew Wood. Agent Based Interaction *in People and Computers IX : Proceedings of HCI'94,Glasgow,UK, August 1994 , pp 239-245*
2. J. Bauman et al. Mole - A Java based Mobile Agent System. *ECOOP'96 Workshop on M obile Object Systems.*
3. H. Peine, T.Stolpmann. The Architecture of the Ara Platform for Mobile Agents. *First international Workshop on Mobile Agents, MA97*
4. D. Johansen, R. V. Renesse and F. B. Schneider. An Introduction to TACOMA Distributed System *Technical report CS-95-23, Department of Computer Science, Institute of Mathematical and Physical Sciences, University of Tromso. http://www.cs.uit.no/DOS/Tacoma/.*
5. D'Agents at Dartmouth. *Computer Science Deptt, Dartmouth college, USA, http://www.cs.dartmouth.edu/ãgent/.*
6. Colin G. and Harrison et al. Mobile Agents: Are they a good idea? *IBM T.J. Watson Research Center Technical Report, 1995.*
7. Sahai A. and Morin C. Towards Distributed and Dynamic Network Management *In the proceedings of IEEE/IFIP Network operations and Management Symposium (NOMS'98), New Orleans, USA, 16-20 February, 1998.*
8. W. Stallings. SNMP, SNMPv2 and CMIP: The practical guide to network management standards. *Addison-Wesley publication, 1994.*

Scalable Service Deployment Using Mobile Agents

Luis Bernardo and **Paulo Pinto**

IST - Instituto Superior Técnico, Lisboa Portugal

Inesc, R. Alves Redol, 9 P-1000 Lisboa Portugal

Phone: +351.1.3100345 Fax: +351.1.3145843

{lflb,paulo.pinto}@inesc.pt

Abstract. Very large networks with thousands of applications and millions of users pose serious problems to the current traditional technology. Moreover, if synchronised client behaviour exists then the limitations are strongly felt. Mobile agent systems can be a suitable technology to answer to these requirements if some aspects of the architecture are carefully designed. This paper proposes a co-operative mobile agent system with a very dynamic and scalable trading service. The system allows applications to deploy servers onto the network to respond to demand making them self-configurable. Clients can also use mobile agents with performance gains. Sets of simulations were performed to study the scalability of the overall system.

1 Introduction

In the current information technology era any new service involves a larger number of end users. Very soon networks with millions of users and thousands of applications will be at work. Despite of the size, which can by itself create operational problems, applications might produce synchronised peaks of traffic due to external events (e.g. lotto draws, sport brokering and interactive TV contests). These peaks can drive parts of the network to a halt if not properly handled. A scalable application implementation must adapt to the intensity and relative distribution of the client load using a dynamic set of servers.

A static approach to the problem, using a fixed number of servers and conventional traders, would lead to inefficient resource usage solutions: either the number of servers is insufficient (during peaks of the load) or there is an over-dimensioning of the servers deployed. A scalable world-wide application implementation should also cover two other aspects: servers must be able to run on an open world-wide set of platforms (to set the maximum load limit as high as possible and to localise interactions); and the server deployment and request binding should be tuneable (to allow service specific optimisations). Most of the traditional scalable service implementations rely on a closed set of servers (WWW cache servers [1], TP monitors [3], task load balancing algorithms [9], smart clients [20], and others). Such systems rely on system load-balancing servers or on a "head" application server (which redirects the requests to other servers), introducing potential bottlenecks. Additionally, the technology must efficiently support the dynamic deployment of new servers: Factory objects and ORB implementation repositories [13] might be used, however they are not optimised to deal with the dynamic creation of new types of servers. The required semantic resulting from all these requirements is met with the mobile agent paradigm: It provides a simple way to deploy personalised services (replica creation from an initial service provider's server) and an open ubiquitous platform where mobile autonomous agents might run.

The solution proposed in this paper is based on a mobile agent system approach and on new scalable algorithms for the trader (called here location service) and services. Servers are implemented using mobile agents, and can deploy new replicas when the demand rises, or migrate towards the location of the majority of the clients. They use the service dynamic topological information from the location service, the client load, and the overall situation of other peer servers, to control the deployment of new servers and adapt precisely to the client load. Server agents are autonomous on their control over server deployment.

Our system assumes a scenario where clients look for a precise service. Clients use the location service to resolve unique application names to single server references. The system does not support service discoveries based on characteristics (price, availability, etc.). Each application server sets an area of the network for its service to be known (server domain). The location service takes into account its own load and server domain sizes to change dynamically its configuration. As other services, the location service is implemented using mobile agents.

The rest of this paper is organised as follows. Section 2 presents a system overview, including the client implementation and location service. Server deployment control and inter-server synchronisation is discussed in section 3. Section 4 presents a study of the dynamic behaviour of servers in face of a rising client demand. Section 5 describes related work and Section 6 concludes. This paper extends a previous one [4] by examining thoroughly the mobile agent utilisation and by extending the dynamic behaviour scalability analysis ([4] restricts its analysis to the server creation algorithm).

2 System Overview

The network provides a ubiquitous platform of agent systems, in which any agent (server or client) can run. Each agent system is tied to a location server (running locally or on another nearby system), where all the interfaces of the local agents are registered. This location server is connected to others to offer a global service.

The proposed architecture does not conflict with the standardisation efforts of OMG [15], or some of the available mobile agent systems (Aglets [10], MOLE [19], Voyager [12], etc). Mobile agents are defined as autonomous objects, which may communicate with other objects or agents through a variety of interfaces [2], and are able to migrate or start agents on remote agent systems. The main differences are the location service requirements.

When a client searches for an application name, the location service helps in the binding process (the association to a server) directing it to the nearest server. If the location server knows more than one server, it will do splitting of client traffic. If it knows that a new, and closer, server was created it will start using the new one, and propagates this information. When a client comes for resolution it will get the best answer for that moment.

The balance between the number of clients, servers and location servers acts as a general load balancing mechanism in the system. The number of application servers will vary with the number of active clients, and the number and range of each location server will vary with both the numbers of active clients and the application servers.

2.1 Clients

Clients may interact with servers using Remote Procedure Calls (RPC) from their location nodes (or other remote interaction mechanism), may migrate to the server's agent system, or do both if, for instance, the first fails. Although not essential, mobility on the client side has advantages in terms of the overall traffic on the network: it gets more asynchronous (less demanding in "peak" network usage), can support unstable connections to mobile computers more easily, and could be tailored to satisfy a set of routing constrains according to a service specific algorithm. Performance models for both approaches ([7], [19]) showed some of the combined RPC/client mobility performance advantages when filtering large amounts of data or when performing multiple interactions over low bandwidth links. However, client migration may also cause the overloading of the servers' agent system. To avoid such effect, the client agent migration destiny is selected using the remote location server. Notice that on the system described here, the impact of variable network latency is lower than on the referred models because of the server mobility, which reduces the "distance" between clients and servers.

The system provides a simple way to integrate legacy system clients, which may interact with server agents using RPC (for instance CORBA IIOP [13]).

2.2 Location Service

The location service is one of the major players for scalability. It has two different roles: at the location server domain (the set of agent systems tied to a server), it must provide detailed local information and balance requests among local available servers (for each service); at a global level, each location server must provide a scalable global trading information service (although not complete). The global load balancing is based on network proximity relations.

The necessity for fast updating during the creation of a server clone, the propagation of frequent updates due to migration, and the dynamic nature of the information in this system (based on dynamic server domains) introduce a high overhead which invalidate some of current technical solutions based on static hierarchic systems (e.g. DNS, X.500 or OMG Trading [14]). See [4] for details.

A scalable and highly mobile system must have the following characteristics: Firstly, the application names must be flat ([18] reached a similar conclusion). Secondly, the location search path, which is now independent from the application name structure, must be performed on a step-by-step basis, through a path of location servers where each one contain routing information indexed by the application names. Thirdly, the load and characteristics of the overall system should tune this step-by-step path.

One important feature is how the location service scales to a large population. We use a mixture of meshed and hierarchic structure where location servers at each hierarchical level interact with some of the others at that level and (possibly) with one above. Higher hierarchic levels offer a broader but less detailed vision of the services available. The hierarchical structure and the scope of the mesh change dynamically according to the load of the system, and to the size of the server domains.

The server domain is service specific. For instance, a car parking service would simply advertise on the surroundings of each car park, while a popular lotto broker service would advertise on a broader range (pricing schemes could be a deterrent to artificially large domains). Clients control their search range. Due to lack of depth, or incomplete information, resolutions can fail, and a deeper search must be tried.

3 Servers

Under the envisioned conditions, server development is a delicate task, because most of the time there will be only a vague forewarn of how high the "peak" of the load will be, or when it will happen. An adaptation algorithm is required, to achieve the service requirements.

3.1 Server Deployment

Several reasons can originate the deployment of a new server (or the migration of an idle one). A new server can help solving problems related to: 1) insufficient processing resources (the overloading of the available servers); 2) insufficient bandwidth (by providing a proxy server which compresses the data); or 3) the support of unstable connections (by providing a local service proxy, which re-synchronises with the remaining servers after connection re-establishment). The proposed algorithm is optimised to deal with the first problem.

A good measure of the quality of service for this system is the global service response time to client requests. For each application, this time must be confined within specific bounds. It includes: the time to resolve the application name to a server reference (at the location service), plus a waiting time due to client load, plus a service time dependent on the application (which depends on whether it is a single RPC or a session, on the overheads for distributed data consistency, etc.).

The adaptation algorithm aims at controlling the number of server agents deployed, but also their locations and each server domain, to keep the waiting time under control due to client load. The most important parameter will be the number of servers. However, the others will influence the relative distribution of clients, and the load induced at the location servers. As clients are bound to servers based on the distance, some unbalancing can exist depending on the relative distribution of clients.

The adaptation algorithm proposed for overloaded servers in this paper is isolated. I.e., each server monitors its local load to detect conditions which violate the application requirements (threshold values are used), and compiles the clients' origins. Any server activity measurement might be used. However, best results are achieved if the load includes a measurement of the queued client requests waiting at the server.

If the load goes above a top threshold value, the server creates and deploys a new server. The replica location is selected amongst the most frequent sources of agents (local or not). The new replica will start running after T_{clone}, which is the time to create a clone on the remote agent system, plus the delays at the location service (dissemination of the new clone's server reference). During this period, new clients continue to bind to an already overloaded server. So, the triggering mechanism of the top threshold value is disabled for a duration dependent on T_{clone}. A simple load measurement is the length of the waiting clients' queue, where the disabled period is converted in an increment of the threshold value (proportional to the clients processed by a new server during its creation). In result, the replica creation rate is controlled by the client request's arrival rate.

If the demand is very high, a server might become crowed with bounded clients (and the waiting time exceeds largely the server response time). A redistribution of clients must then take place to speed up the client's service total response time. The server can unbind some of the clients, or can mutate itself (i.e., close the old interface and create a fresh one). This will force a new resolution phase for all waiting clients and a redistribution of the clients for the available servers.

Dynamically created servers are destroyed using a market based control technique [6]. When a server's load goes below a bottom threshold, it sends messages to the other servers within a maximum range, requesting one of them to take its place. Requested server's answer with bid messages, stating if they can expand their domain and their load. To speed up the overall system response, servers are not blocked for a "bid" time. The resolution phase (load transfer phase) is acknowledged, and the load transfer can be aborted if, for instance, the server had its load increased in result of another ending server and can not handle the new clients. After a load transfer is accepted, the location service is updated, and the originating server dies.

Compared to other approaches based on scheduler objects [3],[9] or inter-server synchronisation [6], the use of an isolated algorithm during overload conditions allows a faster response, and scales to higher levels of client requests. However, it may cause a temporary deployment of a higher number of servers, if for instance, the majority of the origin of the clients moves to another region of the network. During a transition phase, new servers are created while some of the previous ones die.

A complementary algorithm can be used during moderate overloaded conditions (triggered by a lower second high threshold value), or as a response to client maximum delay overrun reports. An example for this algorithm might be a market based control technique that would search for a underused server, prior to creating a new one. The selected server would migrate to the needed region, after delegating its previous server domain.

The presented algorithms also apply to the location servers, with slight modifications. Location servers may create a replica and split a location domain to reduce its load, or may join with another neighbour. The redistribution procedure also applies to the location servers. After a location server mutation, only agents inside the location domain will be able to reach it. Remote clients using RPC which need this location server (even indirectly) will have to wait for interface information dissemination.

3.2 Service Implementation

The proposed system is not restricted to applications which might be implemented with parallel independent servers. It can also be applied both to systems with partial non-mobility requirements (due to a static component or a huge amount of data), or to applications with intra-server synchronisation requirements.

The system is flexible in terms of mobility requirements because even applications with non-mobile components might partially use this scalable feature. If their semantics allow, several smaller interface agents can be deployed in the system. They may implement caches of information (e.g. HTTP [1],[5]), concentrators of client requests or generic proxies (e.g. [8]), reducing the non-mobile components' load.

Depending on the nature of the service, servers might need extra specific synchronisation logic to maintain consistency of shared data between the servers. The average service time will increase with the number of servers. The algorithm will only be applicable when the processing capacity gain of a new server is higher than the average service degradation. It provides better results when servers can work autonomously or have low coherence requirements. An example of the latter kind is the CODA distributed file system [11], where the coherence is implemented on limited points on time, with little or almost no degradation of service time. For applications where a stronger coherence is needed, the improvements may also come from the deployment of interface agents. The maximum intra-synchronisation rate will limit the maximum number of deployable servers, and the maximum client load supported.

4 Dynamic Behaviour

The analysis of the dynamic behaviour of the system was performed with a simulator, developed using the Ptolemy [16] simulation system. The set of tests presented focuses on the study of the adaptation to a constant demand from clients, which originates server overload. Application servers run both the server creation and server destruction algorithms. The effect of the location service was reduced by setting a low-resolution time (compared to the application service time), and by disabling the dynamic change of the hierarchy. Nevertheless, it still runs the application name distribution algorithm, which introduces a delay between the deployment of a new server and the stabilisation of the location service information. The effects of the variation of the latency on the communication between agents were not considered, by setting it to a constant value. This very symmetrical scenario produces highly synchronised reactions on servers, but it is clearly the worst case.

4.1 Simulation Environment

All tests were conducted with the network presented in figure 1 (132 agent systems and 19 static location servers). Results were collected at the end of each measuring interval of 0.5 units of simulation time (0.5 tics). The duration of each simulation was 30 tics.

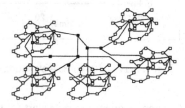

Fig. 1. Simulated meshed network

The simulation assumes an atomic interaction between clients and servers. A client is born and lives until it can make an invocation to the server. Our main results are the client's lifetimes, which are the overall application response times.

The application and location service servers are modelled by a queue defined by a service time probability function, T_s and T_L respectively. For all the experiments reported in this paper, T_L and T_s have deterministic functions with the values 0.001 and 0.1 tics respectively. The transmission time was set to 0.0001 tics, and the clone creation time to 1 tic. Servers use the number of requests on the queue as a load measurement to trigger the creation of servers, and the average utilisation time (a weighted average of measurements in 0.5 tic intervals) as a load measurement to trigger the server destruction. The top threshold value was 15 clients in queue, and the temporary increment due to clone creation was 15 clients (1.5 times T_{clone} divided by T_s). The bottom threshold value was 50% of the processing time. All the reported results were obtained with the same client redistribution procedure: clients waiting in the application server queue are unbound if their waiting time exceeds a duration of 1.5 tics. New clients were generated with a uniform distribution of the inter-server deployment time on the interval [0, 2/ClientLoad] over a group of 125 nodes. *ClientLoad* defines the average number of clients that enters into the system during a time unit.

4.2 Time Evolution

Figure 2 shows the evolution over time of some averages during each measuring interval of: *New Clients*, the number of clients which entered the system; *Unbinds*, the number of clients unbound during the interval; *Pending Clients*, the number of clients waiting on queues (of both application and location servers); *Ending Clients*, the number of clients which died during the interval; and *Processing Capacity*, the maximum number of clients that the servers can process during the interval. The second graphic shows the evolution of the average global response time per client measured on each interval, represented by TT (Total Time). The curves were measured with an average (ClientLoad) of 250 clients per tic (125 per measuring interval) and five initial servers.

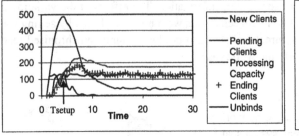 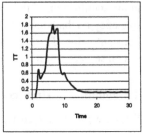

Fig. 2. Service Response – evolution on time of the number of clients and of the total delay

As soon as client requests start (at tic 1), the number of pending clients grows until a point in time where the processing power deployed is enough for the client load, T_{setup}. After that it starts to decrease. TT continues to grow just for a short while after this point (the curves are almost equal because redistribution was used, as curve *Unbinds* show). With the reduction of the number of pending clients, the number of servers decreases. However, the processing capacity is always above the new client rate due to the 50% idle time allowed for each server (the minimum load threshold). It is clear how the system gets stable with a very low and constant response time.

The time measurements used in the remaining sections were: the average value of the client lifetimes, TT_{avg}, and the time value that includes 95 percent of all client lifetimes, *TT95* (which gives a notion of how high the delay peak is). Additionally, the "Processing Capacity Ratio" (ratio between the maximum number of clients that servers can process and the number of clients entering the system) quantifies the availability of processing resources to satisfy the client demand. The variation of the client waiting time depends on the value of the processing capacity ratio (PCR) and on the distribution of clients per server. It gets higher when the PCR is below one and gets lower otherwise (assuming a completely balanced system).

4.2 Results with Weak Inter-server Synchronisation

The algorithm performance depends on a number of parameters and options, which include: the client redistribution procedure, the time to create a clone, the top threshold value, the timeout value (with partial client unbinding), the initial number of servers, and the ClientLoad. The presented results focus on the scalability with ClientLoad. A study on the effect of some of the other parameters on the server creation algorithm can be found in [4].

The next set of experiments study the system response to different client loads (ranging from 125 clients per tic to 8000 clients per tic), using two different numbers for the initial servers (initial processing capacity of 10 and 50 clients per tic). Figures 3a, 3b and 4 show the distribution of TT_{avg}, TT95 and PCR.

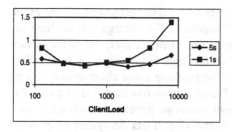

Fig. 3a. TT$_{avg}$

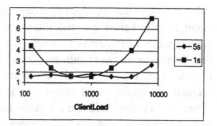

Fig. 3b. TT95

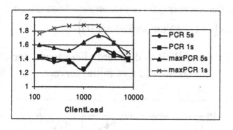

Fig. 4. PCR

The results show a minor variation of the response times (TT95 and TT$_{avg}$) and of PCR compared to the variation on ClientLoad (6400%), which prove the algorithm scalability. The initial number of servers has a great influence on the three parameters, except for the final number of servers deployed (PCR). Location servers (which support a maximum of 1000 requests per tic) influence negatively the system response for ClientLoad values above 1000. This effect in specially noticeable with a single starting server (but also for five starting servers for 8000 clients per tic), where the overloading of the single initial application server's location server occurs. In result, the time to resolve the application names increases, and in consequence, the server clones creation is delayed. For ClientLoad values below 1000 clients per tic, when the load is higher the system has the following characteristics: the adaptation gets done quicker (due to a flooding of servers), is less sensible to the initial number of servers, and has a lower final value of PCR (higher server usage).

The effects of slow response for low ClientLoad values and location server overloading could be compensated. The slow response could be improved by configuring the algorithm parameters (the client redistribution timeout and the top threshold) for a faster response. The use of a higher number of initial application servers would reduce the number of resolutions received at each of the location servers. Nevertheless, the dynamic change of hierarchy of the location service would create new location server replicas, and the load would be redistributed between them. After a transition phase (for local client's requests draining), the service would become available again for the entire network.

4.3 Results with Strong Inter-server Synchronisation

Most services require some state synchronisation between servers. This will introduce a limit to the maximum number of clients (load) which can be processed per tic. It is still possible to use the algorithm on these cases with minor corrections as long as the client load is below the maximum value supported. The average service time increases when a new server is created (and decreases when one dies). When the service time increases, fewer clients are serviced per time unit. In consequence, it takes less time to reach the load top threshold value. The resulting faster clone creation might originate an explosion of server creation. The algorithm was modified to avoid this effect: the top threshold and the client timeout values are incremented when the average service time increases and decremented otherwise. It lets the system adapt more slowly to load peaks.

We tested the approach on a system with a linear degradation for each server (which models a periodic synchronisation between the servers), with the service time given by the following formula: $\text{ServiceTime} = 0.1 \times \left(1 + \alpha \times \left(\text{NumberServers} - 1\right)\right)$.

Figures 5a and 5b show the distribution of TT_{avg} and PCR to different client loads, for nine values of α ranging from 0 (no interference) to 0.07, and five initial servers.

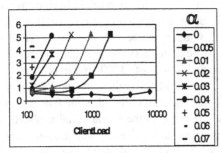 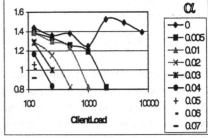

Fig. 5a. TT_{avg} **Fig. 5b.** PCR at tic 30

The main effect of inter-server service degradation time is the existence of a maximum value of ClientLoad[1] for each value of α. When ClientLoad approaches the supported maximum, TT_{avg} increases and the value of PCR decreases. For some ClientLoad values below the maximum, it takes too much time to deploy the necessary servers (PCR below 1), and the system diverges. Although the maximum ClientLoad for the value 0.07 is 143, the system diverges with 125 clients per tic.

5 Related Work

The use of replicated objects indexed by a global location service to support worldwide applications is also proposed on [8], [18]. Their location service is based on a static hierarchic structure, with some scale limitations. Further, they do not handle applications with overloaded servers.

---

[1] MaxClientLoad $= 1 / (0.1 \times \alpha)$

An algorithm to control the location of a mobile but constant set of servers is proposed on [17]. However, it only handles limited bandwidth problems.

Another approach introduces client based scalability [20] by consulting a server directory and scanning for the best available server. This approach needs some client modifications, and implements a limited architecture: the number of servers does not adapt, and each server will always interact with all clients.

6 Conclusions and Future Work

This paper presents a co-operative agent system that allows applications to scale to large networks with millions of users. The dynamic behaviour of the algorithm in face of a strong rise on client demand was studied and several conclusions were drawn based on the results. An overall conclusion is the suitability of such systems and algorithms to respond to "client peak invocations". Traditional approaches do not scale and will create severe bottlenecks if used under these conditions.

The simulation results showed that applications scale with the client load, until a limit defined by the location server capabilities. If the range of values for clone creation, service time, and for name resolution are known, then some quality of service guarantees can be assured. By the correct control on the number of replicas initially deployed and the correct setting of the algorithm parameters, an application may be ready to respond to a roughly predicted rise of the client demand. The inclusion of the dynamic change of the hierarchy of the location server will most likely reduce the dependency on the name resolution time. It is a subject under study.

The use of the mobile agent paradigm provides a sound basis to implement a dynamic service specific algorithm for server deployment. Most of the mobile agent systems available today allow the implementation of the proposed algorithm, if the location service functionality is implemented.

This paper covered atomic interactions between clients and servers. Multi-invocation interactions and session interactions can introduce other requirements to the algorithms and are being studied as well.

Acknowledgements

This research has been partially supported by the PRAXIS XXI program, under contract 2/2.1/TIT/1633/95.

References

[1]   Baentsch, M., Baum, L., Molter, G., Rothkugel, S., Sturn, P.: Enhancing the web's Infrastructure: From Caching to Replication. IEEE Internet Computing, Vol. 1 No. 2, March-April (1997) 18-27

[2]   Baumann, J., Hohl, F., Radouniklis, N., Rothermel, K., Straβer, M.: Communication Concepts for Mobile Agent Systems. In: Mobile Agents - Proceedings of the First International Workshop on Mobile Agents (MA'97), Germany, Springer-Verlag LNCS Vol. 1219, April (1997) 123-135

[3]   BEA: TUXEDO White Paper. (1996) http://www.beasys.com/Product/tuxwp1.htm

[4]   Bernardo, L., Pinto, P.: Scalable Service Deployment on Highly Populated Networks. In: Intelligent Agents to Telecommunication Applications - Proceedings Second International Workshop IATA'98, Paris, Springer-Verlag LNCS Vol. 1437, June (1998)

[5]   Bestavros, A.: WWW Traffic Reduction and Load Balancing through Server-Based Caching. IEEE Concurrency, Vol 5 N 1, January-March (1997) 56-66

[6]   Chavez, A., Moukas, A., Maes, P.: Challenger: A Multi-agent System for Distributed Resource Allocation. In: Proceedings of the International Conference on Autonomous Agents, Marina Del Ray, California (1997)

[7]   Chia, T., Kannapan, S.: Strategically Mobile Agents. In: Mobile Agents - Proceedings of the First International Workshop on Mobile Agents (MA'97), Germany, Springer-Verlag LNCS Vol. 1219, April (1997) 149-161

[8]   Condict, M., Milojicic, D., Reynolds, F., Bolinger, D.: Towards a World-Wide Civilization of Objects. In: Proceedings of the 7th ACM SIGOPS European Workshop, Ireland, September (1996)

[9]   Deng, X., Liu, H.-N., Long, J., Xiao, B.: Competitive Analysis of Network Load Balancing. Journal of Parallel and Distributed Computing Vol. 40 N. 2, February (1997) 162-172

[10]   IBM Aglets Workbench - Home Page. http://www.trl.ibm.co.jp/aglets/

[11]   Kistler, J., Satyanarayanau, M.: Disconnected Operation in the Coda File System. ACM Transactions on Computer Systems Vol. 10(1), February (1992)

[12]   ObjectSpace Voyager V1.0.1 Overview. http://wwwobjectspace.com/voyager/

[13]   OMG Inc.: The Common Object Request Broker: Architecture and Specification, Rev 2.0. July (1995)

[14]   OMG Inc.: Trading Service. OMG TC Document 95.10.6, October (1995)

[15]   OMG Inc.: Mobile Agent Facility Specification. OMG Draft, October (1997) ftp://ftp.omg.org/pub/docs/orbos/97-10-05.pdf

[16]   Ptolemy project home page. http://ptolemy.eecs.berkeley.edu/

[17]   Ranganathan, M., Acharya, A., Sharma, S., Saltz, J.: Network-aware Mobile Programs. Technical Report CS-TR-3659 and UMIACS TR 96-46, Department of Computer Science and UMIACS, University of Maryland, June (1996)

[18]   van Steen, M., Hauck, F., Tanenbaum, A.: A Model for Worldwide Tracking of Distributed Objects. In: Proceedings TINA '96 Conference, Heidelberg, Germany, September (1996) 203-212

[19]   Straβer, M., Schwehm, M.: A Performance Model for Mobile Agent Systems. In: Proceedings International Conference on Parallel and Distributed Processing Techniques and Applications PDPTA'97, Vol. II, Las Vegas, (1997) 1132-1140

[20]   Yoshikawa, C., Chun, B., Eastham, P., Vahdat, A., Anderson, T., Culler, D.: "Using Smart Clients to Build Scalable Services". In: Proceedings of the USENIX'1997, Anaheim, California, USA, January (1997)

Designing a Videoconference System for Active Networks

Mario Baldi, Gian Pietro Picco, and Fulvio Risso

Dip. Automatica e Informatica, Politecnico di Torino
C.so Duca degli Abruzzi 24, 10129 Torino, Italy
Phone: +39 11 564 7067   Fax: +39 11 564 7099
{mbaldi,picco,risso}@polito.it

Abstract. Active networks are receiving increasing attention due to their promises of great flexibility in tailoring services to applications. This capability stems from the exploitation of network devices whose behavior can be changed dynamically by applications, possibly using technologies and architectures originally conceived for mobile code systems. Notwithstanding the promises of active networks, real-world applications that clearly benefit by them are still missing. In this work we describe the design of a videoconference system conceived expressly for operation over active networks. The goal of this activity is to pinpoint the benefits that mobile code and active networks bring in this application domain and to provide insights for the exploitation of these concepts in other application domains.

1 Introduction

The role of computer networks is becoming increasingly important in modern computing. This fact poses unprecedented challenges in terms of performance and flexibility which affect the protocols and standards that constitute the communication infrastructure underlying computer networks, as well as the technologies and methodologies used to build distributed applications.

Researchers are devising approaches coming from different perspectives and addressing different layers of abstraction. However, a set of approaches that exploit some form of *code mobility* is currently emerging among the others as particularly promising and intellectually stimulating. Code mobility can be defined informally as the capability to change dynamically the bindings between the code fragments belonging to a distributed application and the location where they are executed. The rationale for code mobility is to reduce network traffic and increase flexibility and customizability by bringing the knowledge embedded in the code close to the resources [5]. This powerful concept is being popularized by a new generation of programming languages and systems that provide abstractions and mechanisms geared towards the task of relocating code. These technologies, often referred to collectively as *mobile code systems*, are targeted at the development of applications on large scale distributed systems like the Internet.

Concurrently with these developments, other researchers are investigating means to introduce flexibility in computer networks by assuming the availability of next-generation network devices whose behavior can be changed dynamically according to users' needs. These *active networks* are receiving a great deal of attention in industry and academia and seem naturally suited to leverage off of the developments in the field of code mobility. In fact, technologies and architectures conceived for building distributed applications exploiting code mobility can be used for supplying dynamically the network devices with application-dependent code that changes their behavior. In this scenario, networks become active because they take part in the computation performed by the applications rather than being concerned only with the transfer of data.

Researchers presently interpret the idea of active network at least with two different nuances. The first, broader interpretation of the term is that the distinction between network nodes and end-systems becomes blurred in terms of functional characteristics. This approach is embodied for example in the work described in [6] and [18]. In this setting, network devices, e.g., routers, can execute mobile code implementing a distributed application which can benefit by direct access to functionality and information at lower layers in the network stack. This *programmable switch approach* [16] does not affect the way current lower and mid layer protocols are designed and deployed. On the other hand, the second interpretation aims at modifying the heart of network protocols, by extending the control information contained in network packets with code describing how to process the packets at the intermediate nodes along the path to the destination. Protocol deployment is then performed on demand, without requiring software preinstallation and upgrade, and yet is under the control of the applications. A packet augmented in this way, also called *capsule* [16], is reminiscent of what the mobile code community calls a mobile agent—an autonomous unit of mobility containing code and state. Toolkits are being developed [17,7] to support the creation and deployment of capsules.

Active networks and, more generally, code mobility are promising ideas. Nevertheless, despite the great deal of interest and effort in these research areas, contributions that characterize precisely and possibly quantitatively the advantages of the approach are only beginning to appear [11,2], while applications that demonstrate these advantages in real-world domains are still largely missing.

The goal of the research described in this paper is to assess the benefits brought by code mobility in the context of active networks. This is achieved pragmatically by constructing a videoconference system according to the aforementioned programmable switch approach. Videoconference is an increasingly popular distributed application which poses significant challenges and constraints and thus can be considered a reasonable testbed for our purposes. Our long term goal is to characterize qualitatively and quantitatively the implementation currently being completed at our university against conventional ones, in order to identify precisely the tradeoffs involved. However, the work presented here focuses on the *design* of our videoconference application and aims at identifying and suggesting novel architectural opportunities enabled by code mobility and active networks.

The paper is structured as follows. Section 2 discusses briefly the requirements of a videoconference system and how these can be satisfied by an architecture that exploits mobile code on an active network. Section 3 describes in detail the architecture of our prototype, and identifies two variants which feature different degrees of distribution. Section 4 provides information about the ongoing implementation. Finally, Section 5 contains brief conclusive remarks and discusses future lines of research on the subject of this paper.

2 Videoconferencing on an Active Network

Videoconference systems can be split grossly in two categories. In *peer-to-peer* conferencing systems, the participants are connected through a multicast network and the videoconference flow generated by each participant is distributed to the others exploiting multicast delivery. An evident advantage of this first approach is its good scalability. However, conference management is complicated by the characteristics of the architecture, especially as far as security is concerned. A relevant example of this category is the tool suite for MBone, the Multicast Backbone [1].

The alternative, popular especially among commercial systems, employs a *centralized* architecture based on a conference server which receives the conference streams from the clients operated by the participants and replicates such streams back to all the clients connected. Centralization not only simplifies the problem of secure access, but also enables customizability. The server can perform additional computation on an incoming videoconference stream on behalf of the clients instead of simply replicating the stream towards them, thus enabling conference users to get control on the delivered quality of service. A centralized approach is affected by the usual drawbacks in terms of scalability and fault-tolerance. An example of centralized system is CuSeeMe [4], while the H.323 standard [8] defines an architecture that accommodates both categories.

Neither of the two solutions described seems suitable for the large scale scenarios that are being envisioned for the Internet. Let us consider for instance the broadcasting of a sport event. In a multicast network, the conference streams are not tailored to the users: the same stream is routed to all the audience members, no matter whether they are connected through a high-bandwidth local area network or a dial-up connection. Thus, the former get a quality lower than their potential, while the latter get unpredictable quality due to the packets discarded to tailor the rate of the data flow to their low capacity access. On the other hand, a centralized architecture requires a huge amount of computational power in the conference server and overloads the network since separate multimedia streams are maintained through the network between the server and each client.

Ideally, a videoconference system should exhibit features coming from both architectures, thus enabling user customization without preventing the scalability of the architecture. Interestingly, the latter is, by and large, one of the goals that motivated active networks and in general the approaches relying on code mobility. Thus, their exploitation in solving the aforementioned problems seems a natural step.

Our architecture is based on a conference server that we call *reflector*. Customizability and scalability are then provided together by:

1. enabling the users to "upload" application code into the reflector, thus changing its behavior and *customizing* it to their needs;
2. running the reflector on the intermediate nodes of the network, where it can use the information managed by the device to become aware of the status of the network and *adapt* to it;
3. enabling the reflector to *migrate* on a different node as a consequence to adaptation.

The first point provides a degree of customizability even higher than the one provided by centralized systems. Customization is not limited to changing the parameters of the reflector, rather it allows to change the code that governs its behavior. The reflector is then basically a "shell" where each client can plug-in dynamically the code describing some customized processing. Thus, for instance:

- Different coding algorithms can coexist in a flexible way. The reflector does not need to be equipped with plenty of coding algorithms in order to encompass the needs of a wide range of clients. These are linked in the reflector dynamically and on demand.
- The quality of service for the encoded videoconference stream can be changed dynamically to fit user needs. The desired policy can be arbitrarily complex and can be changed at run-time. For instance, it is possible to specify application-dependent criteria to discard packets in presence of congestion, as suggested in [3].
- The videoconference flows coming to a client from different participants can be treated differently. For example, a participant can request the reflector to give higher priority or to guarantee a higher quality of service to some flows, and carry the others with a lower quality. The advantage is that flows can be discriminated according to application level information, like the identity of the current speaker.

Point two, that actually provides the rationale for exploiting an active network, deserves some elaboration. At the time of writing, network devices equipped with a run-time support for execution of mobile code are not widely available. However, many vendors have already announced new releases of their products that feature hardware or software support for the Java language [14]. In the implementation of our prototype we cope with this problem, characteristic of the whole research area, by adopting the approach followed by many researchers: we simulate an active device by running the mobile code on a workstation directly connected to a network device.

Point three is at the core of the work described in this paper. The reflector analyzes constantly the data available on the network device and can trigger a

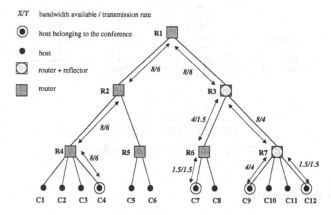

Fig. 1. Cloning reflectors.

migration to adapt to some change in the conditions of the network. We devised two architectural solutions to enable adaptivity through migration. In both cases, the criteria that rule adaptation are embodied in the code of a component of the reflector that is designed to be modular and interchangeable, as described in the next section.

In the first solution, the reflector responds by *relocating* itself in a position of the network that is optimal with respect to some cost function, e.g., distance from the clients. According to the classification presented in [5], the reflector relies on a weak form of mobility where its execution state is not preserved across migration: only its code and a portion of its data state are transferred. This solution is suitable for conferences characterized by a limited number of participants or by heavily clustered participants.

In turn, our second architectural solution is conceived for conferences with a great number of participants. It relies on *cloning* the reflector rather than migrating it; the latter can be regarded as a special case of cloning where the original reflector is terminated. This way, multiple reflectors are injected into the network upon some special event (e.g., when a new participant joins a session), and perform subsequent transformations of the conference streams providing for improved scalability. For instance, Fig. 1 shows a network with two reflectors placed on two different routers, R3 and R7, that are responsible for serving hosts C4, C7, C9, and C12. Notably, the reflectors have been cloned only in the positions of the network where transformation of the videoconference streams is needed. Moreover, whenever possible only one stream is transmitted between reflectors and separate streams are generated close to the participants, thus minimizing the overall network traffic generated by the conference.

The next section illustrates the details of both architectures. In principle, the two architectures can be combined effectively in a single system that, upon the occurrence of some user-specified condition, is capable to switch automatically between the two modes of operation.

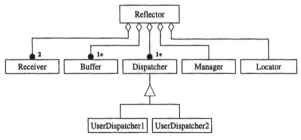

Fig. 2. The components of the reflector.

3   The Architecture

The design described in this section strives for modularity and reconfigurability, in order to leverage off of the opportunities provided by code mobility in changing dynamically the code associated with a component. We specified the design of our prototype using the OMT [12] object-oriented notation. The full OMT design is available in [9].

3.1   The Reflector

The reflector is composed of five classes, depicted in Fig. 2. Receiver, Buffer, and Dispatcher provide the "work power" of the reflector and deal with receiving and transmitting the data packets that constitute the conference streams. The classes Manager and Locator are the "brain" of the reflector. The Manager object is the control component that governs the behavior of the reflector. The Locator object monitors information available on the device the reflector is residing on and can signal to the corresponding Manager object the need for migration or cloning in order to adapt to events in the network. All the aforementioned components are described in the following.

Receiver Instances of this class are responsible for handling the input videoconference streams. Each instance of Receiver contains a separate thread of control that receives the multimedia streams from all the clients. The receiver stores the packets in the element of a buffer pool corresponding to the sender of the packet, identified using information in the protocol headers. The audio and video components are handled as two separate streams which are received on two distinct sockets; thus, two instances of Receiver are spawned in each reflector. The receiver is a key element as far as performance is concerned and keeping it simple is desirable to achieve good performance.

Buffer Instances of this class contain circular lists of packets. The number of buffers contained in the reflector is usually twice the number of clients currently connected to it, in order to separate the processing of audio streams from the one for video streams. Each **Buffer** object is accessed concurrently by **Dispatcher** instances, that can read the packets stored in it by the **Receiver** object in charge of the buffer. Each buffer provides methods to return the packet stored at a given position as well as to determine the index of the packet most recently stored. Clearly, the length of the buffer is a key parameter in the configuration of the reflector, and depends on the bit rate and maximum delay tolerated by each client.

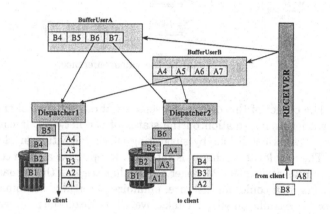

Fig. 3. Exploiting customized **Dispatcher** objects.

Dispatcher Instances of **Dispatcher** have their own thread of control and are responsible for the processing that transforms input streams and replicates them to all the clients. The class **Dispatcher**, in Fig. 2, implements a default behavior that always retransmits the most recent packets in the audio and video buffers. Clients can supply their own classes specialized from **Dispatcher**, in order to benefit by additional, customized processing and possibly adapt to the network conditions. The selection of a customized **Dispatcher** object may take place at setup time, but it can also be performed during the conference, by exploiting mobile code mechanisms such as remote dynamic linking. The customized processing embodied in a **Dispatcher** object may be as simple as an application-aware discarding of frames in order to adapt to network load, or as complex as a recoding of the stream, e.g., to convert it from MPEG to H.261. This scheme can exploit effectively layered encoded video because in presence of bandwidth reduction, e.g. due to congestion, the dispatcher can send to clients only the high priority layers and discard the others with little computation overhead.

Figure 3 illustrates how customized **Dispatcher** objects can filter out differently the same conference streams. In the figure, the leftmost **Dispatcher** object privileges the stream coming from client A, while the rightmost treats both streams the same way, although with reduced bandwidth.

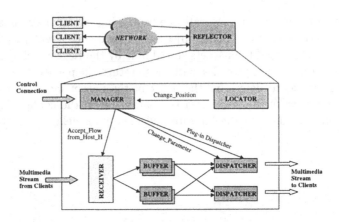

Fig. 4. Managing the videoconference.

Locator The object of this class has a separate thread of control and is responsible for gathering information on the status of the network. It can react to a change in network conditions by suggesting either migration or cloning of the reflector. The new location chosen is supposed to optimize a given cost function, and is communicated to the **Manager** object that triggers the actual relocation.

A cost function could, for instance, minimize a weighted combination of relevant indexes like traffic on selected links, overall traffic on the network, maximum or average delay experienced by conference participants, and economic cost. The data used by the locator to take its decision can be obtained either by monitoring the network or directly from the databases of the network node on which it is running. In the first case, the locator could probe for example the round trip delay of the path to clients using the `ping` mechanism. In the second case the locator exploits directly the information contained in the router on which it is executing, e.g., the status of its queues, the traffic statistics of its interfaces, or the topological database of a routing protocol.

The amount of intelligence and computational complexity embedded in the Locator are implementation dependent. Customized **Locator** classes can be created to cope with different videoconferencing scenarios, and substituted to the default one. Also, the locator can be reconfigurable by applications and users that can tune its parameters and thresholds to better suit their needs. In particular, the strategy for relocation, i.e. migration vs. cloning, can be specified dynamically.

Manager As shown in Fig. 4, the instance of **Manager** coordinates the operations of the reflector to which it is associated with and is in charge of communications with clients. Typical tasks of the **Manager** include joining new members to the conference, accepting incoming code for the dispatchers, dealing with security issues, and taking care of the migration or cloning of the reflector.

The manager handles control communications with the clients through a control connection for sending feedback about the operations of the reflector and receiving requests, e.g., to change transmission parameters. These requests are interpreted and then satisfied by invoking the appropriate methods on the

Dispatcher. The control connection is used, in particular, to inform the clients upon relocation of the reflector so that they can redirect their streams to the new location, as described in the next section.

3.2 Migrating the Reflector

The movement of the reflector should be as transparent as possible to users, to avoid even temporary service disruptions. This is especially important if the locator component is aggressive and movements are frequent. Temporary service disruption could take place if there is a time frame in which the reflector is no longer operational in the old location and is not yet operational in the new one. In order to avoid this situation, migration takes place in two phases:

1. The manager object generates a clone of the reflector which is sent on the network node chosen by the locator. As soon as the new reflector begins its execution on the hosting node, it sends a notification to the manager of the old reflector, which in turn informs the clients about the new location of the reflector. After the clients receive this notification they start transmitting their streams to the new location. The execution state of the reflector is lost, and only a portion of the data space is carried with it. In particular, the buffers are not transferred at destination, as they contain volatile information that is better handled by the old reflector. In contrast, the client profiles are transferred with the reflector clone, in order to maintain the information about the clients currently connected.
2. When all the clients have redirected their flows to the new reflector, the latter sends a control message to the Manager object of the original reflector, which terminates the process running at the old location.

3.3 Using a Capsule to Join the Conference

The minimum setup for a conference includes an instance of Reflector and two clients. Each clients receives the conference streams from the reflector. However, clients can be either *active* or *passive* depending on whether they originate their own streams or not. The startup of a conference session is determined by a client that "rings" another one, the *conference owner*. The identity of the conference owner must be known a priori through some sort of off-line announcement[1]. The conference is associated with an access control list that identifies the conditions under which a client can be allowed to join a conference. If the calling client matches the access control list, the conference owner injects a reflector in the network and the conference begins. Other participants can join the conference in a similar fashion by calling the conference owner.

---

[1] As an example, consider MBone conference announcements which are distributed through sdr and contain the multicast address of the conference. In the framework of our conference system the announcement would contain the address of the conference owner.

This approach does not scale to large distribution events like an Internet TV broadcast, because the conference owner would be overwhelmed by join requests. Also, the component that keeps the conference access control list and that should be responsible for handling new join requests is actually the reflector. However, the difficulty is that the position of the reflector is changing over time and its address cannot be bound to the conference announcement.

A solution to this problem involves the use of a capsule, i.e. an active packet that contains a join request for the client that created it and travels autonomously towards the conference owner, thus actually implementing a mobile agent. At each node, the capsule object checks whether a reflector is running there, and possibly hands the join request to it. The reflector handles the join request by matching it against the access control list and and notifies the sender of the capsule about acceptance or rejection of the request. The capsule contains also additional information about the client needed to setup the connection, like the capability to provide a customized dispatcher.

In case the capsule object does not run into the reflector on its way to the conference owner, this is eventually reached and forwards the capsule to a reflector, whose position is known to the conference owner through its control connection. In case the conference has not yet started and no Reflector instance is executing in the network, the request is handled directly by the conference owner as described above. Sending the join request as a capsule is particularly effective when the cloning approach is exploited. The existence of many reflectors and their displacement increase the probability that the capsule runs into one of them and consequently the join request is handled closer to the client that issued it. The approach can be further extended by allowing a joining client to send the capsule to other conference participants besides the owner. This increases the reliability of the system since the possibility of joining the conference is not conditioned by the status of the conference owner.

4 The Prototype

A prototype of the videoconference system described here is being implemented at our university using the Java language. The support for code mobility is provided by the μCode toolkit developed in parallel by one of the authors [10], which provides a flexible mobile code infrastructure with limited overhead.

The implementation of the client relies on the public domain tools vic and vat to generate respectively the video and audio streams. The streams playback is performed by an application developed using the specialized API of the Java Media Framework (JMF) [15]. In addition, a console written in Java allows the user to communicate with the reflector and manipulate the parameters of the session. A new version of the client integrating the console with the visualization and playback of the conference streams will be implemented as soon as standard capture and encoding support are made available within the JMF. Authentication and access control features are currently not implemented, as we decided to focus on the assessment of the impact of customizability and mobility rather than security.

5 Discussion and Further Work

The work reported here investigates the opportunities opened by code mobility in the context of active networks. The paper focuses on design aspects, describing an original architecture for a videoconference system based on a conference server that migrates or clones itself in order to adapt to events in the network. The proposed architecture provides improved scalability and allows clients to customize the server's behavior by exploiting mobile code.

Our work is inspired by the work described in [11], which describes the implementation of a chat server that migrates to adapt to the position of the participants. In that work, the focus is on the optimization achieved by network-aware positioning of the server with respect to a traditional fixed displacement. In our work the potential of code mobility and active networks has been exploited also in terms of user customization which can be strategic in the videoconference application domain. Also, the aforementioned work is mainly concerned with mechanisms needed to probe and monitor resources. In our work, we focus on the exploitation of code mobility; however, devising and comparing different strategies for relocation to be embedded in the Locator component of the system is the subject of ongoing research. This encompasses individuating and defining which mechanisms and information must be provided at the application level and which information can be assumed to be provided by the active network device—still an open issue in active network research.

The performance of a videoconference system depends strongly on the real-time properties of the transmission services it is based on. This work has not tackled issues related to the provision of quality of service guarantees over an active network and to locator mobility in such a scenario (e.g., the impact on resource reservation of the reflector position changing over time). These topics represent an interesting and broad area for future studies.

Another open issue is a better integration of the Real-time Transport Protocol (RTP) [13] in our prototype. RTP is presently the protocol for multimedia transport most widely used on the Internet, and is engineered for conferences whose attendance ranges from a few clients up to 10,000; more clients cannot be managed due to implosion of control messages. In fact, each participant sends periodically to all the others a report containing its identity and possibly information about the quality of the stream it receives. This information can be used by the sources as a feedback of the quality of service perceived by the receiver. Clearly, this solution is impractical for a very large conference. In the cloning variant of our architecture, control message implosion is reduced because each reflector acts as a virtual participant for other reflectors, and thus "hides" the clients directly attached to it at the same time providing direct feedback about the quality of transmission.

Finally, we are in the process of analyzing quantitatively the benefits and the tradeoffs of our design, along the lines of [2]. This encompasses the definition of an analytical model for comparing the performance (e.g., in terms of traffic or latency) of our architecture with respect to conventional solutions, as well as the validation of such a model through direct measurements on the actual implementation.

Acknowledgments This work has been partially supported by Centro Studi e Laboratori Telecomunicazioni S.p.A. (CSELT), Italy. The authors wish to thank Valerio Malenchino from CSELT for his insightful comments during the development of the work described in this paper. Also, the authors wish to thank Margarita Millet Sorolla for her work on the implementation of the prototype.

References

1. The MBone Information Web. Web page http://www.mbone.com.
2. M. Baldi and G.P. Picco. Evaluating the Tradeoffs of Mobile Code Design Paradigms in Network Management Applications. In *Proc. of the 20th Int. Conf. on Software Engineering*, pages 146–155, April 1998.
3. S. Bhattacharjee, K. Calvert, and E. Zegura. On Active Networking and Congestion. Technical Report GIT-CC-96/02, Georgia Institute of Technology, 1996.
4. Cornell University. CU-SeeMe. Web page http://cu-seeme.cornell.edu.
5. A. Fuggetta, G.P. Picco, and G. Vigna. Understanding Code Mobility. *IEEE Trans. on Software Engineering*, 24(5):342–361, May 1998.
6. J. Hartman et al. Liquid Software: A New Paradigm for Networked Systems. Technical Report 96-11, Univ. of Arizona, June 1996.
7. M. Hicks et al. PLAN: A Programming Language for Active Networks. Technical report, Univ. of Pennsylvania, November 1997.
8. ITU-T Recommendation H.323. *Visual telephone systems and equipment for local area networks which provide a non-guaranteed quality of service*, November 1996.
9. M.A. Millet Sorolla. Realizzazione di un'applicazione su rete attiva. Master's thesis, Politecnico di Torino, Italy, February 1998. In Italian.
10. G.P. Picco. μCODE: A Lightweight and Flexible Mobile Code Toolkit. In *Proc. of the 2nd Int. Workshop on Mobile Agents (MA'98)*, September 1998.
11. M. Ranganathan, A. Acharya, S. Sharma, and J. Saltz. Network-Aware Mobile Programs. In *Proc. of the USENIX 1997 Annual Technical Conf.*, January 1997.
12. J. Rumbaugh et al. *Object-Oriented Modeling and Design*. Prentice Hall, 1991.
13. H. Schulzrinne, S. Casner, R. Frederick, and V. Jacobson. RTP: A Transport Protocol for Real-Time Applications. RFC 1889, January 1996.
14. Sun Microsystems. The Java Language: An Overview. Technical report, Sun Microsystems, 1994.
15. Sun Microsystems. *Java Media Framework*, January 1997. Available at http://java.sun.com/products/java-media/jmf.
16. D. Tennenhouse et al. A Survey of Active Network Research. *IEEE Communications*, 35(1):80–86, January 1997.
17. D. Wetherall, J. Guttag, and D. Tennenhouse. ANTS: A Toolkit for Building an Dynamically Deploying Network Protocols. In *Proc. of IEEE Open Architectures and Network Programming (OPENARCH'98)*, pages 117–129, April 1998.
18. Y. Yemini and S. da Silva. Towards Programmable Networks. In *IFIP/IEEE Int. Workshop on Distributed Systems: Operations and Management*, October 1996.

Author Index

Lecture Notes in Computer Science

For information about Vols. 1–1397

please contact your bookseller or Springer-Verlag

Vol. 1436: D. Wood, S. Yu (Eds.), Automata Implementation. Proceedings, 1997. VIII, 253 pages. 1998.

Vol. 1437: S. Albayrak, F.J. Garijo (Eds.), Intelligent Agents for Telecommunication Applications. Proceedings, 1998. XII, 251 pages. 1998. (Subseries LNAI).

Vol. 1438: C. Boyd, E. Dawson (Eds.), Information Security and Privacy. Proceedings, 1998. XI, 423 pages. 1998.

Vol. 1439: B. Magnusson (Ed.), System Configuration Management. Proceedings, 1998. X, 207 pages. 1998.

Vol. 1441: W. Wobcke, M. Pagnucco, C. Zhang (Eds.), Agents and Multi-Agent Systems. Proceedings, 1997. XII, 241 pages. 1998. (Subseries LNAI).

Vol. 1442: A. Fiat. G.J. Woeginger (Eds.), Online Algorithms. XVIII, 436 pages. 1998.

Vol. 1443: K.G. Larsen, S. Skyum, G. Winskel (Eds.), Automata, Languages and Programming. Proceedings, 1998. XVI, 932 pages. 1998.

Vol. 1444: K. Jansen, J. Rolim (Eds.), Approximation Algorithms for Combinatorial Optimization. Proceedings, 1998. VIII, 201 pages. 1998.

Vol. 1445: E. Jul (Ed.), ECOOP'98 – Object-Oriented Programming. Proceedings, 1998. XII, 635 pages. 1998.

Vol. 1446: D. Page (Ed.), Inductive Logic Programming. Proceedings, 1998. VIII, 301 pages. 1998. (Subseries LNAI).

Vol. 1447: V.W. Porto, N. Saravanan, D. Waagen, A.E. Eiben (Eds.), Evolutionary Programming VII. Proceedings, 1998. XVI, 840 pages. 1998.

Vol. 1448: M. Farach-Colton (Ed.), Combinatorial Pattern Matching. Proceedings, 1998. VIII, 251 pages. 1998.

Vol. 1449: W.-L. Hsu, M.-Y. Kao (Eds.), Computing and Combinatorics. Proceedings, 1998. XII, 372 pages. 1998.

Vol. 1450: L. Brim, F. Gruska, J. Zlatuška (Eds.), Mathematical Foundations of Computer Science 1998. Proceedings, 1998. XVII, 846 pages. 1998.

Vol. 1451: A. Amin, D. Dori, P. Pudil, H. Freeman (Eds.), Advances in Pattern Recognition. Proceedings, 1998. XXI, 1048 pages. 1998.

Vol. 1452: B.P. Goettl, H.M. Halff, C.L. Redfield, V.J. Shute (Eds.), Intelligent Tutoring Systems. Proceedings, 1998. XIX, 629 pages. 1998.

Vol. 1453: M.-L. Mugnier, M. Chein (Eds.), Conceptual Structures: Theory, Tools and Applications. Proceedings, 1998. XIII, 439 pages. (Subseries LNAI).

Vol. 1454: I. Smith (Ed.), Artificial Intelligence in Structural Engineering. XI, 497 pages. 1998. (Subseries LNAI).

Vol. 1456: A. Drogoul, M. Tambe, T. Fukuda (Eds.), Collective Robotics. Proceedings, 1998. VII, 161 pages. 1998. (Subseries LNAI).

Vol. 1457: A. Ferreira, J. Rolim, H. Simon, S.-H. Teng (Eds.), Solving Irregularly Structured Problems in Prallel. Proceedings, 1998. X, 408 pages. 1998.

Vol. 1458: V.O. Mittal, H.A. Yanco, J. Aronis, R-. Simpson (Eds.), Assistive Technology in Artificial Intelligence. X, 273 pages. 1998. (Subseries LNAI).

Vol. 1459: D.G. Feitelson, L. Rudolph (Eds.), Job Scheduling Strategies for Parallel Processing. Proceedings, 1998. VII, 257 pages. 1998.

Vol. 1460: G. Quirchmayr, E. Schweighofer, T.J.M. Bench-Capon (Eds.), Database and Expert Systems Applications. Proceedings, 1998. XVI, 905 pages. 1998.

Vol. 1461: G. Bilardi, G.F. Italiano, A. Pietracaprina, G. Pucci (Eds.), Algorithms – ESA'98. Proceedings, 1998. XII, 516 pages. 1998.

Vol. 1462: H. Krawczyk (Ed.), Advances in Cryptology - CRYPTO '98. Proceedings, 1998. XII, 519 pages. 1998.

Vol. 1464: H.H.S. Ip, A.W.M. Smeulders (Eds.), Multimedia Information Analysis and Retrieval. Proceedings, 1998. VIII, 264 pages. 1998.

Vol. 1465: R. Hirschfeld (Ed.), Financial Cryptography. Proceedings, 1998. VIII, 311 pages. 1998.

Vol. 1466: D. Sangiorgi, R. de Simone (Eds.), CONCUR'98: Concurrency Theory. Proceedings, 1998. XI, 657 pages. 1998.

Vol. 1467: C. Clack, K. Hammond, T. Davie (Eds.), Implementation of Functional Languages. Proceedings, 1997. X, 375 pages. 1998.

Vol. 1468: P. Husbands, J.-A. Meyer (Eds.), Evolutionary Robotics. Proceedings, 1998. VIII, 247 pages. 1998.

Vol. 1469: R. Puigjaner, N.N. Savino, B. Serra (Eds.), Computer Performance Evaluation. Proceedings, 1998. XIII, 376 pages. 1998.

Vol. 1470: D. Pritchard, J. Reeve (Eds.), Euro-Par'98. Parallel Processing. Proceedings, 1998. XXII, 1157 pages. 1998.

Vol. 1471: J. Dix, L. Moniz Pereira, T.C. Przymusinski (Eds.), Logic Programming and Knowledge Representation. Proceedings, 1997. IX, 246 pages. 1998. (Subseries LNAI).

Vol. 1473: X. Leroy, A. Ohori (Eds.), Types in Compilation. Proceedings, 1998. VIII, 299 pages. 1998.

Vol. 1475: W. Litwin, T. Morzy, G. Vossen (Eds.), Advances in Databases and Information Systems. Proceedings, 1998. XIV, 369 pages. 1998.

Vol. 1477: K. Rothermel, F. Hohl (Eds.), Mobile Agents. Proceedings, 1998. VIII, 285 pages. 1998.

Vol. 1478: M. Sipper, D. Mange, A. Pérez-Uribe (Eds.), Evolvable Systems: From Biology to Hardware. Proceedings, 1998. IX, 382 pages. 1998.

Vol. 1479: J. Grundy, M. Newey (Eds.), Theorem Proving in Higher Order Logics. Proceedings, 1998. VIII, 497 pages. 1998.

Vol. 1480: F. Giunchiglia (Ed.), Artificial Intelligence: Methodology, Systems, and Applications. Proceedings, 1998. IX, 502 pages. 1998. (Subseries LNAI).

Vol. 1482: R.W. Hartenstein, A. Keevallik (Eds.), Field-Programmable Logic and Applications. Proceedings, 1998. XI, 533 pages. 1998.

Vol. 1483: T. Plagemann, V. Goebel (Eds.), Interactive Distributed Multimedia Systems and Telecommunication Services. Proceedings, 1998. XV, 326 pages. 1998.

Vol. 1487: V. Gruhn (Ed.), Software Process Technology. Proceedings, 1998. VIII, 157 pages. 1998.

Vol. 1488: B. Smyth, P. Cunningham (Eds.), Advances in Case-Based Reasoning. Proceedings, 1998. XI, 482 pages. 1998. (Subseries LNAI).